BLACK CONDUCTORS

by
D. Antoinette Handy

The Scarecrow Press, Inc.
Lanham, Md., & London
1995

British Library Cataloguing-in-Publication data available

Library of Congress Cataloging-in-Publication Data

Handy, D. Antoinette, 1930–
    Black conductors / by D. Antoinette Handy.
        p.   cm.
    Includes bibliographical references (p.   ) and index.
    ISBN 0-8108-2930-4 (acid-free paper)
    1. Afro-American conductors—Biography.   I. Title.
ML402.H36   1995
781.45′092′273—dc20
    [B]   94-34560

This book is dedicated to black conductors—past, present, and future; my deceased parents (William Talbot Handy, Sr. and Darthney Pauline Pleasant Handy); and my always supportive and loving husband (Calvin Montgomery Miller)

CONTENTS

EXPLANATORY NOTES

1. An asterisk (*) by a name, in Parts II and III, indicates that a full Profile of this individual appears in this book.
2. It was a conscious decision on the part of the author to capitalize the word "Black" when it was used as a noun. When used as a modifier, lower case was applied.

ACKNOWLEDGMENTS

In the early stages of this project, it was clearly evident that the author's professional commitments would delay the research and writing process. Consequently, she solicited assistance from her friend and colleague of more than twenty years, William E. Terry. A special thanks for his collaboration in drafting the correspondence to conductors, designing the Survey Instrument (Appendixes B and C), conducting several interviews, and drafting a few Conductor Profiles. Though completion has been much later than originally anticipated, this work has finally been brought to closure, due in no small part to Terry's efforts.

Material was secured from a variety of sources, including the Moorland-Spingarn Research Center at Howard University, the Library of Congress, the National Archives, and the Martin Luther King Memorial Library (Washington, DC), the Institute of Jazz Studies (Rutgers University), and the Archives for the Performing Arts (San Francisco, CA). Printed sources from the library of the National Endowment for tthe Arts were extremely helpful, as were various publications of the American Symphony Orchestra League.

The author relied heavily on the writings of Eileen Southern, especially the *Biographical Dictionary of Afro-American and African Musicians* and her journal, *The Black Perspective in Music.* Of course the most valuable material was provided by individual orchestra leaders themselves, members of their families, their personal managers, and their orchestras' staffs.

Sincere gratitude is due staff members of the National Endowment for the Arts, particularly those within the Music Program, and to the service organization Affiliate Artists. The assistance of Catherine French, Chief Executive Officer for the American Symphony Orchestra League, was indispensable.

It is imperative that the author acknowledge the following individuals who assisted in various capacities: Janet Edwards, Dorothy Lewis, Margaret Slipek, Keith Stephens, Janice Stunkard,

Marjory Hanson, Camay Murphy, Josephine Harreld Love, Jeanette Jennings, and Carol Quin. For the many hours that my husband spent in different libraries on my behalf, a heartfelt thank you.

Despite all advice, suggestions, and assistance, the author assumes complete responsibility for the final product.

PART I: INTRODUCTION

The Art of Conducting:
A Historical Overview

CONDUCTING AS WE KNOW IT TODAY is less than two centuries old. "Time-beating," on the other hand, as a means of holding players and/or singers together, dates back by several centuries. There is pictorial evidence of such activity as far back as the Middle Ages. In the absence of written notation, the leader's hands indicated the direction of the vocal line. As other vocal lines entered the musical picture (creating polyphony), it became essential that beats be marked. Interpretation, at the time, was an element of no import.

Engravings and miniatures indicate that, in addition to the hands, leaders of instrumental and vocal forces utilized a foot, a pendulum, a stick, a handkerchief, or possibly a roll of paper or parchment. When the element of interpretation entered the picture (seventeenth century), the role of the leader was greatly enhanced. Freedom of interpretation increased the conductor's responsibilities, though no universal practices existed. Gradually the method of "time beating" approached uniformity; as meters became established, so did the conductor's movements, i.e., four distinct movements in 4/4 time and three distinct movements in 3/4 time.

But as conducting and orchestra historian Adam Carse wrote:

> A baton or a roll of paper was ...used in order to give a visible or even an audible time-beat, and was nothing more than a metronomic signal given for the purpose of synchronizing the performance of scattered vocal forces. Instrumentalists...would have considered it a reflection on their musicianship had they been asked to play to a given time-beat; such an elementary aid might be necessary for choir-boys and choral singers, but not for educated and qualified musicians.[1]

During the eighteenth century, particularly in opera, two directors were often required—one directing the singers from a keyboard and the other directing the orchestra from the principal violinist position. On occasion, particularly for large-scale performances, there were three directors: the principal violin, the keyboard player, and a conductor. Orchestras without conductors also existed during this period, a practice continued today in chamber (smaller) orchestra performances.

Gradually the violinist-conductor became more important than the keyboard-conductor, using the violin bow in the same manner that the "little white stick" (baton) would be used later. Early in the nineteenth century, by which time the size of the orchestra had expanded tremendously, an individual standing in front of an aggregation of instruments and instrumentalists, minus an instrument (except for the orchestra itself), had become a fixture.

Carse indicated that

> [b]efore the mid-century was reached, the baton had triumphed; orchestras, choirs, and opera were universally directed as they now are, and a new type of musician began to come into existence— namely, the specialist-conductor.[2]

Any history of "the art of conducting" warrants mention of certain significantly contributing individuals—composers/conductors all. Italian-born, French-educated Jean Baptiste Lully (1632–1687) is generally designated as the first "important" conductor in the history of music. As "director of music" for Louis XIV, Lully

> taught his men a uniform manner of bowing, developed orchestral discipline, and achieved a rhythmic precision unknown till then. His orchestra became the model for all [of] Europe.[3]

It is said that while Lully was conducting his "Te Deum," he struck his foot with a long staff, being used as a baton. An infection developed that led to his death.

German composer Christopher Willibald Gluck (1714–1787) is believed to be "the first great modern conductor." Johann Frederick Reichardt (1752–1814), German composer and music director at the Prussian Court, was perhaps the first to eliminate the keyboard and to conduct standing up or positioning himself seated in front of a conductor's stand. Felix Mendelssohn (1809–1847), often referred to as the first "real conductor" in today's sense of the word, fostered precision and an "exact" realization of the composer's score. With Hungarian composer/conductor Franz Liszt (1811–1886), interpretation by gestures and facial expressions was initiated.

French composer Hector Berlioz (1803–1869), who was not proficient on the piano or an orchestral instrument, was noted as an innovative orchestrator, music critic, and conductor. It was Berlioz

who prepared a pioneering study of modern baton conducting—
L'Art du chef d'orchestre, 1855.

There followed in 1869 Richard Wagner's *On Conducting,* translated by Edward Dannreuther and published by William Reeves,
London, 1887. Though Wagner (1813–1883) was a noted German
composer, he was also an important conductor and writer of his own
libretti and essays. His was the first book devoted exclusively to the
interpretive aspect of the art of conducting. According to Arturo
Toscanini (1867–1957), the twentieth century's stellar maestro,
Wagner's *On Conducting* was "the most perceptive if not the only
worthwhile analysis of the subject."[4]

Wrote conductor, critic, and educator Elliott Galkin in his 1988
treatise, *A History of Orchestral Conducting In Theory and Practice:*

> These specialized publications antedated the creation of conservatory
> instructional programs in conducting. The first such program took
> place in 1905 under the direction of Arthur Nikisch in Leipzig.
> Formal courses in conducting constitute the most recent major
> addition to curricula in conservatories (and in American colleges and
> universities.)[5]

Conductor Training and Competitions

As early as 1943, there took place "an experiment" that potentially offered far-reaching consequences for young American conductors. Music Directors George Szell (Cleveland Orchestra) and
Reginald Stewart (Baltimore Symphony) instituted apprentice-
conductor programs with their respective orchestras. The American
Symphony Orchestra League offered a five-day symposium to fifty
developing conductors in October 1952. The conductors of community, college, and youth orchestras were able to observe Eugene
Ormandy conducting the world-class Philadelphia Orchestra in
rehearsal. A twelve-day workshop led by Cleveland Orchestra Music
Director George Szell and a forum for conductors sponsored by the
Los Angeles Philharmonic followed in 1954.

The American Symphony Orchestra League launched a Summer
Institute of Orchestral Studies in 1956 at the Asilomar Conference
Grounds in Pacific Grove, California. Two years later, the organiza-
tion created an East Coast workshop for conductors and musicians at

Sewanee, Tennessee. The workshop was moved to Orkney Springs, Virginia in 1960. All workshops were under the leadership of outstanding conducting pedagogue Richard Lert (1885–1980), former conductor of the Pasadena Symphony Orchestra.[6]

All of these programs were established "on the premise that certain facilities and conditions are absolutely necessary for professional study of the art and technique of conducting." Each offered a full-scale symphony orchestra, made up of professional players from throughout the country; a master conductor who counseled; and a special artistic coaching staff, collectively "helping many promising conductors to 'see behind the notes'."[7] The orchestral field's service organization had early recognized a need to begin training American conductors—here in America.

A subgroup of the League, the Conductors' Guild, was organized in 1975. This organization played an active role in planning conductors' workshops (in conjunction with the League) until 1985, when the Guild became a separate entity.

Donald Thulean, the American Symphony Orchestra League's Vice President for Orchestra Services (and a conductor) has indicated that

> [t]he conductor is the primary music-maker in the orchestra. Therefore, those of us concerned about the artistic well-being of our orchestras must, as a matter of course, consider how well conductors have been and are being trained. We must evaluate their artistic development and career possibilities. We must nurture their artistic growth.[8]

The League has become particularly sensitive to the absence of American conductors at the helm of our major orchestral institutions and the expressed frustrations of talented but underemployed conductors. In response, the League launched a series of initiatives beginning in the mid-1980s: Conducting Workshops, the American Repertoire Project, a Conductor Mentor Program, and the American Conductors Program—the Conducting Continuum.

Currently three-day Conducting Workshops are held throughout the country. Master conducting teachers make up the faculty. The American Repertoire Project offers in-depth study, rehearsal, and performance of American works; up to four conductors spend one week working with a professional orchestra, under the supervision of a master conductor and a prominent composer. A culminating public concert is attended by managers, music directors, artistic administrators, and the general public.

The Conductor Mentor Program permits gifted conductors to spend a minimum of six weeks with a host orchestra, observing the music director in rehearsal and concerts, experiencing a minimum of two intensive study sessions on the week's repertoire, and conducting for the mentor's critique in a rehearsal setting. The Leonard Bernstein American Conductors Program, renamed to honor the memory of Bernstein (1918–1990), offers three or four conductors the opportunity to rehearse and perform with a prominent (major) orchestra. Under the guidance of conductors of international stature, less well-known conductors, themselves music directors of American orchestras, prepare the orchestra for a public concert before American orchestra leaders during the American Symphony Orchestra League's Annual Conference.[9]

Finally, an extremely prestigious training ground for developing conductors is the Tanglewood Music Center (until 1985 known as the Berkshire Music Center), established in 1940 by Boston Symphony Orchestra conductor Serge Koussevitsky (1874–1951). Worth reading is Helen Epstein's chapter "Learning to Conduct at Tanglewood," included in her book *Music Talks: Conversations with Musicians*. Epstein describes well the "eight-week immersion" of approximately "a dozen young men and the occasional young woman"—all aspiring conductors participating in the conducting seminar at Tanglewood in Lenox, Massachusetts.

The program includes fellows, students, and auditors. The summer experience offers a substitute "orchestra" of two pianos, with only a few high achievers actually conducting the Tanglewood Student Orchestra. The conducting fellows have all survived a rigorous selection process, initially involving roughly 200 applicants. Only the most prominent conductors serve as instructors.[10] Writes Epstein:

> There is no prototype of the young conductor at Tanglewood. The men and handful of women who have studied there have come from all over the world; they are between the ages of twenty and thirty-five; they are mostly bright, well-educated, multilingual, and very polite.[11]

A particularly significant program has been The Exxon/Arts Endowment Conductors Program, administered by the national nonprofit organization Affiliate Artists. Launched in 1973, the program was designed by the National Endowment for the Arts and Affiliate Artists "to bridge the gap between formal training and full-time professional employment." Participating conductors are placed in full-season residencies with leading American orchestras and opera companies for up to three years. Selected participants experience comprehensive involvement in the orchestra's musical and administrative activities.[12] The more than fifty participating conductors (during its more than nineteen-year history) have included several women, as well as Blacks.

"Graduates" of the program have moved on to positions of music director, conductor, resident conductor, associate conductor, principal guest conductor, and artistic director with such established institutions as the Cleveland, Baltimore, New Jersey, Springfield (Massachusetts), Memphis, Akron, North Carolina, Columbus, New Mexico, New Haven, and Oakland East Bay Symphony Orchestras; the Saint Paul Chamber Orchestra; the Australian, San Francisco, Houston, and Dallas Grand Opera Companies; the Paris Opera at the Bastille; and the German Radio Orchestra, Saarbrucken. Exxon support was terminated in 1987, but, with the continued support of the National Endowment for the Arts and that of various private funders, the program continues. The long-range effort, designed to address the issue of career development for gifted conductors in the early stages of their careers, has proven to be overwhelmingly successful.

In 1985, a program conceived by the National Endowment for the Arts for conductors on the threshold of major international careers was launched. Two recipients are chosen biennially. (In one year there were three.) Each receives a $75,000 Career Development Award to pursue individually tailored activities designed to enhance his or her talent and expertise. The custom-tailored, career-planned program is funded by the Seaver Institute (a private foundation based in Los Angeles) and the National Endowment for the Arts. Originally administered by Affiliate Artists, the Seaver/National Endowment for the Arts Conductors Award was subsequently administered by the New World Symphony Orchestra (Miami) and is currently administered by the Juilliard School of Music. An-

nouncement of the recipients is made biennially at the American
Symphony Orchestra League's National Conference.

Many perceive participation in conductor competitions as a valid
method of obtaining career advancement. In addition to offering
prize monies, most competition awards carry with them guest
appearances with various orchestras and in turn provide needed
exposure. Through the years, one of the most important competitions
was the Dimitri Mitropoulos Competition, established in 1961.
Wrote music critic Linda Sanders, however:

> [U]nlike competitions for instrumentalists, conducting contests have
> by and large failed to become a permanent feature of American
> musical life. While many professionals agree that more could be done
> to create performance opportunities for promising talents, the
> question of whether competitions are a just and credible means of
> identifying that talent remains a subject of debate.[13]

Currently only one major competition exists in the United States,
namely the American Symphony Orchestra's [Leopold] Stokowski
Competition. Created in 1979, the Stokowski did not become a
full-fledged competition until 1985. During the first five years, a
promising conductor (as viewed by American Symphony Orchestra
musicians, conductors, and administrators) was "invited" to conduct
the orchestra at a regular subscription concert and given a cash
award. The annual competition is open to young American conductors under the age of 35; the prize, now decided by a panel of outside
judges, includes an engagement with the American Symphony
Orchestra at Carnegie Hall and $5,000.[14]

Many American conductors in pursuit of greater recognition and
additional opportunities see merit in entering foreign conducting
competitions. One can only speculate on the extent to which careers
have been enhanced as a result. Musical America's *International
Directory of the Performing Arts, 1992* listed nine conducting competitions in eight different countries: Denmark, France, Hungary, Italy,
Japan, Netherlands, Poland, and Switzerland.[15] As the reader moves
through the various entries in this publication, more conductor
training programs and competitions will be noted, both here and
abroad.

The Anointed One—Conductor/Music Director

Of the orchestra, former Boston Symphony conductor Charles Munch (1891–1968) wrote:

> The orchestra is not a docile or mechanical instrument. It is a social body, a collection of human beings. It has a psychology and reflexes. It can be guided but it must not be offended.[16]

The individual who guides this unique aggregation of instrumentalists is known as a conductor, who by choice or designation is sometimes music director as well.

A conductor is one who possesses the ability to communicate (as a performing artist) his or her ideas about a composition through his or her instrument, which is the orchestra. Solid musicianship is a given; knowledge of every instrument is most desirable. As has often been stated, the conductor is able to do what he or she wants, but should want only that which he or she can justify.[17] There should exist between the conductor and the orchestra a technical bond, namely musicianship—each a master of his or her instrument.

Norman Lebrecht's *The Maestro Myth: Great Conductors in Pursuit of Power* (1991)[18] forcefully states his case in the opening chapter, "The Making of a Myth." He writes:

> [P]opular heroes are literally mythical,...Cultural gods are no different . . . The Conductor exists because mankind demands a visible leader or, at the very least, an identifiable figurehead. His musical "raison d'être" is altogether secondary to that function...He plays no instrument, produces no music, yet conveys an image of music-making that is credible enough to let him take the rewards of applause away from those who actually created the sound.[19]

Labrecht's opinion notwithstanding, for this writer, the conductor's music-making is certainly more than a mere image and the unified sound of the orchestra is definitely the creation of the individual at the helm.

Wrote maestro William Steinberg (1899–1978):

> To be a conductor, one must be a born leader—but a leader who understands the responsibilities of leadership and is never for a moment deluded with a sense of absolute power or infallibility and

who has the objectivity to withstand the blind hero worship with which amateur listeners may sometimes envelop him. . . . [T]he successful conductor is the one who develops his own method of expressing himself, and that it is the power of his own personality which is his strongest means of commanding his orchestra.[20]

Wrote former *New York Times* music critic Harold Schonberg:

[The conductor] is of commanding presence, infinite dignity, fabulous memory, vast experience, high temperament and serene wisdom. . . . He is many things: musician, administrator, executive, minister, psychologist, technician, philosopher and dispenser of wrath. . . . [H]e is a leader of men.[21]

The conductor is the most visible individual associated with an orchestra. He or she is a communicator of musical ideas, with the prime responsibility of serving the music. As viewed by Leonard Bernstein, requirements of a successful conductor are enormous authority, mastery of conducting mechanics, extensive knowledge, profound perception of music's inner meaning, and uncanny powers of communication.[22]

As one member of an orchestra in search of a music director stated in the mid-1980s:

We want someone who is as technically competent at his profession as we are at ours. We want someone who not only has a clear conception of how a piece should sound, but knows how to obtain that sound from us. We want a conductor who challenges us, who can inspire us to give of our best. We want someone whose foremost interest is his art, not his own career; someone who serves music, not exploits it.[23]

The music director has additional power (and responsibility). It is he or she who makes all artistic decisions, e.g., programming, personnel, guest artists, recording, and touring. The music director takes artistic responsibility and conducts much of the orchestra's season. The musicality of an orchestra depends on the music director who sets the organization's tone and understands that organization's place in its respective community.

The American Symphony Orchestra League has prepared a handbook for orchestra trustees and management (1985), *Selecting a*

Music Director—an important subject, since as one music director indicated, "all music directors should be conductors, but not all conductors should be music directors." As pointed out by the League's publication, the music director of an orchestra today is "a hybrid of artistic, administrative, and social responsibilities[,] daunting in their complexity." Current music directors, in addition to providing artistic leadership and guidance, must assist in selling tickets, fundraising, educating new audiences, and offering community leadership.[24]

The nation's oldest orchestra (the New York Philharmonic, founded in 1842) first offered its designated conductor the title of "musical director" in 1943. Such a title was to exceed the meaning that the word "conductor" had held previously in the Philharmonic's history. The musical director's duties would go beyond those of an "ad hoc" conductor, an artist-conductor, an interpreter-conductor, and complaint-conductor, or even a master-conductor who dictated his will and whim to his "worshiping minions for a few weeks of the season."[25]

Indeed, the terms "conductor" and "music director" are most frequently associated with symphony orchestras. But no publication would be complete without giving attention to leaders in the area of jazz.

Big Band (Jazz) Leaders

In the world of jazz, an assemblage of ten or more players is designated as a big band and is frequently referred to as a "jazz orchestra." Most popular during the 1930s and 1940s, its existence largely coincided with that of the Swing Era. Written arrrangements were favored and instrumental proficiency was the rule.

According to jazz historian Frank Tirro,

> Power, flash, and precision: the big bands had it, and the public loved it. The driving four-beat rhythm, the up-tempo solos, the power of a final riffing chorus with a stratospheric trumpet piercing the orchestration and leading the band to an attack on the final chord—those are the hallmarks of the swing-era, big-band sound.[26]

Fletcher Henderson is the acknowledged creator of the big band concept; but he of course built on the established traditions of James

Reese Europe, Will Vodery, and Will Marion Cook. Expanding on Henderson's creation were such leaders as Count Basie, Cab Calloway, Duke Ellington, Lionel Hampton, Earl Hines, Jimmie Lunceford, and Chick Webb. Bands that these "conductors" fronted reflected their leaders' personalities, built on their leaders' musicianship, reached artistic standards established by their leaders, and survived as a result of their leaders' artistic credibilities.

Big band popularity was enhanced by radio broadcasts and phonograph records. Noting the rapport that existed between the band and its audience when performances were "live," big band historian George Simon wrote:

[T]hey swung freely and joyously and as they swung, they lifted you high in the air with them, filling you with an exhilarated sense of friendly well-being, you joined them, emotionally and musically, as partners in one of the happiest, most-thrilling rapports ever established between the givers and takers of music.[27]

The leader was responsible for it all.

The years 1935 through 1946 are frequently designated as the most important ones for big bands. "[I]t was a time when a great deal of popular music was good and a great deal of good music was popular."[28]

Chicago Tribune entertainment writer Howard Reich recently wrote:

[D]espite the odds, big band music is back, and with a vengeance. . . . The listeners . . . pay rapt attention, regarding this as the sophisticated concert music it is. . . . Veteran groups . . . are proving that great charts by the likes of Count Basie and Duke Ellington still speak to audiences of the '90s. . . . Finally, people are realizing that big-band music is more than just dance tunes—it has become a repertory music.[29]

For a recorded reminder of the period's significance, the reader is encouraged to become familiar with the Smithsonian Institution's six-record set, "Big Band Jazz" (Smithsonian 2200). Worth a visit to the nation's capital is the opportunity to hear the Smithsonian Jazz Masterworks Orchestra (established in 1991) under the direction of composer, author, educator, and conductor, Gunther Schuller, and Indiana University School of Music's Distinguished Professor of

Music, David N. Baker, who is Black. The creation of this orchestra is the result of a Congressional appropriation in recognition of the importance of jazz in American culture.

The writer's choice of profiled music directors active in the area of jazz is purely personal. Perhaps various "authorities on the subject of big band leadership" would wish to add to the author's list, but certainly no one will deny that those profiled here fully deserve inclusion.

In the area of jazz orchestras and bands, press coverage generally emphasizes the ensemble rather than the leader. Consequently, this writer has elected not to include press comments.

For Women Conductors, An Opening Door

Justifying this publication and the need for another, devoted exclusively to women conductors, is the following statement that appears in Galkin's A History of Orchestral Conducting:

> It must be recognized that, as in other professions requiring sophisticated education and enjoying social esteem, opportunities for female conductors and black conductors have become available only during the last half-century. Such musicians, no matter how impressive their abilities, have been restricted to guest appearances; appointment to positions of titular leadership remains isolated.[30]

Both women and Blacks are represented in Galkin's book, only photographically (with captions), by way of a seven-page section entitled "Vanguard."

Toward the end of the 1980s, the following types of articles began to appear throughout the country: "Female Conductors Win New Batons," (Richmond Times Dispatch); "Victoria Bond: Leading Men On," (College Woman); "Female Conductor A Rarity Who's Not Bothered By Press," (San Antonio Light); "A Female First for Phila. Orchestra," (Philadelphia Inquirer); "Women On the Podium: Five Conductors Making Their Mark On Today's Music," (AWC News/ Forum); "Conductor Blazed Her Own Trail to the Podium," (Oakland Tribune); "Female Associate Wields Baton for 'Discovery'," (Dallas Times Herald); "The Opening Door: 'Women in Music' Is Story of Struggle and Opportunity," (Chicago Tribune); "Music, Maestra, Please," (New York Times).

As recently as May 1992, a Cambridge, Massachusetts, writer asked one female conductor if she believed that conducting was a macho profession? Her response:

> Yes, it is, if by macho you mean strong-willed and stubborn. It's also clearly a profession where natural leadership is essential. I don't know how it could be any different. But I don't think these qualities are only manifest in members of the male sex. If you say that women don't have these qualities, then I have nothing further to discuss with you.[31]

Victoria Bond was the first woman appointed as an Exxon/Arts Endowment/Affiliate Artists Conductor and served as assistant conductor to André Previn at the Pittsburgh Symphony Orchestra. When asked "What's it like to be a female conductor?" she responded, "I'm afraid I don't know the alternative."[32]

An inspiration to those women who currently aspire toward conducting careers was certainly the French pedagogue/conductor/composer/organist, Nadia Boulanger (1887–1979), who trained many American conductors and composers, including Leonard Bernstein, Virgil Thomson, and Aaron Copland. She was the first woman to conduct the Boston Symphony Orchestra (1938). Boulanger's charge to her students was, "I did it. Go forth and do likewise."[33] The author wonders if she drew inspiration from the German abbess and composer of sacred music, Hildegard of Bingen (1098–1179), who led an instrumental group in the convent during the twelfth century.

For women conductors who broke through in America in the early years, "their orchestral leadership role was confined to all-female ensembles, except for an occasional guest appearance." Prominent among this group were Eva Anderson, Ethel Leginska, Ebba Sundstrom, Frederique Joanna Petrides, Ruth Sandra Rothstein, Elizabeth Kuyper, and Antonia Brico. "Several 1975 showings of the film 'Antonia, Portrait of a Woman' assisted greatly in bringing the cause of women conductors to the public's attention."[34]

Another "fearless pathfinder" in the male dominated field of conducting is French-born Blanche Honegger Moyse (b. 1911), one of the founders of the Marlboro School and Festival, and founder/artistic director of the Bach Festival in Brattleboro, Vermont.

Margaret Hillis (b. 1921), founder of the Chicago Symphony Chorus, points out that when she started conducting, "no master teacher would take a woman as a student because she had no future in conducting." She points out further that when she began, "There was no path you could go. I had to hoe my own row, . . . I had no role models, so I stumbled an awful lot." Participating on a "Women in Music: Choices and Chances" panel at the Juilliard School in 1989, Hillis said, "Man or woman, it's a difficult field. . ." Nevertheless, she predicted that within the next five years, the picture for women conductors would be brighter.[35]

Still another pioneer is the American-born Sarah Caldwell, founder/director of the Boston Opera Association. She was engaged to conduct the Metropolitan Opera in 1976. By the end of the 1980s, Eve Queler had distinguished herself as founder/conductor of the Opera Orchestra of New York (1967) and as an assistant conductor with the Fort Wayne Symphony Orchestra. The late Judith Somogi (1937–1988) had staked a claim as a noteworthy conductor through her long affiliation with the New York City Opera and as "kapellmeister" at the Frankfurt Opera, a career that regrettably ended too soon.

Heidi Waleson's April 1989 *New York Times* article "Music, Maestra, Please," focused on the new breed of women conductors. She wrote:

> The world of orchestral conducting has not been turned upside down just yet, of course—all the major orchestras are still in the hands of men and resistance to women is far from extinct. But the days when a woman on the podium might have provoked. . . [an] outburst from audiences seems to be fading, albeit only recently.[36]

Ms. Waleson's new breed included: (1) French-born Catherine Comet, a 1988 recipient of the prestigious Seaver/Arts Endowment Conductors Award, a former Exxon/Arts Endowment Conductor and then (1989) in her third year as music director of the Grand Rapids Symphony; (2) Jo Ann Falleta, winner of the Stokowski Conducting Competition (1985) and later conductor of the Queens Philharmonic, Denver Chamber Orchestra, Bay Area Women's Philharmonic, and future music director of the Virginia Symphony; (3) Marin Alsop, then assistant conductor of the Richmond (VA) Symphony, founder/music director of the New York-based chamber orchestra Concordia, future music director of Eugene (Oregon) Symphony, and a recipient of the Koussevitsky Conducting Prize (awarded to a Tanglewood Conducting Fellow); (4) Rachel Worby, music director of the Wheeling (West Virginia) Symphony and music director/conductor of Carnegie Hall's education program; (5) Victoria Bond, music director of the Roanoke (Virginia) Symphony; and (6) Englishwoman Iona Brown, director of the Academy of St. Martin-in-the-Fields and the Los Angeles Chamber Orchestra.

Waleson concluded:

> The obstacles to a career in conducting have not fallen entirely for women, of course . . . . The biggest orchestras still do not have women guest conductors. . . . And American women conductors have the same problem American men have: the preference of American orchestras for foreigners.[37]

Noticeably absent from Waleson's "Maestra" discussion were black women. Perhaps such was not an oversight, since no black woman was leading an "established" ensemble on a regular basis, and none had been championed by any of the nation's leading music critics or managers. Chances were that their "day in the sun" was not yet at hand.

Finally, the extent to which orchestra members, managers, boards, and audiences are today gender-blind remains a matter of speculation. The extent to which these same groups are color-blind is also a matter of speculation.

Brothers and Sisters "Keep on Steppin' "

Slightly more than two decades ago, *New York Times* music journalist Allen Hughes asked the question, "For Black Conductors, A Future? Or Frustration?"[38] The motivation behind his question was no doubt the projected return to the United States of the now immortal black conductor Dean Dixon (1915–1976), absent from this country for 21 years. Dixon was coming back to conduct the New York Philharmonic, the Pittsburgh Symphony, and the Saint Louis Symphony—all major American orchestras. He would guest conduct during the summer of 1970—all post-season events, primarily outdoors.

Dixon's triumphant return in July 1970 was preceded by Beatrice Berg's enlightening article "Dixon: Maestro Abroad, Stranger at Home," also appearing in the *New York Times*. She wrote:

[T]he man who is addressed as "Maestro" in other parts of the world, . . . is a stranger in his own country, virtually unknown to a whole generation of American concertgoers.[39]

Indeed, Dixon was unknown to traditional American concertgoers, but certainly well known in the black community. Negro (Black) History Week always included the name Dean Dixon, along with that of baseball legend Jackie Robinson, diplomat Ralph Bunche, abolitionist Frederick Douglass, et al.

During Dixon's absence, several major black conducting talents had emerged, namely Henry Lewis, James DePreist, and Paul Freeman. Each was determined to succeed—here in America. Lewis was then music director of the New Jersey Symphony, following several years as associate conductor of the Los Angeles Philharmonic. Paul Freeman had recently completed two years as associate conductor of the Dallas Symphony and was about to become conductor-in-residence with the Detroit Symphony. DePreist had been a 1964 first-prize winner in the Dimitri Mitropoulos Conducting Competition and had spent a year as assistant conductor of the New York Philharmonic; but despite a few guest appearances, no significant offers were forthcoming. Consequently, 1970 found DePreist in Europe, where he was experiencing many triumphs. Invitations from the U.S.A for guest conducting experiences were just beginning to arrive (National Symphony, Philadelphia Orchestra, and New York Philharmonic).

Journalist Hughes had in 1970 interviewed five black conductors between the ages of 24 and 37. They were Karl Hampton Porter, Isaiah Jackson, Harold Wheeler, Coleridge-Taylor Perkinson, and James Frazier. Wrote Hughes,

> Their knowledge is immense, their professional credentials are first rate, their capacity for hard work is formidable, and they have guts. All are concerned about their present and future places in the American musical world, and all have perceptive, sometimes challenging comments to make about it. . . . The prospects for their success are better now than ever before, but it remains to be seen if these prospects become realities before another generation of black musical leaders is weakened and scattered by frustration and exile.[40]

Said thirty-year-old Karl Hampton Porter, then conducting the Harlem Youth Philharmonic, "I have the feeling that black conductors are going to save music in this country, . . . Black people are prone to do more with very little, . . ." Twenty-four-year-old Isaiah Jackson, then conductor of the Youth Symphony of New York and assistant conductor to Leopold Stokowski (American Symphony Orchestra), said, "The whole blackness thing is something I'm not very conscious of. . . . I've heard that orchestras are in search of black people, now, . . . but I'd like to be judged as a musician first." Thirty-year-old James Frazier, who in 1969 became the youngest conductor ever to win the Guido Cantelli International competition at La Scala (Milan, Italy) remarked, "Every young conductor is going to be tested by an orchestra . . . but, on the other hand, no group is totally free of biased individuals."

Harold Wheeler, then 26 and associated primarily with the theater, reflected on his role as a conductor trying to reach broader audiences:

> I think the present concert situation does not mean very much to the young . . . I would love to take a Mozart or Tchaikovsky work, or, say Dvorak's "New World Symphony," with which I have already experimented, and, without changing a note of the original score, superimpose a six-piece rhythm section on it to add contemporary rhythms to the music . . . . Conductors should be able to adapt themselves with equal proficiency to everything from Vivaldi to the music of "Blood, Sweat and Tears."

Thirty-seven-year-old Coleridge-Taylor Perkinson, then music director for television's Barbara McNair Show and a successful film composer, "entered the commercial field only after concluding that no other possibility was open to him." Perkinson said:

> I think more opportunities might have been forthcoming had I not been Negro, or black, or who I am. . . . I did my homework here . . . but got my experience in Europe. . . . It hurts that I am not working in my proper field. . . . When I am more secure financially, I would like to go back to Europe and do some more craft-polishing. The doors are still open to me there.[41]

In 1968, Allen Hughes offered an interesting piece to *New York Times* readers, titled "And Now There Are Three." Henry Lewis had only recently been appointed music director of the New Jersey Symphony; the American Ballet Theater had appointed George Byrd as one of its assistant conductors; and James Frazier was about to guest conduct the Detroit Symphony, having already conducted the Royal Liverpool Philharmonic Symphony, the Danish State Radio Orchestra, and the RAI Orchestra in Rome.[42]

Black music journalist Earl Calloway wrote a full-page article in the black *Chicago Daily Defender*, titled "Black Conductors Making Progress." January 8–14, 1972, for his primarily black readership:

> It is unfortunate that too many of our [black] leaders fail to recognize the tremendous progress blacks have made even in the face of adversity. . . . [W]hen a brother makes it through those dismal clouds, let everybody say "Amen," "Right On Brother" and recognize the inch of progress he has made. . . . Realizing that it is difficult for American-born whites, then the situation has been almost impossible for blacks. For too many years there were hardly any opportunities for a black musical director. Thank God the situation is changing, but at a snail's pace.[43]

Calloway's list of those who had made it "through those dismal clouds" included Henry Lewis, Paul Freeman, Isaiah Jackson, James DePreist, Everett Lee, and James Frazier, as well as the black female conductor Margaret Harris and composer/conductor Primous Fountain. Calloway's informational piece also recognized F. Stith, then assistant conductor of the Harvard-Radcliffe Symphony Orchestra. Maestra Harris, musical director of the Broadway musical "Hair" (including the national touring company), had recently conducted the Grant Park Symphony and the Chicago Symphony (summer of 1971) and would soon make her television conducting debut on WBBM-TV, leading the Chicago Chamber Orchestra.[44]

When the black magazine *Sepia* published a feature article, "The New Black Symphony Conductors," in October 1974, it was four years after Dixon's first return visit, in a conducting capacity, to the U.S.A. Then thirty-two-year-old James Frazier was represented rehearsing the Spanish National Radio and Television Symphony on tour. Other featured subjects were James DePreist, then associate conductor of the National Symphony, and Paul Freeman, conductor-in-residence of the Detroit Symphony.

Everett Lee, who made an auspicious New York City debut conducting the Cosmopolitan Little Symphony at Town Hall twenty-six years before and the New York City Opera eighteen years later, had extended his conducting activities with the Norrkoping

Symphony in Sweden to include the Symphony of the New World in New York City. Following six years as music director of the New Jersey Symphony, Henry Lewis was making history as the first Black to conduct the world famous Metropolitan Opera (1972) and the Royal Philharmonic in London's Royal Festival Hall.[45] Not only was there evidence of changing attitudes, but, more importantly, there was every indication that more black Americans were believing that there was for them a future in the area of symphonic conducting—even in their native America.

When Everett Lee made his debut with the New York Philharmonic at Avery Fisher Hall on January 15, 1976, one of the works that he conducted was "Kosbro" by the black composer, David Baker. Literally translated, "Kosbro" means "Keep on steppin', brothers."

Such advice was being heeded not only by "brothers" but by "sisters" as well. In addition to Margaret Harris's conducting involvements, Tania León was in her eighth year as music director of the Dance Theatre of Harlem. Kay George Roberts had recently received a Master of Musical Arts in Conducting from Yale University School of Music and had conducted her hometown orchestra, the Nashville Symphony. Subsequently, Roberts became the second Black and first female to earn the doctorate in conducting from Yale.

During an interview with maestro Lee shortly prior to the Avery Fisher Hall event, black journalist and music critic Raoul Abdul posed the following question to Lee:

> Along with Dean Dixon, you have been a pioneer in the field of conducting for Blacks. How do you feel about the fact that there are now many young Blacks getting the opportunity to conduct major orchestras?

Responded Lee, "I think it is wonderful."[46]

The black magazine, *Ebony*, published an article "The Maestros: Black Symphony Conductors Are Making A Name for Themselves," in February 1989. Wrote Dalton Narine:

> It was in the 1940s, and the man on the podium was Dean Dixon, a Black man. In the audience was young Denis de Coteau, watching with his father as Dixon led the New York Philharmonic, and deciding then and there that he, too, would become a symphony conductor.

Dixon was the first Black to conduct a major symphony orchestra, and de Coteau, now music director of the San Francisco Ballet Orchestra, recalls: "I couldn't believe a Black man was standing there coaxing such beautiful sound from a hundred musicians."[47]

James DePreist had, in 1980, become music director of the Oregon Symphony, following seven years in Canada as conductor of the Quebec Symphony Orchestra. Paul Freeman, music director emeritus of the Victoria Symphony in British Columbia, was in 1989 founder/music director of the newly created Chicago Sinfonietta (1987). Isaiah Jackson was working on both sides of the Atlantic, as music director of the Royal Ballet Orchestra in London and the Dayton Symphony in Ohio.

Raymond Harvey, the first Black to earn a doctorate in conducting from Yale University, was in 1989 music director of the Springfield (Massachusetts) Symphony. Kay George Roberts had become a professor of music at the University of Massachusetts-Lowell and she was then music director of the University's orchestra, as well as frequent conductor of the New York Housing Authority Symphony Orchestra. Leslie Dunner was associate conductor of the Dance Theatre of Harlem's Orchestra and assistant conductor of the Detroit Symphony. Cuban-born Tania León was music director of the Brooklyn Philharmonic's Community Concert series, having made her conducting debut at the Spoleto Festival (Italy) in 1972 and having received the Dean Dixon Conducting Award in 1985.

Willie Anthony Waters represented a rare breed, as artistic director of the Greater Miami Opera Company. William Henry Curry had recently completed five years as associate conductor of the Indianapolis Symphony Orchestra, following positions with the Richmond and Baltimore Symphony orchestras and the Saint Paul Chamber Orchestra. Moving rapidly through the ranks was Michael Morgan, then assistant conductor of the Chicago Symphony. It was Morgan who commented to Narine, "Each generation of conductors paves the way for the next."[48]

Prelude to Black Conductor Profiles

From inception of the idea to prepare this publication, the writer set the following parameters: (1) I was concerned with leaders of instrumental ensembles (ten or more players) performing in all genres of music and performing at any variety of venues; (2) living black conductors would help shape their own profiles; and (3) the author would not attempt to engage in classifying conductors as "great," "less great," "on the verge of greatness," "established," "emerging," "promising," or something similar. A conductor's profile would speak for itself; press reviews would convey critics' assessments of talent and specific performances. The absence of and limitations on press reviews should not reflect negatively on the profiled subject.

Quantity of material would be secondary to quality of material from the standpoint of mainstream assessment. The publication's goal would be to "circulate the word"—black conductors exist, have always existed, and will continue to exist and advance.

One important historian of orchestras and conductors wrote that his "parameters were not fixed" or his "criteria established with any intention of excluding women or blacks [sic]."[49] For the present writer, the parameters were fixed and the criterion of exclusion was established—all are black; all others are intentionally excluded. With the exception of Dunbar, León, and Robertson, all are American-born. These three however, all received American training. Though Dunbar spent much of his life in England, he departed for foreign soil on an American mission. León built her conducting, piano performance, and composing career in America. Robertson and his family moved to the United States from Jamaica when he was quite young. This compilation of profiles may not be as selective as some readers might desire, but the intent in these pages is simply to include those conductors who exhibited presence and involvement in the field, with outstanding achievements along the way.

Notes

1. Adam Carse, *The Orchestra*, New York: Chanticleer Press, Inc., 1949, p. 39.
2. Adam Carse, *Orchestral Conducting*, London: Augener Ltd., 1935, p. 94. Reprint, Westport, Connecticut: Greenwood Press, 1971.
3. Joseph Machlis, *The Enjoyment of Music*, rev. ed. New York: W. W. Norton and Company, Inc., 1963, p. 401.
4. Howard Taubman, *The Maestro: The Life of Arturo Toscanini*, New York: Simon and Schuster, 1951, p. 181.

5. Elliott Galkin, *A History of Orchestral Conducting In Theory and Practice*, New York: Pendragon Press, 1988, p. xxxvi.

6. Chester Lane, "A League of Their Own: The American Symphony Orchestra League Then and Now," *Symphony*, July/August 1992, pp. 58–59.

7. Douglas Merilatt, "Conductor Training and The American Symphony Orchestra League," *Symphony Magazine*, August/September 1986, pp. 43–44.

8. *Ibid.*, p. 43.

9. "Conducting Continuum Created," *Symphony*, January/February 1990, p. 70.

10. Helen Epstein, *Music Talks: Conversations With Musicians*, New York: McGraw-Hill Book Company, 1987, pp. 27–45.

11. *Ibid.*, p. 35.

12. Press Release, April 18, 1984, Affiliate Artists News.

13. Linda Sanders, "Career Advancement and the Conducting Competition," *Symphony Magazine*, August/September 1986, p. 38.

14. *Ibid.*, pp. 37–40.

15. *Musical America: International Directory of the Performing Arts*, New York: Musical America Publishing, Inc., 1981, pp. 682–691.

16. Charles Munch, *I Am a Conductor*, New York: Oxford University Press, 1955, pp. 58–59.

17. Kurt Blaukopf, *Great Conductors*, London: Arco Publishers Limited, 1955, p. 37.

18. Norman Lebrecht, *The Maestro Myth: Great Conductors in Pursuit of Power*, New York: Carol Publishing Group, 1991.

19. *Ibid.*, pp. 1–2.

20. "The Function of a Conductor," *Music Journal*, vol. 26 (April 1968), pp. 27, 60.

21. Harold C. Schonberg, *The Great Conductors*, New York: Simon and Schuster, 1967, pp. 15–16.

22. Leonard Bernstein, *The Joy of Music*, New York: Simon and Schuster, 1967, pp. 122–123.

23. "In Search of Shaw's Successor," *Atlanta Journal and Constitution*, January 19, 1986, p. J4.

24. *Selecting A Music Director* (A Handbook for Trustees and Management), Washington, DC: American Symphony Orchestra League, 1985, pp. 6–7.

25. Howard Shanet, *Philharmonic: A History of New York's Orchestra*, Garden City, New York: Doubleday and Company, Inc., 1975, pp. 296–297.

26. Frank Tirro, *Jazz: A History*, New York: W.W. Norton and Company, Inc., 1977, p. 227.

27. George T. Simon, *The Big Bands*, rev. ed., New York: Collier Books, 1974, p. 13.
28. Gene Lees, "The Big Bands," *High Fidelity Magazine*, September 1977, p. 24.
29. Howard Reich, "Big Band Boom," *Chicago Tribune*, April 26, 1992, Section 13, p. 22.
30. Elliott W. Galkin, *op. cit.* p. xxxviii.
31. D. C. Denison, "Gisele Ben-Dor," *Boston Globe Magazine*, May 17, 1992, p. 8.
32. Dixie Lynam Huthmaker, "Victoria Bond: Leading Men On," *College Woman*, March 1988, p. 14.
33. Benjamin Ivry, "Orchestral Firsts," *Sky* (Delta Airlines Magazine), December 1988, p. 94.
34. D. Antoinette Handy, *Black Women in American Bands & Orchestras*, Metuchen, N. J.: Scarecrow Press, 1981, p. 29.
35. Laura Van Tuyl, "The Opening Door," *Chicago Tribune*, January 6, 1989, p. 3, Section 5 (Tempo).
36. Heidi Waleson, "Music, Maestra, Please," *New York Times*, April 16, 1989, Section 2, p. 1.
37. *Ibid.*, Section 2, p. 36.
38. Allen Hughes, "For Black Conductors, A Future? Or Frustrations," *New York Times*, March 15, 1970, pp. D19, 32.
39. Beatrice Berg, "Dixon: Maestro Abroad, Stranger At Home," *New York Times*, July 19, 1970, p. D11.
40. Hughes, *op. cit.*, p. 32.
41. *Ibid.*
42. Allen Hughes, "And Now There Are Three," *New York Times*, March 17, 1968, p. D19.
43. Earl Calloway, "Black Conductors Making Progress," *Chicago Daily Defender*, January 8–14, 1972, p. 36.
44. *Ibid.*
45. Chris Bockman and Nick J. Hall, "The New Black Symphony Conductors," *Sepia*, October 1974, pp. 18–29.
46. Raoul Abdul, *Blacks In Classical Music*, New York: Dodd, Mead and Company, 1977, p. 194.
47. Dalton Narine, "The Maestros (Black Symphony Conductors Are Making A Name for Themselves)," *Ebony*, February 1989, p. 54.
48. *Ibid.*, pp. 54, 56, 60, 62.
49. Philip Hart, *Conductors: A New Generation*, New York: Charles Scribner's Sons, 1979, p. xviii.

PART II: CONDUCTOR PROFILES, B–H

William "Count" Basie, at Plaza Gardens, Disneyland; Anaheim, California, early 1980's (Photo by Patricia Willard, with permission)

WILLIAM JAMES "COUNT" BASIE, JR.

BIRTHDATE/PLACE: August 21, 1904; Red Bank, New Jersey.
DEATH DATE/PLACE: April 26, 1984; Hollywood, Florida.
EDUCATION: Public Schools of Red Bank, New Jersey.
INSTRUCTORS: Mother and Mrs. Holloway (German Instructor).
AWARDS/HONORS (partial): Metronome Poll (1942–43); Jazz Merit Award, The Lamplighter (1945); Esquire Award (1945); Down Beat International Critics Poll Winner (1952–56); Down Beat Hall of Fame (1958); Honorary Doctor of Music, University of Missouri at Kansas City (1978) and Berklee College of Music (1982); Hollywood Walk of Fame (1982); ASCAP Award and Kennedy Center Honor (1981).
NUMEROUS TRIBUTES.
FILM APPEARANCES: "Cinderella," "Sex and the Single Girl," "Crazy House," "Hit Parade of 1943," "Top Man," "Reveille with Beverly," "Stage Door Canteen," "Choo-Choo Swing," "Made in Paris," "Jamboree," "One More Time," "Man of the Family," "Blazing Saddles."

A COUNT BASIE PROFILE APPEARED in *Down Beat* November 17, 1950. The profile began with a recall of the Basie band's "roar out of the west" fourteen years earlier,

> bursting with a vigor that hit the music business like a charge of dynamite. . . .The storm Basie generated that winter has never really subsided. . . .[T]hey blew the roof off the world and created a style—Kansas City—and a legend that never will disappear.[1]

On the day following Basie's death, a *Washington Post* music critic offered "An Appreciation":

> A central figure in the closed circle of jazz royalty that included King Oliver, Duke Ellington* and Earl Hines.* Count Basie was an elegant man. In his later years, his silver-tinged mutton chops crowded in on a gracious smile that defined his gentleman's demeanor. You never heard bad things about the Count, and you heard little from the Count himself. A witty man who favored a

29

deadpan humor in private, he was genially close-mouthed in public. He preferred to let his band speak for him, and he led them with a subtle body English of shrugged shoulders, lifted eyebrows and cocked head.[2]

William James Basie's elevation to the status of jazz royalty, with the title "Count," can be attributed to a radio announcer in Kansas City who made the designation in the mid-1930s. But a half century later Basie is said to have confidentially disclosed the fact that he hated the title. "I wanted to be called 'Buck' or 'Hoot' or even 'Arkansas Fats'."[3]

"Perpetual catalyst," "jazz monarch," "the sultan of swing," "an institution," "grandmaster of jazz," "the most explosive force in jazz"—the accolades never ceased for the Count, both in life and in death. From the mid-1930s, when Basie departed Kansas City (where his career was launched) for the bright lights—and competition—of New York City to the present, countless commentators (critics, listeners and Basie himself) ventured their opinions of why the band was so extraordinary. Fortunately his music and his music-making are preserved for posterity on hundreds of superb recordings.[4]

Biographer Raymond Horricks, in 1957, gave this assessment of Basie and his organization:

[I]t has been Basie's personal guidance which has been the final determining factor in forging and sustaining the band's unique jazz expression; with him at the helm, the band has overcome all its teeth-ing problems and the various difficulties which have beset it. . . , so that today its reputation stands higher than ever.[5]

Basie's view was somewhat different; he often stressed the importance of the drummer. He indicated that leaders might think they're the boss, but the drummer is generally the head man. But as jazz historian George Simon wrote in 1967:

Basie is strictly in charge at all times. This may not be obvious to those on the outside, though if they watch the band long enough, they'll realize that all the directions come from little, subtle motions from the Count at the piano. He may shrug his shoulders in a certain way to give a specific warning to the drummer. He may cock his head at a special angle to tell the entire band to come way down in volume. Or he may hit just one key note to cue the ensemble into a rousing, roaring finale.[6]

Since Simon had rejected the Basie band initially (in favor of the Kansas City Andy Kirk Band), it is significant to note his assessment of the band and its reason for continued success thirty years later.

> What attracted customers . . . was [the band's] ability to play big band jazz that almost anybody can understand. For the Basie band's appeal has always been basically emotional and surprisingly simple. The beat has always been there, . . . But even more important, Basie's emphasis upon simple, hummable riffs—contagious, swinging melodic figures played by the entire ensemble—has drawn large audiences to his music. . . . Despite great changes in musical tastes . . . the Basie band continued to blow and boom in the same sort of simple, swinging, straight-ahead groove in which it had slid out of Kansas City in the mid-thirties.[7]

Commenting on *Good Morning Blues: The Autobiography of Count Basie*, as told to Albert Murray, *Time* magazine noted:

> Basie had one supreme gift: He knew how to mold a dozen or more idiosyncratic instrumentalists into a single, pulsating organism with a voice of its own, which was always somehow his voice.[8]

But the greatest testimony to Basie's dynamic leadership is the fact that the Count Basie Band has continued (in the Basie tradition), following the monarch's death in 1984, first under the leadership of Thad Jones (now deceased) and then under the leadership of Frank Foster, both veterans of the world class ensemble. Said Foster at the Fourth Annual Congressional Black Caucus's "Jazz Issues Forum" (September 8, 1988; Washington, D.C.), "Now that we have declared jazz an American National Treasure (H. Con. Res. 57), perhaps it is time to declare the Basie Band an American National Treasure."[9]

The Charlie Parker Memorial Foundation (Kansas City) announced in mid-December 1984 that the continuing seventeen-piece Count Basie Orchestra would be housed permanently in Kansas City. The annual schedule for the band projected a one-month residency in Kansas City (essentially to rehearse new material), 40 weeks of touring, and participation in educational activities at the proposed International Jazz Hall of Fame. Approaching the 1990s, all was still at the stage of projection; but the Basie band was continuing, performing both throughout the country and abroad. It was by no means a ghost band; many members had spent twenty-five years or more with the Count himself.

In preparation for the band's appearance at the 16th Annual Convention of the National Association of Jazz Educators (now International Association of Jazz Educators), Production Manager Dennis Wilson wrote a most informative article for the organization's publication, *Jazz Educators Journal*. Wilson addressed the question of "The Count Basie Band: How Do They Do It?" The response was:

> a. Precision ensembles, b. A wide use of the dynamic spectrum, c. Liquid sax soli's [sic], d. A driving rhythmic pulse, e. Soloists that combine personality and technique in a powerful linear presentation, f. A unique "lay back" style, g. An acoustic performance, [and] h. Straight ahead swing.

"The Band," said leader Dr. Frank Foster, "will always maintain the Basie foundation it has built over 50 years."[10]

The Count Orchestra [Band] by then had taken on the mission of jazz education. The answer to the question "How Do They Do It?" would be provided by the Count Basie Band itself, through a clinic program called "The Basie Way." More and more training institutions were "buying in" to the idea.

Returning to the unique individual who created this ensemble that continues in his tradition, it should be noted that his passion for music actually developed gradually. His early interest was show business. The son of a gardener and a domestic, Basie received rudimentary piano instruction from his mother. For a period thereafter, he was given piano lessons, at a cost of 25¢ each, from Mrs. Holloway, who was German.

By age 13, Basie had formed his own band, playing for school dances. Though he was originally the drummer, circumstances forced him to the keyboard: when the pianist failed to show for a job, Basie had to substitute. On that occasion, he relinquished the drums to another famous Red Bank citizen, Sonny Greer. Greer (who later joined the Duke Ellington Band) was so obviously talented that Basie decided that he himself should remain at the keyboard and leave the drumming to his more skilled replacement.

The "pianist" moved to New York City in the early 1920s, where he learned from such black stride masters as Willie "The Lion" Smith, James P. Johnson, and Thomas "Fats" Waller. Basie was a regular visitor to the Lincoln Theatre in Harlem where Waller played the organ. After a time, Waller invited Basie to sit with him in the pit. Basie soon graduated from the status of observer and was permitted to work the pedals. Eventually he was allowed to sit beside Waller at the console.

Basie toured the vaudeville circuit, playing piano at theatres, speakeasies, and hotels. Around 1925, he headed west with Gonzelle White's road show. All was well for close to two years. However, when the show reached Kansas City, the tour fell apart. Basie was stranded. For a year, he played the organ in a silent movie house, the Eblon Theatre, just as Waller had at the Lincoln Theatre in New York City.

In 1928, Basie began playing with Kansas City bands, first with Walter Page's Blue Devils and then with Bennie Moten. By 1935, Basie had formed his own band, organized from remnants of the Moten band, whose leader had died. He secured a booking at the Reno Club where there were experimental broadcasting facilities (W9XBY). With the mighty vocalist Jimmy Rushing now sitting in with the band and a phenomenal rhythm section (including drummer Jo Jones, bassist Walter Page, and guitarist Freddie Green), Basie and his men quickly established an enviable reputation.

Through the airwaves, Basie reached the attention of music journalist and "catalytic agent" John Hammond, who succeeded in getting the band signed by the Music Corporation of America. While Hammond was negotiating a recording contract with Brunswick, Basie himself negotiated a recording contract with the newly-organized Decca label. This was to be "the most expensive blunder in Basie's history." According to Hammond, the contract paid "$750 for 24 sides by a full band, without one penny of artist's royalty, . . ."[11]

During the course of 1935, Basie was beginning to feel that the time was right for the band to seek its fortunes beyond Kansas City—and ultimately in New York City. The first significant appearance outside of Kansas City was an engagement at the Grand Terrace on the south side of Chicago, following the Fletcher Henderson* Band.

The performance of the Basie contingent was less than impressive. However, the fact that the Grand Terrace possessed one of the best radio wires in the country (reaching audiences from coast to coast) justified MCA's decision to book the band at the elaborate supper club. And the fact that the band was "different" caused it to attract notice from "perceptive critics in the trade press."[12] The band benefited musically from the experience, aided tremendously by Fletcher Henderson who generously shared charts that gave the Basie sound a sophistication it had not previously enjoyed.

With a band now enlarged from nine to thirteen, Basie headed east. The band made its debut in the Big Apple at the Roseland Ballroom, December 1936, where it experienced an uncertain reception. According to Ross Russell, there was

> a debacle at the William Penn Hotel in Pittsburgh, and reservations on the part of black audiences at Savoy Ballroom and the Apollo Theatre in New York. . . . Whatever the public felt about the Count Basie Orchestra during its first year, the band rated as an unqualified success with critics and record reviewers, and these voices, although in the minority, had a cumulative effect in upgrading the band and establishing it in the front rank. . . . For the perceptive, the hip, and the aspiring jazz musician, appearances of the Count Basie Orchestra became the most exciting events of those years.[13]

While the band was in Chicago, Hammond had arranged to record five members by the full ensemble (Brunswick-Vocalion); the full band recorded in New York City on January 22, 1937 (Decca). The latter was released only weeks following the session.

On December 23, 1938, Basie and his band participated in the landmark Carnegie Hall Concert "American Negro Music," produced by John Hammond. The event included such musical legends as Albert Ammons, Joe Turner, Sanford Terry, Sidney Bechet, James Rushing, James P. Johnson, Helen Humes and Sister Rosetta Tharpe. Titled "From Spirituals to Swing" and dedicated to the recently deceased blues queen Bessie Smith, the concert began with recorded African Tribal Music and concluded with Swing. Basie's Blue Five (Basie; Shad Collins, trumpet; Walter Page, Bass; Jo Jones, drums, and Hershel Evans, tenor saxophone) and Count Basie and His Orchestra were featured on the program.[14]

From the Reno Club in Kansas City, to the Grand Terrace in Chicago, to Pittsburgh's Hotel William Penn and Boston's Ritz Carlton, to New York City's Roseland and Savoy Ballrooms, the Paramount and Apollo Theatres, and the Famous Door Nightclub, Basie was now making his Carnegie Hall debut. The program notes included a lengthy entry on the maestro, as well as an excellent essay on the subject "The Music Nobody Knows."[15] The concert was repeated the following year (December 24, 1939) at the same locale, but fewer artists were involved. The Basie band shared the stage with Benny Goodman and his orchestra.

The only period during which Basie did not lead a big band was between 1950 and 1952. These were lean times financially and Basie was forced to use combos of six to nine instruments. But his revived big band made the first of its many European tours in 1954. In 1974, shortly following his seventieth birthday "Royal Salute" in New York City, the Basie Band left on its twentieth European tour.

Radio, television, and film appearances were numerous. There was a Command Performance for Queen Elizabeth II; Basie's was the featured band at the Inaugural Ball of President John F. Kennedy. Basie and his band were indeed American institutions. Through the years, it had included in its ranks a most illustrious list of musicians: Buck Clayton, Harry Edison, Joe Newman, Clark Terry, Thad Jones, and Gerald Wilson, trumpets; Dickey Wells, Benny Morton, Vic Dickenson, J. J. Johnson, Benny Powell, Al Grey, and Quentin Jackson, trombones; Lester Young, Herschel Evans, Buddy Tate, Earl Warren, Don Byas, Illinois Jacquet, Paul Quinichette, Ernie Wilkins, Eddie "Lockjaw" Davis, Frank Wess, and Frank Foster, saxophones; Walter Page, bass; Freddie Green, guitar; Jo Jones, drums; and Jimmy Rushing, Billie Holiday, Helen Humes, and Joe Williams, vocalists.

In 1977, the Charlie Parker Foundation held a three-day salute to Count Basie. The festivities included an official welcome from the mayor, a star-studded press conference, and a concert that included, in addition to the Count and his band, guest artists Clark Terry, Max Roach, Eddie "Lockjaw" Davis, Zoot Sims, Dave Brubeck, Jay McShann, Oscar Peterson, and Ella Fitzgerald.[16]

William "Count" Basie was a 1981 Kennedy Center Honoree, along with choreographer Jerome Robbins, actress Helen Hayes, actor Cary Grant, and pianist Rudolf Serkin. Of Basie, *The Washington Post* wrote:

> In a career that began in New York's Roaring Twenties and came to fruition in a wide-open Kansas City in the Prohibition Thirties, Basie has become virtually synonymous with the word "swing," a catalyst and bandleader for five uninterrupted decades. From the good times of the '40s through the hard times of the '60s and '70s, Basie-led bands offered no radical changes, but they could always be counted on to swing madly.[17]

Basie's only expressed regret was that he was alone in receiving the honor. Without the band, Basie was never completely at ease.

In 1982, the Black Music Association honored Basie with a gala at New York City's Radio City Music Hall. Paying tribute were Lena Horne, Stevie Wonder, Joe Williams, Oscar Peterson, and Quincy Jones.

He and the band returned to Kansas City in 1983, to enjoy and participate in the maestro's 79th birthday celebration. Mayor Richard L. Berkley presented the keys to the city and described Basie as "our leading international citizen." Basie responded as best he could for the overflow crowd that had assembled at the Crown Center Square. The victim of a recent heart attack, the leader arrived on stage by way of a motorized cart.

The "Master of Swing" died in Hollywood, Florida on April 26, 1984, at age seventy-nine. The loss was reported as front-page news in *The New York Times* the following day. On May 1, 1984, the front page in the same paper carried the story "Jazz World Bids Farewell to Basie in Harlem." Among the thousands of mourners were "the musicians who swung with Count Basie and the dancers who swung to him." Several verbalized their feelings:

"A legend is lost. And he is the kind of legend who is irreplaceable."—Vibraphonist Milt Jackson

"The last of the A-Team is gone."—Composer, band leader, producer Quincy Jones

"I've hi-de-hi-de-hied and I've hi-de-hi-de-hoed for a long, long time, but I've never been put in a spot like this."—Bandleader Cab Calloway*

"Here was a guy who reached the pinnacle of his success and still sat in the background. As great a musician as he was, he was content to sit back and push someone else. He's the world's greatest accompanist."—Trumpeter Dizzy Gillespie[18]

But "The Basie Way" continues. As the Count's adopted son, Aaron A. Woodward III (chief executive officer and president of Count Basie Enterprises, Inc.), states, "The major contributions of Dad will always be in American history."[19] Now in the hands of leader Frank Foster, "The Basie Way" will always be in world history.

Notes

1. Ralph Gleason, "Basie Will Always Have a Swing Band," *Down Beat*, November 17, 1950, p. 1.
2. Richard Harrington, "Count Basie, the Jazz Monarch," *Washington Post*, April 27, 1984, p. B1.
3. Bert Barnes, "Jazzman Count Basie Is Dead at Age 79," *Washington Post*, April 27, 1984, p. C4.
4. For a selected discography, see Alun Morgan, *Count Basie*, New York: Hippocrene Books, 1984, pp. 72–92.
5. Raymond Horricks, *Count Basie and His Orchestra: Its Music and Its Musicians*, 2nd ed., Westport, Connecticut: Negro Universities Press, 1971, p. 30.
6. George T. Simon, *The Big Bands*, rev. enlarged ed., New York: Collier Books, 1976, pp. 86–87.
7. *Ibid.*, p. 87.
8. "Bookends," *Time*, March 10, 1986, p. 74.
9. Under the auspices of Congressman John Conyers (First District, Michigan), "Jazz" was placed on the Congressional Black Caucus Weekend agenda, beginning in 1985. Topics have been "Jazz: Its Cultural Importance and Its Link to Black Political Empowerment" (1985); "Jazz: An American National Treasure" (1986); "Jazz: A Family Tradition" (1987); "Jazz: The Big Band Tradition" (1988).
10. Dennis Wilson, "The Count Basie Orchestra: How Do They Do It?," *Jazz Educators Journal*, Convention 1989, p. 23.
11. Ross Russell, *Jazz Style in Kansas City and the Southwest*, Berkeley, California: University of California Press, 1971, pp. 139–140.
12. *Ibid.,* pp. 140–141.
13. *Ibid.,* p. 142.
14. James Dugan and John Hammond, "An Early Black-Music Concert: From Spirituals to Swing," *Black Perspective in Music*, Fall 1974, pp. 191–208.
15. *Ibid.*
16. "Count Basie," *Down Beat*, December 1, 1977, pp. 36–37.
17. Richard Harrington, "The Kennedy Center Honors," *Washington Post*, December 6, 1981, p. K1.
18. Samuel G. Freedman, "Jazz World Bids Farewell to Basie in Harlem," *New York Times*, pp. A1, B6.
19. Dennis Wilson, *op. cit.*, p. 24.

Blanche Calloway (Courtesy: Schomburg Center for Research in Black Culture)

BLANCHE DOROTHEA CALLOWAY (JONES)

BIRTHDATE/PLACE: February 2, 1902; Baltimore, Maryland.
DEATH DATE/PLACE: December 16, 1978; Baltimore, Maryland.
EDUCATION: Morgan State College.
INSTRUCTOR: Llewelyn Wilson (voice and piano).†
PRINCIPAL ACTIVITIES: Member of the traveling act "Oma Crosby and Her Five Cubanolas" (singer/dancer); "Shuffle Along" (singer/soubrette) and "Plantation Days" (singer). Appearances with various bands, including those led by Louis Armstrong, Earl Hines, and Cab Calloway (her brother).
LEADER: Blanche Calloway and Her Twelve Clouds of Joy (Joy Boys), 1931–44.
OTHER ACTIVITIES: Manager, Jim Jam Night Club (Philadelphia, Pennsylvania); Disc Jockey, WMBM (Miami, Florida).

THERE WAS A PERIOD WHEN the more famous Cab Calloway* was known simply as "Blanche's younger brother." It was the older Calloway who assisted the younger one in his show business breakthrough, though she advised against it. Cab's book, *Of Minnie the Moocher and Me* (1976), is dedicated to his wife and family and "sister Blanche who introduced me to the wonderful world of entertainment."[1]

In the mid-1920s, Blanche Calloway toured extensively with various traveling revues as singer and dancer. Her departure from Baltimore was to join the traveling act Oma Crosby and Her Five Cubanolas. "Ms. Calloway with her light complexion was one of the 'Cubanolas,' a singer-dancer from Afro-America who had to disguise her origins to get work."[2]

She fronted Andy Kirk's band in 1931 for a residency at Philadelphia's Pearl Theatre. Subsequently she fronted her own bands. Records indicate that the Blanche Calloway Band (all-male)

---

†Other Wilson pupils of distinction: Eubie Blake, Anne Wiggins Brown (the original Bess in George Gershwin's "Porgy and Bess"), Cab Calloway (band leader, singer, actor, and younger brother of Blanche), Avon Long (Sportin' Life in "Porgy and Bess" and star of "Bubbling Brown Sugar"), Ellis Larkins (jazz pianist), Thomas Kerr and Mark Fax (composers).

appeared at New York City's Lafayette Theatre (1931–34), Harlem Opera House (1934–35), and Apollo Theatre (1935–38 and 1941).

Calloway's band once made a five-band tour with Bennie Moten, Andy Kirk, Chick Webb,* and Zack Whythe's bands. Blanche Calloway and Her Joy Boys recorded extensively in 1931 (Victor) and again in 1934 and 1935. Bands under her leadership played in all parts of the United States, including Baltimore, Boston, Atlantic City, Indianapolis, Cleveland, Cincinnati, St. Louis, Kansas City, and Pittsburgh. Playing under her direction were such jazz artists as Cozy Cole (drums), Andy Jackson (guitar), Vic Dickenson (trombone), and Ben Webster (tenor saxophone).[3]

A 1931 *Pittsburgh Courier* Band/Orchestral Survey listed thirty-eight "Leading Negro Orchestras" nationally. Blanche's band (the only one led by a woman) ranked ninth, only five places below Louis Armstrong and well in advance of bands fronted by Jimmie Lunceford,* Chick Webb,* Bennie Moten, Claude Hopkins, and several others that made jazz history.[4]

A 1932 *Pittsburgh Courier* article referred to Blanche Calloway as "one of the most progressive performers in the profession," acknowledging the ownership, management, and directorship of her then popular Twelve Clouds of Joy.[5] In a 1950 *International Musician* article entitled "Dance Bands That Made History," seven female orchestra leaders were singled out for recognition. Blanche Calloway, the only Black, was included in the list.[6]

Calloway studied piano and voice with Llewelyn Wilson, prominent Baltimore music teacher and conductor of the Baltimore City Colored Chorus. She also attended Morgan State College.

She made a mid-1940 appearance as leader of an all-girl orchestra at Club Harlem in Atlantic City, New Jersey, but the group survived only for a short period. She briefly worked as a solo artist, then settled in Philadelphia, where she managed a night club. She was also active in community and political affairs. Blanche later moved to Florida, where she served as executive director (and disc jockey) of Miami's radio station WMBM. Subsequently she founded and served as president of Afram House, Inc., a firm specializing in cosmetics and cosmetic aids for Blacks.[7]

Calloway spent the last six years of her life in her native Baltimore, Maryland. The City's Mayor declared August 13, 1978, "Blanche Calloway Day." On this day, the Waxter Center for Senior Citizens honored the former singer, dancer, soubrette, band leader, business woman, and civic worker. The 76-year-old honoree recalled her various careers by way of narration and slides from her personal scrapbooks. A group of senior citizens, calling themselves The Waxter Free Spirit Motionaires, performed a specially choreographed work titled "In celebration of Blanche."[8]

Multi-talented Calloway was "still going strong," despite her confinement much of the time to a wheelchair. She reminded journalist Earl Arnett,

> Oh, I was something to look at, . . . But I don't feel any differently now. I feel so young. I can't feel old. . . . I've got no regret in the world and would do the same thing all over again.[9]

She continued with words of advice for those seeking a future in show business:

> You need an innate desire to share with the public a talent that you have along with a little love, that's so important coming across that footlight. That love and integrity has got to be in your heart, in your soul so that people can see it being projected. Just be who you are and what you are and get it out so that people can feel it and know it.[10]

Blanche Calloway died four months later. She was eulogized as the 1930's and early '40s "Queen of Swing"—

> the leading female band leader rotating on the Chitterlin' Circuit, playing the Lafayette Theatre on 7th Avenue; the Apollo in Harlem; the Regal in Chicago; the Royal in Baltimore and the old Howard Theatre in Washington.[11]

Notes

1. Cab Calloway and Bryant Rollins, *Of Minnie the Moocher and Me,* New York: Crowell, 1976.
2. Earl Arnett, "The Other 'Hi-de-Ho': Blanche Calloway, 76, Still Young," *Sun (Oasis),* August 12, 1978, p. A7.
3. D. Antoinette Handy, *Black Women in American Bands & Orchestras,* Metuchen, N.J.: Scarecrow Press, 1981, p. 57.
4. "Orchestra Leader," *Pittsburgh Courier,* September 5, 1931, p. 6, Section 1.

5. "Blanche Calloway," *Pittsburgh Courier,* January 16, 1932, p. 7, Section 2.

6. "Dance Bands That Made History," *International Musician,* October 1950, pp. 20, 22, 35.

7. Handy, *op. cit.,* pp. 57–58.

8. "Waxter Center Remembers," *Sun (Oasis),* August 12, 1978, p. A7.

9. Arnett, *op. cit.*

10. *Ibid.*

11. "Remembering Blanche Calloway," *Richmond Afro-American,* December 30, 1978, p. 19.

Cabell ("Cab") Calloway (Courtesy: Camay Murphy)

CABELL "CAB" CALLOWAY

BIRTHDATE/PLACE: December 25, 1907; Rochester, New York.
DEATH DATE & PLACE: November 18, 1994; Hosckessin, Delaware.
EDUCATION: Public schools of Baltimore, Maryland (pupil of Llewelyn Wilson); private voice study with Llewelyn Wilson and Ruth Macabee; Crane College (Chicago).
BAND LEADER: Alabamians, 1928–29; Missourians, 1930; Cab Calloway Band, 1931–48.
PERFORMANCES WITH SYMPHONY ORCHESTRAS (partial): National, Richmond, Cincinnati, San Diego, Baltimore Symphony Orchestras; Los Angeles, Tulsa, Rochester, Buffalo Philharmonic Orchestras; Houston, Chicago, New York, Toronto, Philly Pops.
FILM APPEARANCES (partial): "The Big Broadcast of 1932," "International House," "Stormy Weather," "Sensations of 1945," "St. Louis Blues," "Ali Baba Goes to Town," "Dixie Jamboree," "The Cincinnati Kid," "A Man Called Adam," "Brother Can You Spare A Dime," "The Blues Brothers."
AWARDS/HONORS: 1988, Ebony Lifetime Achievement Award; 1993, National Medal of Arts.
THEATRE APPEARANCES: "Plantation Days," "Connie's Hot Chocolates," "Cotton Club Revue," "Porgy and Bess," "Pajama Game," "Hello Dolly."
AUTHOR: Of *Minnie the Moocher and Me* (with Bryant Rollins), Autobiography, Crowell, 1976.

THE DOCUMENTED HISTORY OF BIG BAND JAZZ does not always include the name Cabell "Cab" Calloway. Even when his contributions are acknowledged, they are most often overshadowed by negative assessments of his unique musicianship. A 1952 statement of one recognized jazz historian is typical:

> Calloway made hundreds of records, most of which are mainly vehicles for the leader's ostentatious vocals, full of exhibitionistic "scat-singing" which brought him the name of the Hi-De-Ho Man. Occasionally an odd solo on the records suggests that Calloway could perhaps have done

something more worthwhile with his band, but today he is playing the same tunes as he was in 1930—and in the same style.[1]

But big band historian George Simon suggests that he should be remembered as the director who

led one of the truly great outfits of the big band era, one that too few people seem to remember . . . [T]hat band, with its rich, clean ensemble sounds, its brilliant soloists, and its persuasive swing and great spirit, must go down as Calloway's greatest contribution to American music.[2]

A band that included in its personnel such stars as Chu Berry, Ben Webster, Dizzy Gillespie, Jonah Jones, Milt Hinton, Doc Cheatham, Quentin Jackson, Tyree Glenn, Panama Francis, Eddie Barefield, and Cozy Cole demands recognition. A band that survived for almost two decades and garnered the successes that it did, can in no way be discounted from the history of big bands. A leader who was able to attract the interest of such musicians as those cited above certainly merits recall. His value as a leader is enhanced by the fact that he was able to continue with smaller ensembles or as a single act even after the big band era ended.

Though Calloway played no instrument, he is indisputably one of the giants of show business. It is Calloway's assertion (one corroborated by others) that he served as the model for the character of Sportin' Life in George Gershwin's folk opera "Porgy and Bess."[3]

In an interview with C. Gerald Fraser of *The New York Times*, just prior to his two-concert Carnegie Hall appearance at age 80, Calloway proclaimed, "I'm a legend. You can't be in show business for 60 years and not be a legend." And as Fraser wrote, "The Calloway legend has many facets: his band-leading . . . his singing . . . his acting in films . . . his acting on stage . . . and his composing."

The Carnegie Hall concerts followed recent performances in San Diego, Buffalo, Cincinnati, and Los Angeles, several university appearances (tributes), and a tour of Europe in the Summer of 1987. For the occasion, a band of Calloway veterans was assembled, along with a chorus line of former Cotton Club showgirls. Calloway sang throughout the concert and was backed by a seventeen-member chorus in the singing of "It Ain't Necessarily So."[4]

Bryant Rollins, co-author of Calloway's autobiography *Of Minnie the Moocher and Me,* suggested that Calloway's success as a band leader was partly based on his early failure as a saxophonist himself and the respect for musicians of quality that resulted from his own thwarted efforts.[5] On the subject of Calloway and the saxophone, it has often been both said and written that when he began directing bands, tenor saxophonist Chu Berry consented to join on the condition that the leader agree never to play the instrument.

The style of singing for which Calloway was most noted was scat-singing (a nonsense-syllable technique of vocalizing, with the singer often mimicking the sound of an instrument). It all began one night in 1931, with Calloway fronting his band as vocal soloist. As he tells the story,

> [I] forgot the words of a song. When memory failed, scat-singing came to the rescue. And it went over so big that I kept right on doing it. It became a style that people began to identify me with. . . . I scat the same way they used to take the chorus in a hot jazz number, where the player is improvising.[6]

Cab Calloway's family was a musical one: His mother was a church organist and both his brother (Elmer) and sister (Blanche) became professional musicians. Blanche Calloway*—a singer, nightclub entertainer, and most importantly, jazz bandleader—was instrumental in getting her younger brother "Cab" established in the music business. Though it was the lawyer father's plan for son "Cab" to follow in his path, the route to a legal career terminated abruptly with his withdrawal (after a brief enrollment) from Chicago's Crane College. It was not the yen to study that had drawn Cab from Baltimore to Chicago anyway. Rather, it was the attraction to and admiration for his sister Blanche's many artistic endeavors. So, when the opportunity to become involved in Blanche's world arose, he took advantage of it.

Cab was accustomed to work: he had spent his high school years shining shoes, working as a stable boy, selling newspapers on the streets of Baltimore, and singing in local nightclubs. He also, in the early years, sang in the church choir (prompted, no doubt, by both the love of performing and the prodding of his church organist mother).

In 1927, in Chicago, his career was firmly launched with an appearance in the musical revue "Plantation Days." Two years later, he organized his first band, The Alabamians, which toured briefly and then appeared at Harlem's Savoy Ballroom. When the band failed to catch fire in New York, Calloway decided to accept the singing role in the musical "Connie's Hot Chocolates" (1929).

Still in New York the following year, Calloway fronted a group called "The Missourians," which soon recorded under the name "Cab Calloway's Band." The group appeared with great success at the exclusive Cotton Club in 1931–32 and later became the house orchestra that replaced Duke Ellington's* Band. Recording contracts followed and in 1934 the group made a tour of Europe.

In October 1939, the band participated in the week-long Silver Jubilee Festival of the American Society of Composers, Authors and Publishers (ASCAP) at Carnegie Hall, along with jazz bands led by Noble Sissle, Louis Armstrong, and Claude Hopkins. This concert, the second to be entitled "From Symphony to Swing" (the first was in 1938), employed a 350-voice chorus, accompanied by a 75-piece orchestra. For the 1939 gala, composers William C. Handy, Harry T. Burleigh, and J. Rosamond Johnson were challenged to secure "the best Negro talent of the nation."[7]

Though the Calloway band disbanded in 1948, the career of its leader continued. He returned to the stage as "Sportin' Life" in the 1952 revival of "Porgy and Bess" (1952–54) (which starred Leontyne Price as Bess and William Warfield as Porgy) and in the all-black version of the Broadway musical "Hello, Dolly!" (1967–71).

Calloway's film career began with a featured role in the Big Broadcast series. Other appearances included "The Singing Kid" (with Al Jolson), "Stormy Weather" (with Lena Horne), "St. Louis Blues" (with Nat King Cole), "The Cincinnati Kid" (with Steve McQueen), and, most recently, "The Blues Brothers" (with Dan Ackroyd and John Belushi). In recent years, he has appeared as soloist with numerous symphony orchestras, including the Tulsa, Rochester, and Los Angeles Philharmonic Orchestras; the San Diego, Buffalo, National, Cincinnati, Chicago, and Cleveland Orchestras; and the Houston and Philadelphia Pops Orchestras.

Calloway received *Ebony* Magazine's highest accolade, the Ebony Lifetime Achievement Award, at the Seventh Annual American Black Achievement Awards' televised ceremony in 1988. It was announced in late December 1988 that the 81-year-old entertainer had collapsed during a show in Tokyo, suffering from exhaustion. One year later, Calloway performed at the National Association for the Advancement of Colored People's (NAACP'S) Image Award Ceremony.

At Chicago's Cotton Club, a room has been established in his honor. With actor/comedian Bill Cosby chairing an April 1990 event, the jazz faculty of New York City's New School for Social Research saluted "The Hi-De-Ho Man." In January 1992, Calloway was the featured performer at the Moon Over Miami Ball in Miami Beach (Florida), the kickoff event of Art Deco Weekend. In October 1993, Calloway was awarded the National Endowment for the Arts generated National Medal of Arts.

Through all of Cab Calloway's many careers, the overriding concern was to make his audiences feel the fullness of life as he felt it and lived it. As he wrote in his autobiography:

> Put me in the spotlight, give me two or three thousand people and a decent group of men behind me with instruments, and you can't give me more. . . . Let me feel that the people out there have for just a moment understood that it is possible to follow your dreams and to be free with your emotions and to express what you feel deeply.[8]

Notes

1. Rex Harrison, *Jazz,* rev. ed., London: Penguin Books Ltd., 1952, pp. 181–182.
2. George Simon, *The Big Bands,* rev. enlarged ed., New York: Collier Books, 1976, pp. 86–87.
3. Cab Calloway did not appear in the original production, due to other commitments.
4. C. Gerald Fraser, "Cab Calloway, at 80, Is Still Doing the Old Hi-De-Ho," *New York Times,* January 7, 1988, p. C 18.
5. *Ibid.*
6. C. A. Bustard, "Cab Calloway: Irresistable Character Still Strutting After 72 Years," *Richmond-Times Dispatch,* January 11, 1981, J 1.
7. Eileen Southern, *The Music of Black Americans: A History,* 2nd Edition, New York: W. W. Norton and Company, Inc., 1983, pp. 438–439.
8. Cab Calloway and Bryant Rollins, *Of Minnie the Moocher and Me,* New York, N. Y.: Thomas Y. Crowell Company, 1976, p. 250.

Will Marion Cook (Courtesy: *The Black Perspective in Music*)

WILL MARION COOK

BIRTHDATE/PLACE: January 27, 1869; Washington, D.C.
DEATH DATE/PLACE: July 19, 1944; New York, N.Y.
EDUCATION: Oberlin Conservatory, National Conservatory of Music (New York City), Hochschule für Musik (Berlin).
MAJOR INSTRUCTORS: Amos Doolittle (Oberlin); Josef Joachim (Berlin), Antonin Dvorak and John White (National Conservatory of Music).
ORCHESTRAL AFFILIATIONS: Cook's Chamber Orchestra, Williams and Walker Company Orchestra, The Memphis Students, The Clef Club, The Southern Syncopated Orchestra (aka The New York Syncopated Orchestra), American Syncopated Orchestra.

THE *NEW YORK TIMES* ANNOUNCED COOK'S 1944 death accordingly:

> Will Marion Cook, Negro composer, whose works had a great vogue during the early part of this century and rank with the best of American Negro compositions, died late Wednesday night in Harlem Hospital after an illness of four weeks. His age was 75.[1]

Two months later, the prestigious music journal *Etude* reported,

> Will Marion Cook, Negro composer, whose many songs and operettas have enjoyed great popularity, died on July 19 in New York City. . . . He organized three orchestras, one of which, the American Syncopated Orchestra, toured Europe after the first world war.[2]

Though Cook is best remembered for his compositional skills, it is with the last mentioned activity—conducting—that this entry is primarily concerned.

A native of Washington, D.C., Cook's musical gifts were recognized at an early age. His chosen instrument was the violin. At fifteen, he was sent to Oberlin Conservatory (Oberlin, Ohio), where his mother, father, uncle, and elder brother had received their training. He was enrolled in the high school (which he did not

50

complete) and later in the conservatory (another program he did not complete).[3] Upon the recommendation of his professor, Amos Doolittle, he journeyed to Berlin in 1887 to study at the Hochschule für Musik with Josef Joachim. He had financial assistance from the abolitionist and writer Frederick Douglass and from a benefit concert that he gave in Washington prior to his departure. He had acquired recital experience at the conservatory and made additional solo appearances at a local Oberlin Church.

Cook was introduced to Antonin Dvorak, the Director of New York City's National Conservatory of Music, by the black baritone, composer, and arranger Harry Thacker Burleigh (a student at the conservatory and friend of Dvorak's) in 1892, by letter. Though his exact enrollment date remains an unknown, we are certain that he was a member of the violin section of the conservatory's orchestra (conducted by Dvorak) that performed at the *New York Herald*'s Free Clothing Benefit Concert at Madison Square Garden on January 23, 1894.[4]

In 1890 violinist-composer Cook launched his conducting career in Washington, D.C., conducting a chamber orchestra. With Frederick Douglass serving as its president, the group toured the eastern seaboard, traveling as far as Boston for a concert in 1891.

Cook was the designated music director for Colored American Day (August 25, 1893) at the Chicago World's Fair. The program was to include his work "Scenes from the Opera of Uncle Tom's Cabin." Though all indications are that the event did not materialize, Cook did appear on another concert in Chicago during the month of August, with popular black singers Harry T. Burleigh, Marie Selika, and Sidney Woodward.

Arriving in New York City for enrollment at the National Conservatory, Cook soon came in contact with vaudeville and ragtime. Within a short while, he realized that the world of show business perhaps offered more professional recognition and financial rewards, particularly for a Black. His first major success occurred when, in collaboration with the black poet Paul Laurence Dunbar as lyricist, his musical sketch "Clorindy, or The Origin of the Cakewalk" was performed at the Casino Roof Garden on Broadway during the summer of 1898. This was the first time that a black show had played at a "major" theater—patronized exclusively by whites— and attracted such wide interest.

Wrote author and diplomat James Weldon Johnson,

"Clorindy" was the talk of New York. It was the first demonstration
of the possibilities of syncopated Negro music. Cook was the first
competent composer to take what was then known as rag-time and
work it out in a musicianly way. His choruses and finales in
"Clorindy," complete novelties as they were, sung by a lusty chorus,
were simply breathtaking. Broadway had something entirely new.[5]

Cook later wrote of the opening night experience,

When I entered the orchestra pit, there were only about fifty people
on the Roof. When we finished the opening chorus, the house was
packed to suffocation. . . . When the last note was sounded, the
audience stood and cheered for at least ten minutes. . . . It was
pandemonium. . . .[6]

The following year, Cook became composer-in-chief and musical
director of the George Walker and Bert Williams Company,
continuing in that capacity until the group's demise in 1908. The
Cook, Walker, and Williams association lasted through the productions of Cook's "The Sons of Ham" (1900), "In Dahomey" (1902),
"In Abyssinia" (1905), and "In Bandanna Land" (1907). Apparent in
each of these productions was Cook's opposition to the minstrel
tradition; not always acknowledged (by Cook) was reflection of his
"classical" background. When "In Dahomey" was taken abroad in
1903, maestro Will Marion Cook was at the helm.

He interacted regularly with other black artists of the day, who at
the turn of the century congregated in Black Bohemia, with the
Marshall Hotel, between Sixth and Seventh Avenues on West 53rd
Street as headquarters. There Cook enjoyed professional associations
with James Weldon and J. Rosamond Johnson, Bob Cole, and Ernest
Hogan, to name a few.

It was Ernest Hogan who organized the singing-dancing troupe
known as the Memphis Students (none were students and none were
from Memphis)[7] that made its debut at Proctor's Twenty-third Street
Theatre in New York City. The unorthodox instrumental combination (banjos, mandolins, guitars, saxophones, a violin, a double bass,
a couple of brass instruments, and drums) was led by Will Dixon,
"the dancing conductor." But it was Will Marion Cook who trained
the group. Wrote philosopher and literary critic Alain Locke:

> The organization was the first truly genuine Negro playing unit; like the original "Jubilee Singers" they blazed a trail to Europe their first season [late 1905] and with their demonstration of the difference, real jazz was in the making and Negro music had burst the Nordic strait-jacket unwise imitation had imposed. . . . Will Dixon was the conductor, but the genius of Cook was back of the whole thing.[8]

When in October 1905 the Memphis Students went abroad, Cook was the conductor. The black press accused him of abducting the students; but legal efforts to prevent the group's sailing were unsuccessful.

The "coming-out party" for Negro music took place at Carnegie Hall, May 2, 1912.

> That night the cinderella of Negro folk music found royal favor and recognition and under the wand of Negro musicians put off her kitchen rags. At that time ragtime grew up to full musical rank, and the golden age of jazz really began.[9]

James Reese Europe* organized the Clef Club in 1910 in New York City, essentially as a black musicians' union. It was a Clef Club orchestra of 145 musicians that offered the 1912 Carnegie Hall event and it was Cook's composition "Swing Along" (which he rehearsed) that was designated by one critic as "the hit of the evening" and the "one number on the program well worth the price of admission."[10]

The next major musical event for Cook took place in 1918. The years immediately preceding this date found Cook occupied with conducting various Clef Club ensembles, lecturing, teaching and coaching, and collaborating with others to write musicals ("The Traitors," 1912, and "In Darkeydom," 1914). Cook's 1918 organization of The Southern Syncopated Orchestra (aka The New York Syncopated Orchestra) is frequently referred to as "his greatest adventure."

Following an American tour in early 1919, the group of approximately forty instrumentalists and singers toured England, opening in London at Philharmonic Hall July 4, 1919. Of the opening event, the local press reported:

> It would be a pity if people not overwhelmingly enamoured of syncopation should stay away from the performances of "The Syncopated Orchestra" . . . from fear that ragtime fills the whole bill.

Because they would miss much else worth hearing. . . . The orchestra played . . . in first-class style. Like their conductor, Mr. Will Marion Cook, they appear to be soaked in syncopation, running over with racy rhythms. Their music is part of them, and they part of it.[11]

Adding to the excitement that followed, The Syncopated Orchestra appeared at Buckingham Palace on August 9, 1919.

Included in the ensemble was the outstanding jazz clarinetist Sidney Bechet. Ernest Ansermet, later the famed conductor of L'Orchestre de la Suisse Romande, expressed profound approval of the ensemble and was overwhelmed with the improvisational capabilities of Bechet.

The business manager of the organization was George William Lattimore. Orchestral control soon became an issue and settlement was placed in the hands of the British courts. An April 1920 advertisement announcing the appearance of the Southern Syncopated Orchestra in Nottingham listed E. E. Thompson as conductor.[12]

Under the caption "Will Preserve and Cultivate the Music of the Colored Race," *Musical America* announced that James R. Saville "took hold of the American Syncopated Orchestra, . . . scarcely half a year" prior to the date of publication, February 7, 1920:

It was at a time when the season had just about closed and Will Marion Cook, the conductor and master mind of the organization, was undetermined on his future public course. Mr. Saville saved the situation by taking charge of the management and while Mr. Cook was abroad re-organized the band and the singers and booked them extensively throughout the country, but particularly on the western coast in California.[13]

Note the new name, "American" Syncopated Orchestra.

The article indicated further that the organization was in Chicago the week prior, following appearances

throughout the far west. . . . At Sacramento, Will Marion Cook returned from Europe and assumed the conductorship of the company. . . . The remainder of the tour is to be spent in St. Paul, Minn., for one week, in Minneapolis, another week, and at Indianapolis, the second week in February.

The article concluded, "The concerts have been received by the general public with unalloyed pleasure and enjoyment."[14]

Recalling the *Etude* announcement of Cook's death, the question arises, did this group subsequently go abroad? One suspects that Cook and the "American" Syncopated Orchestra did venture to Europe (no doubt under the management of Mr. Saville), supporting the customarily registered date of 1922 as his return to America.

Between 1922 and 1944, Cook organized and promoted concerts and renewed his association with Clef Club ensembles. More compositions were written, including the opera "St. Louis 'ooman." His Negro Folk Music and Drama Society sponsored various concerts under the title "Negro Nuances." Additionally he continued to teach, coach, and advise, including in the list of "those assisted" black female choral conductor Eva Jesseye, ragtime pianist Charles "Luckey" Roberts, pianist-composer Eubie Blake, and pianist-composer-bandleader Edward "Duke" Ellington.* Ellington referred to Will Marion Cook as "His Majesty the King of Consonance," and added, "That time with him was one of the best semesters I ever had in music."[15]

Notes

1. "Will M. Cook, 75, Negro Composer," *New York Times,* July 21, 1944, p. 19.
2. "The World of Music: Here, There, and Everywhere In the Musical World," *Etude,* September 1944, p. 493.
3. S. Frederick Starr, "Oberlin's Ragtimer: Will Marion Cook," *Oberlin Alumni Magazine,* p. 13.
4. Maurice Peress, "Dvorak and African-American Musicians, 1892–1895," *Black Music Research Bulletin,* Fall 1990, pp. 27–28.
5. James Weldon Johnson, *Black Manhattan,* New York: Alfred A. Knopf, 1930, p. 103.
6. Will Marion Cook, "Clorindy, the Origin of the Cakewalk," *Theatre Arts,* September 1947. Reprinted in *Readings in Black American Music,* Eileen Southern, ed. New York: W. W. Norton and Company, Inc., 1971, pp. 217–223.
7. According to Alain Locke, "The name Memphis was well-chosen; it was the early tribute of those who knew the true folk source of this musical style." In *The Negro and His Music,* Washington, D.C.: The

Associated Publishers, 1936. (Reprint, New York: Arno Press and *New York Times,* 1969, p. 65).

8. *Ibid.*

9. *Ibid.,* p. 68.

10. Lester A. Walton, "Concert at Carnegie Hall," *New York Age,* May 9, 1912, p. 12 in *Black Perspective in Music,* Spring 1978, p. 75.

11. "Southern Syncopated Orchestra," *The Era,* July 9, 1919, p. 10.

12. Paul Oliver, ed. *Black Music in Britain,* Philadelphia: Open University Press, 1990, p. 48.

13. "Will Preserve and Cultivate the Music of the Colored Race," *Musical America,* February 7, 1920, p. 47.

14. *Ibid.*

15. Duke Ellington, *Music Is My Mistress,* Garden City, N.Y.: Doubleday, 1973, pp. 95, 97.

Jackson C. Crawford, Jr. (Photo: Lilo Werner Afin)

JACKSON COLLIER CRAWFORD, JR.

BIRTHDATE/PLACE: March 11, 1943; Thomasville, Georgia.

EDUCATION: B. S., Florida A & M University (Tallahassee, Florida), 1965; San Francisco State University, 1969–70; University of California at Hayward, 1971–72; Institute of Musicology, Sorbonne (Paris), 1972–73; Conservatorio di Musica di Roma, St. Cecilia, 1974–76; Institute for New Music (Darmstadt, West Germany), 1982; University of West Virginia (Morgantown, West Virginia), Conductors Guild Summer Institutes, 1984–86.

MAJOR INSTRUCTORS: Donald Carroll, Philip Fields, Ruffie London, Saxophone and Clarinet; Franco Ferrara, Dimitri Chorafas, Harold Farberman, Herbert Blomstedt, Pierre Dervaux, Sergui Celibidache, Richard Schumacher, Hugo Ruf, Peter Eötvös, Daniel Lewis, Samuel Jones, Enrico Boni, Conducting.

FOUNDER/CONDUCTOR: L'Orchestra Internazionale di Roma (Italy), 1976–80.

MAJOR APPOINTMENTS: Assistant Conductor, Solingen Orchestra Association, 1980–84; Assistant Conductor, State of Westphalia's Youth Symphony Orchestra; and Conductor, Colophonia Chamber Orchestra in Köln, 1989– .

GUEST CONDUCTOR: National Orchestra of Santa Cecilia, 1975–76; Solingen Symphony Orchestra, 1982; Remscheid Symphony Orchestra, 1983; Cologne Sinfonietta (Fall Tour), 1985; State Youth Orchestra of Rheinland-Pfalz, 1987; State Youth Orchestra of North Rhein-Westphalia, 1989; All-European Youth Orchestra (Saumar, France), 1991; Mainz Chamber Orchestra, 1992.

AWARD: Cabot Trust Grant (for furtherance of conducting career).

THE ELDEST OF FOUR CHILDREN, Crawford's early musical influence and support came from his mother, a pianist and choir director. How he came to select conducting as a career choice is "totally unknown," wrote the maestro. He also indicated that he does not feel limited by his racial identity: "It simply means that I must work harder to achieve."

The American-born, European-based conductor considers the most significant milestone in his conducting career to be his selection as a Fellow by the Yehudi Menuhin Foundation (France) in 1991. There he conducted the All-European Youth Orchestra.

He is a graduate of an historically black institution, Florida A and M University, and The University of Paris. Training in conducting has been secured in both the United States (California and West Virginia) and Europe (France, West Germany, and Italy). Conducting teachers and coaches have included Jean-Phil Caillard, Richard Schumacher, Peter Eötvös, Dimitri Chorafas, Franco Ferrara, Pierre Dervaux, Enrico Boni, Herbert Blomstedt, Harold Farberman, Daniel Lewis, and Samuel Jones. His training has also included opera repertoire and new music composition. With a particular interest in music from the Classical and Romantic periods, his conducting repertoire ranges from the Baroque to the modern era.

While studying at the Conservatorio di Musica di Roma, Santa Cecilia (Rome, Italy), 1974–76, Crawford organized the International Orchestra of Rome. Of this experience he wrote:

> When I founded L'Ochestra Internazionale di Roma, it was a lot of work for a committee of one. But I can look back with pride to two important concerts in Rome's Chiesu St. Agnese in Piazza Navona for the World Council of Churches. I began with seven musicians and I saw the orchestra grow to twenty-six, performing music from Bach to Beethoven.[1]

Since 1989, Crawford has served as conductor of the Colophonia Chamber Orchestra in Köln and Assistant Conductor of the State of Westphalia's Youth Symphony Orchestra. Between 1980 and 1984, he was Assistant Conductor of the Solingen Orchestra Association in Gast.

Crawford's solo saxophone and clarinet experiences have been extensive, including appearances with the Huy Chamber Orchestra (Belgium), 1983; State Orchestra of Solingen, 1985; Orchester der Beethovenhalle (Bonn, Germany), 1988; Hessisches Stadtstheater Orchestra (Wiesbaden, Germany), 1989; and Orchester Philharmonia Hungarica (Marl, West Germany), 1989. Crawford greatly values his appearances as a classical saxophone soloist with various ensembles (including professional symphony orchestras), his work as a saxophone clinician, and his participation in several International Saxophone Congresses.

When asked if he feels any obligation to program the music of black composers, he responded,

> Neglecting to do so denies the public, other conductors, musicians, and orchestra administrators the opportunity of becoming culturally and socially enriched, thereby restricting the value of the black composer's talent and dedication. Lack of programming also denies the black composer a source of income and prestige.[2]

His personal identity is that of "an American." Yet he offers this advice to aspiring black conductors (since he is one of them):

> Study with the best teachers; participate in international courses; learn several languages; follow rehearsals and concerts [of others] regularly; conduct, even an ensemble of ten.[3]

As of this writing, there are no indications of Crawford's desire to return to the States on a permanent basis. European critics have responded favorably to his conducting, describing him as "a commanding musician completely at ease on the podium" and "a conductor who possesses the ability to communicate his musical ideas and feelings to other musicians." Orchestral players praise his personal and musical commitment, and appreciate his "clear and controlled technique as well as his dynamic and intelligent approach" to the musical score. Fully appreciated abroad, the absence of a desire for immediate return to his place of birth is completely understandable.

Press Comment

{Crawford} is a prominent, trained conductor . . . a sensitive musician and a strong interpreter of 'fine points' through his flexible and smooth {conducting} style. {His} controlled and economical gestures were understandable to all . . . {I}n constant contact with the musicians, they were able to perform in a delicate manner.

Bergische Morgenpost
(Remscheid, Germany)

Notes

1. Correspondence, Crawford/Handy, March 25, 1992.
2. *Ibid.*
3. Questionnaire, March 25, 1992.

William Curry

WILLIAM "BILL" HENRY CURRY

BIRTHDATE/PLACE: June 30, 1954; Pittsburgh, Pennsylvania.

EDUCATION: Oberlin Conservatory, University of Pittsburgh, Carnegie-Mellon University, American Symphony Orchestra League's Conductor's Workshops (Summers, 1973 and 1974).

MAJOR INSTRUCTORS/COACHES: Richard Lert, Samuel Jones, Phillip Spurgeon, and Robert Baustian (Conducting); Richard Hoffman (Composition); Eugene Reichenfeld and William Berman (Viola).

MAJOR APPOINTMENTS: Music Director, Carnegie Institute Theatre (1969–71); Assistant Conductor, Wilkinsburg and Murrysville (Pennsylvania) Symphony Orchestras (1970–72/1971–72 respectively); Associate Director, Kennerdell (Pennsylvania) Baroque Music Festival (1971–76); Assistant Conductor, Wilkinsburg Youth Orchestra (1972); Conductor, Oberlin Conservatory Reading Orchestra (1972–75); Music Director, Oberlin Contemporary Music Chamber Ensemble (1972–75); Assistant Conductor, Oberlin Orchestra (1974–75); Conductor, Richmond (Virginia) Sinfonia Student and Community Concerts and Richmond Symphony Youth Wind Ensemble (1975–76); Assistant Conductor, Richmond Symphony and Richmond Sinfonia (1976–77); Principal Conductor, Richmond Symphony Youth Orchestra (1976–77); Principal Guest Conductor (1977–78) and Resident Conductor, Baltimore Symphony (1978–82); Resident Conductor, St. Paul Chamber Orchestra (1983–85); Associate Conductor, Indianapolis Symphony Orchestra (1983–88); Featured Conductor, "Serious Fun at Lincoln Center," Contemporary Music Festival, 1989; Music Director, "X" (The Life and Times of Malcolm X), Touring Company and Recording (Gramavision), (1988–90); Resident Conductor, New Orleans Philharmonic (1990–91).

GUEST CONDUCTOR: Carnegie-Mellon String Orchestra, Pittsburgh Youth Orchestra, Oberlin Wind Ensemble; New Orleans, San Diego, Atlanta, Detroit, National, Syracuse, Denver, Florida, New Mexico, Savannah, Phoenix, Columbus (Ohio), American, and Indianapolis Symphony Orchestras; Ohio Chamber Orchestra, St. Luke's Chamber Orchestra (Recording), New York City and Houston Grand Opera Companies.

AWARDS/HONORS: Carnegie Mellon Composition Contest—First Prize (1970); Cleveland Orchestra Conductor's Symposium—Finalist (1975); Leopold Stokowski Conducting Competition Winner (1988).

"BILL CURRY IS A YOUNG MAN WHO IS a living example of being in the right place at the right time," according to Walt Amacker of the *Richmond {Virginia} News Leader.* Amacker was reacting to an overwhelmingly successful performance of Beethoven's Ninth Symphony by the Richmond Symphony, with Assistant Conductor William Henry Curry on the podium.

William ["Bill"] Curry had received the news only in the morning that he would conduct the Richmond Symphony that evening in a performance of the monumental work—without rehearsal. Fortunately he had studied the score the night before, as he always did before a rehearsal or concert. He even awakened in the middle of the night for additional study.

The orchestra's principal conductor had become ill. Early in the morning the orchestra's manager called to inquire, "How well do you know Beethoven's Ninth?" According to Curry, he was tempted to say, "I studied it all night!"

Of his thoughts as he strode to the podium, the twenty-one-year-old maestro commented:

> All I could think was that sometime within the next hour-and-a-half, I would be able to walk back into the wings and it would all be over. But the audience was so warm in their reception, and I felt they were really with me. It wasn't an "Oh no, I wonder if he can do it reaction," and that was very encouraging.

In an interview with Amacker a few days later, Curry stated:

> I was a little nervous during the first piece, the overture. I could feel the audience behind my back. After that I forgot about them and things settled down. I didn't feel on the spot . . . in fact, I sort of enjoyed it. I knew if I did well the reaction would be good[1]

It is worth noting that the evening's event represented several firsts for Curry: the first time he had conducted the Beethoven Ninth, the first time he had conducted the orchestra in its own hall (The Mosque), the first time he had conducted before a paying audience, and the first time he had conducted a chorus.

The April 12, 1976 triumph with the Richmond Symphony followed closely on the heels of Curry's elevation within the orchestra's conducting ranks. Only recently had he been named the orchestra's assistant conductor.[2]

Curry arrived in Richmond at the beginning of the 1975–76 season to fulfill three simultaneous responsibilities: violist, Richmond Symphony; conductor of the 18-member Richmond Sinfonia (core orchestra of the symphony) for its student and community concerts; and conductor of a 40-member youth wind ensemble, through an arrangement with the symphony's youth orchestra. He was invited to join the Richmond Symphony during the previous season, after having been observed as one of the finalists among thirty contestants competing in the Cleveland Orchestra's Conducting Competition. Though accepting the Richmond offer necessitated interrupting his final year of study at the Oberlin College Conservatory of Music, Curry felt the opportunity was too important to resist.

Bill Curry grew up in Pittsburgh, Pennsylvania, in a musically enlightened family. Both parents studied music as teenagers. His paternal grandmother was a well-trained organist (first black woman admitted to Boston University as an organ major) and his maternal grandfather was a leading baritone in a black opera company.

Curry's first musical interest was the piano, but his parents could not afford an instrument. He enrolled in the school band in the sixth grade and was assigned to the clarinet, with less than encouraging results. As time passed, he explored various other instruments: clarinet, violin, and eventually viola. It was Curry's viola teacher, Eugene Reichenfeld (a music supervisor in the Pittsburgh school system), who recognized his musical leadership potential, and appointed Curry as student conductor of the junior high school orchestra. He also arranged for Curry to make his conducting debut at age 14 (conducting a rehearsal of a community orchestra in suburban Pittsburgh). Reichenfeld was able to arrange other conducting opportunities for young Curry with several community orchestras in the Pittsburgh area. These experiences sparked his enthusiasm and allowed the budding conductor to test his skills. As *Richmond Times Dispatch* journalist Alison Griffin noted, "When the air cleared with the passing of adolescence, he realized that all of these spreadout and sometimes confusing musical preoccupations pointed in a single direction: He wanted to be a conductor."[3]

Of the initial and subsequent early experiences, Curry reflected,

It was sink or swim. . . . I don't remember a thing about that first rehearsal—except that when it was all over, I was smiling. . . . The thing that really attracted me to conducting . . . was my realization that I could express my emotions that way. It could be scary, too, of course. I remember my first conducting teacher telling me, "If anything goes wrong during a performance, it's *your* fault." I nearly lost my mind worrying about that.

But it was a good lesson, because it taught me to be self-analytical. It taught me to ask after every performance, "Did I know the score? Did I rehearse it thoroughly? What did I do to make the performance exciting?"[4]

Both William and his younger brother Ralph (currently a cellist with the Cleveland Symphony Orchestra) were members of the Pittsburgh Youth Orchestra. Upon completion of high school, William Curry engaged in the study of harmony, counterpoint, composition, and chamber music at Carnegie-Mellon University and conducted intensive research (cantatas of J. S. Bach and the instrumental works of Olivier Messien) at the University of Pittsburgh. These activities were all "extra-curricular"; Curry was concurrently pursuing a degree in music theory and composition at Oberlin Conservatory.

His interest in, and talent for, composition led to the creation of ten chamber works, four overtures, two concerti (for trumpet and baritone horn), and two symphonies, as well as miscellaneous works for chorus and symphonic band. His "Mysticum" for orchestra won the 1970 first prize in the Carnegie-Mellon University Composition Contest. His "Night Poems"—a song cycle for contralto and chamber ensemble—was performed at the Kennedy Center in the nation's capitol in 1978.

The Richmond experience was by no means Curry's introduction to professional conducting. Many assignments had intervened between his debut at age 14 and the Richmond posts: Assistant Conductor of the Wilkinsburg and Murrysville (Pennsylvania) Symphony Orchestras and the Oberlin Conservatory Orchestra; Music Director of the Carnegie Institute Theatre and the Oberlin Contemporary Music Chamber Orchestra; Assistant Conductor of the Pennsylvania Opera Workshop; Music Director of Pittsburgh area theatre productions ("Camelot," "Sound of Music," "The King and I"), and numerous guest conducting appearances.

In the spring of 1977, at twenty-three, Curry left Richmond to serve as Guest Conductor with the Baltimore Symphony. The competition for the position had been intense. All contenders except Curry had ten or more years of professional conducting experience. Two finalists emerged: William Curry and James Frazier* (another Black American).

By the end of the calendar year, Curry had been named Resident Conductor, beginning with the 1978–79 season. With that assignment, Curry became "the youngest person to hold such a position with a major American orchestra . . ."[5]

During his first year, Curry conducted nearly eighty performances, including subscription, school, pops, and out-of-town concerts. His interest in new, local composers was particularly significant. He arrived in the city with intentions "to look into composers in Baltimore and promote interest in them. . . . I would like to leave a legacy behind of composers I was able to find." In addition, Curry was keenly interested in the black community. As he explained to the local press:

> I'm not self-conscious about blackness . . . I don't think that every black person has a responsibility to go out in the black community, but this is something I'm genuinely interested in. I want to help in finding out what the black community wants. There's a block, a barrier there between symphonies and black communities, and I don't really understand why. It doesn't have to be there.[6]

While in Baltimore, he also served as Music Director/Conductor for the Peabody Conservatory and the Baltimore School for the Performing Arts.

Curry was appointed Resident Conductor of the St. Paul Chamber Orchestra (SPCO) in April 1983. Three conductors auditioned for the position with the orchestra; two returned to conduct an SPCO rehearsal. Following the season-long search, Curry was offered a one-year contract, beginning with the 1983–84 season. His SPCO duties included conducting one set of baroque concerts, a Friday morning performance, two Thanksgiving concerts, several "Perspective" programs, regional tour engagements, and youth concerts. He was also designated as substitute conductor, in the event maestro Pinchas Zukerman or a visiting conductor might suddenly be unable to appear.[7]

In an interview with Roy M. Close of the *St. Paul Pioneer Press,* Curry said that he preferred to be thought of as a conductor without

labels of any kind. He explained: "I guess I've never felt black, or
male, or 28 . . . I don't feel any special need to promote anyone's
music, and I don't want to be pigeonholed myself."[8] Months earlier,
Curry said to the same writer, "My identity has nothing to do with
who and what I am. I have no problem putting myself in the
emotional situations of Brahms, or Tchaikovsky, or Pachelbel or
whatever."[9]

While he was still affiliated with the St. Paul Chamber Orchestra,
Curry made his Indianapolis Symphony Orchestra debut in an
all-Beethoven "Symphony on the Prairie" series concert at Conner
Prairie (Indiana). He continued to serve as artistic director of the
series until his formal departure from Indianapolis in 1988. His
"Symphony on the Prairie" Independence Day Celebration concert in
1985 drew over 10,000 people (the largest single audience in the
orchestra's history). As Associate Conductor of the ISO (1983–88),
Curry's assignments included several Classical and Family Series
concerts, appearances with the ISO Chamber Orchestra, run-out
concerts across the state and school concerts throughout the city, free
park concerts, and the annual Contemporary Music Festival concerts
at Indiana State University in Terre Haute.

In 1988 William Henry Curry won the prestigious Leopold
Stokowski Conducting Competition, sponsored by the American
Symphony Orchestra. Over 75 applications from around the country
had been received for the annual competition, open to American
conductors under the age of 35. From the group of nine semi-
finalists, one of whom was black conductor Leslie Dunner* (then
Assistant Conductor of the Detroit Symphony and Associate Conductor of the Dance Theatre of Harlem), four finalists emerged.[10] From
the field, Curry took first honors. His prize included an engagement
with the American Symphony Orchestra at historic Carnegie Hall,
$5,000, and performances with the Florida Symphony Orchestra
(Orlando).

While fulfilling his first major professional assignment with the
Richmond Symphony, Curry made clear that his life's ambition was
to be a successful music communicator, "someone who has the ability
to turn people on to music, to share his enthusiasm for music with
them."[11] In addition to his staff conducting assignments, he
delivered his message with such organizations as the New Orleans,
San Diego, Atlanta, Detroit, National, Syracuse, Denver, New
Mexico, Savannah, Phoenix, Columbus (Ohio), and American Sym-

phony Orchestras, as well as the Ohio Chamber Orchestra. He assisted in identifying, acknowledging, and recommending rewards for artistic excellence of various art institutions by serving as a panelist for the Indiana State Arts Council and the National Endowment for the Arts. At age thirty-five, he terminated his five-year relationship with the Indianapolis Symphony Orchestra and took to the road. During the 1988–90 season, he appeared as music director of black composer Anthony Davis's ensemble Episteme, performing the concert version of Davis's opera "X" (The Life and Times of Malcolm X) on tour. Curry also conducted the Gramavision recording of the same work.

Following a highly successful guest appearance with the New Orleans Philharmonic in 1989, Curry assumed the position of Resident Conductor for the Orchestra's 1990–91 season. He made his debut with the New York City Opera in October 1991, conducting the American premiere of Leroy Jenkins's opera-ballet "The Mother of Three Sons," choreographed by the popular Bill T. Jones. Jenkins and Jones are both African Americans.

Curry made his debut with the Houston Grand Opera the following year, conducting the same work.[12]

Press Comments:

"If there were any doubts that young Curry wasn't up to the tremendous task thrust upon him {Beethoven's Ninth Symphony, upon twelve-hour notice and without rehearsal}, he erased them quickly. He possessed a strong and self-assured presence and beat. . . . He gave clear, distinct directions to his performers, and they followed him admirably." {Age 21}

Richmond News Leader

"In many respects, the program {Richmond Sinfonia} was the most satisfying of the season. The playing, under the able leadership of William Curry, reached a high degree of proficiency early and stayed at that level throughout the program."

Richmond News Leader

"The orchestra {Richmond Symphony} was ably led by William Henry Curry, . . .{He} is a delight to watch. He has a stick so clear you can follow it from the balcony."

Richmond Times-Dispatch

"Not many men managed to upstage Ludwig van Beethoven. Take a well-deserved bow, William Curry. . . . {I}t was clearly William Curry's night."
                                                    Richmond Times-Dispatch

"Curry is one of those rare conductors who is actually interested in the music of his own time, which is why he conducts it so well."
                                                    Minneapolis Star and Tribune

"Curry's stature as associate conductor of the ISO (Indianapolis Symphony Orchestra) leaped to premiere prominence as an imaginative, dynamic and tireless maestro with a soul for the big sound."
                                                    Indianapolis Star

"The results were favorable . . . energetic, emphatic style. . . . {B}oth the pizzicato passage during the adagio that precedes the finale and the noble melody that heralds the finale proper {Brahms First Symphony} glowed under Mr. Curry's direction. . . ."
                                                    New York Times

"After intermission came the evening's real highlight, a sensitive and moving performance of Dvorak's 'New World' Symphony. A conscientious, hard-working, talented and energetic man, Curry . . . is certainly in his element with something like Dvorak."
                                                    Indianapolis News

Notes

1. Walt Amacker, "Right Place," *Richmond News Leader,* April 17, 1976, p. A41.
2. Douglas Durden, "Conducting Was Hectic Surprise," *Richmond Times-Dispatch,* April 14, 1976, p. B1.
3. Alison Griffin, "Varied Instrumental Background Led Bill Curry to Conducting, " *Richmond Times-Dispatch,* January 18, 1976, p. H1.
4. Roy M. Close, "SPCO's Resident Conductor Underplays His Uniqueness," *St. Paul Dispatch,* February 23, 1984, p. 9B.
5. Earl Arnett, "BSO's New Conductor Seeks New Composers," *Baltimore Sun,* July 20, 1977, p. B1.
6. *Ibid.*
7. "SPCO Picks Curry As Resident Conductor," *Minneapolis Star and Tribune,* April 28, 1983, p. 5C.
8. Roy M. Close, "Curry Is Veteran Conductor At 28," *St. Paul Pioneer Press,* May 9, 1983, p. 8C.

9. ———, "SPCO's Resident Conductor Underplays His Uniqueness, " *op. cit.*

10. An earlier winner of the Leopold Stokowski Competition was black conductor Calvin Simmons.

11. David Manning White, "The Lively Arts" (William Curry's "Magical" Decade), *Richmond,* August 1976, p. 11.

12. Interview, Handy with Curry, December 7, 1991, Washington, D.C.

Charles Darden

CHARLES DARDEN

BIRTHDATE/PLACE: August 28, 1946; Galveston, Texas.
EDUCATION: San Francisco State University, School of Music (1963–66); San Francisco Conservatory of Music (1968–70); San Francisco Symphony Orchestra, Apprentice Conductor (1970–71); Tanglewood Berkshire Music Festival, Conducting Fellow (1971–72); Curtis Institute of Music, Diploma in Conducting (1973); Accademia Nazionale di Santa Cecilia, Roma, Diploma in Conducting (1973).
MAJOR INSTRUCTORS: Ross Taylor (French Horn); Seiji Ozawa, Max Rudolf, Leonard Bernstein, and Franco Ferrara (Conducting).
MAJOR APPOINTMENTS: Instructor/Conductor, U.S. Navy School of Music (1966–68); Founder/Conductor, Berkeley Free Orchestra (1968–70); Founder/Conductor, Philadelphia Free Orchestra (1971); Conducting Assistant, The Cleveland Orchestra (1975–76); Music Director, Ballet Rambert, London (1977–79); Resident Conductor, Bombay Philharmonic Orchestra (1980–81); Conductor, Washington Square Music Festival Orchestra (1982–86); Principal Conductor, Dance Theatre of Harlem (1985–86).
GUEST CONDUCTOR: Schwetzinger Festspiele, Das Radio-Sinfonieorchester Stuttgart, Oslo Philharmonic Orchestra, Bergen Festival Orchestra, Norwegian Radio Orchestra, Gotteborgs Symfoniker, Royal Danish Orchestra, Den Norske Opera Orchestra, Ballet Rambert Chamber Ensemble, San Francisco Chamber Orchestra, Bombay Philharmonic, Copenhagen Radio Symphony Orchestra, Brooklyn Philharmonic Orchestra; Cleveland, Atlanta, North Carolina, St. Louis, Indianapolis, American, Pittsburgh, and San Francisco Symphony Orchestras.

BORN IN GALVESTON, TEXAS, Darden moved with his family to Berkeley, California, just prior to his entrance into the fourth grade. His music career began with French horn study in the Berkeley public schools at age 14. He was soon invited to join the Young People's Symphony Orchestra in Berkeley and, before long, was appointed principal horn player. Piano study began in junior high school and continued through the twelfth grade. Senior high school provided many opportunities to accompany the glee club and choir,

73

and a chance to appear as the King in Rodgers and Hammerstein's "The King and I."

While a student of Ross Taylor (principal horn, San Francisco Symphony), Darden matriculated at San Francisco State University from 1963 to 1966. During those years he taught both privately and in the parochial school system. Upon graduation he enlisted and was assigned to the U.S. Navy School of Music, teaching music theory and French horn and doing some conducting.

Several months short of fulfilling his military obligation, Darden auditioned for the newly-established Martin Luther King, Jr. Memorial Fellowship offered by the San Francisco Conservatory of Music. As a result, he was offered the school's $10,000 four-year scholarship. As Darden explained to journalist Jack Otter,

> I wrote President Johnson a personal letter explaining how I had gotten this fellowship in King's name and all. . . . When I returned from leave, the Pentagon had ordered my immediate release from active duty.[1]

While enrolled at the Conservatory, Darden organized the Berkeley Free Orchestra and served as the group's director-conductor, fundraiser, and general manager. At the same time, he was assistant conductor of Berkeley's Young People's Symphony Orchestra.

In recognition of his innate conducting talent, Darden was invited in 1969 both to participate in an important conducting competition and to audition for a promising conducting position—the Dimitri Mitropoulos International Conducting Competition in New York City *and* to assist maestro Seiji Ozawa of the San Francisco Symphony, respectively. During the summer of 1970, he participated in the St. Louis Orchestra's Institute of Orchestral Conducting and returned to San Francisco in the fall to work with Ozawa as an apprentice conductor. The San Francisco Symphony Association also provided him the opportunity to work as special instructor in the orchestra's In-School Concert Program.

David Schneider, San Francisco Symphony historian (also former member of the violin section and once chairman of the orchestra committee), reported on Darden's role with the San Francisco Symphony in his 1983 book, *The San Francisco Symphony: Music, Maestros, and Musicians:*

. . . Charles Darden, a 23-year-old black man, was appointed "apprentice" in conducting. This new position was created for Darden, who had shown great talent at the audition yet was not ready to assume the assistant conductor post. Unfortunately, Darden had no specific duties with the orchestra. Rather, he was an advanced student poised to step up to a conducting position when he was considered sufficiently schooled. He left after a very short time to study in New York [?] and Europe and has never returned.[2]

During the summer of 1971, Darden participated as a conducting fellow at the Tanglewood Berkshire Music Festival, where Ozawa served as an artistic advisor and the Boston Symphony Orchestra made its summer home. He enrolled at the Curtis Institute of Music in the fall of 1971 and shortly after his arrival, *The Philadelphia Tribune* published a feature story about the young, rapidly developing talent, who had just organized a forty-piece symphony orchestra,

consisting of Black and white youths from throughout the city. . . . The Philadelphia Free Orchestra, led by Charles Darden. . .[would] stage an informal concert . . . featuring works by Dukas, Mozart, Stravinsky and Beethoven.

With a two-year grant from Curtis Institute, Darden had been in the city only three weeks before assuming this orchestral responsibility.

Within that short period, Darden [had] been able to put together the Philadelphia Free Orchestra consisting of students at Curtis, the Philadelphia Academy of Music and the New School of Music. . . . Darden talked of a new type of symphony orchestra that has been formulated in this new orchestra of his. "We're trying to do away with the old structure. We're an orchestra made up of young people and it's the cooperative type of orchestra."

In this exclusive interview with *Philadelphia Tribune* reporter James Cassell, Darden said:

My greatest hope is to get more Blacks interested in the classics. My work with young people in The Philadelphia Free Orchestra . . . is the first step in that direction. There are many young Black potential conductors who never get the opportunity to show what they can do. By working closely with the youths in this orchestra, I hope to be able to help prepare them for a brighter future.

I like to reach everyone . . . In order to achieve this we're prepared to
do some concerts in the key schools and churches in the city where we
can attract youngsters from the ghetto.[3]

He was one of several black conductors who attempted to explain
the profession, their place in it, and the route to a successful career to
Bryant Mason, for Mason's 1972 *Essence* article "And the Beat Goes
On." Darden contributed the following:

The problem with Black conductors and musicians is study. If you are
not from a family that disciplined you, you must learn to do it
yourself. . . . You have to serve under someone first . . . and then you
will catch somebody's eye.[4]

Subsequent activities confirmed and reinforced his stated convic-
tions. In 1973, he received his conducting diploma from Curtis
Institute and a conducting diploma from Accademia Nazionale di
Santa Cecilia in Rome. He also participated in master classes of
Franco Ferrara's at the Accademia Chigiana in Siena, upon the
recommendation of Leonard Bernstein. He obviously "caught someone's eye," for he was selected to serve as conducting assistant to
Lorin Maazel at the Cleveland Orchestra during the 1975–76 season.
The exposure and experience this prestigious appointment would
provide could be crucial to his receiving other conducting invitations, which would in turn boost his career.

A May 1977 article in *The Sun,* focused on black conductors'
optimism about the future, reflected on one of Darden's Cleveland
accomplishments. Specializing in contemporary music and educational concerts, Darden's "liaison with Cleveland's black community
is credited with increasing its appearance in the audience."[5]

The same year, Darden was hired as music director and conductor
of the Ballet Rambert in London. There he remained for two seasons.
Several guest conducting appearances followed: Schwetzinger
Festspiele, Das Radio-Sinfonieorchester Stuttgart (1979), Den
Norske Opera (1980), the Oslo Philharmonic (1981), the Bergen
Festival Orchestra (1981), and the Norwegian Radio Orchestra
(1981). He served as Resident Conductor of the Bombay Philhar-
monic Orchestra during the 1980–81 season.

During this period of guest conducting, Darden continued in the
pursuit common to young conductors building careers: the search for

an orchestra. To support Darden's quest, New York Philharmonic's music director Zubin Mehta, in a letter of introduction wrote:

> I have observed Mr. Charles Darden at work and I find he is a conscientious musician who has obviously had very good training.
>
> I feel Mr. Darden's qualities as both a musician and a human being would be a great asset to an orchestra looking for a young gentleman who is willing to spend time and energies in building up such an organization to a level of excellence.[6]

Darden made his New York debut conducting the Brooklyn Philharmonic, which performed with the Norwegian National Ballet in its season at the Brooklyn Academy of Music in 1982–83. Shortly thereafter, he launched a four-year affiliation with New York's Washington Square Festival Orchestra. In late January 1985, Dance Theatre of Harlem announced the appointment of Charles Darden as its principal conductor for the 1985–86 season.

Beyond conducting, Darden's musical experiences have been extensive. When in 1985 the Metropolitan Opera performed George Gershwin's opera "Porgy and Bess," Darden was on stage as Jazzbo Brown, the piano player in the opening scene.

Since 1986, Darden has performed a one-man show "Great Scott," where from the keyboard he chronicles the life of ragtime composer-pianist Scott Joplin through music and narration. As he explained to journalist Jack Otter, "I wanted to turn around and face the audience." Otter added:

> He attributed his departure from the podium to several factors, including frustration with the profession, fatigue from traveling, and the simple desire to tickle the ivories.[7]

Currently a resident of Sag Harbor on Long Island and New York City, Darden "tickles the ivories" on Friday and Saturday nights at Bobby Van's Restaurant in Bridgehampton, Long Island, entertaining audiences with old standards.

> Gone is the dinner jacket, and in its place is a turtleneck shirt and velour sweater. Audience members set their drinks down on the piano and sing along. If they like what he plays, they sometimes drop a few dollars in an oversized brandy snifter sitting on the piano.[8]

For Charles Darden, musical life and fulfillment continue. But the appeal of a conducting podium was at least attractive enough to steer him back long enough to conduct the Indianapolis Symphony Orchestra during the 1990–91 season. The writer is convinced that there will be many other appealing orchestral leadership experiences.

Press Comments

"... Mr. Darden exhibited admirable podium skills. ... {H}is easy bearing and economy of gesture made him seem a natural for his calling."

New York Times

"{H}is interpretations ... were characterized by nice sensitivity to lyric lines and expressive nuance."

New York Times

Notes

1. Jack Otter, "An 'Itinerant' Piano Man," *East Hampton Star,* March 9, 1989, p. 11–24.
2. David Schneider, *The San Francisco Symphony: Music, Maestros, and Musicians,* Novato, California: Presidio Press, 1983, p. 178.
3. James Cassell, "Youth Conductor to Lead New Orchestra in Concert Here," *Philadelphia Tribune,* November 9, 1971, p. 25.
4. Bryant Mason, "And the Beat Goes On," *Essence,* November 1972, pp. 51, 81.
5. "Black Conductors Are Optimistic About Appointment to Orchestras," *Sun,* May 31, 1977, p. B9.
6. Correspondence prepared by Zubin Mehta on behalf of Charles Darden, dated January 8, 1982.
7. Otter, *op. cit.*
8. *Ibid.*

Denis de Coteau (Courtesy: *The Black Perspective in Music*)

DENIS MONTAGUE de COTEAU

BIRTHDATE/PLACE: June 12, 1937; Brooklyn, New York.

EDUCATION: B.A. and M.S., New York University; D.M.A., Stanford University.

ADDITIONAL STUDY: Juilliard School of Music.

MAJOR INSTRUCTORS/COACHES: Ruvin Heifetz, Violin; Wilhon Persim, Hans Strowski, Richard Lert, Henrich Goldsmith, Conducting.

MAJOR APPOINTMENTS: Faculty, Grinnell College; Professor of Music, California State University (Hayward); Conductor, Oakland Symphony Youth Orchestra (1970–79); Conductor, San Francisco Chamber Orchestra; Assistant Conductor, San Francisco Ballet, 1970–1974; Music Director and Conductor, San Francisco Ballet, 1974—; Conductor of the Orchestra, San Francisco Conservatory of Music; Music Director and Conductor, Flagstaff (Arizona) Festival of the Arts.

GUEST CONDUCTOR: Oakland East Bay Symphony, BBC Scottish Symphony, Tokyo City Philharmonic, Toronto Chamber Orchestra, Oakland Ballet, Symphony of the New World, San Francisco Symphony, New Orleans Philharmonic, Yomiuri Orchestra (Tokyo), Saint Louis Symphony, National Philharmonic (London), Detroit Symphony Orchestra, International Youth Orchestra, Australian Youth Orchestra.

AWARDS/HONORS: Pierre Monteux Conducting Prize (1969); ASCAP Award for Adventuresome Programming (1976); Resolutions of Commendation from the California State Legislature and the San Francisco City Council (1974, 1976, 1978).

LIKE SO MANY OTHER SUCCESSFUL CONDUCTORS, Denis de Coteau began his musical training with piano study, at age three. No doubt his interest was stimulated by his parents; his father played the violin and his mother the piano. By the time he was six, he decided to switch to the viola, largely because he considered his twin brother to be a more accomplished pianist than he. And though instruments provided his practical introduction to music, his conducting interest was stimulated early in his life as well.

[M]y father used to take my brother and me to concerts at the
Brooklyn Museum, Carnegie Hall, and the NBC Studio 8H, where
Toscanini used to conduct. I had decided that I wanted to be a
musician or a diplomat... But at the age of nine or ten I went to hear
the New York Philharmonic, where to my complete surprise there
was a black man standing in front of an orchestra conducting. It
turned out to be Dean Dixon.*[1]

Though de Coteau was young, the experience of seeing Dixon was
pivotal; he determined then to be a conductor. Not long thereafter,
he began a three-year period of study (score reading, counterpoint,
and harmony) with the maestro at Dixon's home on Convent Avenue
in New York. De Coteau was never able to study conducting with
Dixon; by the time de Coteau was ready to begin, Dixon had left for
Europe because there was no work in the United States for black
conductors. However, de Coteau considers Dixon crucial to his
success:

> [Dixon] got me started and gave me the discipline that is required to
> be a conductor. He was a difficult task-master. Never let up the
> pressure even though I was only ten or eleven when I started studying
> with him.[2]

At age 15 de Coteau was enrolled at New York City's Music and
Art High School, having been a scholarship winner at the Chatham
Square Music School (where he studied violin with Ruvin Heifetz,
father of the famed violinist Jascha Heifetz). Because he was
considered to be an excellent violinist (after only five years of study),
he was accepted for membership in the Brooklyn NAACP Interracial
Orchestra. He was also a track star, having won four local medals in
the 60-yard dash. "I go in for track as a sideline...I do it for relaxation
and recreation and also to keep myself in shape for my musical
career." But that recollection of Dixon, conducting the New York
Philharmonic, was both strong and lasting. "My main ambition is to
become an orchestra conductor like Dean Dixon. I think I have the
ability to demonstrate. I do much better in my music lessons at
school than at all my other courses." Already he had conducted the
orchestra at Music and Art High School several times.[3]

After graduating from Music and Art High School, de Coteau
attended New York University, from which he received both

bachelor's and master's degrees. Fulfilling an early ambition, he studied conducting at the Juilliard School of Music. During those New York years, de Coteau studied with a number of Germans who had fled Hitler's regime: Wilhon Persim, a former assistant conductor to Richard Strauss; Hans Strowski, former conductor of the Vienna Philharmonic; Richard Lert, former chief conductor at the Munich Opera House; and Henrich Goldsmith, opera coach and conductor in Berlin before it was partitioned.[4] Thereafter he earned his doctorate of musical arts degree in conducting at Stanford University.

After serving on the faculty of Grinnell College in Iowa, de Coteau accepted appointment to California State College, Hayward. In 1970, he became conductor of the Oakland Symphony Youth Orchestra (which in 1974 won the Silver Medal at the Herbert von Karajan International Festival of Youth Orchestras in West Berlin[5]). In the same year, de Coteau was appointed assistant conductor of the San Francisco Ballet, and in 1974 became its conductor and music director. De Coteau reports that his lengthy tenure with the Ballet started as a fortuitous accident: "The conductor was sick, I was asked to fill in, and I've been there ever since."[6]

Though de Coteau maintains an active schedule of conducting orchestral concerts, ballet and opera in the United States and around the world, ballet occupies the central position in his musical life. The critical difference in his ballet conducting is the consideration of tempi:

> You have a paramount concern for tempo because it is the whole thing on which the dancers hang their hats. The dancer could be injured by a radically wrong tempo....I have always thought of my work in the pit as a concert by the orchestra, to which there just happens to be dancing.... We still try to make the most gorgeous music we can. We just make sure that it is tailored to suit the dancing needs.[7]

Inevitably, black conductors are asked about how their careers have been effected by their race. De Coteau says:

> There were many barriers . . . I don't talk about them because I spend the better part of my life dealing with the present and the future. The past gives us a reference point. It helps us understand where we are and what we have to do. But to dwell in the past is dangerous.[8]

And with regard to being called a black conductor, the maestro feels strongly

> . . . that it is all a matter of semantics. I am a conductor who happens to be black, so in a sense I am a black conductor. The problem with that, of course, is that one runs into the risk of setting up a category-a category of musicians who are apart from any other musician. So you have good conductors, bad conductors, and black conductors. No one refers to Ozawa as a Japanese conductor. He is a conductor.[9]

Press Comments

". . . the youthful {San Francisco Ballet} orchestra—a full-time resident orchestra—played even the most demanding symphonic scores with virtuosic elegance under the knowing leadership of Denis de Coteau."

Los Angeles Times

". . . in the concluding Stravinsky Divertimento Mr. Coteau obtained the best ensemble effort of the afternoon, and invested the music with an appropriately relaxed, ingratiating reading."

New York Times

Notes

1. Anne Lundy, "CONVERSATIONS with Three Symphonic Conductors: Denis de Coteau. Tania Leon, Jon Robinson [sic]," *Black Perspective in Music,* Vol. 16, No. 2, Fall 1988, pp. 213–214.
2. *Ibid.*
3. "Youthful Violinist Seeks Orchestra Leader's Career," *Afro-American,* April 7, 1945, p. 16.
4. Lundy, *op. cit.* p. 214
5. "Speaking of People," *Ebony Magazine,* June 1975, Chicago, Illinois, p. 7.
6. Joette Dignan Weir, "His mission is music: conductor to lead symphony," *Daily Review* (Alameda County, California), April 20, 1989, p. 2.
7. Lundy, *op. cit.* p. 216.
8. Weir, "His mission is music," p. 2.
9. Lundy, *op. cit.* p. 217.

James Anderson DePreist

James DePreist, Conducting Oregon Symphony Orchestra

JAMES ANDERSON DePREIST

BIRTHDATE/PLACE: November 21, 1936, Philadelphia, Pennsylvania.
EDUCATION: B. S. (Economics), 1958 and M. A. (Film and Communication), 1961, University of Pennsylvania; Philadelphia Conservatory of Music (Composition), 1959–61.
MAJOR COMPOSITION INSTRUCTOR: Vincent Persichetti.
MAJOR APPOINTMENTS: Music Director, Contemporary Music Guild (Philadelphia), 1959–62; American Specialist in Music (Bangkok, Thailand), United States State Department, 1962–63; Conductor-in-Residence, Bangkok, Thailand, 1963–64; Music Director, Station WCAU-TV (Philadelphia), 1965–66; Assistant Conductor, New York Philharmonic, 1965–66; Principal Guest Conductor, Symphony of the New World, 1968–70; Associate Conductor, National Symphony Orchestra, 1971–75; Principal Guest Conductor, National Symphony Orchestra, 1975–76; Music Director, Quebec Symphony Orchestra, 1976–83; Music Advisor, Grand Rapids Symphony, 1985–86; Music Director, Oregon Symphony, 1980—; Music Director and Conductor, Peter Britt Gardens Music and Arts Festival, 1988—; Music Director, Malmo (Sweden) Symphony Orchestra, 1991–1994; Music Director Designee, Monte Carlo (French Riviera) Philharmonic, 1994.
GUEST CONDUCTOR: New York and Los Angeles Philharmonic Orchestras; Chicago, National, Boston, Indianapolis, Denver, Houston, Detroit, Pittsburgh, Atlanta, Utah, and Syracuse Symphony Orchestras; Cleveland, Philadelphia, and Minnesota Orchestras; Cosmopolitan Young People's Symphony; Juilliard Orchestra; Grant Park Symphony; Aspen, Sun River, and Blossom Festival Orchestras; Helsinki, Rotterdam, Israel, Amsterdam, Stockholm, and Zagreb Philharmonic Orchestras; National Orchestra of Monte Carlo; Toronto, Honolulu, and Budapest Symphony Orchestras; Radio Orchestras of Belgium, Munich, Bavaria, Stuttgart, and Berlin; Netherlands Radio Philharmonic; Tonkünstler Orchestra of Vienna; Naantali (Finland) Music Festival Orchestra; Opera South (Mississippi); and Portland Opera.
AWARDS/HONORS/PRIZES: First Prize, Dimitri Mitropoulos International Conducting Competition, 1964; Martha Baird Rockefeller Award, 1966; Merit Citation from the City of Philadelphia, 1969; The Governor's Award (Oregon Arts Commission); eleven honorary degrees, from such

institutions as Pennsylvania and Portland, Laval (Quebec), St. Mary's, Pacific, Lewis and Clark, Forest Grove, and Linfield.

PUBLICATIONS (Poetry): *This Precipice Garden* and *A Distant Siren* (1986 and 1989 respectively).

COMPOSITIONS: (ballet scores): Including "Vision of America," "Tendrils," and "A Sprig of Lilac."

RECORDINGS (partial): The Toronto Symphony, the Delos and Los Angeles Chamber Orchestras, the Royal, Helsinki, and Stockholm Philharmonic Orchestras; the Quebec and Oregon Symphony Orchestras.

DURING HIS YEARS OF GUEST CONDUCTING only (1966–71), James DePreist insisted that his talent not be ghettoized: "I want to know they want a conductor, not just a black conductor." In a 1975 interview, he said:

> When people call me "the first black conductor" I don't know what that means. The first to amass the knowledge? The first they've let through? I'm a human being first, a musician second, and a Black American after all that. . . .[1]

More than a decade later, having obtained membership in the select group of American conductors leading (as music director) a major American orchestra, DePreist emphatically stated:

> I have always found it pointless to look for, presume or in an ex-post-facto way attribute to prejudice things that did not come about. I don't think it's possible to live an examined life as a black American without sooner or later encountering examples of prejudice.
>
> What becomes important is that you have to go beyond that, you almost assume that it can be there, not that it will be there, but never use it as the operative reason why something doesn't happen, because then it becomes both a crutch and an excuse.[2]

DePreist also had strong opinions about black audience participation and expressed them in a 1974 interview with the *Rocky Mountain News* (just prior to guest conducting the Denver Symphony): "[We should be] widening horizons, enticing them into concert halls where they will hear sounds at their best."[3] Fourteen years later DePreist led the New York Philharmonic in its debut concert at the legendary Apollo Theatre on 125th Street in Harlem.[4] The concert was a gala benefit for the Boys Choir of Harlem, the Harlem School of the Arts (founded in 1966 by black concert artist Dorothy Maynor), and the Philharmonic itself. The maestro was scheduled to lead two weeks of New York Philharmonic subscription concerts around the same time, at Avery Fisher Hall.

The concert, titled "Take the 'A' Train," was a collaboration of the Boys Choir of Harlem, the Modern Jazz Quartet, and the New York Philharmonic. DePreist said of the event,

> Usually a venue does not have a history that affects one's program. But when you bring the New York Philharmonic to the Apollo Theater, I think a respect for the theater's history dictates that one should pay homage to what the Apollo has been, while also pointing in the direction of what it can become.[5]

The program included Leonard Bernstein's "Chichester Psalms," John Lewis's "Tales of the Willow Tree," and Duke Ellington's* "Praise God and Dance."

In his usually profound and articulate manner, DePreist further explained,

> There was a time when classical music was believed to be irrelevant to the black experience. . .But my contention is that classical music is relevant to the human experience, and that to the degree that we regard ourselves first as human and then as black, it is relevant to everyone. Being so clearly visible, it's difficult for there not to be connotations attached to what one does. But I think it would be wrong to construe this concert as an outreach program. Rather, it is an intriguing juxtaposition of two institutions that would not normally be spoken of within the same paragraph, and a concert that shows the versatility of the forces and the multiplicity of the music.[6]

One year prior, DePreist led the Philharmonic in a program featuring works by George Gershwin and Duke Ellington at Avery Fisher Hall. The program included a saxophone concerto entitled "Ellingtones" by the black composer David Baker, with Dexter Gordon (star of the film " 'Round Midnight") as soloist, and black concert pianist Leon Bates, as soloist in Gershwin's "Rhapsody in Blue." On that occasion, DePreist remarked:

> I have assiduously avoided concerts of this sort in the past. . . . I won't allow myself to be just a symbol. But I like this program, and I

already had two weeks of subscription concerts with the orchestra coming up next season and so felt these performances would be understood as part of my larger relationship with the Philharmonic.[7]

Reviewing a late 1970 concert of the Symphony of the New World, *New York Times* music critic Donal Henahan wrote:

James DePreist. . .looms more and more as the Great Black Hope in the American conducting arena. . . .[But], [I]t is too simple to praise Mr. DePreist as a good black conductor; the fact is that few Americans of any age or color could handle as successfully the many-styled symphonic program he offered [Mozart's Symphony No. 34 in C, Schubert's "Unfinished" Symphony, Mahler's "Kindertolenlieder," and Jan Carstedt's Symphony No. 2—"A Symphony of Brotherhood"].[8]

DePreist served as Principal Guest Conductor of the Symphony of the New World from 1968 to 1970. Then 34 years of age, DePreist already had taken top honors in the Dimitri Mitropoulos International Conducting Competition (1964); had served as Assistant Conductor of the New York Philharmonic (1965–66); had become a resident of Rotterdam, whence he guest conducted throughout Europe; and was beginning to receive conducting invitations from prestigious orchestras in his native country.

One such invitation came in 1970 from the National Symphony in the nation's capitol. The concert venue was Constitution Hall, the site that in 1939 had refused to permit the appearance of his famous aunt, world renowned contralto Marian Anderson. He subsequently explained the Constitution Hall/National Symphony experience to black music journalist Raoul Abdul:

Antal Dorati [Music Director of the National] asked me to come to Washington to conduct the National Symphony. . . when they were still in Constitution Hall. That was a very emotional moment because that was the same hall where my aunt could not appear. But it was so simple for me. I just went in and walked on the stage. That was a very special moment.[9]

The St. Louis Post-Dispatch music critic James Wierzbicki assessed DePreist's guest conducting appearance with the St. Louis Symphony in March 1989:

[He] has a solid reputation as one of the most reliable—and most thoughtful—of this country's conductors, a musician as famous in recent years for his ability to step in on short notice and solve an orchestra's immediate problems as for his consistant, high-quality work as music director of the Oregon Symphony.[10]

Obviously much had transpired in the intervening years: in addition to his many guest conducting appearances, he had served as associate and principal guest conductor of the National Symphony, as music director of L'Orchestre Symphonique de Québec, and since 1980, as music director of the Oregon Symphony.

The musical ascent of James DePreist from a multi-talented twenty-five-year-old "in search of direction" to one of the select and talented circle of American-born and trained conductors of international stature is indeed interesting. Let us consider the first quarter of a century of this exciting life.

DePreist was born and raised in South Philadelphia, an ethnically diverse community. The DePreist residence was filled with classical music; but young Jimmy's private listening also included Tony Bennett, Rosemary Clooney, Johnny Mathis, Nat "King" Cole, and Stan Kenton. The fact that his aunt was a celebrity made little impression in the early years.

I knew she sang on the radio and I liked the way she sounded, but it was difficult, especially without television, for me to relate the disembodied voice I'd hear on the Bell Telephone Hour to my aunt whom I visited summers on her Connecticut farm. She'd be like any other aunt, giving warmth and affection and time and attention.

I think when I was 12 I realized who she was. . . . People always comment on the fact, the biological accident, that I'm her nephew. I don't think I've used that connection to help my career. But there's no way of getting around it. . . . People see it as a tradition.[11]

He studied both piano and percussion and played the latter in the citywide high school orchestra. At fourteen, his famous aunt gave him some classical recordings and the orchestral scores to accompany them. The seed was planted, devoid of any personal realization.

DePreist entered college with plans of preparing for a career in law. During the undergraduate years he formed the Jimmy DePreist Quintet that in 1956 was one of the best jazz ensembles in the East, capturing a Music Society of America award and appearing on The Tonight Show with Steve Allen. The DePreist Quintet performed in and around Philadelphia, at various jazz festivals, and in concert. Leader DePreist also worked briefly as an arranger for Stan Kenton. He graduated in 1958 with a degree in economics.

With second thoughts about a future in the law, DePreist entered graduate school at the Annenberg School of Communication of the University of Pennsylvania and in 1961 received his master's degree in film and communication. Concurrently, he matriculated at the Philadelphia Conservatory, studying music history, theory, and orchestration. He also studied composition with the distinguished American composer Vincent Persichetti. Throughout his University of Pennsylvania years, he participated in the symphonic and marching bands.

Despite his many talents and numerous fulfilling experiences, DePreist was late in settling on a career direction. Yet, as he later stated:

> Because I was so curious, and because I had the opportunity to explore a variety of things, I never felt frustrated. . . . The real frustration was in not being able to make up my mind.[12]

His first experience before an orchestra took place in the late 1950s when members of the Philadelphia Orchestra, following a rehearsal, remained to read through a DePreist score—a commissioned work for the Philadelphia Dance Academy. Remarked DePreist:

> They were on an incandescent high after playing with him [Leopold Stokowki] and then here I was, this little novice. . . .It was not an enviable position, but I guess it kindled what had been a subliminal interest in me to be a conductor.[13]

Upon the recommendation of black concert pianist Natalie Hinderas, who had taken an interest in DePreist's compositional skills and jazz talents, the young musician, still in search of direction, was invited by the State Department to tour a number of countries in the Far East, teaching and lecturing on jazz specifically and American music generally. Prior to his 1962 departure, aunt Marian Anderson arranged for him to meet with Leonard Bernstein (then music director of the New York Philharmonic), who suggested that the Asian experience would no doubt help him to make a career selection.

It was in Thailand that DePreist had the opportunity to conduct the Thai Orchestra in a rehearsal of Schubert's Symphony in C, studied only by a recording. As he later explained:

> Suddenly everything was clear. . . .I was conducting and I loved it. It was as if I had done all this the day before, when there actually had been a three-year lapse since I'd studied the score. It was as if it had all entered a part of my head and stayed there.[14]

Soon after this marvelous experience, DePreist contracted polio, which left him paralyzed from the waist down. Flown back to America, DePreist began a tedious recovery in a Philadelphia hospital, where he spent many hours poring over orchestral scores. Upon the suggestion of Bernstein, DePreist entered the 1963 Mitropoulos International Conducting Competition and made it to the semifinals.

After returning to Thailand on another brief tour, thereby acquiring additional experience, he entered the 1964 Mitropoulos Competition and emerged a first prize winner. He was selected by Leonard Bernstein to be an assistant conductor of the New York Philharmonic for the 1965–66 season, becoming the first American winner of the Mitropoulos Competition to serve as Mr. Bernstein's assistant.

Between the competition and assuming his duties as assistant conductor of the New York Philharmonic, DePreist worked with a group of talented young instrumentalists in New York City who made their formal debut at Carnegie Hall in December 1964 as the Cosmopolitan Young People's Symphony Orchestra. This was but one of many of DePreist's involvements with young musicians.[15] For several seasons in the mid-1970s, DePreist was a participating maestro in the American Federation of Musician's Congress of Strings, a summer program designed to assist aspiring young string players and enhance their career-building opportunities. Shortly following his "concise, witty, and inspiring" remarks delivered at the opening general luncheon of the American Symphony Orchestra League's 43rd National Conference (Chicago, 1988), he led an open rehearsal of the Chicago Youth Symphony Orchestra. The enthusiasm for sharing his skills and knowledge with "developing" orchestral musicians in 1988 was as genuine as it was in the mid-1960s.

Following his fulfilling season with the New York Philharmonic, his only offer of a job in this country was at the Westchester Music and Arts Camp in Croton-on-Hudson. In 1967, he took up residence in Rotterdam and remained in Europe for several years. He later recalled:

> The only opportunities I was getting here. . .were for pops concerts, which didn't seem like the right thing to do for someone with serious ambitions that had not yet been realized. I thought it would be better to starve slowly over there than instantly over here.[16]

DePreist offered another assessment of the situation:

> There was a time when you didn't see blacks conducting symphony orchestras because you didn't see Americans conducting the major orchestras in this country. It's the same way people feel about handbags and shoes and scarves—imported is better. You don't begin by conducting in Boise, Idaho, and working your way up. Your Boise, Idahos have to be in Europe. There's a greater opportunity to learn about serious music abroad. Everybody is waiting for some stamp of approval; you know, get more experience and we'll hire you.[17]

An extremely successful European debut in 1969 with the Rotterdam Philharmonic represented the first of many offers to guest-conduct in Europe. Upon recommendation of maestro Antal Dorati, DePreist was invited to make his Scandinavian debut with the Stockholm Philharmonic. He returned two weeks later to substitute for an ailing "scheduled" conductor. Return guest engagements were becoming routine in the life of DePreist, on both sides of the Atlantic. From his Rotterdam residence, he journeyed to such additional places as Brussels, Amsterdam, and Berlin, and, in the United States, to Chicago, Minnesota, Washington, Philadelphia, and New York City.

New York City's Symphony of the New World, an orchestra established in 1965 to "right the wrongs in hiring practices in major symphony orchestras," sought to take advantage of DePreist's growing popularity and ability. He was the orchestra's principal guest conductor from the 1968 season through the 1970 season.

DePreist's overwhelmingly successful guest appearance with the National Symphony in 1970 led the orchestra's music director, Antal Dorati, to ask DePreist to join him the following year in Washington as the orchestra's associate conductor. During DePreist's final season with the orchestra in 1975–76, his title was that of principal guest conductor.

The time had arrived for DePreist to lead his own orchestra, bringing to an end his "second-in-command" status. In 1976, he accepted the position of music director of Quebec's oldest orchestra, L'Orchestre Symphonique de Québec.

> For young, would-be conductors, the trip to the podium is never short—and most who start out in this fiercely competitive field never make it. For James DePreist, the journey encompassed 13 years, an attack of polio and periods of near total despair. . . .For DePreist, it is a double triumph. Quebec, the hotbed of Francophile sentiment, has picked not only an American, but a black one at that.[18]

As for DePreist's reaction:

> Things happen when they're supposed to,. . .Shifting from guest to permanent conductor is like shifting from lover to husband—you lose the privileges of an affair.[19]

DePreist was *Musical America*'s "Musician of the Month" in March 1977. The fact that this orchestra, largely subsidized by the Canadian government, would select an American, "and a black one to boot," aroused the curiosity of journalist Jack Hiemenz, who set out early in the maestro's tenure to interview him. The burning question was "How has all this come about?"[20]

When Hiemenz arrived at the music director's New York City apartment, DePreist was reviewing an opera score by black composer Ulysses Kay that he would conduct for the black opera company Opera South (Mississippi), while arranging solo replacements with the Quebec Orchestra for ailing violinist Isaac Stern and recently deceased pianist Gina Bachauer. During the course of the interview, DePreist described his appointment as "enigmatic, an unforeseen development." Wrote Hiemenz:

> The warm outgoing persona is another likely reason for his appeal to the Quebec music community; talking with James DePreist is like standing before a sunlamp.[21]

He had first conducted the Quebec orchestra in 1974, as a substitute guest. He returned the following year "unaware at the time that the orchestra was looking for a music director." But an offer was made and he accepted. The schedule—fourteen weeks of subscription concerts, with the music director conducting nine of them, plus a choral event—allowed ample time for continued guest conducting. Other bonuses existed: he loved the city and would be forced to learn French, the official language.

One year following his appointment, the Symphony's federal subsidy went from $333,000 to $500,000. The orchestra also played its first concert in Washington, D.C., and made its first recording for RCA. The ensemble grew from sixty-seven to seventy-five; the season was lengthened, as well as the repertory. Just prior to the orchestra's October 1977 visit, DePreist signed a contract for three additional years.[22]

In December 1979, following a ten-month search, the Oregon Symphony appointed forty-three-year-old James DePreist as its music director. Having signed a three-year contract, he would assume his new duties with the 1980–81 season, while continuing his Quebec tenure until 1983. This appointment distinguished DePreist as "one of only two black conductors of major symphony orchestras in the United States."(The other was Henry Lewis, music director of the New Jersey Symphony Orchestra, 1968–76.)

When the announcement was made, he had only recently completed a three-week, fifteen-concert engagement with the Israel Philharmonic. Future guest assignments included conducting engagements in Finland, Sweden, Manitoba, Seattle, and Utah.[23]

Within a few years (and with a renewed contract), DePreist had become one of Oregon's most popular figures and the orchestra the most powerful performing arts group in the city of Portland. He was successful in increasing attendance at all concerts—classical pops, and family—enlarging the playing roster, and in doubling the orchestra's operating budget.

Under his leadership, the Oregon Symphony released several recordings, all commercially viable. He presided over the orchestra's move from the Civic Auditorium to the newly renovated Arlene Schnitzer Concert Hall. When he arrived in Portland, many players were receiving a mere $9,000 annually. By the 1984–85 season, players were receiving more than $20,000 annually.

Though such rapid growth brought on an accumulated deficit,

DePreist's background in economics and "way with people" provided the wherewithal to assist in balancing the budget. Cleverly, he

> devised an ingenious plan to sell "Symphony Shares" for a dollar
> apiece, ensuring that support for the orchestra came not just from an
> elite group of corporate and private donors, but from the entire
> community.

Additionally, the orchestra expanded its outreach by carrying its
musical message to shopping malls, high school auditoriums, college
gymnasiums, and state fairs.[24]

Moving from one success to another, "with his own orchestra,"
DePreist maintained the following vision for both himself and the
Oregon Symphony:

> We have to be conscious of meeting the demands of the community
> and the demands of our mission statement: young people, educational
> programs, helping communities around the state afford the orchestra.
> We don't ever want to get to the position that in the name of fiscal
> responsibility, we neglect service to the community. My job is to
> make certain that we don't lose sight of what we're about.[25]

Success and recognition were now routine. By the end of the
1980s, his honorary degrees numbered eleven. In 1987, the University of Portland established an annual James DePreist humanitarian
award, honoring a "renaissance man of enduring values and ideals."[26]
Through most of the 1980s, DePreist was a regular guest conductor
of the Aspen (Colorado) Festival Orchestra. In 1988, he became the
artistic director and conductor of the Peter Britt Gardens Music and
Arts Festival in Medford, Oregon.

In late June 1987, *The Philadelphia Inquirer* carried an article titled
"Today, Another Side of Conductor James DePreist." The article
focused on his return to Philadelphia on behalf of the American
Poetry Center to give a poetry reading from his book, *This Precipice
Garden* (University of Portland Press, 1986), as a fundraiser for the
Center. *Philadelphia Inquirer* staff writer Leonard W. Boasberg
indicated that DePreist's poetry writing began by accident more
than a decade earlier:

> He was trying to write a letter to a friend and, finding considerable
> difficulty saying exactly what he wanted to say, started making notes

in the margin: "The marginal notes became numerous and, in short order, more significant to me than the letter."[27]

A second book of DePreist's poetry was published in 1989—*A Distant Siren* (Willamette University Press).

DePreist continues to reach wider audiences—readers, listeners, and viewers alike. He and the Oregon Symphony were featured subjects on CBS-TV's program "Sunday Morning," broadcast nationally May 15, 1988. On June 16, 1988, he was the Opening General Luncheon speaker for the American Symphony Orchestra League's 43rd National Conference in Chicago. He shared his thoughts on the subject "Money Is Not the Bottom Line," insisting that the essential mission of symphony orchestras is the presentation of quality music:

> Symphony orchestras are not artistically credible because they have raised millions of dollars. They have raised millions of dollars because they are artistically credible. And it is the hunger for that artistic credibility that we must elevate to a benign addiction.[28]

An abbreviated version of that speech was published in the August/September 1988 issue of *Symphony Magazine,* the official publication of the American Symphony Orchestra League.

The Oregon Symphony, under DePreist's leadership, made history during the 1988–89 season, when it was heard weekly performing the theme music on the popular television program "The Cosby Show." The request to arrange and record the theme came from Bill Cosby, DePreist's friend from Central High School in Philadelphia.

Ovation magazine's senior editor Charles Passy wrote a feature story for the January/February 1989 issue of *Symphony Magazine,* "Heart and Mind: The Musical Ascent of James DePreist." Passy informed readers of DePreist's strength as a human being, talent as a poet, ability as a speaker, and his nontraditional route to a successful reign as leader of the Oregon Symphony.[29]

Travelers on Northwest Airlines during the month of May 1989 were invited to experience "Airborne Symphonies" with host Paul Rogers and guest artist James DePreist. Displaying the maestro's photograph, Northwest's *Portfolio* made available to in-flight passengers recordings of Richard Strauss's "Don Juan" and Rachmaninoff's "Vocalise," Op. 34, No. 14, with the Oregon Symphony; Hindemith's March and Pastorale from "Nobilissima Visione," with the Royal Philharmonic Orchestra; and Mozart's Symphony No. 4 in D-Major, K. 19, featuring the Los Angeles Chamber Orchestra. For each Delos recording, DePreist conducted.[30]

DePreist was one of eight individuals featured in United Airline's April 1989 magazine *Vis à Vis*. When writer David Stabler commented on DePreist's approaching fifty-second birthday, he recalled DePreist's response: "Actually, age doesn't bother me. The opportunities are coming. The meat of a conductor's career comes between 50 and 75." Continued Stabler:

> If the telephone is any measure, DePreist is right. It rings every few minutes: Baltimore wants him in April, Philadelphia in June, Monte Carlo in July. Whether he's whipping the New York Philharmonic into a Tchaikovskian froth or pleading before Congress for more Mozart with its missiles, DePreist is a maestro on the move.[31]

In September 1991, the Oregon Symphony held a two-night gala, honoring its music director of eleven years. The local press referred to DePreist as "a folk hero," "an Oregon treasure," "a Renaissance man," "Oregon's premier ambassador of the arts." During his tenure, the Orchestra had grown from eighty-three part-time musicians to eighty-six full-time employees. The budget had grown from $2.5 million to $8.3 million; the endowment had grown from $2 million to $10 million. He had also guided the orchestra into the ranks of the major United States orchestras.

The board, management, musicians, and the community firmly believed that the DePreist years had been significant ones for the orchestra. Celebration was in order. On September 11, 1991, a "Tribute to Jimmy" black-tie dinner was held; on September 12, 1991, there took place a Special Oregon Symphony Concert, featuring renowned pianist André Watts as soloist. For the tributary dinner, Board President Gerard K. Drummond wrote:

> Your leadership of the Symphony is commanding, your talent awesome and your ability to inspire people to achieve excellence is unparalleled . . . .[W]e are most fortunate because we have someone as special as James DePreist to work with and to call our friend.[32]

Press Comments

"There seems no question that he {James DePreist} has emerged as one of the most important American conductors of the day. He is an imaginative program builder, and he can reach out to his players and secure the kind of response that denotes superior leadership."

Chicago Sun-Times

"Few American conductors can claim the kind of musical charisma that James DePreist commands."

Cincinnati Inquirer

"It was splendid to hear this marvelous, homegrown ensemble {Philadelphia Orchestra} led, for once, by an American conductor."

New York Times
(Carnegie Hall Debut)

"James DePreist . . . brought forth a performance that rang with clarity. . . . Clearly DePreist has that special magic many conductors lack, the magic to inspire professional musicians to give their best."

Detroit Free Press

"DePreist is an imposing presence on the podium. He approaches the music with wit and a real delight in the melodic possibilities of each piece. He and the orchestra seemed well suited to each other. He conducts with an economy of gesture; there is no false showmanship, and yet his control is generally first rate."

Detroit Free Press

"The confidence he radiates is so solid that it can be viewed as an integral part of him and the way he makes music . . . {S}uch an unrestrained warm and full tone like the one which streamed into the big hall one really does not hear everyday."

Dagens Nyheter (Stockholm)

"When an orchestra is in top form; when it plays music of a composer with whom it feels an affinity; when its conductor has the ability, in performance to somehow say, 'Here, look at this; look at this piece from this angle and from that light,' well, then, you're in for a whirlwind ride. The Oregon Symphony Orchestra, conducted by James DePreist . . . took Bartok's Concerto for Orchestra and Brahms Second Piano Concerto through just such a treatment."

News Tribune (Tacoma)

". . . DePreist clearly has an affinity for large scale playing and instrumental splendor."

Philadelphia Inquirer

"A perennial topic of discussion in the music business is just who, really, are the conductors of today . . . the conductors who really know how to make music. . . . It usually does not take very long for the name of James DePreist to come up."

Sunday Star-Ledger (Newark, New Jersey)

"{I}mmediately projected an image of immense authority . . . DePreist's interpretation . . . was among the most eloquent this critic has ever heard."

New York Daily News

"Few of his American colleagues are held in such high esteem and respect within the field as James DePreist. And few have established so outstanding a reputation for musicality, taste, versatility and technical expertise."

Star-Ledger

"To play under such thorough, electric competence must be a thrill."

Bangkok Post

"Mr. DePreist led a performance of power, sensitivity and maturity."

New York Times

". . . one of the finest conductors this nation has produced."

Chicago Tribune

Notes

1. Maralyn Lois Polak, "James DePreist: 'I'm At Home At the Top'," *Today/Philadelphia Inquirer,* February 9, 1975, p. 8.
2. Leonard W. Boasberg, "Today, Another Side of Conductor James DePreist," *Philadelphia Inquirer,* June 24, 1987, p. 3-C.
3. Marjorie Barrett, "Young Conductor Found Musical Route Circuitous," *Rocky Mountain News,* March 22, 1974, p. 58.
4. The New York Philharmonic began performing concerts in Harlem in 1980, at the famous Abyssinia Baptist Church. These concerts continued through the 1986–87 season.
5. Allan Kozinn, "Philharmonic At Apollo: Taking the 'A' Train," *New York Times,* April 25, 1988, p. C 17.
6. *Ibid.*

7. Michael Kimmelman, "A Maestro's Evolution: DePreist's Difficult Path," *New York Times*, June 5, 1987, p. C3.

8. Donal Henahan, "DePreist Conducts Subtly and Surely," *New York Times*, December 21, 1980, p. 48.

9. Raoul Abdul, *Blacks in Classical Music: A Personal History*, New York: Dodd, Mead and Co., 1977, p. 204.

10. James Wierzbicki, "DePreist Leads Symphony As Guest Conductor," *St. Louis Post Dispatch*, March 26, 1989, p. 2C.

11. Polak, *op. cit.*

12. Charles Passy, "Heart & Mind: The Musical Ascent of James DePreist," *Symphony Magazine*, January/February 1989, p. 54

13. Kimmelman, *op. cit.*

14. Donal Henahan, "Suddenly, On Tour, A Call To Conduct," *New York Times*, August 25, 1971, p. 44.

15. Raymond Ericson, "Youth Symphony Bows at Carnegie," *New York Times*, December 28, 1964, p. C 33.

16. Will Crutchfield, "Musician's Own Path To Podium," *New York Times*, July 24, 1984, p. C13.

17. Polak, *op. cit.*

18. Barbara Kevies, "Conductor James DePreist Fought and Won—an Orchestra," *People*, November 24, 1975, p. 71.

19. *Ibid.*

20. Jack Hiemenz, "Musician of the Month: James DePreist," *High Fidelity/Musical America*. March 1977, pp. 8–9, 35.

21. *Ibid.*

22. *Ibid.*

23. "DePreist Wins Post in Oregon," *Philadelphia Inquirer*, December 30, 1979, p. F11.

24. Passy, *op. cit.*, pp. 55–56.

25. David Stable, "DePreist, Symphony Think Music Instead of Money Now," *Sunday Oregonian*, October 25, 1987, p. 12.

26. Boasberg, *op. cit.*

27. *Ibid.*

28. James DePreist, "Money Is Not the Bottom Line," *Symphony Magazine*, August/September, 1988, pp. 20–21.

29. Passy, *op. cit.*

30. "In Concert," *Portfolio* (Northwest Airlines Magazine), May 1989, p. 98.

31. David Stabler, "Maestro On the Move: James DePreist," *Vis à Vis* (United Airlines), April 1989, p. 86.

32. *Jimmy,* Souvenir Booklet (Oregon Symphony Orchestra), September 1991.

(Charles) Dean Dixon (Courtesy: National Archives)

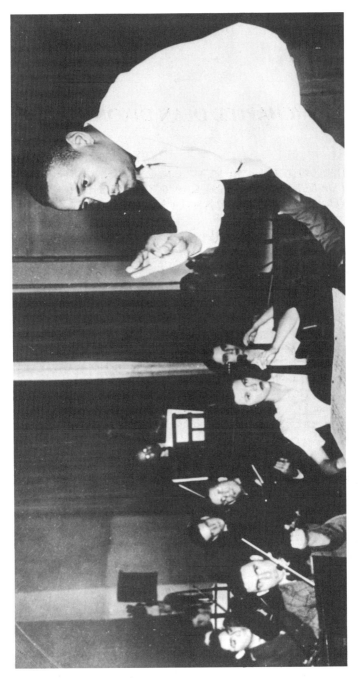

(Charles) Dean Dixon Rehearsing the American Youth Orchestra at Carnegie Hall (1944) (Courtesy: National Archives)

(CHARLES) DEAN DIXON

BIRTHDATE/PLACE: January 10, 1915; New York, N. Y.
DEATH DATE/PLACE: November 4, 1976; Zug, Switzerland.
EDUCATION: B.S., The Juilliard School of Music, 1936; M. A., Columbia University Teachers College, 1939.
MAJOR INSTRUCTORS: Mary Mandelen (Violin); Albert Stoessel (Conducting).
MAJOR APPOINTMENTS: Göteborg Symphony (Sweden), 1953–60; Hesse Radio Symphony Orchestra (Frankfurt, Germany), 1961–74; Sydney Symphony Orchestra (Australia), 1964–67.
FOUNDER/CONDUCTOR: Dean Dixon Symphony Orchestra, 1932; New York Chamber Orchestra, 1939; American Youth Orchestra, 1944.
CHORAL CONDUCTOR: Dean Dixon Choral Society, American Peoples Chorus, Long Island University Chorus;
OPERA/MUSICAL THEATER CONDUCTOR: "John Henry," 1939 and Shoestring Opera Company, 1943.
GUEST CONDUCTOR: Chamber Orchestra of the League of Music Lovers; NBC Symphony Orchestra; New York Philharmonic; Philadelphia Orchestra; Kansas City Philharmonic; Pittsburgh, Minnesota, St. Louis, National, Chicago, Detroit, San Francisco, and Milwaukee Symphony Orchestras; French National Radio Orchestra (first appearance outside of the U.S., 1949); Symphony and Radio Orchestras in Amsterdam, Athens, Barcelona, Belgrade, Berlin, Bern, Brussels, Budapest, Buenos Aires, Cologne, The Hague, Copenhagen, Florence, Hamburg, Helsinki, Leipzig, London, Melbourne, Mexico City, Milan, Monaco, Munich, Naples, Oslo, Poland, Prague, Rome, Salzburg, Stockholm, Tokyo, Vienna, and Zurich Symphony Orchestras.
CONTRIBUTING WRITER: The Musical Courier, Music World Almanac, The Music Educators Journal.
AWARDS/HONORS: Rosenwald Fellowship, 1945–47; ASCAP Award of Merit, 1945; Newspaper Guild Page One Award, 1945; Alice M. Ditson Award as Outstanding Conductor of the Year, 1948.

MUSIC JOURNALIST RAOUL ABDUL appropriately referred to Charles Dean Dixon as "the first full-time black American conductor of symphonic music."[1] Though other Blacks had preceded him on symphonic podiums, none engaged in the business of conducting as a primary activity. Before his death in 1976, Dixon attained the distinction of "the first black American to achieve recognition as a conductor of international stature."

Bernard Jacobson wrote in his entry "(Charles) Dean Dixon," appearing in the *New Grove Dictionary of American Music* (published in 1986): "In a sense Dixon's career as a conductor paralleled Marian Anderson's as a singer: he opened several important doors to black musicians. . . ."[2] Consequently, there was a time when the name Dean Dixon was synonymous with the label "black (Afro-American, Negro, or Colored) conductor."

In pursuit of his life's ambition, Dixon often heard, "Why bother? A Negro doesn't have a chance." Such a possibility was unacceptable to the Dixon family. That her only child would be a musician was decided by his Barbadian mother, McClara Dean Ralston Dixon. She imbued her son with her love of music and had young Dean reading music before he knew his ABCs. When he was a mere three-and-a-half years old, Mrs. Dixon purchased a violin for $15 at a Harlem pawnshop. The schedule of three lessons per week began immediately, and his mother monitored all practice sessions.

His attendance at Carnegie Hall events began shortly thereafter. His Jamaican father, Henry Charles Dixon, had been trained as a lawyer; but when he came to America, the only work that he could find was as a porter in a hotel. The sacrifice to support Dean's aspirations were great; both parents shared a vision of their son's musical potential. The father however did not live to see Dean realize any of his dreams.

At age thirteen, Dixon's teacher advised his mother that he should abandon the thought of a career in music. Both mother and son disregarded the advice, though mother Dixon began to make preparations for her son to pursue a medical career. As he approached graduation from DeWitt Clinton High School in 1932, Harry Jennison, head of the music department (who was determined that the young violinist should pursue music) exerted his influence to secure Dixon's acceptance at The Institute of Musical Art (subsequently The Juilliard School). Admitted on the basis of a violin audition, Dixon received his B.S. degree from The Juilliard School in 1936. He received his M.A. degree from Columbia University in 1939 and completed all course work for the doctorate shortly thereafter. At Juilliard he first followed the course of study in violin and after the first half year, the course of study in music pedagogy. Upon completion of the undergraduate degree, he successfully auditioned for a graduate fellowship in conducting, while concurrently continuing his academic studies at Columbia.

At twenty-eight Dixon had already achieved a status that merited a chapter in David Ewen's book *Dictators of the Baton,* originally published in 1943. But it was only in the revised and enlarged 1948 edition that Dean Dixon was included, along with thirty-two other conductors.

In the spring of 1948 Dixon received Columbia University's Alice M. Ditson Award of $1,000 "for outstanding contributions to American music." Dixon earned such recognition by virtue of his appearances with the Dean Dixon Symphony, the National Youth Administration Orchestra, the New York Chamber Orchestra, the League of Music Lovers Chamber Orchestra, the NBC Orchestra, the New York Philharmonic, the Philadelphia Orchestra, the Boston Symphony, the American Youth Orchestra, routinely programming music of American composers and featuring American artists. Wrote Ewen:

> Dixon's career is the triumph of talent over the greatest obstacle which can be placed in the way of a young musician acquiring conductorial assignments: race prejudice. . . . It is not an easy road that has brought a Negro to the conductor's stands of two [?] great American orchestras and the winning of a major award. That the road has, at last, been traversed speaks well both for Dixon's capabilities and for the capacity of true talent to assert itself.[3]

Though Dixon did not gain inclusion in Ewen's original publication, he did attract the attention of Blanche Lemmon in 1943, who featured the young maestro and an ambitious project on which he was working in an article for *Etude* magazine. The project was known as the Dean Dixon New Talent Contest. According to Lemmon, though it was an accepted fact that artistic democracy reigned as to welcoming foreign artists to our concert halls and classrooms,

> it was also well known that in past years our own young people had a difficult time in wedging their way into our top-ranking musical organizations . . . [O]ur attitude toward them was one of noninterference: they had to learn to swim somewhere else—or sink . . . [W]e

had no organization which could risk prestige by presenting unknown artists or unknown works in debut performances.[4]

Dixon's experience to date was a clear example of what a "break" could do for a young musician. The opportunities granted Dixon "provoked a genuine desire to make a reciprocal beneficial gesture and one as democratic as the opportunity that had been extended to him."

In 1939, Dixon and some of New York City's finest instrumentalists banded together to form the New York Chamber Orchestra. This aggregation of musicians he culled from players in major New York symphonic organizations. When the young conductor proposed the idea of assisting emerging young musicians of exceptional talent, his associates responded favorably. The New Talent Contest, which existed for at least three years, was open to citizens of the United States, Canada, and Central and South American nations, who were under twenty-six years of age, and who had not had a Town Hall or Carnegie Hall concert or debut with newspaper criticisms. The prize—for singers, keyboardists, or instrumentalists—was "a public performance or debut with an orchestra of quality before a metropolitan audience."

Dixon further evidenced his concern for the development of youth through his involvement in the late 1930s with various music projects under auspices of the Works Progress Administration (WPA) and work with the National Youth Administration Orchestra. Programs with the latter were challenging—a Beethoven cycle on Friday nights, a series of Sunday afternoon broadcasts, and a group of Saturday morning music appreciation sessions on the municipal radio station, WNYC. Friday night events "included concerts presented with young 'name' soloists, and the premiere performance of new works by such young contemporaries as Morton Gould and Paul Creston. The quality of the music produced was good, by any standards."[5]

The enterprising Dixon started his orchestral conducting activities in 1932, as leader of "one" violinist and "one" pianist (both his students), rehearsing at the Harlem Branch of the YMCA. Within a short period of time, the Dean Dixon Symphony Orchestra consisted of seventy musicians—men and women, boys and girls, black and white. From the group's inception, Dixon was also a full-time student at Juilliard. When time permitted, he taught violin and piano privately. All earnings (as well as lunch money) were put to good use—purchasing scores, covering the cost of rehearsal space, and occasionally purchasing an instrument for a student.

The Dean Dixon Symphony Orchestra struggled, giving annual concerts, until 1937, when a women's group became interested in Dixon's musical venture and offered subsidy. In 1938, he conducted his first professional orchestra, the League of Music Lovers Chamber Orchestra, at Town Hall. A year later, he served as music director for Jacques Wolfe-Roark Bradford's short-lived musical "John Henry," starring the black actor and concert singer, Paul Robeson.

Soon the work of Dixon reached the attention of first lady Eleanor Roosevelt, who arranged for the Dean Dixon Symphony Orchestra to present a concert at Heckscher Theatre, May 18, 1941. This was the kind of "break" that Blanche Lemmon referred to in her 1943 article.

In attendance at the Heckscher Theatre concert was Samuel Chotzinoff, music director of NBC. He was so impressed that he contracted the young conductor to direct famed Arturo Toscanini's NBC Symphony Orchestra for two concerts. The first appearance took place in 1941. In early 1942, Ella Davis wrote for *The New York Times:*

> In a few days the 27-year old Negro conductor will, for the third time in seven months, step to the podium in Studio 8H and put the NBC Symphony Orchestra through its musical paces—for the benefit of a nation-wide radio audience. . . . On August 10 [1941] Dean Dixon took the New York Philharmonic Symphony in his stride at the Lewisohn Stadium.[6]

During the summer of 1943, Dixon conducted the Philadelphia Orchestra at Robin Hood Dell and the following year made his first appearance with the Boston Symphony Orchestra as conductor for "Coloured American Night." Also in 1944, he organized his American Youth Orchestra, which was, like the Dean Dixon Symphony Orchestra, a fully integrated ensemble. The average age of the players was twenty, with each having been selected on the basis of successful completion of "a blindfold test," i.e., each auditioner displaying his or her skills with the maestro's back turned.[7] The orchestra was endorsed by such prominent musical personalities as Yehudi Menuhin, Leonard Bernstein, Aaron Copland, Bruno Walter, and Oscar Hammerstein II.[8]

Not long after its founding, the American Youth Orchestra began offering "Concerts for Three Year Olds," which permitted the youngsters to sit on stage among the musicians. Announcing the first of a series of "Symphony at Midnight" concerts (offered to those whose work did not permit them to attend concerts at the regularly scheduled hour) in Town Hall by the American Youth Orchestra, Olin Downes of *The New York Times* reminded his readers of the orchestra's objectives:

> To inculcate a love of worthwhile orchestral music in the youth of America; to stimulate musical education and participation; to furnish gratuitous training; to provide free concerts or concerts at a nominal cost to the general public, and particularly to the underprivileged; to assist and encourage American composers, soloists and musicians; to establish and perpetuate a democratic youth orchestra open to all youth regardless of race, creed, color, religion, nationality or sex.[9]

Youths who worked with Dixon in the American Youth Orchestra recall with fondness his outstanding leadership ability and skill at working with young people. It was told to the author over the years by many students, "He never raised his voice." "He was a master teacher." "He conveyed without lengthy explanations just what he wanted from the various instruments." "He was a player and was familiar with the difficulties and limitations of every instrument in the orchestra." "He knew the music thoroughly."

Despite Dixon's impressive conducting record (even in the big league of major orchestras), little of real significance happened between 1944 and 1949. In 1949 he was invited to conduct concerts in Paris by the Radio Symphony Orchestra of the French National Radio. Thus began Dixon's "self-imposed exile" from America.

Dixon would no longer "skirt the musical fringes." In search of a full-time conducting post following his many high marks as a guest conductor, he resolved to try Europe. As he later explained, "I felt like I was on a sinking ship and if I stayed here, I'd drown . . . I'd made a start. I had the critics. But for five years after that, nothing happened."[10]

Though a concert review of a May 1950 New York Chamber Orchestra concert at Town Hall indicated that Dixon was at the helm, Dixon stated in an interview with Ernest Dunbar in the late 1960s that after he left in 1949, he returned to America for only "two quick trips," not conducting on either occasion. Regardless, it should be noted that the May 20, 1950 concert featured a "program of symphonic music by [six] Negro composers from five countries"— William Grant Still and Ulysses Kay, American; Samuel Coleridge-Taylor, English; Amadeo Roldan, Cuban; Ingram Fox, British Guianian; and Michael Moerone, South African.[11]

By mid-1952, Dixon's activities outside of his native America began attracting the attention of the American press. In an article titled "Spreading the Word," *Time* magazine reported:

> In the courtyard of the Doges Palace sat the 88-piece La Fenice Theater Orchestra; on the podium stood the U.S.'s most active musical ambassador to Europe, Manhattan-born conductor Dean Dixon, 37; on the racks, instead of the usual outdoor fare, was music by modern composers, e.g., Walter Piston, Bernard Herrmann, Benjamin Britten.
>
> Venetians came to satisfy their curiosity, stayed to enjoy themselves. They admired the conductor's vigorous command of the orchestra, warmed to his obvious sympathy for the music.[12]

Dean Dixon was by then a resident of Sweden.

The *Time* article indicated that during the previous season, Dixon led thirty-two concerts, conducted in nine countries, and during the 1952–53 season, would become resident conductor of the Göteborg (Sweden) Symphony. Maintaining a strong commitment to American music, he had conducted about ninety American scores, including those of black Americans, during the past eighteen months.[13]

In 1953 Dean Dixon was appointed permanent conductor of the Göteborg Symphony, remaining in that position until 1960. Before receiving that appointment, he guest conducted symphony and radio orchestras in Amsterdam, Athens, Barcelona, Belgrade, Berlin, Berne, Brussels, Budapest, Buenos Aires, Copenhagen, Florence, Hamburg, The Hague, Helsinki, Leipzig, London, Melbourne, Mexico City, Milano, Monaco, Munich, Naples, Oslo, Poland, Rome, Salzburg, Stockholm, Tokyo, Vienna, and Zurich.

According to Australian journalist Anne Cattarnes, Dixon was offered several posts outside of America that he was unable to accept. These offers included the Helsinki City Orchestra, the Mozarteum Orchestra in Salzburg, the Brussels Philharmonic, the Cologne Radio Symphony, and the Bavarian Radio Orchestra in Munich.[14]

In 1961 Dixon became principal conductor of the Hesse Radio Symphony Orchestra in Frankfurt am Main, Germany, where he then made his home. This position he held until 1974. Between 1964 and 1967, he was also principal conductor of the Sydney (Australia) Symphony Orchestra, an assignment that consumed three and a half months each year.

Shortly before Dixon's resignation in 1967 from the Sydney post, symphony member Helen Bainton, violist, published her book *Facing the Music.*[15] Excerpts appeared in *The Sydney Morning Herald,* under the heading "My Boss Dean Dixon." The violist wrote:

> Dean Dixon first came to Australia in 1962, making an immediate and overwhelming impact upon the audience. . . . [He] presented a Mozart Festival at the end of 1962, . . . which was accorded high praise by the critics.
>
> Nobody was surprised, therefore, when on February 23, 1963, the A. B. C. (Australian Broadcasting Commission) management officially announced his appointment as resident conductor. . . . [H]e is the youngest conductor we have had in Sydney as musical director. . . . He is a painstaking worker with a definite plan of action; his demands are considerable but not overtaxing. . . . A man who can captivate the hearts of young people and endear himself to listeners of all ages as Mr. Dixon is able to, possesses a wonderful gift which should be fostered, not only to build but to sustain musical standards of our city.[16]

Writer Ernest Dunbar, curious about the several black expatriates that he encountered abroad during the course of his various writing assignments, returned in the late 1960s specifically to ask them some questions.[17] One of Dunbar's interviewees was Dean Dixon who was then living "with his second wife,[18] a Finnish noblewoman, and their children on a quiet, tree-lined street behind the American Consulate in Frankfurt."[19]

Dixon spoke quite candidly with Dunbar on a wide range of subjects. Dunbar included this interview in his 1968 publication, *The Black Expatriates: A Study of American Negroes in Exile.* On the subject of his nationality, Dixon noted that at the time of his birth, his West Indian parents were not yet citizens. "So actually there is a lot of legal questioning as to whether I am an American or whether I only have an American passport."

When asked if he always wanted to conduct, he responded, "No. I wanted to play ball, to go running with other boys, talk with the girls and so forth. . . . I had been coming along on the violin . . . but I hated it." When he began playing on the radio at age nine, his playmates who had been calling him a sissy began offering to carry his violin case into the studio. "So that began to have a status symbolism. I said, well, maybe this thing is not so bad."

On the formation of the Dean Dixon Symphony Orchestra in 1932, Dixon pointed out that in the early 1930s, civil rights organizations were beginning to ask for more antibias legislation. He firmly believed that the day would come when orchestrally, the doors would be opened and the requests would follow. "All right, fine, we don't want to have any trouble—there's a place for violinists, please bring us a Negro violinist, we'll let him play and we'll see what happens." Those whose musical involvement was limited to jazz would be ill-prepared. He felt that Harlem needed a symphony orchestra.

> If once a week at least . . . these men had a chance to go through the symphonic literature, at least they'd know the difference between the jazz rhythms they are playing and the way Beethoven writes the same rhythm and the way you have to play it differently.

When the Dean Dixon Symphony expired a decade later, it had played in forty special concerts.

Asked if he could live in the States again, the expatriate responded:

> No, no, no, no, no. I think I could visit America as a guest conductor or with my own orchestra, preferably with my own orchestra. . . . But this would be in order to balance the scales, to set the record straight. . . . Mainly, I would go back to show our own people—Negroes— that I do exist, that it is not completely lost, and that the lies spread about our intellectual inferiority, and the myth that only jazz can come out of us really is a myth. . . . I have a great desire to come back to America, but I don't come back as a "Negro" conductor, I come back as an "international" conductor.[20]

A most significant event took place in 1970: Dixon returned to America. Beatrice Berg wrote of the momentous event for *The New York Times* in an article titled "Dixon: Maestro Abroad, Stranger at Home." She began:

The exile returns. On Tuesday night Dean Dixon, native New Yorker, will conduct the New York Philharmonic in Central Park—the first appearance on an American podium since he left his country 21 years ago. . . . . Now, the man who is addressed as "Maestro" in other parts of the world, whose face and music are known all over Europe and as far away as Australia . . . is a stranger in his own country, virtually unknown to a whole generation of American concertgoers. He has guest-conducted as many as 125 concerts a year in Europe . . . and since 1960 has lived in Germany where . . . he conducts "every day of the year, except for three weeks' vacation."[21]

Gail Stockholm wrote of the return for *Music & Artists:*

Conductor Dean Dixon, an American long relegated to Europe, is a remarkable man for many reasons, not least of which is his humane response to conditions that characterized various stages of his career. . . . His calm, relaxed, honest manner indicates that as a critically watched example for his race he has not only vindicated the negro's right to enter this field, but also that he has established himself as an artist in the fullest sense of the word. He has no need to make excuses or to indulge in recriminations.[22]

Dixon conducted the New York Philharmonic in three park concerts and enjoyed a guest conducting stint with the Pittsburgh Symphony at Temple University's Ambler Festival and with the St. Louis Symphony at the Mississippi River Festival. In response to Stockholm's query concerning what effect his "American splash" might have on the careers of upcoming young black conductors, Dixon responded:

I don't see that what I do will suddenly make any of them better conductors in anyone's eyes. But it could make it easier for the reluctant places to give them the chance to prove themselves. And I think it should help Negro instrumentalists who want to play classical music.[23]

A 1971 conducting tour sponsored by the Schlitz Brewing Company included the Kansas City, Minnesota, Milwaukee, and Detroit Symphony Orchestras. The tour continued in 1972, with appearances before the National, Chicago, and San Francisco Symphony Orchestras, as well as the Prague Symphony Orchestra at the Academy of Music in Philadelphia.

In 1975 Dixon reflected again on his native America and his experiences within it, with Australian journalist Maria Prerauer:

On New York City in 1949: "Building out of bounds to Negroes. . . . My concert master was in that out-of-bounds building, . . . and they wouldn't let me see him. Before that, my violin teacher had to stop my lessons. The whites were complaining. A Negro in the apartment. Not nice."

On his return guest offer from the United States in 1970: "It was not because I was suddenly a better conductor. But because black was suddenly beautiful. And what could be more beautiful than a black conductor?"

On mid-1970s black attitudes toward him personally, his departure from America, and his conducting career generally: "The young Negroes in the States accuse me of having opted out. . . . They won't understand that there would have been no battle if I had stayed . . . .[E]very success I have anywhere in this world is also a success for them. By getting away I have helped those at home. I have shown what can be done."[24]

After a six-year absence, Dixon returned to Australia and the Sydney Symphony Orchestra for a two-week season. Accepting the title of chief conductor, Dixon returned in 1975 to conduct the Sydney and Melbourne Symphony Orchestras on a twenty-four–concert tour of Australia, accompanied by his third wife, a German. The Australian press reported that both were vegetarians, environmentalists, experimental cooks, and fitness fans. Husband Dean had also evolved into an amateur inventor, termed "essential to his sanity away from the conductor's podium." His inventions included a special lavatory cistern, a transparent piano top, and a reusable dishwashing liquid. The local press also reported on evidence of Dixon's failing health. He had only recently retired as musical director of the Frankfurt Radio Orchestra.[25]

Only nine concerts were completed before it was necessary for Dixon to return to Switzerland because of suspected heart problems. Dixon underwent open-heart surgery in December 1975. He resumed his guest conducting activities in early 1976, but was stricken again and died on November 4, 1976.

News of his death appeared in *The New York Times* (as it did throughout the world), on November 5, 1976: "Dean Dixon, 61, Dies; Conductor in Exile/First Black to Lead Philharmonic/Left the

U.S. in 1949 to Build His Reputation in Europe." Reporter Ronald Smothers wrote:

> It took a 21-year self-imposed exile from the United States and a sojourn as conductor of orchestras in Sweden, Denmark, Germany, France, Italy, Spain, Japan and Australia for Dean Dixon to win the title of "maestro." It was a title that had for the most part eluded him in more than 10 years of work as a conductor in New York and despite reviews through the early 1940s terming him a "coming man" and "ranking conductor."
>
> Throughout this time, Mr. Dixon was outspoken on the racial barriers he faced in the United States in trying to establish himself as a conductor. He ruefully told of the insults from one concert manager after another, ranging . . . from polite protestations that there was little work for any conductors to ridiculous suggestions that he conduct in white-face, wearing white gloves.[26]

Shortly following his death, the ABC radio broadcast what was referred to by a presumed "letter to The Australian editor" as "a workmanlike obituary." The writer noted that the broadcast "scrupulously avoided mentioning that he [Dixon] was a Negro, or was black." The letter writer concluded:

> This point is essential to his musicianship and also helps measure his incredible feat of reaching the top in a white-dominated profession.
>
> The ABC might like us to think it is non-racist and that an artist's color is irrelevant but I think it is failing in its duty to its non-white audience by not reporting the achievements of a colored artist.[27]

More than eight years following Dixon's death, Noah André Trudeau paid due respect to the maestro in an article for *High Fidelity*. Under the title "When the Doors Didn't Open: A Cool Classicist and a Soldier for Social Equality," Trudeau wrote:

> What kind of conductor was Dean Dixon? His recorded legacy provides the opportunity for evaluation. That legacy is surprisingly large, though scattered among many small labels. . . . Dixon records often require some effort to track down, but many are worth it.

Trudeau recommended Haydn's Symphonies 48 and 92 on Musicaphon SL 1709, two symphonies of Carl Maria von Weber on SL 1710 (available from Andre Perrault in Virginia Beach, Virginia), and Howard Swanson's Fourth Symphony and Short Symphony, on AR 6 and ARS 116 respectively. Trudeau also suggested that it is "a simple matter of both moral and artistic justice to recognize the man as what he always sought and preferred to be: Dean Dixon, conductor."[28]

Press Comments

"Mr. Dixon . . . led a dramatic and striking performance . . . and demonstrated that his control over serious modern music can be as effective as his performance of older works."

New York Herald Tribune

"{T}echnical precision . . . and sensitivity to the rhythmic values."

Il Gazzattino

"Mr. Dixon conducted with his accustomed sensitivity and authority, accomplishing particularly meritorious work . . . {F}inely tinted, richly textured and deeply felt."

New York Times

"Dean Dixon directed the orchestra with an awe-inspiring command. . . . {T}he orchestra responded with a rich, integrated ensemble tone. . . . There was a buoyancy, litheness and freshness of spirit . . ."

Telegraph (Australia)

"Once in a while a conductor sets people listening afresh."

Daily Express (London)

"Mr. Dixon imparted new bloom and sheen to the famous BBC Orchestra which has had its share of the world's most famous conductors."

The Times (London)

"There he was, back with the Sydney Symphony Orchestra in the opera house for the first time in 1975 . . . and after only a brief rehearsal period, the SSO was sounding as it hasn't sounded since he was last here. . . . It is also a better sound . . . It is rich, strong, weighty, determined. It is as if the nap had been restored to a worn carpet. Everything takes on more colour, firmness, body and resilience."

Sydney Morning Herald

"It was a notable occasion, disclosing to the audience that the race has produced a stalwart figure in the musical world. . . ."

New York Age

The American Press—Post Exile (Beginning 1970)

"A superb conductor, an absolute master of the orchestra."

Daily Mirror (New York)

". . . {M}oved with freedom and confidence as he led an interpretation . . . that was clear, direct, authoritative and filled with attention to expressive detail. There was a warmth and radiance of feeling in his projection . . . that made him seem, indeed, a conductor whose work we should have been familiar with during his 21-year exile in Europe and Australia."

New York Times

"Dixon knew what he wanted and got it. He is not addicted to flashy conducting and the orchestra {Prague Symphony} is not given to straining for maximum effects."

Evening Bulletin (Philadelphia)

"Last night, he was greeted by audience and the Philadelphia Orchestra players alike with an affectionate, respectful ovation reserved for the real musical heroes of this world. . . . Dean Dixon is still very much a conductor to reckon with. A permanent major post should be open to him somewhere in his own country. His belated debut with the Philadelphia Orchestra was brilliant and exciting."

Evening Bulletin

"He is a mature musician and the {Philadelphia} orchestra responded to his economical style with playing that was at once graceful and full of tension built on concentration. . . . Dixon sorted all the colors clearly and paced the reading for full dramatic effect.

Philadelphia Inquirer

"His experience and expertise were very much in evidence . . . an authoritative conductor, though not an authoritarian. . . . Mr. Dixon conducted . . . in a dignified manner, with a steady rhythmic pulse, plenty of strength and a fine feeling for the arbitrary touches. . . . This kind of sober approach is not calculated to knock an audience dead, but the integrity of the conductor demanded respect. Judging from the hearty audience response, Mr. Dixon made his point most successfully."

New York Times

"{Dixon's} control of the orchestra is complete . . . and his delineation of little niceties of expression is always in evidence."

Kansas City Star

"He is no showboat conductor, yet he showered his program with a lilting lyricism and controlled grace. And he gave Brahms' Second Symphony a rich, romantic sweep

that brought the great throng {75 thousand} to its feet in a standing, especially thrilling ovation."

Newsweek

Notes

1. Raoul Abdul, *Blacks in Classical Music: A Personal History,* New York: Dodd, Mead and Co., 1977, p. 191.
2. Bernard Jacobson, "(Charles) Dean Dixon," *New Grove Dictionary of American Music,* vol. 2, ed. by H. Wiley Hitchcock and Stanley Sadie, New York: Grove's Dictionaries of Music, Inc. 1986, p. 634.
3. David Ewen, *Dictators of the Baton,* rev. and expanded ed., Chicago/New York: Ziff-Davis Publishing Company, 1948, p. 275.
4. Blanche Lemmon, "Democracy in Music," *Etude,* March 1943, p. 148.
5. *Ibid.*
6. Ella Davis, "Conductor from Harlem: Dean Dixon Makes His Way With Baton Despite Many Hazards," *New York Times,* January 11, 1942, p. 6, Music Section.
7. S. J. Woolf, "In the Groove With Bach and Beethoven," *New York Times Magazine,* June 17, 1945, pp. 16, 38.
8. Mark A. Schubart, "A New Orchestra for American Youth," *New York Times,* December 10, 1944, p. 9, Music Section.
9. Olin Downes, "At Midnight: Dean Dixon's American Youth Ensemble To Begin Series Next Month," *New York Times,* January 18, 1948, Section 2, p. 7.
10. Beatrice Berg, "Dixon: Maestro Abroad, Stranger at Home," *New York Times,* July 19, 1970, p. D11.
11. R. P., "Music Composed By Negroes Heard," *New York Times,* May 22, 1950, p. 17, Arts and Leisure Section.
12. "Spreading the Word," *Time,* July 21, 1952, p. 81.
13. *Ibid.* Also, Gail Stockholm, in a June–July 1970 article for *Music & Artists* ("Dean Dixon: A Return With Laurels," pp. 7, 10–12, 14–15) pointed out that Dixon introduced Europeans to such Americans as Douglas Moore, Howard Swanson, Randall Thompson, Edward McDowell, Howard Hanson, Robert Ward, Ulysses Kay, William Schumann, Henry Cowell, Walter Piston, Samuel Barber, Aaron Copland, Arthur Foote, Peter Mennin, Leo Sowerby, Otto Luening, Norman Dello Joio, Bernard Herrman, Vladimir Dukelsky (Vernon Duke), Carl Ruggles, and others.
14. Anne Cattarnes, "Dean Dixon: The Man for the Job," *Bulletin,* March 9, 1963, p. 18.

15. Helen Bainton, *Facing the Music: An Orchestral Player's Notebook,* Sydney: Currawong Publishing Co., 1967.

16. ———, "My Boss Dean Dixon," *Sydney Morning Herald,* July 15, 1967, p. 12.

17. Other black musicians interviewed and included in Dunbar's subsequent publication were opera and concert singers Reri Grist (Zurich), Gloria Davy (Berlin), and Mattiwilda Dobbs (Stockholm).

18. Dean Dixon's first wife was pianist Vivian Rivkin, a classmate at the Juilliard School of Music. See "Interracial Romance Blooms: Director Dean Dixon Weds Brilliant Pianist," *Afro-American,* August 9, 1947, p. 1.

19. Ernest Dunbar, Editor, *The Black Expatriates: A Study of American Negroes in Exile,* New York: E. P. Dutton and Co., Inc., 1968, p. 189.

20. *Ibid.,* pp. 188–200.

21. Berg, *op. cit.*

22. Stockholm, *op. cit.,* p. 7.

23. *Ibid.,* p. 12.

24. Maria Prerauer, "I'll Never Go Back," *Australian* (Weekend), September 20, 1975, p. 5.

25. Snellen O'Grady, "Maestro Takes the Plunge To Stay Sane," *Australian,* August 30, 1975, p. 3.

26. Ronald Smothers, "Dean Dixon, 61, Dies; Conductor in Exile," *New York Times,* November 5, 1976, p. A22. Note: The "white-face, wearing white gloves" incident did not occur in the United States; it was proposed by a Swedish impresario in 1952. Dixon often remarked that he rejected the idea but had since conducted in the involved Swedish city "10 to 15 times a year—in blackface."

27. "Obituary," *Australian,* November 16, 1976.

28. Noah André Trudeau, "When the Door Didn't Open: A Cool Classicist and a Soldier for Social Equality," *High Fidelity,* May 1985, pp. 57–58.

W. Rudolph Dunbar (Courtesy: National Archives)

W. RUDOLPH DUNBAR†

BIRTHDATE/PLACE: April 5, 1907†; Nabaclis, British Guiana [Guyana].

DEATH DATE/PLACE: June 10, 1988; London, England.

EDUCATION: Diploma, Institute of Musical Art (Juilliard), 1924 (clarinet, piano, and composition); University of Paris (Journalism and Philosophy).

MAJOR INSTRUCTORS: Sergeant-Major E. A. Carter (Clarinet), British Guiana; Louis Cahuzac (Clarinet), Philippe Gaubert (Conducting), Paul Vidal (Composition), Paris; Felix Weingartner (Conducting), Vienna.

MAJOR APPOINTMENTS: African Polyphony Orchestra (early 1930s); London stage show "Black Rhythm" (1934); Foreign Correspondent, Associated Negro Press (1939–?); Correspondent, Allied Forces in France (1944–?).

GUEST CONDUCTOR: The Over-Seas League Symphony Orchestra (1942); London Philharmonic Orchestra (1942 and 1955); Liverpool Philharmonic (1942); Association des Concerts Colonne, Association des Concerts Pasdeloup, Orchestre Nationale, L'Orchestre de la Societe des Concerts du Conservatoire—American Festival of Music, Paris (1945); Hollywood Bowl Orchestra (1946); British Guiana Militia Band (1951); Philharmonic Orchestra of Port-Au-Prince, Haiti (1952); Wroclow Philharmonic and Lublin Philharmonic, Poland (1959); Orquesta Sinfonia Nacional, Cuba (1962); Leningrad Philharmonic (1964); Moscow State Symphony Radio and Television Orchestra (1964); Baku Philharmonic (1964).

FOUNDER/INSTRUCTOR: The School of Modern Clarinet Playing - London (1940s).

---

†Though this publication is concerned with American conductors, Dunbar's close association with this country (training, employment, and the fight for racial justice) legitimize his inclusion. A native of British Guiana, he was a British subject and resided in that country for more than half-a-century. He studied in America and was a champion of American music, long before it was fashionable.

---

†According to Britisher Jeffrey Green, 1907 is the date Dunbar finally settled on. Other possible birthdates are 1904 and 1899, the latter based on passport information recorded in the 1930s.

AUTHOR: Treatise on Clarinet Playing (1939).
COLUMNIST: "Technical Expert," *The Melody Maker,* London (1931–38).

MUSICOLOGIST EILEEN SOUTHERN, EDITOR of the journal *Black Perspective in Music,* attributed several "firsts" to Rudolph Dunbar, among them:

> first black man and youngest of any race (at that time) to conduct the London Philharmonic (1942), first black man to conduct the Berlin Philharmonic (1945), first person to conduct a Festival of American Music in Paris (1945), first black man to conduct orchestras in Poland (1959) and Russia (1964), and first conductor to promote in Europe the compositions of black composers, particularly those of William Grant Still.[1]

Born in British Guiana, the son of a druggist, Dunbar apprenticed with the British Guiana Militia Band for a period of three years and studied clarinet with Sergeant-Major E. A. Carter. At twelve (possibly fifteen or twenty; see note on date of birth), his father sent him to the United States for further study. In New York City, he soon enrolled at the Institute of Musical Art, studying clarinet, piano, and composition. He next settled in Paris in 1925, having first gone to Europe on tour with the revue "Dixie to Broadway," and finally in London in 1931, which remained Dunbar's home base until his death in 1988.

An obituary in the *The Guardian* (London), quoted Dunbar's friend, C. L. R. James (another prewar black musician and journalist who pursued an international career, also with London as his base):

> Dunbar was a striking example of his musical period. He was first of all a master of popular music—jazz—but he always insisted . . . of the importance of classical music. His distinguished work must be seen in relation to the strong prejudice against coloured classical artists.[2]

Not only did Dunbar insist upon the importance of classical music, but he very much involved himself in its creation and interpretation.

For several years, beginning in 1929, Dunbar toured the Continent as a solo clarinetist. The widow of Claude Debussy hosted one of Dunbar's clarinet recitals in her home in the early 1930s.[3] The French and British press recorded impressive criticisms: "a serious virtuoso and an accomplished musician"; "His tone is luscious and refined, his technic is polished, and his attitude entirely serious and that of a matured artist"; ". . . facility and breathing powers that seem inexhaustible"; "a concert virtuoso."[4]

An announcement of a Dunbar recording (Oriole P114) included the following impressive remarks:

> Rudolph Dunbar, the coloured musician, is undoubtedly the leading authority on Clarinet playing in this country [Britain]. While his articles in the "Melody Maker" have earned him world wide renown as a past master of the theory as well as the practice of his instrument, his purity of tone, phrasing, and innate musicianship all stamp him as a virtuoso of the first rank.[5]

After settling in London (and establishing on the Continent what many considered a new school of clarinet playing), Dunbar continued his clarinet activities by offering instruction through his clarinet studio. He published his *Treatise on Clarinet Playing* in 1939, a well utilized method that by the early 1980s had reached its tenth edition.

In 1931, the London press reminded its readers that when "the all-coloured revue 'Blackbirds' . . . caused such a sensation at the London Pavilion some few years ago," Rudolph Dunbar was the hot first alto in the all-Negro band, "which was one of the hottest things London had ever heard." In 1934, the *Tropical Times* alerted its readers to an "All-British Coloured Band," led by Dunbar, that at the time was performing at London's Cossack Restaurant. According to the reporter, it was also the first "all-British coloured band to be heard over the air" (BBC, August 22 and 23, 1934). The reporter added, "Rudolph Dunbar and his band are probably the only people we have who are cultured men with the rhythmic instinct. . . ."[6] While in New York City (1919–25), Dunbar had been active in both jazz and classical circles, including the Harlem [Symphony] Orchestra, under the direction of E. Gilbert Anderson and the Plantation Orchestra, under the direction of Will Vodery.*

Dunbar was for many years European correspondent for the Associated Negro Press. He joined the Allied Forces in France as a newspaper correspondent and covered the Normandy invasion and the liberation of Paris. With his pen, he campaigned furiously against racism, always maintaining an alliance with Blacks in the United States, Europe, and Africa.

Despite his varied careers and abilities (solo clarinetist/clarinet instructor and journalist), Dunbar's lifelong ambition was to conduct a symphony orchestra. He made his conducting debut with the London Philharmonic Orchestra in 1942 and his French conducting debut at Paris with the Association des Concerts Pasdeloup Orchestra in 1944. Perhaps the highlight in Dunbar's conducting career was leading the Berlin Philharmonic on September 2, 1945. The invitation had come that summer from the orchestra's regular conductor, who was tragically shot a few days prior to Dunbar's appearance "by American sentries when the limousine in which he was riding failed to heed orders to halt at a military traffic post." The invitation was approved by the Allied Control Council, which believed that Dunbar's performance could assist in alleviating racial prejudice. The Berlin audience was composed of 3,500 German civilians and a few allied service men.[7]

A major event for both American composers and Dunbar occurred in 1945, when Dunbar conducted four of France's leading orchestral ensembles in the Festival of American Music in Paris. Though other conducting opportunities followed, they were both few and infrequent.

Though we are uncertain about the details—even place and by whose invitation—Dunbar returned to New York in 1938 to conduct a performance of his "Dance of the Twenty-first Century." He returned again during the summer of 1946, making concert appearances in New York, Boston, Chicago, and the West Coast, where he conducted the Hollywood Bowl Orchestra.

Included in his itinerary for the 1946–47 season was a visit to Howard University in Washington. Addressing faculty and students in Rankin Chapel, Dunbar emphasized, "The success I have achieved through sacrifice and struggle is not for myself but for all the colored people. . . ." He stressed "sacrifice and hard work as the key to success. . . . [C]ollege training is only the beginning . . . the foundation to climb to higher goals."[8]

Following his death in mid-1988, a "Celestial Banquet" took place in his honor in London on October 23, 1988, under the direction of his nephew Ian Hall (an organist and drummer).[9] The two hour "celebration of a distinguished life" was held at St. James Church in central London's Piccadilly and included members of London's black musical community. The program included a steel band from Brixton (south London's black neighborhood); a rendition of "Deep River," a Negro Spiritual; and a work by William Grant

Still (an African-American composer whom Dunbar consistently programmed).[10]

Much of Rudolph Dunbar's memorabilia is housed at Yale University. British music journalist Jeffrey Green alerts us to the fact that Dunbar's autobiography is forthcoming.

Press Comments

"Members of the orchestra {Berlin Philharmonic} . . . agreed that Mr. Dunbar was a musical topnotcher. The audience of 3,500 . . . applauded Mr. Dunbar's conducting of works by Tchaikovsky and von Weber, but saved its loudest cheers for . . . William Grant Still's 'Afro-American Symphony'."

New York Times

"Parisians who doubted it . . . had opportunity tonight to discover that there is modern American music other than jazz. . . . But they were enthusiastic about the spirited and clean-cut conducting of slender and youthful Rudolph Dunbar . . ."

New York Times

Extracts from the Polish Press (following a series of six concerts with various Polish orchestras, at the invitation of the Minister of Culture):

"Dunbar is very dynamic and full of temperament. . . . {He} gave an extraordinary sensitivity to the colour of sound."

"Dunbar received an enthusiastic reception with superlative comments. That Dunbar is able, gifted and talented I do not deny. He feels the music and is a wonderful musician with great culture on a very high artistic level."

Notes

1. "In Retrospect: W. Rudolph Dunbar, Pioneering Orchestra Conductor," *Black Perspective in Music,* Fall 1981, p. 193. (Note: for this entry, we have relied heavily on "In Retrospect: W. Rudolph Dunbar," pp. 193–225, with permission.)
2. "A Conductor's Baton In His Knapsack," *The Guardian,* July 7, 1988.
3. *Ibid.*
4. *The Black Perspective in Music, op. cit.,* pp. 195–196.

5. *Ibid.,* p. 197.

6. *Ibid.,* p. 196.

7. "Negro Wins Plaudits in Berlin," *New York Times,* September 3, 1945, p. 25.

8. "Rudolph Dunbar Came Up Hard Way; Now Tops in Field," *Afro-American,* February 1, 1947, p. 4.

9. See A. Twumasi-Ankra Ofori, "Conversation With Ian Hall, The Proud 'African'," *Black Perspective in Music,* Fall 1976, pp. 313–319.

10. Correspondence, Jeffrey Green (London) to Eileen Southern, December 1, 1988. Used with permission.

Leslie Byron Dunner

LESLIE BYRON DUNNER

BIRTHDATE/PLACE: January 5, 1956; New York, New York.

EDUCATION: University of Rochester; B. A., Eastman School of Music (Clarinet Performance), 1978; M. A., Queens College (New York City) (Music Theory and Musicology), 1979; D. M. A., College Conservatory of Music, University of Cincinnati (Orchestra Conducting and Clarinet Performance), 1982.

ADDITIONAL STUDY: American Symphony Orchestra League Conducting Workshops; Tanglewood Music Festival Conducting Seminar; Academie Internationale d'Ete.

MAJOR INSTRUCTORS/COACHES: Donald Hunsberger, Gustav Meier, Taavo Virkhaus, Gerhard Samuel, Elmer Thomas, John Lehman, Maurice Abravanel, Pierre Boulez, Zubin Mehta, Jorge Mester, Edo de Waart, Max Rudolph, Leonard Slatkin, Ricardo Muti, Leonard Bernstein, Igor Markevitch, Seiji Ozawa, Gunther Schuller, Pierre Dervaux, Fernand Quattrocchi.

MAJOR APPOINTMENTS: Assistant Conductor, New Mexico Music Festival, 1979–80; Assistant Conductor, Pacific Northwest Ballet Company, 1981; Music Director, Orchestral Programs, Carleton College, 1982–86; Music Director, St. Cloud Civic Orchestra, 1983–86; Assistant Conductor, Colorado Philharmonic Orchestra, 1983–86; Associate Conductor, Dance Theatre of Harlem, 1987–89; Assistant Conductor, Detroit Symphony Orchestra, 1987–89; Principal Guest Conductor, Dance Theatre of Harlem, 1989—; Music Director, Dearborn Symphony, 1989—; Music Advisor, Harlem Festival Orchestra, 1989—; Associate Conductor, Detroit Symphony Orchestra, 1990—.

GUEST CONDUCTOR: Dallas and National Symphony Orchestras; Louisville Orchestra; San Diego, Columbia, and Windsor (Ontario) Symphony Orchestras; Minnesota Orchestra; New York City Ballet; Opera Ebony.

AWARDS/HONORS: Beamon-Hough Arts Fund Award, in Recognition of Achievement in the Arts; Cincinnati Symphony and Oregon Symphony Orchestras, Assistant Conductor Finalist; Exxon/Arts Endowment Conductor's Program, St. Louis Symphony, Assistant Conductor Finalist; Membership, American Society of Composers, Authors and Publishers (ASCAP); Recognition as first American to win a prize in the International Toscanini Competition (Parma, Italy); Letters of recognition from New York's Governor, State Senator, Manhattan Borough President, the Italian and

Barbadian Consulate General Offices, New York State Governor's Advisory Committee for Black Affairs (NYC); "Man of the Year," Eta Lambda Zeta Chapter, Zeta Phi Beta Sorority; Semi-finalist, Herbert von Karajan International Conducting Competition (Berlin); One of six semi-finalists (and only American to place), International Competition for Young Conductors (Besançon, France); First Prize Winner (and first winner), Colorado Philharmonic Orchestra's National Conducting Competition; McKnight Foundation Composition Award.

THOUGH LESLIE DUNNER GREW UP IN EAST HARLEM (New York City), his early life was, through a serendipitous occurrence, molded largely outside of his home community. When he was in the second grade in a Harlem public school, his teacher decided he should be tested for a special program which placed talented minority students in schools elsewhere in the city. As a result of his high scores, Dunner was bussed to the predominantly Jewish Stuyvesant section of Manhattan, where he continued his elementary schooling. There, Dunner received his first exposure to concert music; several of the assembly programs held throughout the year were lecture-demonstrations presented by chamber music ensembles.

Just prior to his entering junior high school, Dunner was tested for aptitude in music and art. His scores indicated high potential for both fields, a determination that was borne out by subsequent activities. He began studying the clarinet in the seventh grade, though by default; his primary interest was the piano. However, his parents would not allow him to take piano lessons unless his older sister agreed to study as well. Because of her lack of interest, the piano was out. Instead, the two studied African dance (which Dunner continued until age seventeen, and at which he became sufficiently proficient to perform with an ensemble at the 1963 New York World's Fair). At the same time, Dunner continued to develop his interest and skills in the visual arts. When he was in the eighth grade, one of his drawings was included in an exhibition at the Museum of Modern Art.[1]

During his seventh grade year, the teachers at Dunner's junior high school went on strike. He was returned to Harlem (where schools were open), where he made a startling discovery; though he and his downtown schoolmates were advanced in mathematics and science (areas in which Dunner was both keenly interested and considerably apt), the Harlem students were ahead in reading skills. And beyond that, they were reading the works of African-American writers, to whom he had had little exposure. That experience awakened in Dunner an interest in African-American literature that he actively maintains.

During his junior high school years, Dunner's interest in music surged ahead of his interest in art and science. He applied for, and was admitted to, the High School of Music and Art. At the same time, he enrolled in the precollege division of the Manhattan School of Music. There, he studied clarinet privately; participated in the choir, orchestra, and opera productions; and took classes in theory and ear training.

Before his graduation from high school, Dunner's parents, concerned about how their son would make a living, convinced him to undertake a nonmusic major in college. He applied to both Oberlin College and the University of Rochester. Oberlin was his first choice, and he was accepted, but only as a math major. Rochester offered him an engineering scholarship, which he accepted. In his freshman year, he studied only mathematics and science.[2]

His second year at Rochester was critical for Dunner's career decision. He petitioned his advisor for some relief from the concentration in science and mathematics; he wanted to add liberal arts and music courses. His advisor refused the request. The following day, his optics professor suggested to the students in a very small class that because the field was so specialized they would be working closely with each other for the rest of their professional lives. Dunner looked around and, after that class, changed his major to music. He elected to continue at the University of Rochester, but at the Eastman School of Music. Dunner left Rochester before the end of his senior year (though the University did award him the degree), and transferred to Queens College. He had decided he didn't want to be a performer, though he wanted to continue in music.

Dunner remained at Queens College for a master's degree. His rewarding experience with a course in performance practice caused him to reconsider his decision against being a performer. However, the clarinet was gently nudged into a second-place position when, as the final requirement for a course in contemporary music, he was compelled to conduct a program. His interest was strong and immediate. He decided to apply for a conducting program at the College-Conservatory of Music at the University of Cincinnati, and emerged three years later with a doctorate in conducting, with a cognate in clarinet performance.[3]

In 1982, Dunner accepted appointment as assistant professor of music and music director of Orchestral Programs at Carleton College in Northfield, Minnesota, a post he held until 1986. Besides conducting, his duties included instruction in clarinet and music theory. The four years at Carleton were accompanied by his leadership of the St. Cloud Civic Orchestra (1983–86), where he planned and executed the orchestra's concert season, selected guest artists, and adjudicated concerto competitions. During the 1983–84 season, Dunner was assistant conductor of the Colorado Philharmonic Orchestra, the result of his having won first prize in the Orchestra's First National Conducting Competition. Also during those years, Dunner's reputation was enhanced through both his initial association with the prestigious Dance Theatre of Harlem and his participation in increasingly more significant competitions.

The Second Arturo Toscanini International Competition for Orchestra Conductors, held in 1986, began with 140 applicants worldwide and was reduced to thirty-four auditioners and six finalists.[4] The fact that Dunner was the only American finalist was sufficient justification for Dance Theatre of Harlem's founder and executive director, Arthur Mitchell, to extend to Dunner the invitation to guest conduct. So impressive was Dunner's debut that Mitchell engaged the thirty-year-old as the company's Associate Conductor. Wrote *Saint Louis Post-Dispatch* critic James Wierzbicki of Dunner's conducting of the 19th century classic "Giselle":

> Conductor Leslie B. Dunner . . . seemed utterly in control. The playing he drew from the pit orchestra was surprisingly refined, and his accompaniment. . .was always sensitive to the very real physical needs of the dancers.[5]

Success in the Toscanini Conducting Competition also resulted in letters of recognition from New York Governor Mario Cuomo, State Senator David A. Paterson, Manhattan Borough President David Dinkins, the Italian and Barbadian Consulate General Offices, and the New York State Governor's Advisory Committee for Black Affairs. The United Pioneers of New York City sponsored "A Harlem Tribute" and the Office of the Council President, City of New York, declared March 1, 1987 "Dr. Leslie Byron Dunner Day" in New York City.

The 1987–88 season was indeed a busy one for Dunner with the

Dance Theatre of Harlem; Salzburg Music Festival; Tivoli Gardens Music Festival (Copenhagen, Denmark); Pasadena and San Diego, California; Kennedy Center (Washington); a Soviet Union tour (Moscow, Leningrad, and Tbilisi); New York International Arts Festival and City Center of Music and Dance; and a tour of Great Britain. During the same period, he served as guest conductor for the State Ballet of Missouri.

Dunner joined the Detroit Symphony Orchestra as assistant conductor on September 1, 1987. He was chosen from a field of eight candidates who had auditioned before the orchestra four months earlier. In its press release June 1, 1987, the Detroit Symphony wrote:

> Each candidate was evaluated on conducting ability, musicianship and personality while rehearsing or conducting the orchestra. Three finalists were then asked to repeat the exercise and a single vote on that performance was cast by each musician. Final selection was determined by Music Director Gunther Herbig who, in this case, confirmed the impressions of the musicians.

Said Maestro Herbig:

> Clearly, Dr. Dunner was the best candidate for the position. . . He is extremely talented and has the maturity and the experience to command the respect of a major orchestra. He has already conducted a wide range of symphonic, choral, opera and ballet works. I am very happy he will be joining us.[6]

The appointment received front-page coverage in the *Detroit News* on June 2, 1987, under the heading "Black Wins DSO Post." Of particular interest was the following:

> The Detroit Symphony Orchestra, recently criticized by state lawmakers [State Senator David Holmes and State Representative Morris Hood, both Black] for failing to increase the number of blacks in its membership, has hired its first black assistant conductor[7]. . . . Although a top symphony official said race played no part in Dunner's appointment, the decision could help mute criticism of the orchestra for its lack of black members.[8]

Three days later, the appointment received editorial consideration in the same newspaper. With equal concern for the issue, there was this added comment from the appointee:

I don't think race played a factor in my selection. I think I was judged on my qualifications, my credentials, and my ability to communicate with the orchestra.

The editorial continued:

We invite Sen. Holmes (Chairman, Senate Appropriations Committee) to recognize a good faith effort and progress in the face of a new beginning. . . . There are symphonic stars yet to be discovered, white and black. A non-discriminatory selection process, such as that used by the DSO, is the best insurance that Detroit will get its fair share of them.[9]

The season's opener was scheduled for September 17, 1987, and Dunner's debut for October 23. Unfortunately, the orchestra was on strike (not returning to work until mid-December).

Dunner's conducting duties for that first season included several dates on the 1987–88 Merrill Lynch Weekender Pops Series, the Hudson Metro Tour, three concerts on the 1987–88 Young People's Concert Series, and the Educational Concert Series. He assumed the music director's duties of the Detroit Symphony Civic Orchestra (a pre-professional training orchestra with emphasis on the identification and development of minority talent), was one of the two conductors on the 1988 Upper Peninsula Festival Tour, and shared responsibility for "coverage" for Detroit Symphony rehearsals and performances. ("Coverage" meant being prepared to conduct in case of an emergency, often without rehearsal.)[10]

Shortly after Dunner joined the Detroit Symphony, the *Detroit Monthly* released an article entitled "Who's Your Next Boss?" focusing on seventy "hot professional properties, careers with a bullet, the best of the bosses-to-be." Writers Marney Rich and Julie Hinds labeled the seventy, one of whom was Leslie Dunner, "youthquakers who, if they play their cards right, will be moving and shaking this town in the next five to ten years."[11]

For the 1988–89 season, while Dunner continued in his post with the Detroit Symphony he fulfilled his responsibilities with Dance Theatre of Harlem as well. In addition to his conducting the orchestra for the company, he assisted in the television production of "Giselle" and served as Music Advisor for the television taping of "Fall River Legend."

In 1989, Dunner realized that ambition shared by all conductors building careers, i.e., appointment to the primary artistic leadership position with an orchestra. Dunner was offered and accepted a three-year contract as music director of the Dearborn (Michigan) Symphony.

Finally, Dunner's talent as a composer and a performing clarinetist must be recognized. Since 1976, Dunner has appeared as a solo and chamber clarinetist throughout the country, including such cities as Minneapolis, Los Angeles, Cincinnati, and New York City. A member of the American Society of Composers, Authors, and Publishers (ASCAP) since 1985, he has been featured composer (and performer) on Minnesota Public Radio. In 1985, he received a McKnight Fellowship Grant for composition of a children's ballet ("Noah's Ark"). His "Short Rhapsody for Clarinet" was recorded in 1989, with the composer performing. Also in 1989 the Minnesota Composers Forum released a recording of his songs entitled "Motherless Child," with Dunner as the featured clarinetist.

Press Comments

"He is by any definition, impressive . . ."

Detroit News

"The concert began with the perennial audition piece, Strauss' "Don Juan," a complicated work . . . which conductor Leslie B. Dunner conducted from memory. Dunner's . . . performance was well-reasoned and thoroughly prepared . . . He paced the piece very well, and he elicited a healthy sound from the Philharmonia."

Cincinnati Enquirer

"In the first and last analysis, much of the success of this intense and talented group of musicians lies with the unique conducting and directing skills of its leader . . . An evening of delight awaits every serious friend of the St. Cloud Orchestra."

Escape Magazine, Minnesota

"Dunner did more than simply hold his forces together, He shaped the music lovingly, injecting a spirit and intensity into its measures that emphasized its artistic value."

Detroit Free Press

"Dunner appears to have a natural command of the orchestra and possesses a gesture that evoked an impassioned performance from his peers . . ."

The Cincinnati Post

"Dunner oversaw the disparate forces skillfully . . .

Detroit Free Press

"Associate Conductor Leslie B. Dunner{'s} . . . reading of the Ravel {"Alborado Del Gracioso"} was very much reflective of a lively jester's morning song, which is the work's name in English. It was energetic and had a satiric bite. The effect was . . . true to the original and well worth the hearing."

Grosse Pointe {Michigan} News

Notes

1. Interview, William E. Terry with Dunner, July 8, 1989, Detroit, Michigan.
2. *Ibid.*
3. *Ibid.*
4. "Dunner Wins Conducting Prize," *Symphony Magazine,* December, 1986, p. 57.
5. James Wierzbicki, "'Giselle' Successful Despite 'Relevancy'" *Saint Louis Post-Dispatch,* October 20, 1986, p. 4B.
6. "Detroit Symphony Appoints Leslie B. Dunner as Assistant Conductor," Press Release, *Detroit Symphony News,* June 1, 1987.
7. It should be noted that black Paul Freeman* was Conductor in Residence with the Detroit Symphony Orchestra from 1970 to 1979. Also, several black conductors have made guest appearances with the orchestra.
8. George Bulanda, "Black Wins DSO Post," *Detroit News,* June 2, 1987, p. 1A.
9. "The DSO Reaches Out," Editorial, *Detroit News,* June 4, 1987, p. 22.
10. Press Release, *Detroit Symphony News, op. cit.*
11. Marney Rich and Julie Hinds, "Who's Your Next Boss?," *Detroit Monthly,* October 1987, p. 91.

Edward Kennedy ("Duke") Ellington conducting a master class at the University of Wisconsin, July, 1972. (Photograph by Patricia Williard.)

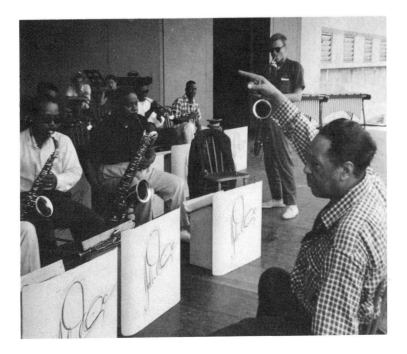

Edward Kennedy ("Duke") Ellington rehearsing his reed and brass sections, with baritone saxophonist Gerry Mulligan at Lewisohn Stadium, New York City, 1958. (Photograph by Patricia Williard.)

EDWARD KENNEDY "DUKE" ELLINGTON

BIRTHDATE/PLACE: April 29, 1899; Washington, D. C.
DEATH DATE/PLACE: May 24, 1974; New York, N. Y.
EDUCATION: Armstrong High School; Washington, D. C. (Diploma received in 1971).
INSTRUCTORS: Mrs. Clinkscales (piano); Henry Grant (music theory); Unofficial—Oliver "Doc" Perry (piano), Will Vodery and Will Marion Cook (orchestration).
PROFESSIONAL DEBUT: Pianist (1916).
MAJOR AFFILIATIONS: Pianist, Composer, Arranger—Duke's Serenaders (1923) and Duke Ellington Orchestra (1924–74).
MOST MEMORABLE COMPOSITIONS: "Mood Indigo," "It Don't Mean a Thing," "In a Sentimental Mood," "Solitude," "Concerto for Cootie," "Sweet Thunder," "Creole Love Call," "Caravan," "Black, Brown and Beige," "Sophisticated Lady," "My People," "The River" (ballet), Sacred Concerts I, II and III; Film Scores: "Symphony In Black," "The Asphalt Jungle," "Anatomy of a Murder," "Paris Blues," "Assault On a Queen," "Change of Mind."
DOCUMENTARY FILMS: "On the Road With Duke Ellington" (1974); two-part documentary (American Masters), "A Duke Named Ellington" (1988).
AWARDS/HONORS/MEMBERSHIPS (Partial): Spingarn Medal, NAACP (1959); Gold Medal, President Lyndon B. Johnson (1966); Grammy Awards, National Academy of Recording Arts and Sciences (1968, 1969, 1973); National Association of Negro Musicians Award (1964); National Council on the Arts, National Endowment for the Arts (1968); Pied Piper Award—American Society of Composers, Authors and Publishers (1968); Presidential Medal of Freedom, President Richard M. Nixon (1969); Fellow, American Academy of Arts and Sciences (1971); Member, Royal Swedish Academy of Music (1971); Honorary Gold Card Life Membership, American Federation of Musicians (1972); French Legion of Honor (1973); Proclamations—States of New York (1969), New Jersey (1969), Kentucky (1970), Nebraska (1970), Tennessee (1970), New Mexico (1970), Wisconsin (1972); Keys to Cities—Amsterdam, Cincinnati, Jacksonville (Florida), Kingston (Jamaica), Madison (Wisconsin), Phoenix (Arizona), Washington, San Francisco, Chicago, Niigata (Japan); *Down Beat* Awards (Duke

Ellington Band)—First Place, 1946, '48, '59, '60, '62–72; *Esquire Magazine* (Duke Ellington Band)—Gold Award, 1945, '46, '47; Eleanor Roosevelt International Workshop in Human Relations: International Humanist Award (1972); Honorary Doctorates: Wilberforce, Milton, Columbia, Assumption, Rider Colleges; Howard, Morgan, Columbia, Wisconsin, St. John's, Yale, Washington, Brown Universities.
AUTHOR: Music Is My Mistress, Autobiography (1973).

OFTEN WRITTEN, OFTEN SPOKEN, and always implied is the following: To tell the story of Edward Kennedy "Duke" Ellington is to tell the story of jazz; to tell the story of his orchestra is to tell the story of his compositions. The man, the music, the life that he lived, the compositions that he wrote, and the orchestra that he fronted were one and the same. Such is readily apparent from a reading of his autobiography, *Music Is My Mistress* (published in 1973, one year prior to his death),[1] a work that musicologist Eileen Southern classified as a memoir, rather than an autobiography in the strictest sense of the word.[2]

As his personal friend and biographer, Stanley Dance wrote:

> Duke Ellington stands alone in jazz as a composer for and performer on, the unique instrument that he himself invented and perfected—the Ellington Orchestra. . . . As a bandleader he indulged with consummate skill his own predilections as composer and arranger, developing musicians whose creative thinking suited his own—or, as often, actually stimulated his own. . . . Ellington constantly sought out musicians who could give his imagination something new to work on and who also made his band sound different from any other.[3]

Born in Washington, D.C., Edward Kennedy, as a child, "was pampered and pampered, and spoiled rotten."[4] His father was a butler, caterer, and a blueprint-maker for the Navy Department, who worked occasionally at the White House (where his son would later perform on many occasions). Both parents played the piano, the mother "by note" and the father "by ear." Ellington began taking piano lessons at age seven, studying with a local piano teacher, Miss Clinkscales. As many lessons were missed as were taken, though payment was regular. Duke's inability to stick to the printed page presented problems for both teacher and student.

Since baseball offered a much greater attraction, piano lessons were eventually terminated. He later studied harmony with Henry Grant, having heard and been inspired by such ragtime pianists as

Gertie Wells, Louis Thomas, Louis Brown, and Oliver "Doc" Perry, and stride pianists Willie "The Lion" Smith and James P. Johnson.

Formal academic study was terminated three months short of finishing high school. He received his high school diploma from Armstrong High School in 1971, long after having received many honorary doctorates. Nevertheless, with his customary charm, he stated, "I needed this diploma more than anything else."[5]

The sobriquet "Duke" was acquired from a childhood friend, in recognition (and admiration) of his impeccable taste in dress, food, and lifestyle. He carried himself like one of great means, financially, socially, and mentally. This self assurance was of course inherited. As Duke Ellington wrote:

> J. E. [my father] always acted as though he had money, whether he had it or not. He spent and lived like a man who had money, and he raised his family as though he were a millionaire. . . . Maybe he was richer than a millionaire? I'm not sure that he wasn't.[6]

Ellington informed us that "Duke" was not the only nickname given to him. Others were "Cutey," "Stinkpot," "the Phoney Duke," "Wucker," "The Kid," "Apple Dumpling," "Dumpy," "Pops," "Big Red," "Puddin'," "Maestro," "Governor," and "Govey."[7]

A talented young artist, Ellington was offered a scholarship to Pratt Institute but turned it down. His first job was selling "peanuts, popcorn, chewing gum, candy, cigars, cigarettes, and score cards" at the baseball park. His next job was working the soda fountain at the Poodle Dog Cafe, the inspiration for his first composition, "Soda Fountain Rag," written at fifteen.

Ellington formed his first band, The Duke's Serenaders, in 1917. During the day, he operated a sign and poster business. He was also playing with one of contractor Louis Thomas's bands. Noting the contracting benefits, he soon began sending out bands himself.

He and his Serenaders made their first trip to New York City in 1922, working in a vaudeville show with clarinetist/leader Wilbur Sweatman. Having experienced limited success, the group returned to Washington after only a few weeks. The following year, pianist Thomas "Fats" Waller persuaded Ellington and the others to give the "Big Apple" another chance.

Under the leadership of banjoist Elmer Snowden and the name "The Washingtonians," the five-piece band secured work at the

Hollywood Club (later called the Kentucky Club). Ellington assumed leadership of the group in 1924 and soon expanded the membership to nine. By the time the band moved into the famous Cotton Club in 1927, he had enlarged the band to eleven pieces.

> The Cotton Club was a perfect place for him to develop his skills as a composer. There were new stage shows frequently and Ellington was required to write fresh music to accompany the shows, dance routines and tableaux. His tenure at the Cotton Club led to important recording contracts and between 1928 and 1931 he made more than 160 recordings.[8]

The fame of the Ellington band was enhanced by the nightly radio broadcasts from the Cotton Club, heard throughout the country. Musicians of all genres were drawn to the Club—to hear, to see, to experience the rich tonal colors generated by the fabulous Ellington ensemble.

Ellington and the band played their first Broadway musical, "Show Girl," in 1929, and the first of many films, "Check and Double Check," in 1930. Four years later the band appeared in "Murder at the Vanities" and "Belle of the Nineties." The following year they appeared in the short film "Symphony in Black." In 1937 the band appeared in the Marx Brothers film "A Day at the Races" and in 1942 and 1943, "Cabin in the Sky" and "Reveille with Beverly," respectively.

The composition "Mood Indigo," written in 1930, brought worldwide recognition to Ellington. His experiments with extended compositions began in 1931, with the writing of "Creole Rhapsody." He inaugurated a series of annual concerts at Carnegie Hall in New York City, in January 1943, with the band performing his monumental work "Black, Brown and Beige." Other extended works for these annual events, which continued until 1952, included "Liberian Suite," "Harlem," "Night Creature," "Such Sweet Thunder," "Suite Thursday," "New World A-Comin'," and "Deep South Suite." Not often recalled is his show "My People," written and produced by Ellington in 1963 for the Century of Negro Progress Exposition in Chicago. He wrote the first of many full-length film scores in 1959, for Otto Preminger's "Anatomy of a Murder."

The band's first trip to Europe took place in 1933, followed by another in 1939. Foreign tours became more and more frequent, including one to the USSR in 1971. Other European tours took place in 1950, 1958, 1959, and yearly from 1962 through 1966. The band made its first tour of Japan in 1964 and of the Far East and Australia in 1979.

Ellington devoted an entire section of *Music Is My Mistress* to the State Department Tour in 1963.[9] He referred to the trip as "one of the most unusual and adventurous" the band had ever taken. The tour included Damascus, Jordan, Jerusalem, Beirut, Kabul, and New Delhi. As on the occasion of all of his foreign travels, the general public "loved him madly" and foreign leaders accorded wonderful receptions.

For most of his professional life, he survived on 20-hour days, beginning at noon and ending at dawn. *Time* magazine reported in 1964 that

> In the past 100 days, the Duke has given 25 concerts, made an LP and taped four television shows, all while working on a new musical called "Sugar City" that is scheduled for Broadway this fall.[10]

The press (as well as his peers) consistently referred to Ellington as "the busiest man in the business."

As written in the entry "Duke Ellington" in the piano version of *Sacred Concerts* (complete),

> The incomparable Ellington Orchestra, which, in a typical month, spanned the spectrum of sacred concerts in churches and synagogues, performance with major symphony orchestras, at college dances and symposia, in nightclubs, dance halls, television specials and Las Vegas hotels, was the only musical aggregation in the world playing 52 weeks a year and rarely with a day off. They presented concerts in Japan, Thailand, Taiwan, Laos, Okinawa, Singapore, Australia, Burma, New Zealand, Canada, France, Switzerland, Norway, Sweden, Italy, Germany, Great Britain, Monaco, Portugal, Spain, Luxembourg, Czechoslovakia, Yugoslavia, Netherlands, Belgium, Finland, Africa, India, The Middle East, and nearly every state in the United States. In 1969, they toured most of Central and South America. Little wonder that President Nixon appointed the personable Dr. Duke Ellington official goodwill envoy for American music abroad.[11]

Ellington's bands were noted for proper behavior, decorum, and real class. When traveling through the South in early years, Duke chartered two pullman sleepers and a seventy-foot baggage car.

Dining car and room service were available. Upon arrival in a city, the cars were parked and connections were made for water, steam, sanitation, and ice.

The Duke rarely featured himself as a soloist, though he was an extremely capable pianist. Instead, he fed ideas to the band, provided rhythmic energy, and contributed to the overall effect. Wrote Eileen Southern, "His music represented the collective achievement of his sidemen, with himself at the forefront rather than the sole originator of the creative impulse."[12]

Compositions were often team efforts, since Ellington was a firm believer in "freedom of expression." Big band historian George Simon, considering what it was like for a newcomer to the Ellington Band, quoted tenor saxophonist Al Sears:

It's not like any other band where you just sit down and read parts. Here you can sit down and read the parts and suddenly you find you're playing something entirely different from what the rest of the band is playing. It's not logical. You start at the beginning of the arrangement at letter 'A' and go to letter 'B' and then suddenly, for no reason at all, when you go to letter 'C', the rest of the band's playing something else which you find out later on isn't what's written at 'C' but what's written at 'J' instead. . . . See, I'm the newest man in the band and I haven't caught on to the system yet.[13]

As jazz historian and archivist Dan Morgenstern indicated:

The development of Ellington's band followed that of jazz bands in general. His originality expressed itself in what he did with this format and instrumentation, which was to imbue it with an unprecedented richness of timbre, texture and expressiveness. . . . Each member of the ensemble was an individual voice, each had a special gift, each contributed to the totality of what could be called an organism as well as an organization.[14]

The collection of instrumentalists playing Ellingtonia for close to half a century included Cat Anderson, Harold Baker, Sidney Bechet, Aaron Bell, Louis Bellson (the first white to join the band), Barney Bigard, Jimmy Blanton, Wellman Braud, Lawrence Brown, Harry Carney, Willie Cook, Wilbur DeParis, Mercer Ellington (Duke's son), Tyree Glenn, Paul Gonsalves, Sonny Greer, Jimmy Hamilton, Otto Hardwick, Johnny Hodges, Quentin Jackson, Freddie Jenkins,

Wendell Marshall, Andres Meringuito, Bubber Miley, Ray Nance, Joe "Tricky Sam" Nanton, Oscar Pettiford, Russell Procope, John Sanders, Al Sears, Ernie Shepard, Jabbo Smith, Willie Smith, Elmer Snowden, Rex Stewart, Billy Strayhorn (Duke's collaborator, protégé, and alter ego), Clark Terry, Juan Tizol, Ben Webster, Arthur Whetsol, Cootie Williams, Booty Wood, Jimmy Woode, Britt Woodman, and Sam Woodward. His vocalists included Ivie Anderson, Kay Davis, Marie Ellington (the future Mrs. Nat "King" Cole), Al Hibbler, Herb Jeffries, June Norton, Jimmy McPhail, and Betty Roche.

Discussing the band's longevity, Ellington commented in 1963:

> It's a matter of whether you want to play music or make money, I guess. I like to keep a band so that I can write and hear the music the next day. The way to do that is to pay the band and keep it on tap fifty-two weeks a year. If you want to make a real profit, you go out for four months, lay off for four, and come back for another four. Of course you can't hold a band together that way, and I like the cats we've got. So by various little twists and turns, we manage to stay in business and make a musical profit. And a musical profit can put you way ahead of a financial loss.[15]

One of several appendices in *Music Is My Mistress* is titled "Honors and Awards."[16] Several merit particular attention: The Spingarn Medal, presented by the NAACP (1959); membership on the National Council on the Arts (National Endowment for the Arts), appointed by President Lyndon B. Johnson (1968); Presidential Medal of Freedom, presented by President Richard M. Nixon (1969); election as a Fellow of the American Academy of Arts and Sciences (1971); membership in the Royal Swedish Academy of Music (1971); Duke Ellington Fellowship Program at Yale University (established in 1972); the Legion of Honor, by executive order of French President Georges Pompidou (1973); sixteen honorary doctorates (including the University of Wisconsin; Yale, Howard, and Brown Universities; and the Berklee College of Music); and three Grammy Awards, National Academy of Recording Arts and Sciences (1968, 1969, and 1973).

In 1965, the Pulitzer music committee recommended Ellington for a special award. The full Pulitzer committee turned down the recommendation. Nearly a quarter of a century later, *Washington Post* journalist Jonathan Yardley wrote:

Thus it was that . . . the board charged with such matters rejected the recommendation of the jury reporting to it and refused to award Ellington a Pulitzer Prize in music. . . .

The decision of course said far more about the personages who then occupied the Pulitzer board than it said about Ellington himself; it was a confession, however unwitting, of the cultural establishment's hostility to the new and the different and the unsanctioned.[17]

Ellington wrote of the denial:

Let's say it had happened. I would have been famous, then rich, then fat and stagnant. And then? What do you do with your beautiful, young, freckled mind? How, when, and where do you get your music supplement, the deadline that drives you to complete that composition, the necessity to hear the music instead of sitting around polishing your laurels, counting your money, and waiting for the brainwashers to decide what rinse or tint is the thing this season in your tonal climate?[18]

The institution that administers Joseph Pulitzer's Will, Columbia University, awarded Ellington an honorary doctorate at its annual commencement exercise in 1973.

From the standpoint of composition (and performance), Ellington devoted much of the final decade of his life to liturgical music. The first of his sacred music concerts was performed on September 16, 1965, at Grace Cathedral Church in San Francisco, California; the second on January 19, 1968 at the Cathedral of St. John the Divine in New York City; and the third, on United Nations Day, October 24, 1973, at Westminster Abbey in London.

As the composer/leader Ellington wrote:

As I travel from place to place by car, bus, train, plane . . . taking rhythm to the dancers, harmony to the romantic, melody to the nostalgic, gratitude to the listener . . . receiving praise, applause and handshakes, and at the same time, doing the thing I like to do, I feel that I am most fortunate because I know that God has blessed my timing. . . . When a man feels that that which he enjoys in his life is only because of the grace of God, he rejoices, he sings, and sometimes dances.[19]

Stanley Dance concluded his publication *Duke Ellington,* prepared for the Time-Life Records' Giants of Jazz series, with the following:

The climax of his career might have been the premiere of his "Third Sacred Concert" in Westminster Abbey. . . . But by then he himself was too ill and the band too weak to present his new music with the éclat the occasion demanded. He spent his remaining strength on an exhausting tour of Europe and Africa, followed by a last string of one-nighters in the United States. A few months later, on May 24, 1974, he died. . . .[20]

It was decided that the Ellington Orchestra would continue, under the leadership of Duke's son Mercer. Mercer departed (with the band) from his father's funeral to honor Duke's eleven-day commitment to perform in Bermuda.

Postscript

- A national and international press gave notice of the maestro's death; the world mourned.

- *International Musician,* the voice of the American Federation of Musicians, published the following in its "Farewell to a Musical Giant":

  From the standpoint of continuous achievement, no other figure in the world has managed more successfully to meet the demands of music as an art form, entertainment business and as an economic imperative of twentieth century life. (June 1974, p. 10)

- Western High School was designated as the location for the District of Columbia's "Workshop for Careers In the Arts." Following Ellington's death, the building was renamed The Duke Ellington School for the Arts. The Calvert Street Bridge, also in the nation's capitol, was renamed The Duke Ellington Bridge.

- The first of The International Duke Ellington Conferences was held in 1983, in Washington, D. C. The Tenth International Duke Ellington Conference was held May 28–31, 1992, in Copenhagen, Denmark.

- In June 1984, fifty boxes of unreleased Duke Ellington studio tapes were donated to Radio Denmark by Duke's son Mercer.

- The United States Postal Service issued a 22-cent commemorative stamp on April 29, 1986, honoring Ellington.

- New York City's Jazzmobile presented "A Celebration of Ellington's Sacred and Inspirational Music," directed by jazz pianist/composer/

television commentator Billy Taylor. The program included narrations by actor Douglas Fairbanks, Jr., dancing by Ballet Tap U.S.A. and an Alvin Ailey Special Performance Group, solos by guitarist Kenny Burrell, trumpeter Joe Newman, pianist Billy Taylor, and vocalist Jon Hendricks, as well as the Jazzmobile Orchestra.

- On April 26, 1988, the National Museum of American History of the Smithsonian Institution in Washington, acquired more than 200,000 pages of documents reflecting the life and career of Duke Ellington, following more than three years of negotiation with the Ellington estate. The acquisition was made possible by a special $500,000 appropriation from Congress. Included were more than 3,000 original and orchestral compositions, 500 audio tapes, scrapbooks of world tours, more than 2,000 photographs, programs, posters, awards, citations, and medals. The Ellingtonia will be housed in the museum's Archives Center, available for scholarly research and exhibitions. The scores would also form the basis of a major publication project under the joint auspices of the museum's Department of Music History, the Smithsonian Press, and Oberlin College.

- The American Masters series, focusing on the cultural contributions of prominent American artists, included a two-part documentary on the music and influence of Ellington; "A Duke Named Ellington" was aired on PBS July 18 and 25, 1988.

- The Duke Ellington International Festival took place throughout the month of April in 1989 in Washington, D. C., commemorating the 90th anniversary of Ellington's birth. A special exhibition of original compositions and world tour posters were on view at the Museum of American History. At the same location there were daily events, including lectures, performances, and a symposium assessing Ellington's legacy. Dances from the famed Cotton Club were recreated; Ellington alumni performed. In mid-April, the first American-Soviet co-production of a Broadway musical opened at the Kennedy Center Opera House, Ellington's "Sophisticated Ladies." At 10:00 A.M. on the actual birthdate (29th), the building now on the site where Ellington was actually born (2129 Ward Place NW) was redesignated as the Duke Ellington Building and a plaque was unveiled. There followed a musical caravan across the Duke Ellington Bridge.

- The memorable Carnegie Hall debut of Duke Ellington and His Orchestra on January 23, 1943, was re-created in July 1989, Maurice Peress conducting at Carnegie Hall.

- On April 28, 1990, a dedication ceremony took place at 2728 Sherman Avenue, NW, Washington, D.C., where Ellington lived with his wife Edna and infant son Mercer, between 1919 and 1922.

- A Duke Ellington Youth Project was announced in early 1991, presented by the National Museum of American History. The project was designed to introduce junior and senior high school students to the legacy of Ellington. The pilot project for the D.C. public schools offered in-school music performances, planned curriculum activities for teachers and students, and the first annual Duke Ellington Festival. Five schools were selected for the project. Music, art, social studies, and English teachers at the five schools engaged their students in multifaceted, interdisciplinary approaches to the music and life of Ellington.

- In September 1991, the Smithsonian Institution unveiled a collection of musical scores and manuscripts acquired from Ruth Ellington (Duke's sister), adding an additional 900 original scores to the Archives Center.

Notes

1. Edward Kennedy Ellington, *Music Is My Mistress,* Garden City, N.Y.: Doubleday & Company, Inc., 1973.
2. Eileen Southern, *Black Perspective In Music,* Fall 1974, p. 211 (review of *Music Is My Mistress*).
3. Stanley Dance, *Duke Ellington* (Giants of Jazz Series), Alexandria, Va.: Time-Life Books, Inc., 1978, p. 3.
4. Ellington, *op. cit.,* p. 6.
5. Joe Elam, "Endless Ellington Era," *Dawn Magazine,* July 27, 1974, p. 16.
6. Ellington, *op. cit.,* p. 10.
7. *Ibid.,* p. xi.
8. Joel Dreyfuss, "Duke Ellington: Musician of Elegance," *Washington Post,* May 25, 1974, pp. B6 and 7.
9. Ellington, *op. cit.,* pp. 301–330.
10. "The Duke's Day," *Time,* June 6, 1964, p. 60.
11. Duke Ellington, (Foreword) *Sacred Concerts Complete/Duke Ellington, Inspirational Music,* Miami Beach, Florida: Hansen House, 1984, n.p.
12. Eileen Southern, "Ellington, Edward Kennedy ("Duke")," in *Biographical Dictionary of Afro-American and African Musicians,* Westport, Conn.: Greenwood Press, 1982, pp. 125–126.
13. George T. Simon, rev. ed., *The Big Bands,* New York: Collier Books, 1974, p. 191.

14. Dan Morgenstern, "The Ellington Era," *Listen,* December 1963, p. 16.

15. Stanley Dance, *The World of Duke Ellington,* New York: Da Capo Press, Inc., 1981, pp. 25–26 (reprint of 1970 Edition, Charles Scribner's and Sons).

16. Ellington, *op. cit.,* pp. 476–490.

17. Jonathan Yardley, "The Duke, Our Unrecognized Royalty," *Washington Post,* May 1, 1989, p. B2.

18. Ellington, *op. cit.,* p. 286.

19. Duke Ellington, (Foreword) *Sacred Concerts Complete,* n.p.

20. Dance, *Duke Ellington* (Giants in Jazz Series), *op. cit.,* p. 32.

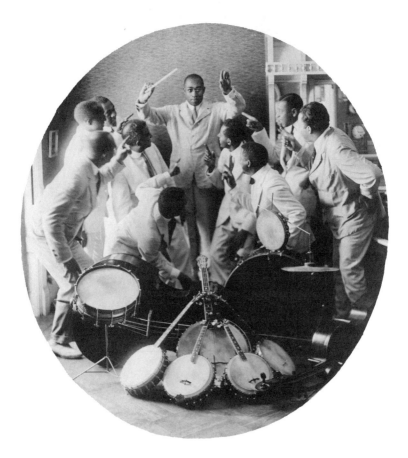

James Reese Europe and the Clef Club Orchestra (Courtesy: The Black Perspective in Music)

James Reese Europe and the Clef Club Orchestra (Courtesy: The Black Perspective in Europe)

JAMES REESE EUROPE

BIRTHDATE/PLACE: February 22, 1881: Mobile, Alabama.
DEATH DATE/PLACE: May 9, 1919; Boston, Massachusetts.
MAJOR INSTRUCTORS/COACHES: Harry T. Burleigh and Melville Charlton, composition; Joseph Douglass, Enrico Hurlei, violin.
BROADWAY DIRECTOR/CONDUCTOR: "The Shoofly Regiment" "Mr. Lode of Koal."
FOUNDER/CONDUCTOR: The Clef Club, 1910; The Clef Club Orchestra, 1910; The Tempo Club, 1914, The National Negro Orchestra, 1914; Europe's Society Orchestra (also called the New York Society Orchestra); Europe's Double Quintet; 369th Infantry Regiment Band ("Hell Fighters"), 1918.
COMPOSITIONS: "Too Much Mustard," "Castle House Rag," "Castle Walk," "The Visitor," "The Lame Duck Waltz," "The Half-And-Half."

SELDOM IS ANY INDIVIDUAL WIDELY PERCEIVED and acknowledged to be as significant to his own time, in that time, as was James Reese Europe. An article on the editorial page of the *New York Times* on May 12, 1919 (three days after his death), offers what appears to have been a common appraisal of Europe's importance in developing

> . . . a different sort of music which may eventually possess considerable merit . . . Ragtime may be Negro music, but it is American Negro music, more alive than much other American music; and Europe was one of the Americans who was contributing most to its development.[1]

The honor intended by that press piece might have been received by Europe with less enthusiasm than the writer would have expected. Europe did not like his music categorized as ragtime. Rather, he described the music he played as "syncopated rhythms," and characterized it as "the music of the American Negro." To him "ragtime" was "merely a nickname or a fun-name given to Negro rhythm by our Caucasian brother musicians many years ago."[2]

152

Europe's aversion to the term ragtime, though hardly shared by most other black musicians of his time, was not surprising, considering his middle-class birth and upbringing in a household of classically trained musicians. To people striving to promote the highest standards of black cultural achievement, the word ragtime and the milieu it connoted could only reinforce the notion among whites that the art of black people was not worthy of serious critical attention and respect.

James Reese Europe was born February 22, 1881. He was the second child, born between an older brother (John) who became a reputable ragtime pianist, and a younger sister (Mary) who pursued a career as a music teacher and a choral director. The Europe family moved from Mobile, Alabama, to Washington, D.C., when James was ten years old. There he continued to study the piano (building upon the instruction given by his mother) and began learning the violin. According to his sister, his first violin teacher was Joseph H. Douglass, son of the abolitionist Frederick Douglass.[3] Later he studied with Enrico Hurlei.

In 1903 Europe moved to New York and joined the ranks of other young black musicians trying to make their way in the flourishing world of black Broadway musical shows. Europe continued his musical studies with, among others, composer, arranger, and concert singer, Harry T. Burleigh. To earn a living, he hired himself out as a violinist and pianist for social functions and cabaret shows. He experienced some success as an entertainer in New York and Philadelphia society and for a period became the "official musician of the famous Wanamaker family."[4]

Europe's first residence in New York was the Marshall Hotel on West 53rd Street. The Hotel was both home and gathering place for numbers of black artists, entertainers, and celebrities, including such vaudeville and Broadway personalities as Robert Cole, J. Rosamond and James Weldon Johnson, Bert Williams and George Walker, Ernest Hogan, Will Marion Cook,* Ada Overton, Abbie Mitchell, Theodore Drury, Will Dixon, and Ford Dabney. Europe quickly immersed himself in this world and within a few months discovered a way to become a working member of this new society. In 1905, Europe became a member of a musical group called the Memphis Students, organized by Ernest Hogan. (The name was misleading; they were neither students nor from Memphis.) The twenty-member ensemble debuted at Proctor's Twenty-Third Street Theatre in the spring of 1905 and then fulfilled a five-month engagement at the Victoria Theater. Their New York success served as the springboard for a European tour that included the Olympia in Paris, the Palace in London, and the Schumann Circus in Berlin. The Memphis Students are said to have introduced the concept of the dancing conductor (in the person of Will Dixon), as well as the novelty of the singing band (the musicians sang four-part harmony—without any necessary correspondence between the line a musician played and the one he might sing).

From 1906 to 1910, Europe was active as a composer and music director for a series of black musical shows that played on Broadway and toured. In 1906, he served as music director for "The Shoofly Review," presented by Bob Cole and the Johnson brothers. Thereafter he directed the Bert Williams show, "Mr. Lode of Koal." However, Europe's timing was a bit off. The black musical was slipping swiftly from its pinnacle of success, and Europe was forced to seek other outlets for his musical talents. He turned to dance music and the bands that social dancing required.

In 1909, Europe and a group of musicians (including Ford Dabney, Joe Jordan, William Tyers, and Will Vodery*) formed the Clef Club. The organization was officially incorporated June 21, 1910, and headquartered in a house the group bought on West 53rd Street. The Clef Club served as a booking agency, union, and clearinghouse for black musicians in New York. The Club boasted that it could provide a dance orchestra numbering three to thirty players, day or night, from its roster of more than 200 musicians. Europe served as the organization's first president and conductor of the Clef Club Orchestra, numbering more than 100 players. The Orchestra gave its first concert in October 1910 at the Manhattan Casino in Harlem. The *New York Age* reported: "Never before has such a large and efficient body of colored musicians appeared together in New York City in a concert . . . nearly one hundred in all."[5]

The Manhattan Casino concert was merely a preview of the spectacular musical offerings the concert-going public was to receive from James Reese Europe. On May 2, 1912, the Clef Club gave a performance at Carnegie Hall, billed as "Concert of Negro Music," that dazzled, mystified, and entertained music critics and audience alike. The concert was a benefit for the Music School Settlement for Colored People, founded by David Mannes (violinist, educator, and later founder of the Mannes School of Music in New York). The program included marches, waltzes, liturgical music, popular songs, and vaudeville tunes, composed by such significant black musicians as Samuel Coleridge-Taylor, J. Rosamond Johnson, Harry T. Burleigh, Will Marion Cook,* and, of course, Europe himself. In addition to the Clef Club Orchestra, the performers included the Clef Club Male Chorus (led by Will Marion Cook), the Choir of St. Philip's Church, the Royal Poinciana Quartet (male), the Versatile Entertainers Quintette (male), J. Rosamond Johnson (piano), and Miss Elizabeth Payne (contralto). The Clef Club Orchestra was the greatest single attraction, owing largely to its highly unusual complement. In addition to the conventional orchestral instruments, the ensemble included grand pianos, mandolins, banjos, harp guitars, and saxophones. According to Europe, the mandolins and banjos took the place of the second violins, thus providing a strumming accompaniment, something like that of a Russian balalaika orchestra. The 10 pianos provided ". . . a background of chords which are essentially typical of Negro harmony."[6]

In writing about the event, black poet James Weldon Johnson (brother of J. Rosamond Johnson) observed:

New York has not yet become accustomed to jazz; so when the Clef Club opened its concert with [Europe's Clef Club march] playing it with a biting attack and an infectious rhythm, and on the finale burst into singing, the effect can be imagined. The applause became a tumult![7]

The Musical Quarterly reported:

Music-loving Manhattan felt a thrill down its spine such as only the great performances can inspire. . . . There were many violins, violas, cellos and double basses; but it was a motley group of plectrum instruments of all sorts and sizes—mandolins, guitars, banjos and a few ukeleles . . . an assortment of reed and wind instruments . . . drums and tambourines, big and little, whose sharp accents danced across the jagged syncopations of the music, recalling the elaborate drum-orchestras of Africa. . . .[8]

In an interview published in the *New York Evening Post* two years later, Europe stated his intention not to imitate the white orchestras of his day but rather to develop "a kind of symphonic music that, no matter what you may think, is different and distinctive, and that lends itself to the peculiar compositions of our race."[9]

The success of the Clef Club was both immediate and tremendous. By 1913, Europe's bands were playing in cabarets and dance halls and for social events all over Manhattan and beyond. Europe made a practice of stopping for a few minutes to lend his presence to each engagement. Clef Club bands were heard, and danced to, at the Tuxedo Club, Sherry's, Delmonico's, and the Plaza, Biltmore, and Astor hotels. In 1913, Europe was signed to a recording contract by Victor. In February of that year Europe and a Clef Club Orchestra, with his assistant conductor William H. Tyers, played again at Carnegie Hall, this time in celebration of the fiftieth anniversary of the Emancipation Proclamation.

In mid-1914, jealousies and ill feelings among some members of the Clef Club compelled Europe to resign from that organization and to form the Tempo Club. Again, Europe was able to assemble a large band of musicians that became known as the National Negro Symphony Orchestra. Europe took that group to Carnegie Hall in 1914 for the third concert of Negro music. The Tempo Club prospered in its mission to serve black musicians and is reported to have garnered $100,000 in bookings in 1915.[10]

During this period, social dancing in clubs was sweeping the country, spurred largely by the dance team of Irene and Vernon Castle. In 1914, Europe and an eleven-piece premier orchestra accompanied the Castles on the "Whirl Wind tour" of thirty-five cities in twenty-six days. The Castles credited Europe with introducing them to the fox trot. Europe himself gave the credit to W. C. Handy, feeling that the dance was born from Europe's playing of Handy's "Memphis Blues."[11] Europe's association with the Castles continued until Vernon's death in 1918. His Society Orchestras, with Tyers and Ford Dabney as assistant conductors, toured the United States and abroad with the Castles. On occasion, the Castles would appear in Europe's concerts at Harlem's Manhattan Casino. At a performance there on October 3, 1915, the Castles presented Europe with a bronze statuette of themselves, and demonstrated the fox trot.[12]

In 1917, Europe was asked by Colonel William Hayward to organize a band for the Fifteenth Infantry. Europe was commissioned first lieutenant and given $10,000 to pay the higher salaries required to recruit musicians of the caliber the band would require. Europe doubled (to more than 50 players) the size of the regular military band,

and recruited widely in the United States and Puerto Rico. The band, known as the "Hellfighters" of the 369th Infantry (the former Fifteenth Infantry, now a segregated unit), landed in France on New Year's Day, 1918. The band was originally assigned a six-week tour of duty entertaining American troops at Aix-les-Bains. At the end of that stint, the Hellfighters toured extensively, entertaining French and American military personnel and civilians. The band also performed for the Congress of Women in Paris in 1918. The Hellfighters traveled more than 2,000 miles before being disbanded, becoming the most popular American military band in Europe. For several months thereafter, the men of the unit were assigned to combat stations prior to being reassembled for a final concert before going home.

As tremendous as the band's reception in Europe was, it paled compared to the American homecoming. On February 17, 1919, the Hellfighters marched in triumph up Fifth Avenue to Harlem. The streets were lined with spectators estimated at one million. The band marched past the reviewing stand at 60th Street (on which sat Governor Al Smith, former Governor Charles Whitman, Acting Mayor Robert L. Moran, and William Randolph Hearst), turned west on 110th Street, and continued north up Lenox Avenue. As they made the turn at Lenox Avenue, the band, which until that time had been playing marches and military tunes, struck up "Here Comes My Daddy Now." The *New York Times* reported, "the multitude went wild with joy." The *New York Age* wrote, "The Hellfighters marched between two howling walls of humanity . . . from the rooftops thousands stood and whooped things up . . . so frantic did many become that they threw pennants and even hats away."[13]

A month following the Fifth Avenue parade, Europe's band gave a concert with an augmented Hellfighters band at the Manhattan Opera House. That performance was the beginning of a tour around the country that was projected to develop into a world-wide tour. Concurrently, the band produced two dozen new recordings for the Pathé label.

Tragically, that international tour was never to materialize. On May 9, 1919, during a performance at Boston's Mechanics' Hall, Europe was stabbed in the neck by the band's drummer, Herbert Wright (whom Europe had reprimanded). The wound, inflicted in Europe's dressing room, seemed superficial. However, doctors at the hospital to which he was rushed discovered that the jugular vein had been severed. According to Noble Sissle,† Europe identified Wright to the investigating officer but pleaded for leniency for his attacker. And Europe, still conscious, authorized the doctors to proceed with surgery.[14] However, the bleeding could not be stopped and Europe died several hours later without regaining consciousness.

On May 13, 1919, James Reese Europe was given the first public funeral ever accorded a black person in New York City.[15] Thousands lined the streets along the route of the procession, and crowded into St. Mark's Church for the service. A second service was held in Washington, D.C., the following day, and Europe was buried with full military honors at Arlington National Cemetery on May 15, 1919.

Reflecting upon Europe's contributions to the development of American music, musician, critic and historian Gunther Schuller observed:

> James Europe was the most important transitional figure in the, pre-history of jazz on the East Coast. . . . In some ways Europe was to orchestral jazz the same kind of catalyst Jelly Roll Morton was for piano music.[16]

Notes

1. Quoted in Dan Morgenstern, "The Night Ragtime Came to Carnegie Hall," *New York Times,* July 9, 1989, p. H32.
2. Jervis Anderson, "Styles in Ragtime," *This Was Harlem,* New York: Farrar Straus Giroux. 1982, p. 78.
3. Noble Lee Sissle, *Memoirs of Lieutenant "Jim" Europe,* unpublished manuscript, October 1942, Manuscript Division, Library of Congress, NAACP Papers 1940–55, p. 7.
4. *Ibid.,* p. 13.
5. Anderson, *op. cit.,* pp. 76–77.
6. Morgenstern, *op. cit.*
7. Gale Dixon, "How the First Black Musicians Union Began," *Allegro* (publication of Musicians' Local 802, American Federation of Musicians, New York City), February, 1989, p. 16.
8. *Ibid.*
9. Morgenstern, *op. cit.*
10. *Ibid.*

---

†Noble Sissle was drum major with Europe's popular 369th Band, as well as guitarist/vocalist with his Clef Club Orchestra.

11. *Ibid.*
12. *Ibid.*
13. Anderson, *op. cit.,* pp. 118–119.
14. Sissle, *op. cit.,* p. 2.
15. Eileen Southern, *Biographical Dictionary of Afro-American and African Musicians,* Westport, Connecticut: Greenwood Press, 1982, p. 129.
16. Gunther Schuller, *Early Jazz: Its Roots and Musical Development,* New York: Oxford University Press, 1968, pp. 249–250.

Harvey Felder (Photo: Hart Hollman; Courtesy: Affiliate Artists)

HARVEY FELDER

BIRTHDATE/PLACE: November 2, 1955; Milwaukee, Wisconsin.
EDUCATION: B. Mus., University of Wisconsin–Madison (Music Education), 1977; M. Mus., University of Michigan (Music Education, Conducting), 1982; Specialist Degree in Music (an additional thirty credit hours), University of Michigan (Conducting), 1982.
MAJOR INSTRUCTORS: Elizabeth Green, Maurice Abravanel, Gunther Schuller, Seiji Ozawa, Max Rudolf, and David Zinman.
CONDUCTOR-IN-RESIDENCE: The New School of Music Symphony Orchestra (Philadelphia), 1985–86.
FOUNDER/CONDUCTOR: Contemporary Chamber Orchestra of Philadelphia, 1987–88.
MAJOR APPOINTMENTS: Conductor, Livonia (Michigan) Youth Symphony, 1982–84; Assistant Conductor, Ann Arbor Symphony, 1983–84; Music Director/Conductor, Haverford/Bryn Mawr Symphony, 1984–88; Johns Hopkins Symphony, 1987–90; Fox Valley (Wisconsin) Symphony, 1990—; Chairman, Haverford College Department of Music, 1986–88; Affiliate Artists/National Endowment for the Arts Conductor, Milwaukee Symphony Orchestra, 1988–91; Assistant Conductor, Milwaukee Symphony Orchestra, 1991–94; Music Director, Tacoma Symphony Orchestra and Assistant Conductor, Saint Louis Symphony Orchestra, 1994—.
GUEST CONDUCTOR: Milwaukee Symphony Orchestra ("Music Under the Stars," age 16); Spokane Symphony; Concerto Soloists of Philadelphia Chamber Orchestra; Redlands, Waukegan, and West Virginia Symphony Orchestras; Chicago and American Symphony Orchestras (Young People's Concerts); and Colorado Philharmonic.
RECOGNITION: One of America's Promising Young Conductors (*Symphony Magazine,* Fall 1983).

IN LATE 1989, *MILWAUKEE JOURNAL* MUSIC CRITIC Tom Strini wrote of his seven-year-old child's reaction to a Milwaukee Symphony school concert. He was impressed by the conductor, less by the music. "He was nice . . . really nice," said the younger Strini. The father inquired about the conductor's race, realizing that it appeared to be a nonissue to the youngster. After a moment of hesitation, the son responded, "[H]e was black." Continued the critic:

161

The conductor in question was Harvey Felder, the 33-year-old Affiliate Artists conductor of the Milwaukee Symphony under a fellowship. While Nick barely noticed his race, it is an arresting fact to most symphony goers. Felder stands between an orchestra with only one black musician and an audience more than 99% white.[1]

This was well into Felder's second year of affiliation with the orchestra.

"Position at MSO [Milwaukee Symphony Orchestra] Dream Come True for Milwaukeean"—so read the title of an article that appeared in the *Milwaukee Sentinel,* July 19, 1988, fourteen months earlier. French hornist Harvey Felder, then music director and conductor of the Johns Hopkins Symphony in Baltimore and the Haverford/Bryn Mawr Symphony (as well as chairman of the Haverford College Music Department), had dreamed of joining the Milwaukee Symphony Orchestra's staff since 1972. That was the year a sixteen-year-old Felder conducted the orchestra at Lincoln Park, "the prize for having won the 'Music Under the Stars' youth conducting competition."[2]

The article was announcing Felder's three-year appointment as Affiliate Artists Conductor with the Symphony. He would serve primarily as an assistant to Milwaukee Symphony Orchestra's music director Zdenek Macal. His assistantship required that Felder be prepared to cover in rehearsal or performance in the event that Macal was unable to fulfill his conducting responsibilities.

Native Milwaukeean Felder was a member of the first black family in his Northwest Side neighborhood. Consequently, he was familiar with minority status, though he recalled no specific incidents. The son of a social worker father and a nursing professor mother (at the University of Wisconsin-Milwaukee), home for only son Harvey was a welcomed haven. For his interest in music, he credited his father:

> My dad was one of the first people in the world to own a hi-fi. He was much more than a dilettante when it came to listening. He'd acquired a taste for all kinds of music, from jazz to opera to oratorio. He had a pretty extensive record collection.

Between home and Lancaster Elementary School, where the Felder children were the first Blacks to enroll, music became an essential part of the future conductor's life. Soon, inspired and encouraged by interested teachers, "music became a part of who I was, inseparable from my personality."[3]

Sixteen years after the "Music Under the Stars" concert and with much formal training behind him, the Milwaukee post was indeed "a dream come true." Said Felder, "My parents . . . are just beside themselves. . . . They think they've died and gone to heaven . . ."[4]

The following appeared in the *Milwaukee Journal,* October 14, 1988, only a few weeks following his return to the city, under the caption "Felder Fills Ailing Macal's Shoes Well":

> At 8:30 Thursday morning, Zdenek Macal called the Milwaukee Symphony Orchestra office to say he was too ill with the flu to conduct that day's concert. At 11 a.m., Harvey Felder, 32, was on the podium at Uihlein Hall of the Performing Arts Center, leading his first classical subscription concert. . . . Felder should be pleased with his work, and the orchestra and management should be pleased to have a steady hand to take the helm in an emergency.[5]

As announced by Affiliate Artists, Felder would regularly conduct the orchestra and participate in a full range of other musical and administrative activities throughout the season. Under an internship designed to develop young American conductors, Felder would concurrently study with both the music director and the executive director, gaining from the latter an understanding of the nonartistic aspects of running an orchestra. Conducting assignments would include youth and senior citizen concerts, subscription SuperPops and summer concerts.

Only a week prior to the "substitute" appearance, Felder made his formal debut with the Milwaukee Symphony, opening the Super-Pops season with singer Tony Bennett as the featured artist. As reported in the *Milwaukee Sentinel:*

> The beginning was made by Harvey Felder, the young man who has come home to become the orchestra's new affiliate artists conductor.

> Felder . . . demonstrated sensitivity from the podium in his graceful response to the music. . . . Felder courageously chose driving tempos for the upbeat expressions [i.e., curtain raisers—Reznicek's "Donna Diana" and Kabalevsky's "Colos Breugnon," the first act prelude from Verdi's "La Traviata" and the introduction and waltz from Tchaikovsky's "The Sleeping Beauty"]. He also did a fine job in shaping the numbers' dramatic dynamics.[6]

Felder had prepared himself well for the assignment and for other musical responsibilities, should conducting not become a career reality. He received the B.Mus. degree, with a major in music education, from the University of Wisconsin-Madison and the M. Mus., with a concentration in music education and conducting, from the University of Michigan. By completing thirty credit hours beyond the Master's degree, Felder acquired certification as "Specialist in Music," in conducting.

He regularly participated in conducting institutes and master classes, most by invitation. There were professional interactions with Michael Tilson Thomas and the Pittsburgh Symphony (1987); Otto Werner-Mueller and Curtis Institute of Music Symphony (1987, 1988); Max Rudolph and the Concerto Soloists Chamber Orchestra of Philadelphia (1985, 1986); Gustav Meier, Seiji Ozawa, and Ghennadi Rostdestvensky at Tanglewood Music Center (1986); Jon Robertson and the Redlands Conducting Institute (1986); Louis Lane, Larry Newland, Otto Werner-Mueller, and Harold Farberman at the American Symphony Orchestra League's Conductor's Guild Institute (1983).

In an August 1988 telephone interview with music critic Nancy Miller, just prior to his homecoming, Felder indicated that it was the "Music Under the Stars" appearance with the Milwaukee Symphony that confirmed his direction in life. Said the young maestro:

> I'd always planned to be a musician, but wasn't sure what path to pursue. Before, conducting had always been an option but never a goal. But afterward, I knew what I wanted to do.[7]

As an Affiliate Artists conductor, Harvey understood that his term with the Milwaukee Symphony was for a two-year term with an optional third. The three-year term expired September 1, 1991, but as early as February of that year, the *Milwaukee Journal* announced that Felder's MSO contract was likely to be extended. The orchestra's general manager confirmed the extension, to be financed by the orchestra's own money (the original appointment was funded by the National Endowment for the Arts and private sponsors).

Now at age 35 and close to three years of experience (February 1991) with a "Major" orchestra behind him, Harvey remarked:

> I've decided that I have a good 20 years before I have to decide whether I'm a failure. . . . The obvious next step is to become an

associate director somewhere, and get more podium time with the serious repertoire. But who knows what the future will bring? Eight years ago, if you had told me I'd be conducting professional orchestras for a living, I'd have laughed. But here I am. Right now, the future looks bright.[8]

Beginning September, 1994, Harvey Felder becomes Music Director of the Tacoma Symphony Orchestra in Tacoma, Washington. and Assistant Conductor of the Saint Louis Symphony—one of America's premiere orchestral ensembles.

Press Comments

"Felder . . . projected a conductorial profile that was efficient, poised, and well-shaped."

Milwaukee Sentinel

"Affiliate Artists conductor Harvey Felder . . . and the Milwaukee Symphony Orchestra and Chorus treated 'Porgy and Bess' like great music. The dozen numbers from Gershwin's landmark opera . . . were passionate, intelligent, and alive. . . . Felder was the key to it."

Milwaukee Journal

"Felder is elegant, cool and precise on the podium, and a suave, articulate and amusing pops concert host."

Milwaukee Journal

"This was Felder's classical series debut . . . and he knows what to do with a complex and serious piece of music . . . {T}he orchestra gave Felder everything."

Milwaukee Journal

". . . a thoughtful and sincere musician with a stylish, poised podium presence."

Milwaukee Sentinel

Notes

1. Tom Strini, "Scoring A Success," *Milwaukee Journal*, November 5, 1989, p. 35.
2. Nancy Miller, "Position at MSO Dream Come True for Milwaukeean," *Milwaukee Sentinel*, July 19, 1988, p. 5.
3. Strini, "Scoring A Success," *op. cit.*

4. Miller, *op. cit.*
5. Strini, "Felder Fills Ailing Macal's Shoes Well," *Milwaukee Journal,* October 14, 1988, Section B, p. 5.
6. Jay Joslyn, "Bennett, Symphony Please Crowd," *Milwaukee Sentinel,* October 8, 1988, Part 1, Page 11.
7. Miller, *op. cit.*
8. Tom Strini, "Felder's MSO Contract Likely to be Extended," *Milwaukee Journal,* February 17, 1991, p. E16.

Dingwall Fleary

DINGWALL FLEARY

BIRTHDATE/PLACE: June 2, 1940; St. Louis, Missouri.

EDUCATION: University of Kansas; L'Accademia Musicale di Siena, Italy (Conducting).

MAJOR INSTRUCTORS: Alleda Ward Wells and Jan Chiapusso (Piano); Samuel Nicholas (Organ); Clayton Krehbiel, Robert Baustian, Franco Ferrara, Vladimir Golshmann, and Kenneth Billups (Conducting).

MAJOR APPOINTMENTS: Faculty, Vassar College; Music Director/ Principal Conductor, Wappinger Falls (NY) Little Symphony; Hudson Valley Opera Company; Staff Pianist and Conducting Assistant, Hudson Valley Philharmonic; Music Director, Oratorio Society of Charlottesville-Albemarle; Director of Music and Organist, Christ Church, Arlington, Virginia, and Emmanuel Lutheran Church, Bethesda, Maryland; Music Director/Conductor, D.C. Community Orchestra (1979–1990); Music Director, International Children's Festival (1989—); Music Director/ Conductor, McLean Symphony (formerly McLean Chamber Orchestra/ McLean Orchestra) (1972—).

GUEST CONDUCTOR: Baltimore, National, Fort Worth, and St. Louis Symphony Orchestras.

BOARD MEMBERSHIP: Virginia Commission for the Arts (1984–89).

AWARDS/HONORS: Semi-Finalist, Mitropoulos Conducting Competition (1971); Outstanding Contribution to the Arts, McLean Community Center and McLean Citizens Association.

IN HIS NATIVE ST. LOUIS, MISSOURI, Dingwall Fleary received his early musical training: piano, Alleda Ward Wells; organ, Samuel Nicholas; and conducting, Franco Ferrara, Vladimir Golshmann, Kenneth Billups, and others. The late black master teacher Kenneth Billups wrote of his pupil:

> Dingwall Fleary is a product of the musical atmosphere of the Sumner High School; the same that has produced Robert McFerrin, first black to sign a Metropolitan Opera contract, and Grace Bumbry, a leading soprano on the roster of the Metropolitan Opera Company. I was the vocal teacher for both prior to their signing professional contracts, and Fleary was their accompanist. He is an unusually talented and

sensitive musician. His talent as a conductor was apparent even then, but after experiencing his Beethoven Ninth [St. Louis Symphony and Summer Chorus] . . . I seriously regard Mr. Fleary as a promising young conductor.[1]

Fleary graduated from the University of Kansas and studied the "art of conducting" at L'Accademia Musicale di Siena in Italy. He was a semi-finalist in the 1971 Mitropoulos Competition for Conductors (NYC). Early conducting experience included: Wappinger Falls (NY) Little Symphony, Hudson Valley Philharmonic, and the Hudson Valley Opera Company, as well as guest conducting appearances with such "Majors" as the Baltimore, National, and Saint Louis Symphony Orchestras. Occasionally he met the challenges of musical theater.

The District of Columbia's *Guide to Recreation and Leisure-Time Activities,* Fall/Winter 1986, included in its listing of "Cultural Arts Programs" activities of a D.C. Community Orchestra. Made up of professionals as well as highly trained nonprofessionals, the orchestra's purpose is "to bring city residents a program of symphonic concerts as well as a variety of educational events."[2] Four concerts were listed for the fully integrated orchestra's 1986–87 Concert Series, all free to the public.

The D.C. Community Orchestra has been in existence since 1934, when it was called the Washington Civic Symphony. Through the years, the orchestra has persisted "not as a staid institution sought out only by the exclusively refined but as an extroverted band of music makers not afraid to play for all the members of the city's neighborhoods."[3] Leading the orchestra from 1979 through 1990 (as music director/conductor) was Dingwall Fleary.

Commenting on the Orchestra's 1981–82 rehearsals in a junior high school auditorium, Fleary recalled:

> People would come in off the street and were completely amazed that a symphony orchestra was there. . . . That was something people could bring their children to and say, "This is what you can do some day; this is something to aspire toward."[4]

Northern Virginia has for many years taken pride in its McLean Chamber Orchestra, resident orchestra of the McLean Community Center. The volunteer orchestra is made up of government workers, teachers, business professionals, retirees, housewives, and students.

Fleary has served as this orchestra's music director since the orchestra's founding in 1972.

Orchestra publicity includes the following tribute to Fleary:

> His dynamic personality, combined with unquestionable musician-ship, careful and shrewd programming, and firm leadership, are his hallmarks. He has guided MCO to its present stature among the nation's community orchestras. . . . The rapid growth of The McLean Orchestra bears witness to his credits.[5]

Fleary and his musicians received the ASCAP (American Society of Composers, Authors and Publishers) Community Orchestra Award "for adventuresome overall programming in 1979" and honorable mention in the same category on two subsequent occasions.

During the summer of 1986, a contract dispute arose between Fleary and the McLean Orchestra's Board of Directors. Fleary and most of the orchestra's players resigned and formed the McLean Symphony.[6]

> Fleary said he resigned his $19,000-a-year part-time position as music director and conductor of the orchestra because of a contract the board drew up that prohibited him from serving in a similar job for "any other orchestra, symphony or similar music organization in the metropolitan Washington, D.C. area." As a free-lance musician, Fleary said, "that was something I could not accept."[7]

Season subscriptions and contributions for the new (continuing) McLean Symphony grew; support was forthcoming from the Virginia Commission on the Arts and the Fairfax County Council of the Arts. A new McLean Orchestra was formed, under leadership of George Mason's Performing Arts Department's chairman.

Washington Post journalist Courtland Milloy attended a February 1989 concert and reported the following comments from involved individuals with the McLean Symphony: one player—"He's a joy to work with, . . . He commands respect." Another player—"I forgot he was black about five years ago." A board member—"When you get to know people, race doesn't make a difference." These were relevant opinions, since as Milloy indicated, the power struggle was "fraught with social and racial overtones," a point worth noting since the organization is overwhelmingly nonblack.[8]

Maestro Fleary wrote to his patrons:

For me, the 1989–1990 season of The McLean Symphony marks 18 continuous years of sharing a wonderful variety of full symphonic and chamber music with you and the talented avocational musicians who make up the symphony. . . . The increasing number of ardent followers and supporters bear witness to my commitment to high performance standards and to the presentation of well-rounded thoughtful programs ranging from contemporary works—many by musicians based in our Northern Virginia and Washington, D.C. area—to those of the established master composers.[9]

Well into the 1990s, it is believed that the full-size, all-volunteer McLean Symphony is well positioned to continue into the 21st Century, fulfilling an important role in its community and meeting the needs of its players and audiences alike. Additionally, the orchestra could offer a more diverse repertoire than professional orchestras which are obligated to pay greater attention to the bottom line.

Well into the 1990s, Dingwall Fleary also enjoys an impressive reputation as an accomplished harpsichordist, coach, teacher, chamber musician, and accompanist. In addition, his talents are shared with the congregation of Emmanuel Lutheran Church in Bethesda, Maryland, where he serves as director of music and organist.

Press Comments

"Last night the McLean Chamber Orchestra gave their first public concert. They set an extremely high standard for community orchestras to follow. The conductor Dingwall Fleary, a young man whose work is becoming increasingly known, led the ensemble to play sensitively, with fine balance . . ."

Washington Star

"Superb! 'The Creation' was given a reading by conductor Fleary that moved a capacity audience to respond with a well-deserved standing ovation at the end of the evening."

Daily Progress (Charlottesville, Va.)

"The Beethoven Ninth—Summer Choir-St. Louis Symphony Orchestra . . .— conductor Dingwall Fleary . . . Ingredients for greatness . . . and greatness was achieved!"

Saint Louis Post Dispatch

"American conductor Dingwall Fleary exhibited talent, taste and authority . . . A truly fine concert."

De Rotterdammer

Notes

1. Publicity material, Dingwall Fleary. Billups was then a member of the Board of Directors and Advisory Committee, Saint Louis Symphony.
2. D.C. Department of Recreation, "Cultural Arts Programs," *Recreation Guide,* Fall and Winter 1986, p. 5.
3. Elaine Lembo, "Classical Diversity," *Washington Post,* October 30, 1983, p. F3.
4. *Ibid.*
5. McLean Chamber Orchestra Program, May 23, 1983.
6. Vince Stehle, "New Name, New Music For McLean Symphony, *Washington Post,* December 11, 1986, p. 16 (Virginia).
7. Barbara H. Blechman, "Disharmony Splits McLean Musicians," *Washington Post,* p. 1 (Virginia).
8. Courtland Milloy, "The Music of Proud Black Men," *Washington Post,* February 14, 1989, B3.
9. McLean Symphony 1989–90 Brochure.

James Frazier Rehearsing the Philadelphia Orchestra at the Academy of Music, January 1971. (Courtesy: Adrian Siegal Collection, Philadelphia Orchestra Archive.)

JAMES FRAZIER, JR.

BIRTHDATE/PLACE: May 9, 1940; Detroit, Michigan.
DEATH DATE/PLACE: March 10, 1985; New York, New York.
EDUCATION: Diploma (Piano), Detroit Conservatory of Music, 1958; B.S. (Chemistry), Wayne State University; M.M., University of Michigan, 1966.
ADDITIONAL STUDY: Conductors' Seminar, Interlochen (Michigan); Berkshire Music Center (Boston Symphony Orchestra, Tanglewood, Massachusetts).
MAJOR INSTRUCTORS/COACHES: Joseph Blatt, Elizabeth Green, Gunther Schuller, Joseph Silverstein, William Smith, Erich Leinsdorf, Eugene Ormandy, Conducting.
MAJOR APPOINTMENTS: Assistant Conductor (Summer Season), Philadelphia Orchestra, 1974; Founder/Music Director, National Afro-American Philharmonic Orchestra (Philadelphia), 1978–80; Artistic Director and Conductor, Bogotá Philharmonic Orchestra (Colombia), 1981–82.
GUEST CONDUCTOR: London, Liverpool, Leningrad, Bogotá, Los Angeles Philharmonics; New Philharmonia (London); BBC (London), RAI (Rome), French National Radio, Indianapolis and Detroit Symphony Orchestras; Danish State and Nashville Symphonies; Symphony of the New World.
AWARDS/HONORS: Winner, Piano Competition, National Association of Negro Musicians, 1962; Winner, Guido Cantelli International Conductors' Competition (Milan), 1969.

THE OBITUARY OF JAMES FRAZIER, JR., that appeared in *Variety* (the entertainment industry trade paper) on March 27, 1985 began:

> James Frazier, Jr., 44, conductor who was the first black to lead the Philadelphia Orchestra and who in 1978 founded the National Afro-American Philharmonic, died March 10 in New York after a long illness.[1]

That lead paragraph reflects, in an understated way, the priorities that dominated Frazier's musical life: achieving excellence as a conductor within the Western orchestral tradition; providing opportunities for the training and employment of black musicians; and exposing black audiences (particularly youth) to the full range of music that can be presented within the context of a symphony orchestra concert.

Frazier was born and reared in Detroit, a city whose musical riches included a symphony orchestra, strong church and choral music traditions, a thriving and vital jazz community, and a contemporary music ("The Motown Sound") unparalleled anywhere else in the world. All of these resources influenced the life of this talented son of a visionary sanitation worker. Frazier was able to begin piano lessons at age five because his father was willing to set aside part of his take-home pay for his son to study at the Detroit Conservatory of Music. Young James continued lessons (piano, organ, theory and composition) at the Conservatory until he graduated from high school.

With his parents' strong support and encouragement, Frazier progressed rapidly. At age 11, he became organist at Second Grace Methodist Church and was later appointed choir director. At 16 he conducted Handel's *Messiah*. However, Frazier never considered himself a prodigy:

> I hated to practice the piano. I used to stare out the window, wishing I could get out with the guys and play ball. Or watch Howdy Doody on the tube. But my mother wouldn't have any of that. And she knew enough about music to know when I was practicing or just fooling around.[2]

After graduating with honors from Chadsey High School in 1958, Frazier enrolled in the School of Music at the University of Michigan at Ann Arbor. He had originally intended to be a concert pianist.

> Yet the more I learned about music the more I realized I didn't have what was needed to be a great concert pianist. Prof. [Elizabeth] Green convinced me I could be a conductor. She pleaded with my parents to convince me I must continue.[3]

But Frazier was not to be convinced. He left the University of Michigan and enrolled in a premed program at Wayne State University in Detroit; he graduated with a bachelor's degree in chemistry. During the Wayne State years he continued his musical activities at People's Community Church, and at age 19 he succeeded George Shirley, noted black opera singer and native Detroiter, as music director. He is still remembered in Detroit for performances of Mendelssohn's "Elijah" in 1962 and 1963 that he organized and conducted at Ford Auditorium. (The first of these performances featured black bass-baritone William Warfield, best known for his stage role as Porgy in "Porgy and Bess" and the screen portrayal of Joe in "Showboat." The second performance featured George Shirley.)

The role and influence of the church was always highly significant to Frazier:

> To the blacks in America, their churches are the most important social structures. I give them credit for any successes I have attained. In the early years of my development the church is where I received the most encouragement and opportunity. Some doors are closed to blacks, but never their churches. . . . One of my staunchest supporters was Dr. Carlyle Stewart, of the People's Community Church. . . . [I]t was in his church I got a chance to grow as a musician.[4]

Professor Green persisted in her efforts to steer Frazier into conducting. She finally persuaded him to participate in a conductors' seminar at the National Music Camp at Interlochen, Michigan. There he conducted Mendelssohn's Overture to "Fingal's Cave." Among those who heard the performance was Eugene Ormandy, then the illustrious conductor of the famed Philadelphia Orchestra. Later in the day of the performance, Ormandy spotted Frazier crossing the campus and invited him over. "I was very pleased with your conducting," the maestro assured Frazier, then turned, in perfect seriousness, to a couple of his musicians. "Gentlemen," he said, "someday this young man may well be your conductor."[5] Ormandy's championing of Frazier led to important conducting opportunities later in his career, which, after the Interlochen experience, became clearly focused on conducting.

Prior to the Interlochen performances, appeals by Blacks and others to the Detroit Symphony Orchestra for Frazier to guest conduct had been rejected. Ormandy made a personal request and the opportunity was granted. At age 24, Frazier debuted with the Detroit Symphony Orchestra on November 8, 1964, in a program at Ford Auditorium that benefited the United Negro College Fund and People's Community Church. The program included works by Beethoven, Vaughan Williams, Richard Strauss, and Rachmaninoff.

Earlier in the year, Frazier had entered the International Conductors Competition, sponsored by the Royal Liverpool Philharmonic

Society. Though he did not win the competition, his conducting skills were acknowledged by the orchestra's general manager and secretary, Gerald McDonald, who wrote:

> [A]lthough you were not called to the Final of our recent International Conductors Competition your work here made a great impression, in view of your youth and lack of opportunities for conducting large scale professional forces. You had a very remarkable success and for this reason the Directorate awarded you a special prize of £25 "for encouragement" . . . Your feat in memorizing so effectively all the scores of the competition was in itself a proof of your seriousness and your ability.[6]

Frazier had hoped that his first engagement with the Detroit Symphony Orchestra would lead to other invitations to conduct his hometown orchestra. He was disappointed; none were immediately forthcoming. Nonetheless, he had decided to make conducting the focus of his musical career. He returned to the University of Michigan on a teaching fellowship and earned the Master of Music degree in 1966. Thereafter, Frazier accepted a position teaching music and biology at Inkster High School (Detroit). Simultaneously he served as music director of Detroit's Second Baptist Church.

Though the years immediately following his graduation from the University of Michigan did not fulfill his expectations for important guest conducting opportunities beyond home, they did begin to bring him the recognition he felt he deserved locally. On March 24, 1968, Frazier conducted the Detroit Symphony Orchestra in Beethoven's Ninth Symphony, a performance sponsored by the Detroit Civic Opera Company. In May of that same year, he conducted members of the orchestra in a series of concerts in local schools. (He was invited back for similar concerts in 1973 and 1974.) In the fall of 1968, Detroit Symphony Orchestra Music Director Sixten Ehrling invited Frazier to conduct Bach's Orchestral Suite No. 3 in concerts at Ford Auditorium and in Windsor, Canada. And, on May 9, 1969. Frazier conducted the Detroit Symphony Orchestra in a performance of his own composition, a tribute to Dr. Martin Luther King, Jr. entitled "King Requiem."[7]

Frazier took a bold step in 1969 when he entered the prestigious and highly competitive Guido Cantelli International Conductors' Competition in Milan. He emerged as the first American winner of the prize (then offering $1,600 in cash and the opportunity to conduct the La Scala Orchestra, once headed by Arturo Toscanini). He made an impressive debut two days later, conducting Beethoven's *Seventh Symphony.*

Frazier's winning the Cantelli Competition was noticed with pride by his old supporter Eugene Ormandy. In January 1971, at Ormandy's invitation, Frazier made his debut with the Philadelphia Orchestra at the Academy of Music, conducting Schumann's Fourth Symphony. Though he shared the podium with the orchestra's assistant conductor William Smith, his appearance was history-making: Frazier became the first black American conductor to lead the Philadelphia Orchestra in its winter home (the Academy) in a major work.

Ormandy continued to assist the career development of James Frazier. On the strength of his first exposure to Frazier at Interlochen and Frazier's debut with the Philadelphia Orchestra, Ormandy urged his colleagues in Leningrad to invite the young conductor to Russia. So on November 14, 1971, Frazier stood before the Leningrad Philharmonic (Russia's oldest and most prestigious orchestra) and conducted a daring program: Schubert's Fifth Symphony, Richard Strauss's "Don Juan," and Moussourgsky's "Picture at an Exhibition." He was the youngest American and the first conductor of African descent to receive the honor of leading the Leningrad.[8] As reported in the *Detroit Sunday News Magazine:*

> The concert ended with 'Pictures at an Exhibition.' "For a full 10 seconds," recall[ed] Frazier, "the huge auditorium was so quiet it was eerie. So many people there, and yet it seemed as if each one was holding his breath. There was not a sound. Suddenly, everything seemed to break loose at once. There were yells and rhythmic clapping such as I'd never heard in my life anywhere. It was deafening. They started clapping in cadence. They liked me. I was stunned."[9]

The Leningrad triumph led to other important conducting engagements; prominent among them were appearances with the New Philharmonia Orchestra (London) and the London Philharmonic.

Frazier's relationship with the Philadelphia Orchestra continued to develop. In 1974, he was named Assistant Conductor for the Robin Hood Dell season, substituting for William Smith, who was taking a sabbatical. In that position, Frazier had to "cover" (learn all the programs and step in to conduct should a scheduled conductor not be able to appear), as well as conduct all children's concerts. In announcing the appointment, Frederic R. Mann, President of Robin Hood Dell Concerts, Inc., noted that Frazier was selected "not because he is black, but because of his success with children's concerts, his musicianship, and his experience . . ."[10] Frazier was invited back the following summer (1975) to conduct three children's concerts. President Mann cited both the excellence of his programming and a noted increase in attendance at the 1974 children's morning concerts as reasons for the re-engagement.[11]

During the early 1970's, even as his conducting career was surging forward, Frazier was occupied with other music projects as well. He was busily revising the "King Requiem" and was completing the musical "Twelfth Street," which he described as a "soul musical." The work tells the story of black Americans living in Detroit's ghetto and focuses on the period leading up to the 1967 Detroit riot. Additionally, it draws upon those other musical riches—gospel, rhythm and blues—that exist in Detroit on what most consider "the end of the spectrum most distant from the symphony orchestra."

> "West Side Story" was a landmark because it brought jazz, real jazz, to the stage. "Hair" did the same thing for acid rock . . . In my "Twelfth Street," I had come to grips with a philosophical as well as a musical problem. I want to bring rhythm and blues and gospel music within the formal structure of a symphony. And, I'd like it to be a landmark.[12]

Frazier hoped his work would serve two musical purposes: to enrich the symphonic form with musical elements from the African-American culture, and, through the use of music that is familiar and accessible, to remove the barriers that often prevent racial and ethnic minorities from participating in the life of a symphony orchestra. The notions that good music is good music, and that quality music in all genres and idioms should be accepted, appreciated, and enjoyed without value judgment, were important to Frazier:

> I grew up hearing and playing gospel and rhythm and blues, and what is more, I dig them. Anyway, how can I not respect the music and tastes of others and then wish them to begin to understand what I'm doing on the podium?[13]

In 1975, Frazier experimented on national television with this theory that presenting pop music and jazz with an orchestra could make the experience of symphonic music more accessible for ". . . the young black in the ghetto as well as the child of the affluent suburbia."[14] He brought together for a television taping in Detroit the Detroit Symphony Orchestra, singer Melba Moore, trumpeter Donald Byrd and the Blackbyrds, and the jazz-rock group Blood, Sweat and Tears. The show ("Soul and Symphony"), which was aired nationally on NBC, October 21, 1975, was hosted by popular top-40 radio host Wolfman Jack.

That broadcast, directed particularly to youth, was not an isolated attempt to bring symphonic music to new audiences by combining the familiar with the remote. Earlier in the same year, Frazier and the Music Department of Zion Baptist Church in Philadelphia presented "Symphonic Soul: A Tribute to the Black Composer." That concert, held at the Academy of Music, included the music of William Grant Still, Duke Ellington, Quincy Jones, Margaret Bonds, George Walker, Kenneth Gamble and Leon Huff, Nicholas Ashford and Valerie Simpson, Tom Bell and Linda Creed, Stevie Wonder, William Dawson, Hall Johnson, and Ludwig van Beethoven. Singer Diahann Carroll was the Honored Guest Artist (along with an orchestra, two church choirs, and other soloists) in a remarkable program whose scope included academic music, jazz, soul, and spirituals.

Though the concept was Frazier's, the impetus came from the Rev. Leon H. Sullivan (Pastor of Zion Baptist Church and founder/board chairman, Opportunities Industrialization Centers of America, Inc.), who had met Frazier when he was conducting the Dell concerts. Sullivan was searching for ways to interest the communities around the church in concert music. He had a vision that his church would be filled with young people playing instruments. Frazier proposed a concert that would show the relationship between commonly labeled "popular" and "classical" composers, and that would combine the symphonic tradition with the musical heritage of African-Americans.

This meeting and subsequent conversations between Frazier and Sullivan were fortuitous: each man had a dream that could be realized with the help of the other. Sullivan's dream of exciting his communities about a different kind of music from that to which its members were accustomed, and of filling the church with young people playing instruments were at least partially fulfilled through "Symphonic Soul" and other concert ventures. Frazier's position as

Minister of Music at the church provided him the opportunity to create programs that would bring in young people to study, practice, and perform. Frazier's dream of conducting an orchestra composed entirely of black musicians was fulfilled in 1978, three years after "Symphonic Soul." On May 22, 1978, the National Afro-American Philharmonic Orchestra made its debut at the Academy of Music. The program, which featured black pianist Armenta Adams in Beethoven's *Third Piano Concerto,* also included music of Shostakovich and Schubert, the world premiere of black composer Arthur Cunningham's "Night Bird" (commissioned by the Zion Baptist Church, and featuring Donald Byrd and the Blackbyrds), and Frazier's "King Requiem."

The debut was a remarkable event. The sixty-odd member orchestra had drawn musicians from Detroit, Chicago, and New York as well as Philadelphia. A two-and-a-half-hour session the day prior to the concert was the orchestra's only rehearsal. The *New York Times* reported:

> Under these circumstances, the orchestra did remarkably well. It began quite brilliantly with Shostakovich's spirited little "Festive Overture". . . . The problems were greater in the succeeding *Symphony No. 2 in B flat* of Schubert and the *Piano Concerto No. 3 in C minor* of Beethoven. These are scores where the writing is more exposed. Not surprisingly, small mistakes were made, and the strings had pitch trouble. In most any orchestra nowadays, the string section is the weakest. That was the case here. The playing was honorable . . .[15]

Frazier and Sullivan had ambitious plans for the National Afro-American Philharmonic. They hoped to establish a summer residence on the campus of Temple University, where performers could practice, play in smaller ensembles, and give concerts in surrounding communities. Frazier stated:

> The Institute will be modeled after those at Tanglewood and Aspen [Colorado], and include lectures by Black musicologists on the Baroque and other historical periods of the music world.[16]

Frazier always planned that a major portion of each season would be devoted to touring. During the 1979–80 season, members of the orchestra toured with Stevie Wonder. The 1980–81 tour season was scheduled to begin at Washington's Kennedy Center, and include

Richmond (Virginia), Hampton (Virginia), Westchester County (New York), Wilmington (Delaware), Pittsburgh, Philadelphia, New York City, Chicago, Detroit, Gary (Indiana), Minneapolis, St. Louis, Kansas City, Denver, Dallas, Houston, Atlanta, Nashville, and Los Angeles.[17] However, lack of adequate financial support restricted the orchestra's touring, as well as its performing to its home, Philadelphia.

In April 1981, Frazier was appointed artistic director and conductor of the Bogotá Philharmonic Orchestra in Colombia and committed himself to twelve weeks of the orchestra's forty-three–week season. He resigned after the first season, citing the unstable political situation in Colombia. He returned to Philadelphia, resuming his work at the Zion Baptist Church with the National Afro-American Philharmonic. However, his declining health caused him to gradually withdraw from both ventures. As his condition worsened, he returned to Detroit for treatment. He was hospitalized there, but in early March 1985 he flew to New York on business, where he died on March 10.

Press Comments

"His gestures were clear, precise and in general restrained. . . . The New Philharmonia Orchestra played for him as they have rarely played recently—with a cohesiveness and expressive warmth that called back all the glories of their performances in the fifties and early sixties."

The Guardian

"{Frazier demonstrated} a lively sense of rhythm and equally a feeling for melodic flow."

The Times (London)

"Frazier had a solid beat and showed moderation in all things—sustained chords, pauses and other dramatic devices. . . . His control of the extremely rapid close was impressive."

Evening Bulletin (Philadelphia)

"His reading of the Schumann in D minor was, on the whole, conservative. Especially in the opening movement. Frazier stressed breadth rather than drama. But the music always flowed easily, and the expressive Romanza was followed by a Scherzo with the vigorous and lyric sections contrasted in proper proportion, while the introduction to the Finale was carefully graduated and the last movement . . . fairly sang."

Philadelphia Inquirer

Notes

1. "Obituaries," James Frazier, Jr., *Variety,* March 27, 1988, p. 110.
2. Noble, William T., "A Detroiter Whose Baton Conquered Russia," *Sunday News Magazine* (Detroit), January 16, 1972, p. 21.
3. *Ibid.,* p. 34.
4. *Ibid.,* p. 21.
5. Bims, Hamilton, "A New Breed of Maestro," *Ebony Magazine,* May 1972, p. 148.
6. Letter to James Frazier from Gerald McDonald, general manager and secretary, Royal Liverpool Philharmonic Society, June 17, 1964.
7. Carr, Jay, "Symphony, Chorus Premiere Requiem for Dr. King," *Detroit News,* May 10, 1969, p. 7B. The concert was originally scheduled for January 5, 1969, but was postponed because flu decimated the ranks of the chorus.
8. Bims, "A New Breed of Maestro," p. 141.
9. Noble, "A Detroiter Whose Baton Conquered Russia," p. 21.
10. "Black Composer Named to Conduct Philly Orchestra," *Jet Magazine,* March 28, 1974, p. 18.
11. Patricia Spollen, "Frazier Returning to the Dell to Lead Children's Concerts," *Evening Bulletin,* February 21, 1975, p. A21.
12. "Black Conductor Is Writing Soul Musical," *Denver Post,* June 20, 1972, p. 31.
13. Bims, "A New Breed of Maestro," p. 148.
14. "Dell Conductor Strives to Reach Kids," *Evening Bulletin,* June 16, 1975, p. 21.
15. Raymond Ericson, "Music: Black Symphony," *New York Times,* May 24, 1978, p. C21.
16. Dean Nolan, "Dean Nolan's Music and Musicians," *Michigan Chronicle,* May 6, 1978. Section B, p. 5.
17. *Ibid.*

Paul Douglas Freeman (Courtesy: Chicago Sinfonietta.)

PAUL DOUGLAS FREEMAN

BIRTHDATE/PLACE: January 2, 1936; Richmond, Virginia.
EDUCATION: B. Mus., M. Mus., and Ph.D. (Theory), Eastman School of Music, 1956, 1957, 1963 respectively.
ADDITIONAL STUDY: Höchschule für Musik (Berlin, Germany), 1957–59; L'Ecole Monteaux; American Symphony Orchestra League Workshops.
MAJOR INSTRUCTORS: Maurice Williams, General Music (High School); F. Nathaniel Gatlin, Clarinet; June Carpenter, Cello; Ewald Lindemann, Richard Lert, Pierre Monteux, Conducting.
MAJOR APPOINTMENTS: Director, Hochstein Music School and Opera Theater of Rochester (Rochester, New York), 1960–66 and 1961–66 respectively; Director, San Francisco Community Music Center and Conductor, San Francisco Conservatory Orchestra, and San Francisco Little Symphony Orchestra, 1966–68; Associate Conductor, Dallas Symphony Orchestra, 1968–70; Conductor-in-Residence, Detroit Symphony Orchestra, 1970–79; Principal Guest Conductor, Helsinki Philharmonic Orchestra, 1974–76; Music Director, Saginaw Symphony Orchestra, 1978–80; Artistic Director, Delta Summer Festival, 1978–79; Principal Conductor, Alaska Festival, Summer 1983; Music Director, Victoria (Canada) Symphony Orchestra, 1979–88; Director Emeritus, Victoria (Canada) Symphony Orchestra, 1988—; Music Director and Conductor, Chicago Sinfonietta, 1987—; Principal Guest Conductor, Zagreb Symphony Orchestra, 1990—.
GUEST CONDUCTOR: Rochester, Buffalo, New Orleans, and New York Philharmonic Orchestras; Minnesota and Cleveland Orchestras; San Francisco, Atlanta, Baltimore, Oklahoma City, Chicago, Denver, Richmond, Toledo, St. Louis, Houston, Indianapolis, Tucson, Sacramento, Glendale, and Springfield (Massachusetts) Symphony Orchestras; Opera South, Opera Ebony, and Pacific Opera Companies (USA); Calgary and Hamilton Philharmonic Orchestras, Edmonton, CBC, CJRT, Thunder Bay, and Windsor Symphony Orchestras; Orchestra Nova Scotia (Canada); Slovenic Philharmonic, Radio-Television Orchestra of Ljubljana, and Sarajevo Philharmonic (in the former Yugoslavia); leading symphony and radio orchestras in England, Scotland, Ireland, Germany, Denmark, Netherlands, Sweden, Belgium, Iceland, Poland, Italy, Norway, Finland, Luxembourg, Israel, Austria, and Mexico.

185

RECORDINGS: Columbia Records, Serenus (USA); Fanfare Recordings, Marquis, Total Records (Canada); Finlevy (Finland)—more than sixty releases. Artistic Director, Columbia Black Composers Recording Series and the Canadian Music Educators Association's Artists Recording Series.

AWARDS/HONORS: Fulbright Fellowship, 1957–59; Winner, Dimitri Mitropoulos International Conductors Competition, 1967; Spoleto Festival of Two Worlds Award, 1968; Koussevitsky International Recording Award, 1974; Vols. I–IV, Black Composers Series, top 1974 classical records listing, *Time* Magazine; Grammy Nominee, 1974; Critics' Choice— *Grammaphone* Magazine (England), 1986; Distinguished Alumni Citation, University of Rochester, 1975; CFAX Award for "Arts Leader of the Community" (Victoria, B.C.), 1984.

THOUGH NEITHER PAUL FREEMAN'S MOTHER NOR FATHER was a musician, both felt that their children should be exposed to music. Family radio listening included the Metropolitan Opera and all available symphony orchestra broadcasts. Each of the twelve children studied at least one musical instrument and son Paul Douglas began studying the piano at age five. By the third lesson, young Paul had reached the second book. But his interest in the keyboard soon waned; band and orchestral instruments offered far more appeal.

Young Paul's seventh Christmas brought a trumpet and a clarinet to the Freeman household. Three valves of the trumpet seemed to offer a faster route to performance than the instrument with many holes and keys. But a brother three years his senior had first choice.

With encouragement and frequent instruction from Maurice Williams, director of instrumental music at Armstrong High School in Richmond, Virginia, Paul's clarinet progress was rapid, even while he was still in elementary school. As he advanced to high school, arrangements were made for Freeman to travel the thirty-five miles from Richmond to Petersburg to study with F. Nathaniel Gatlin, the Oberlin-trained clarinetist who was head of the Department of Music at Virginia State College (now Virginia State University). In Petersburg, Freeman acquired his first meaningful instrumental ensemble experience, performing with the Virginia State College Concert Band and the Little Symphony Orchestra (both conducted by his clarinet teacher). Recalled Freeman:

> By age twelve, I was giving full clarinet recitals. As tedious as this must have been for the audience, it was an exciting venture for me. By this time, both Williams and Gatlin were encouraging me to think

of going into music seriously. My first experience at conducting happened when I was fourteen or fifteen years old. Williams had taken ill and the high school band was scheduled to perform at the PTA meeting. Instead of playing in the Armstrong High School band, I conducted it. Although the ministry was an earlier career interest, a maestro was born that evening.[1]

Williams advised Freeman to study a string instrument if he wanted to be an orchestral conductor. Consequently he began studying cello with Richmond Symphony cellist June Carpenter. Williams also advised Freeman to enroll in a conservatory. Following that advice, he submitted applications to Juilliard and Eastman Schools of Music and The Curtis Institute. Since financing a college education was a major issue for a family whose head-of-household was a produce merchant, the final decision was based on the size of the scholarship offer. The Eastman scholarship was the largest, and so to Eastman Paul Freeman went.

The Eastman years were rewarding ones, and he was able to study with Pierre Monteux during the summer months in Hancock, Maine. During his sophomore year, he worked as head of Eastman's Recording Department. Said Freeman:

> At Eastman, a student was permitted to be in charge of recording orchestra rehearsals and student recitals. I had a staff of three or four students, as well as a secretary. I started out working under Joseph Henry, who was a senior. When he left to join the army, I took over. Henry had also organized the Hillel Little Symphony Orchestra, that rehearsed regularly at B'nai Brith in Rochester. I was also able to take over this ensemble when Henry left. What a great experience.[2]

Also during the Eastman years, he met his wife Cornelia, a piano and organ major at the same institution.

His bachelor's degree, awarded in 1956, was quickly followed by a master's degree the next year. Freeman then received a Fulbright Fellowship and matriculated at the Höchschule für Musik in Berlin, Germany. Under the tutelage of Ewald Lindemann, he studied both operatic and orchestral conducting in an international class of eight students from five different countries. Students met with Lindemann five days a week, from three to six hours each day.

> It was wonderful being able to study in the great conducting tradition and to hear so many Berlin Philharmonic [and other

orchestra] concerts conducted by [Herbert] von Karajan. I attended every concert that he conducted. Another benefit was that Lindemann had played violin under [Wilhelm] Fürtwangler and these traditions he communicated to his students.[3]

Upon completion of his Fulbright studies, Freeman returned to Eastman, where he received the doctorate in 1963. During and immediately following this period of advanced study, Freeman served as director of the Höchstein Music School in Rochester, New York (1960–66). While he was director, the school's enrollment increased from two hundred students to more than seven hundred. During the same time, he conducted the Opera Theater of Rochester (1961–66) and the Höchstein Symphonia (which he organized), an ensemble of advanced Eastman students, Eastman faculty, and community members.

In a radio interview with tenor George Shirley on Shirley's broadcast series, "Classical Music and the Afro-American" (1973),[4] Freeman reflected that the doctorate provided security for an uncertain future in his chosen profession:

> I was still not sure that it would be possible for me to earn a substantial living as a conductor. Not only was I Black, but I was also American. I had noted that of the thirty major orchestras, there were very few native-born music directors. There were a few more assistant and associate conductors. That said something about the state of the conducting art in America.[5]

The Freemans moved to San Francisco in 1966. There he directed the San Francisco Community Music Center (1966–68), and conducted the San Francisco Conservatory Orchestra (1966–67) and the San Francisco Little Symphony (1967–68). During the San Francisco years, Freeman entered the Mitropoulos Conducting Competition, emerging as a winner in 1967. Shortly after Freeman's return from the competition, André Cluytens became ill and was unable to fulfill his commitment as guest conductor with the San Francisco Symphony.

> On about a six-day notice, I was asked to take over his three subscription concerts. This was really my first important conducting break in America. From there I went to other professional American orchestras, generally as guest conductor.[6]

Of that performance, the *San Francisco Examiner*'s Alexander Fried wrote enthusiastically under the headline "Symphony's First Negro Maestro—A True Gift." The black-oriented magazine *Sepia* paid tribute to the young maestro in an April 1968 "Salute" by Sonny Wells. The caption read, "Dr. Paul Freeman Is To Symphonic Music What Jackie Robinson Was To Baseball."[7]

Also during the San Francisco years, the New Orleans Philharmonic's conductor Werner Torkanowsky invited Paul Freeman to lead his orchestra in two concerts, one in Houston, Texas, and the other in Baton Rouge, Louisiana. Consequently, Freeman is believed to have been the first Black to conduct a major southern orchestra in the South.[8]

In 1968 Freeman was one of nearly twenty finalists in the Dallas Symphony Orchestra's search for an associate conductor. For his final audition, he shared half a concert with the orchestra's music director Donald Johannas. Immediately following that event, the orchestra extended the invitation and Freeman accepted.

Paul Freeman is widely acknowledged as the person most singularly responsible for interest in the symphonic music of black composers that emerged and developed in the 1970s and 1980s. His leadership in this development was clearly established when he shared the podium with Atlanta Symphony Orchestra conductor Robert Shaw in a series of reading sessions of music of southeastern composers at historically black Spelman College in Atlanta, Georgia, in 1967. The inclusion of works by lesser-known black composers sparked an interest that led to a research collaboration with musicologist Dominique-René de Lerma (then Director of the Black Music Center at Indiana University and subsequently Associate Director for Special Projects with the Afro-American Music Opportunities Association—AAMOA,[9] based in Minneapolis, Minnesota) that would prove to be highly significant for the promotion, documentation, performance, and preservation of works of black composers.

Soon after, Freeman conducted a concert of works by black symphonic composers with the Dallas Symphony Orchestra, where he was by then associate conductor. The program was subsequently aired as a ninety-minute special on National Educational Television, supported by the Irwin-Sweeney-Miller Foundation. Freeman soon thereafter joined the roster of guest conductors of the Baltimore Symphony Orchestra who participated in a week-long American

Composers Project (including works by black composers) funded by the Rockefeller Foundation.

These activities, which included black composers broadly as regional and American composers, led to a series of public readings of new scores and the performance of older ones, all by black composers, with the Baltimore, Houston, Minneapolis, and Detroit Symphony Orchestras (1973–76). For the first Symposium (Baltimore) in 1973, Freeman wrote:

> Those of us in education, performance, and research are proud of our people in such fields as jazz and rhythm-and-blues, but we lament conditions which encourage us and the general public to regard Black symphonic composers as insignificant. . . . Documentation proves that Black composers have been active in many media in the United States, Africa, Europe, and Latin America for at least two hundred years, and that these composers have not only used successfully folk materials in a highly sophisticated context, but have also absorbed other significant influences which surrounded them.[10]

Freeman and de Lerma (along with AAMOA) joined efforts and sought to "develop a project which would make their research available in a massive way to the general public." Following additional research and negotiations with Columbia Records, the team projected a recording project of tremendous magnitude: the issuing on Columbia's "regular Masterworks Series approximately twenty recordings of works by international Black composers, covering two centuries of creativity."[11] By this time Freeman was conductor-in-residence with the Detroit Symphony (1970–79).

With Paul Freeman as Artistic Director of Columbia Records' Black Composers Series, nine albums were released between 1974 and 1977. According to Freeman, "some thought we were ghettoizing the music; others . . . saw it as bridging the gap at a time when fewer than two dozen works by black composers had been recorded."[12]

Responding to the first four releases, *Newsweek*'s Hubert Saal wrote:

> It's hard enough for serious white composers to get a hearing. Try being black. . . . Happily, Columbia Masterworks has just issued the eye-opening first four records in a five-year series devoted to black composers; reaching as far back as the extraordinary eighteenth-

century Frenchman, the Chevalier de Saint-Georges. . . . What this series of records documents is both the richness and the diversity of black composition. It also confronts the question of whether such a thing as black music exists.[13]

Though many of the younger generation of black composers insisted that "Exploitive racism has a profound effect on the way the black composer reinterprets the world," Freeman simply responded, "It's notes on a white page."[14]

Largely because of Freeman's perseverance, other ventures were mounted. The New York Philharmonic offered five concerts in five days—August 29 through September 2, 1977—under the billing "Celebration of Black Composers." Three of the concerts were orchestral and two were recitals (one of solo piano music and the other of art songs). The orchestral concerts were a conducting collaboration of two Richmond, Virginia conductors, both Black— Leon Thompson, director of educational activities with the New York Philharmonic and Paul Freeman, friends from childhood.

Wrote Lon Tuck of the *Washington Post:*

> The festival represents a sort of culmination of a 10-year effort by Paul Freeman . . . to put music by black composers on the musical map.[15]

Wrote Francis Church in the conductor's hometown newspaper (*Richmond News Leader*):

> The chief significance of the black music festival . . . was that it showed black composers of our day wrestling with the challenge of synthesizing the best of 20th century music. . . . Richmonders . . . could be proud. . . . It was a cause for celebration.[16]

New York Times critic Harold C. Schonberg wrote of Freeman's leadership:

> Mr. Freeman conducted the entire evening in an energetic fashion. . . . [He] is an experienced conductor . . . [He] had the scores in his head and was able to get the message across.[17]

Under the heading "Orchestral Leave-Takings . . ." the Detroit Symphony Orchestra paid tribute to its conductor-in-residence in its May 10, 11, and 12, 1979 program, formally announcing Freeman's departure at the end of the month to become Music Director of the Victoria Symphony Orchestra in British Columbia. Following are excerpts from that entry:

> Versatility has been the hallmark of Paul Freeman's career with the Detroit Symphony Orchestra. Not only has he conducted a wide variety of subscription concerts . . . but he has also appeared at many unique concerts outside the regular DSO calendar. . . . There is hardly a type of DSO concert which Dr. Freeman has not conducted during his time in Detroit. . . . He was founding conductor of the Detroit Symphony Youth Orchestra in 1970–75, and he arranged and conducted the annual Summer Music Theatre during the same period. . . . Around his service to the DSO, Paul Freeman has built a national and international career, . . . [H]e is fast becoming one of the most-recorded young conductors on the scene. . . . In addition to his new post in Victoria, Dr. Freeman will retain his position as Music Director of the Saginaw Symphony and the Delta Summer Festival. . . . [We] wish him all success as his career moves forward.[18]

Victoria Symphony publicity expressed great excitement over the arrival of its new conductor. After the opening of the second season, a local critic wrote:

> The opening pair of Victoria Symphony concerts . . . left little doubt that the 1980–81 season—the society's 40th—will be every bit as good and musically probably even better, than the last. Having assimilated, and been assimilated by Victoria, music director Paul Freeman is now working from a vantage point he did not have at the start of last season.[19]

Following the second year, the next season's brochure read: "Maestro Paul Freeman has moulded the Victoria Symphony into a Canadian musical 'tour de force!' With this year's exciting program, the orchestra will approach its finest hour."[20] The Freeman/Victoria Symphony Orchestra relationship continued through the 1987–88 season.

Always seeking new challenges (and new conducting opportunities), Freeman set out in 1987 to organize a new orchestra in Chicago. Perhaps the greatest appeal of the Windy City was a musical climate perceived to be receptive to Freeman's programming ideas. During 1986 he led both the Grant Park Symphony in a well-received concert of music by black composers and the Orchestra of Illinois in a "Symphony in Black" concert, featuring the outstanding talents of trumpeter Wynton Marsalis and flutist Hubert Laws at the city's famed Orchestra Hall.

The Chicago Sinfonietta, a mid-sized orchestra consisting of thirty-two to forty-five professional musicians from the area, was incorporated in April 1987. The orchestra's special mission was "[T]o offer minorities an opportunity to nurture their talents and become role models for future artists, and make symphonic music accessible to those who do not normally attend symphony concerts."

The Sinfonietta gave its debut concert at Rosary College in River Forest (where it is in residence) on October 11, 1987, and two days later, its debut performance at Orchestra Hall. A documentary about the events, "Birth of an Orchestra," was aired on WFMT Chicago on November 18, 1987.

As music director and conductor of the Chicago Sinfonietta, Paul Freeman became Chicago's first black senior conductor. To the orchestra's credit were the following statistics: approximately forty-three percent of the board, twenty-one percent of the orchestra, and fifty percent of the staff represented a combination of Black, Hispanic, and Asian heritages. Women represented almost half of the orchestra membership.[21]

Reviewing the opening concert of the Sinfonietta's second season in September 1988, Howard Reich wrote for the *Chicago Tribune,* under the headline "1-Year-Old Sinfonietta Gets Better With Age":

> What a difference a season makes. . . . [T]he Sinfonietta launched its second season with some exquisite sounds and obvious self-assurance.
>
> The transformation bodes as well for this mid-size orchestra as it does for Chicago's musical scene. . . . Freeman is making impressive strides. . . . Freeman and the orchestra turned in a skilled and sensitive performance.[22]

Because Freeman is always the optimist and always the worker giving support to his optimism, there is every reason to believe that his latest adventure will be successful and that his conducting career will continue to expand. Since the evening when he stood in for his ailing band director at Armstrong High School in Richmond, Virginia, Freeman had come a long way. Reflecting back, Freeman said:

> Although I came along at a time when things were just beginning to open up for Blacks in classical music, I am sure that some of the

engagements that I received initially were because I was Black. But receiving a repeat engagement was certainly because I had done a good job previously. I am pleased to say that I have conducted over 65 orchestras in about 15 countries. To date, I have done over 55 recordings [including Columbia, Vox, Orion, and Finlevy]. As for a music directorship, perhaps this might have come sooner, had I not been Black, based upon the experience I had. But the field of conducting is not an easy one. I don't concentrate on whether I got something or didn't get something. One must always be appreciative for what one has been able to accomplish.

I shall be delighted if my career continues as it has thus far. I am pleased about my being selected as Music Director of the Chicago Sinfonietta. This brings me back to the States and allows me to continue with the Victoria Symphony. And, I am continuing to fill guest conducting engagements abroad.[23]

Foreign engagements during the 1989–90 season extended to Yugoslavia, where he scored successes with the Slovenic Philharmonic, the Radio-Television Orchestra of Ljubljana, and the Sarajevo Philharmonic. Following these successes, Freeman was named principal guest conductor of the Zagreb Symphony Orchestra, with whom he would conduct concerts in both its Masterworks Series and its Special Programs Series. He would also record a minimum of five compact disc recordings.

Back in Chicago, the Sinfonietta's fourth season brochure announced a 170 percent gain in the previous season's subscribership. It also announced that the orchestra was living up to its credo:

> to provide increased performing opportunities for the most talented professional musicians from the Chicago area's varied racial and ethnic elements—and to draw first-time listeners to its exciting concert events, along with the musically sophisticated audience it has already attracted.

And it publicized the fact that Paul Freeman was still "dynamic, charismatic, lauded and applauded everywhere—AND HE'S OURS."[24]

In early 1992, Paul Freeman and the Chicago Sinfonietta were featured on "Sunday Morning," CBS. Both conductor and ensemble were now reaching a national audience. They reached an international audience in late 1992 when the orchestra performed in fifteen

German cities including the world renowned Gewandhaus in Leipzig. The orchestra made its Kennedy Center (Washington, D.C.) debut in March 1993.

Press Comments

"Freeman's reading {of Tchaikowsky's 'Romeo and Juliet Overture-Fantasy'} expressed the drama, the passion and the poignancy reflected in a rendering that had a rare quality of inspiration with sensitive playing from all sections of the orchestra."
Times-Colonist (Victoria, British Columbia, Canada)

"Never before within memory has the Victoria Symphony achieved such galvanizing virtuosity. . . . Freeman proved that he really does have an orchestra that, when challenged, is capable of precision and brilliance beyond most people's imagining."
Times-Colonist

"This third program in the 1980–81 series {Victoria Symphony under Paul Freeman} was, from first to last at different moments, joyous, charming, stirring, exuberant, absorbing. It strengthened and extended the orchestra's reputation under Paul Freeman and further established the choice of Freeman for this difficult post, as a brilliant one."
Times-Colonist

"At the Opera House last night it was apparent from the very beginning when he caught a perfect tempo for the first movement of Brahms' 'Variations on a Theme of Haydn' that Freeman has a true gift for conducting."
San Francisco Examiner

"Freeman proved an adroit baton technician with a manner all his own. His control . . . result{ed} in invariably clear and balanced textures, rich sonorities and a gloss pointing to successful rehearsals."
Los Angeles Times (Glendale Symphony)

"Freeman proved that he can control orchestral forces with ample precision indeed . . . {T}his concert epitomized what happens when high inspiration is matched with consummate technical control. . . . Freeman turned in one compelling performance after another, each representing a different set of musical and technical accomplishments."
Chicago Tribune

"Under the baton of Paul Freeman . . . the Chicago Sinfonietta was characterized with a supple lyricism, a contracted inventive imagination and dynamic brilliance."
Chicago Defender

"A charismatic conductor. . . . A dynamic performance. . . . The real marvel of Freeman's work was the clarity of his tone painting."

Chicago Tribune

"Freeman made a strong case for the {Joseph} Joachim Orchestration {Schubert's Grand Duo for piano four-hands}, drawing exquisite lyric playing from his young orchestra in the first movement and a perfectly appropriate transparency of texture in the third. . . . Freeman made the most of its musical possibilities."

Chicago Tribune

Notes

1. Correspondence, Freeman/Handy, June 28, 1987.
2. *Ibid.*
3. *Ibid.*
4. Reference, George Shirley's 1973 "Classical Music and the Afro-American" radio series, Parkway Productions, aired originally on WNYC. The list of interviewees included composers Ulysses Kay and George Walker; pianists Natalie Hinderas and Armenta Adams; singers Grace Bumbry, Robert McFerrin, Camilla Williams, Leontyne Price, and Arthur Thompson; timpanist Elayne Jones; and conductors Henry Lewis, James DePreist, and Paul Freeman.
5. Freeman Interview with George Shirley, *ibid.*
6. Correspondence. Freeman/Handy, *op. cit.*
7. Sonny Wells, "Salute" *Sepia,* April 1968, p. 37.
8. "Hemidemisemiquavers," *New York Times,* June 18, 1967, p. D17.
9. The Afro-American Music Opportunities Association (AAMOA) was organized in 1969. Based in Minneapolis, Minnesota, its basic goals related to support for black music and black musicians, essentially in the areas of education, research, and performance.
10. Paul Freeman, "A Welcome from Dr. Freeman," Souvenir Program, Symposium of Symphonic Music by Black Composers, Baltimore, Maryland, September 24–30, 1973, n.p.
11. *Ibid.*
12. Clarke Bustard, "Guest Maestro Finds Familiar Faces," *Richmond Times-Dispatch,* March 7, 1986, p. D3.
13. Hubert Saal, "Black Composers," *Newsweek,* April 15, 1974, p. 82. (Note: Only nine albums were released. These nine languished in Columbia's vaults for almost a decade. Through the efforts of the College Music Society, all nine were rereleased in 1987.)
14. *Ibid.*
15. Lon Tuck, "In Celebration of Black Composers," *The Washington Post,* August 28, 1977, p. L2.

16. Francis Church, "Black Music Celebration," *Richmond News Leader,* September 10, 1977, p. A42.
17. Harold C. Schonberg, "Hailstork, Walker and Cordero In a Black Composers Concert," *New York Times,* September 3, 1977, p. C7.
18. Detroit Symphony Orchestra Program, 65th Season, 1978/79, May 10, 11, and 12, p. 716.
19. Audrey Johnson, "Success Marks Concert Opening," *Times-Colonist,* October 7, 1980, p. 33.
20. Season Brochure, 1981–82, Victoria Symphony.
21. Chicago Sinfonietta publicity material, "History and Activities," 1988.
22. Howard Reich, "1-Year-Old Sinfonietta Gets Better With Age," *Chicago Tribune,* September 28, 1988, Section 2, p. 9.
23. Correspondence, Freeman/Handy, *op. cit.*
24. Season Brochure, 1990–91, Chicago Sinfonietta.

F(lowers) Nathaniel Gatlin

F(LOWERS) NATHANIEL GATLIN

BIRTHDATE/PLACE: July 5, 1913; Summit. Mississippi.
DEATH DATE/PLACE: April 16, 1989; Petersburg, Virginia.
EDUCATION: B. Mus. Oberlin Conservatory, 1938; M. Mus., Northwestern University, 1945; D. Mus. Ed., Columbia University Teachers' College, 1960.
MAJOR INSTRUCTORS: Elmo Von Roesler, Fritz Holhauer, George Waln, Gustave Langenus, Clarinet; Karl Gehrkens, Maurice Kessler, Domenico DeCaprio, George Dasch, Norval Church, Conducting.
MAJOR APPOINTMENTS: Director of Instrumental Music, Bennett College (Greensboro, North Carolina), 1938–43; Director of Instrumental Music, Lincoln University (Jefferson City, Missouri), 1944–47; Director of Instrumental Music and Director of Bands, Virginia State College (now Virginia State University, Petersburg, Virginia), 1947–51; Acting Head, Department of Music, Virginia State College, 1951–54; Head, Department of Music, Virginia State College, 1954–76; Music Director, Petersburg (Virginia) Symphony Orchestra, 1977–89.
AWARDS/HONORS: Doctor of Humane Letters, Iowa Wesleyan College, 1954; one of ten most outstanding music directors in the United States and Canada, *School Musician Director and Teacher,* 1975.

IN THE WORDS OF F. NATHANIEL GATLIN in August 1987, "Becoming a conductor—being black in America—was not a reasonable option available to me during my development."[1] When approached by the author, Gatlin questioned the validity of his being included in a volume about conductors. Though his national reputation was based primarily on his accomplishments as a solo clarinetist, music educator, band director, and workshop consultant, his post-retirement accomplishments fully justified the authors' decision to include him.

One year following his retirement from Virginia State College (now Virginia State University) in Petersburg, Virginia, Gatlin set out to create a community symphony orchestra in that city. In an interview with *Richmond Times Dispatch* staff writer Robert Merritt, Gatlin said:

> For 25 years I have dreamed of forming a community orchestra in
> Petersburg. . . . It is something I have been thinking about ever since
> I came . . . to Virginia State in 1947.[2]

Gatlin said of his first rehearsal:

> I didn't know what to expect . . . It was hard to believe, but over
> seventy people showed up at the first rehearsal. It was so much fun,
> and that's what music should be.[3]

He set May 6, 1979 as his target date for a first public
performance. A review of orchestra programs reveals however that
"concert number one" took place on April 29, 1979, with the
Petersburg Chamber of Commerce as the orchestra's sponsor. The
program notes included the following comments:

> The Petersburg Symphony Orchestra Personnel include: high school
> students, college undergraduates, students pursuing advanced de-
> grees, military personnel, business persons, retired persons, house-
> wives, public school teachers, college professors, and unemployed
> persons. . . . The Petersburg Symphony Orchestra is committed to
> confirming a permanent cultural institution in the City of Petersburg
> for the expression of the talent of its members and for the enjoyment
> and inspiration of all who will seek the privilege to hear it.[4]

October 18, 1987 marked the beginning of the Petersburg
Symphony Orchestra's tenth season. Four major concerts, featuring
three soloists, were scheduled. "Pops" (as Gatlin was known to his
many students) proudly announced that the orchestra now attracted
its membership from the Petersburg area and fourteen adjoining
communities. And, in addition to its regular concert season, small
orchestra ensembles were performing in area high schools, under
sponsorship of the Chesterfield Board of Supervisors. Further, the
orchestra was providing accompaniment for the annual "Winterfan-
tasies" performances presented by the Petersburg Ballet Company.
F. Nathaniel Gatlin was always at the helm. With strong support
from the Petersburg Chamber of Commerce and partial support from
the Virginia Commission for the Arts, the Petersburg Symphony was
striving to become "a permanent source of enjoyment for the
community" and a source of training, nurturing, and encouragement
for aspiring young musicians.

Gatlin, through his own experience, recognized the value of nurture and encouragement. From the time he started learning music in the fourth grade in the Gary, Indiana public schools, his interests were supported by his family (none of whom were themselves musical), friends, and teachers. He was, in fact, practically adopted by his first music teacher (who remained his teacher through the 11th grade) Elmo Von Roesler, with whom Gatlin lived while attending high school. Roesler, himself a clarinetist, provided Gatlin with not only excellent training, but also with a role model that encouraged Gatlin to consider a career as a clarinetist and teacher.

At the end of the 11th grade, Gatlin was encouraged to accept the invitation of Frederick C. McFartland to accompany him to Dayton (Ohio), where he had been appointed the first black principal of the all-black Paul Lawrence Dunbar High School. With the advent of McFartland's principalship, the entire professional staff of the school was to be black. McFartland believed that Gatlin's presence could be helpful in establishing the image of strong, positive, and successful black leadership. So, again, Gatlin was "adopted."

He accompanied McFartland on speaking engagements in the Dayton community and performed before and after McFartland's speeches (which always emphasized the fact that Gatlin was trained by black professionals). The relationship with McFartland provided Gatlin not only opportunities to perform but also support and encouragement for his career aspirations. When Fritz Holhauer, the band director at Steele High School (which Gatlin attended in his senior year and from which he graduated) announced that the Oberlin Conservatory would be recruiting students for the freshman class, it was McFartland who drove Gatlin to Oberlin for the audition. Gatlin was admitted on a four-year scholarship and graduated in 1938.

During the Oberlin years, Gatlin encountered the preconceptions and stereotypes so prevalent—then and now—about blacks and music:

> Friends of mine didn't understand my interest in pursuing a career in academic music. I was so often referred to the popular black dance people. But I was bitten by the classical music bug. I was not interested in the "red hot and low down." Many factors led me to this. I came to the attention of splendid teachers, especially the private ones. Playing in the Conservatory ensembles, large and small;

playing in the Conservatory's symphony orchestra, playing the great symphonic literature just overwhelmed me. I committed myself completely. I sought to associate myself with classical music because this kind of music was not popular with my black brothers. I thought of myself as an ambassador—a disciple if you will—not only as a soloist but by leadership at the college level. I felt I could sell great music to my black brothers as well as others.[5]

Within a week of graduation from Oberlin, Gatlin accepted a job offer that provided his first opportunity to test his teaching skills. That first post, director of instrumental music at Bennett College (a black women's school in Greensboro, North Carolina), brought him into daily contact with the illustrious black composer, choral conductor, educator R. Nathaniel Dett, who was his supervisor. Of his responsibilities, Gatlin recalled:

I saw as my first task the development of an orchestra. This was my first opportunity to try my hand at conducting. Ah, that proved to be a most inspiring experience. I found conducting to be a matchless medium for the total and most complete expression of music.[6]

In response to his challenge, Gatlin developed a fifty-piece women's orchestra.

Gatlin's devotion to large instrumental ensembles, and the joy and satisfaction he derived from conducting, soon became central to his career. In 1944, he joined the faculty of Lincoln University in Jefferson City, Missouri, where he directed the marching and symphonic bands and the Little Symphony Orchestra. Three years later, he accepted the invitation of black educator J. Harold Montague to develop an instrumental music program at Virginia State College, which had long been known for its vocal and choral music programs. His successes with creating and conducting bands and orchestras there were largely responsible for his being named head of the music department in 1954, a post he maintained for twenty-two years.

Though conducting continued to be his first love, Gatlin maintained an active schedule of solo performing during those Virginia State years. He performed clarinet recitals in schools and colleges in seventeen states, and appeared as soloist with the St. Louis Symphony, conducted by Vladimir Golschmann, a performance that garnered him critical acclaim.

The Virginia State post offered Gatlin ". . . my greatest opportunity for musical growth and expression."[7] News of his successes in Petersburg gradually spread to secondary schools, colleges and universities, first in the immediate environs, and in time throughout the country. By the mid-1960s, Gatlin was much sought after as a guest conductor, clinician, adjudicator, and consultant in not only the East and South, but all over the nation. In April 1975, *The School Musician Director and Teacher* named him one of the ten most outstanding music directors in the United States and Canada for that school year.[8]

The passing of time only increased the demands for Gatlin's services, which were sought by post-collegiate and professional ensembles as well. In the 1970's, Gatlin was invited on six occasions to conduct the Richmond (Virginia) Concert Orchestra (composed primarily of members of the Richmond Symphony) at the city's summer festival site, Dogwood Dell.

In 1976 Gatlin retired from Virginia State College as professor emeritus. That change in professional activities created the opportunity for which Gatlin had long waited:

> I had always wanted to share my love for the orchestra with the world, so to speak. Wherever I have worked and there did not exist a symphony orchestra, I was moved to create one. And thus it is that upon my retirement in 1976 from VSC, I laid plans for the creation of a Petersburg Symphony Orchestra. The plans were initiated in 1978.[9]

Nine years later, *Richmond Times-Dispatch* writer LeeNora Everett reported:

> "Pops" Gatlin has accomplished what many regarded as an impossible dream. He has brought blacks and whites of all ages, from all walks of life, together for a common purpose—music.[10]

Though he spent a major portion of his professional life on a podium, Gatlin's enthusiasm had always been tempered by a saddening reality:

> Although always interested in conducting and a continuing student of conducting, I have not had the desire to make conducting my sole career interest, due primarily to my awareness that there are practically no opportunities for black conductors to gain employment in America. If this was not the case, I am sure that I would have sought to be one of America's outstanding conductors.[11]

On April 15, 1989, the Petersburg Symphony Orchestra was performing a special concert celebrating the inauguration of Dr. Wesley C. McClure as the eleventh president of Virginia State University. Gatlin had conducted the first half of the concert and, after having received two ovations, was being presented an award for his many years of outstanding service to the University and the community. He suddenly dropped to the floor, striking his head. He was rushed to Southside Regional Medical Center, where he died the following morning.[12]

Press Comments

"Under the leadership of Dr. Gatlin, the orchestra met the challenge handsomely."
                                                                    Progress-Index (Petersburg)

"Under the expert guidance of Dr. Nathaniel Gatlin, founder and permanent conductor of the orchestra, the ensemble was able to handle the extraordinary quick changes of tempo, texture and dynamics along with the dazzling figuration for the various instruments of the orchestra."
                                                                    Progress-Index

Notes

1. Interview, D. Antoinette Handy with F. Nathaniel Gatlin, August 1987.
2. *Ibid.*
3. *Ibid.*
4. Petersburg Symphony Orchestra program, April 29, 1979.
5. Interview, *op. cit.*
6. *Ibid.*
7. *Ibid.*
8. *The School Musician Director and Teacher,* April 1975.
9. Interview, *op. cit.*
10. "Musician Realizes Dream in Petersburg Symphony," *Richmond Times-Dispatch,* August 12, 1987, p. D-2.
11. Interview, *op. cit.*
12. See Secondary Profile, Ulysses Kirksey.

Lionel Hampton (Courtesy: Lionel Hampton School of Music, University of Idaho.)

LIONEL HAMPTON

BIRTHDATE/PLACE: April 20, 1908; Louisville, Kentucky.

EDUCATION: Holy Rosary Academy (Kenosha, Wisconsin); University of Southern California (Los Angeles, California).

MAJOR INSTRUCTORS: Sister Petra, Holy Rosary Academy (drums); N. Clark Smith and James Clifford ("Snags") Jones (drums); James ("Jimmy") Bertrand (xylophone).

PROFESSIONAL MEMBERSHIPS: Vernon Elkins Band, Paul Howard's Quality Serenaders, Les Hite (Louis Armstrong) Band (1930–34); Benny Goodman groups (1936–40).

LEADER: Lionel Hampton Band, 1934–36 and 1940—.

OTHER INVOLVEMENTS: Chairman of the Board, Glad Hamp Records, Glad Hamp Music Publishing Co. Inc., Swing and Tempo Music Publishing Co., Lionel Hampton Housing, Lionel and Gladys Hampton Foundation; Lionel Hampton Enterprises.

FILM APPEARANCES: "Pennies from Heaven" (1936); "Hollywood Hotel; (1938); "A Song Is Born" (1948); "Rock and Roll Revue" (1955); "The Benny Goodman Story" (1956); "Mister Rock and Roll" (1957); "Rooftops of New York" (1960).

TELEVISION APPEARANCES: One Night Stand (1971); Kup's Show (1975); Black Pride (1975); Mike Douglas Show (1975); Dinah (1976); Festival of Lively Arts for Young People (1976).

AWARDS/HONORS: "Band of the Year," Metronome (1943); Metronome Poll (1944–46); Esquire's New Star Band Award (1945); Down Beat Critic's Poll (1954); Handel Cultural Award, New York City (1966); Papal Medal from Pope Paul I; New York Governor's Award for Fifty Years of Music (1978); Alumnus of the Year, University of Southern California (1983); American Jazz Master Fellowship, National Endowment for the Arts (1988); Kennedy Center Honor (1992); keys to various cities, including New York, Los Angeles, Chicago, and Detroit.

HONORARY DOCTORATES: Allen, Pepperdine, Xavier (Louisiana), Daniel Hale, Howard, and Alabama A & M Universities; Glassboro State College; the University of Liège (Belgium), the University of Southern California, and the University of Idaho.

"THERE'S NO DOUBT ABOUT IT, Lionel Hampton must go down in history as one of the most inspiring and surely the most perspiring jazz musicians of all times."[1] Such was the assessment of *The Big Bands* author George T. Simon in 1967. As late as 1986, when Hampton was 77 years of age, jazz journalist Stanley Dance wrote:

> He is still out front with his mallets, beating the vibes, selling the band with his personality and simultaneously bringing out the best in the youngsters behind him, who are apparently free to express themselves in whatever contemporary idiom they prefer.[2]

In addition to "beating the vibes," it should be noted that Hampton occasionally performs as drummer, vocalist, and "two-finger pianist" as well.

Lionel Hampton has been out front as a band leader for more than half a century, leading bands that included such talents as Cat Anderson, Clifford Brown, Dizzy Gillespie, Benny Carter, Johnny Hodges, Fats Navarro, Joe Newman, Quincy Jones, Nat Adderley, Benny Powell, Jerome Richardson, Illinois Jacquet, Charles Mingus, Kenny Dorham, Art Farmer, Joe Williams, Dinah Washington, and Betty Carter. He has been out front as a vibraphonist since 1930. According to Broadcast Music Incorporated's Burt Korall, "Others had played vibes . . ., but Hamp really brought the sound into the foreground." As Hampton explained, "I had a good background for it . . . I'd studied marimba and had been playing orchestra bells, which has the same keyboard as vibes, since I was a kid."[3]

The early Hampton years were ones of good musical preparation. Born in Louisville, Kentucky, he grew up in Chicago, where he was reared by his grandparents. He attended the Holy Rosary Academy in Kenosha, Wisconsin, and was a member of the school's fife-and-drum corps. Dominican Nun Petra taught him the drum rudiments. His percussion study later included the snare drum, tympani, and marimba. In Chicago Hampton came under the tutelage of black master musician N. Clark Smith, director of the Chicago Defender Newsboys Band, of which Hampton was a member.

Moving to California in 1928, young Hampton became drummer with a band led by Les Hite. There followed brief stints as drummer with bands led by Vernon Elkins and Paul Howard (Quality

Serenaders). Rejoining the Les Hite Band in 1930 meant a new direction for Hampton, one that was to prove extremely beneficial to him personally and all of the world.

When Louis Armstrong took over as leader of the Hite Band in late 1930, Armstrong challenged Hampton to play vibes rather than drums. The result was Hampton's first recording as a vibraphonist— "Memories of You," the first of many recording successes.

Hampton organized his own band in 1934 and in 1936, joined the Benny Goodman quartet, along with Theodore ("Teddy") Wilson and Gene Krupa. This small hot unit within Goodman's larger unit was historical for several reasons, not the least of which was musical integration. "[A]ny use of Negroes in a big white band that toured the plusher location spots of the nation was clearly a victory for good music over prejudice."[4]

One of the most celebrated figures of the swing era, Hampton left Goodman to form his own band in 1940. Two years later the band recorded "Flying Home" for Decca. This Hampton composition "compiled over a million performances on radio and TV. It provided the impetus for an enormous breakthrough for Hampton. Widespread acceptance has been his since then."[5]

The band's repertoire ranged from swing to avant-garde, forever adapting to changing styles and popular demand. Beginning in the early 1950s, the band made regular "goodwill" tours to Europe, Japan, Australia, Africa, the Middle East, and elsewhere, and recorded prolifically.

In addition to Hampton's ability for identifying and incubating talent, he is credited with having been the first to establish the vibraphone as a standard band member rather than a novelty instrument, and the first to add to his ensembles the electric organ and the electric bass. Big bands or small ensembles, Lionel Hampton consistently led with vigor, inspiration, flexibility, and tremendous emotional excitement.

Hampton represented the President of the United States when the King of Swaziland died. He was vice chairman of the New York Central Committee for the Republican Party and goodwill ambassador for President Eisenhower. His bands appeared at Inaugural affairs for Democrats and Republicans alike.

In a 1986 interview with Burt Korall, Hampton outlined his plans for the future:

I'm thinking about helping to build a university of the arts right in Harlem. I want to do as much as I can for everyone who needs help. I'm always speaking to people in government . . . about what has to be done to improve things in the country.[6]

Wrote Maynard Good Stoddard for *The Saturday Evening Post:*

First, the man became a musician, the musician became a celebrity, and the celebrity became a legend. Finally, when the appeal of the music and the qualities of the man had transcended fame, Lionel Hampton became an institution: The Lionel Hampton School of Music on the campus of the University of Idaho.[7]

That historic day was February 28, 1987. Wrote the University's President Richard D. Gibb:

We at the University of Idaho are indeed privileged to name the School of Music in honor of Lionel Hampton. Mr. Hampton's commitment to music, education, the arts, and all mankind is not only to be envied but is an example for all to follow.[8]

Robert Miller, director of the School of Music, added:

Mr. Hampton's achievements as a musician and humanitarian are a matter of record; he is a national treasure, a legend in his own time. He set a model to which all can aspire; a model of commitment, dedication, humility, sincerity, and what those attributes can achieve, excellence.[9]

The University highly publicized the number of firsts that the decision to so designate its School of Music created: (1) the first state school or department of music dedicated by name; (2) the first school of music dedicated to a person "whose significance is in the field of jazz and humanitarian endeavors"; and (3) the first school of music dedicated to a black person.[10]

Dedicatory events came at the conclusion of the 20th Annual Lionel Hampton-Chevron Jazz Festival, an event that owes much of its success to Hampton's involvement. Held each winter on the University of Idaho campus, the Festival brings student musicians together with internationally acclaimed jazz artists. According to the School, Hampton lent to the Festival not only his name but a significant amount of money.

Lionel Hampton was one of three distinguished American Jazz Masters honored by the National Endowment for the Arts in 1988, joining a list that included such names as John Birks ("Dizzy") Gillespie, Thelonious Sphere Monk, Miles Dewey Davis, Ella Fitzgerald, Gil Evans, Benny Carter, and William ("Count") Basie. The other two 1988 recipients were Arthur ("Art") Blakey and William ("Billy") Taylor.

The National Endowment for the Arts panel that designated Hampton an American Jazz Master (with the approval of the National Council on the Arts) cited

> his mastery of swing, flawless execution of the mallets, directorship of a school through which passed many future jazz celebrities, and his established record as a philanthropist (housing, racial equality, and education).[11]

The award carried with it a $20,000 Fellowship grant to support a project of his choice.

Lionel Hampton's life story was released in late 1989, titled simply *Hamp: An Autobiography.*[12] The book (written in collaboration with English Professor James Haskins) is dedicated to Gladys Riddle Hampton, his wife, mentor, manager, and commercial partner for thirty-five years. According to sports journalist A.S. "Doc" Young, the Lionel/Gladys relationship was

> one of the most unique and profitable marital relationships in the history of show business. Hamp played the music and Gladys managed the money.[13]

Following her death in 1971, Hampton stated,

> She was the smartest of all the band managers. . . . She knew how to work with the wolves on Broadway. Gladys during the war times and during the '50s, was always good to book $1 million to $2 million a year. She knew how to bargain. She knew how to say "yes" and "no."[14]

It was Gladys Riddle Hampton who urged Hamp to form his own band, to venture into the music publishing business, and to invest in real estate. The latter resulted in The Lionel Hampton and The Gladys Hampton Houses for moderate and low-income residents.

Proceeds from these and other projects have been used to support The Lionel and Gladys Hampton Scholarship Fund.

Master of the vibes and legendary leader of bands, Hampton continues a full schedule of performances. For Hampton, "the secret is keeping busy, and loving what you do." In February 1993, he returned to Moscow, Idaho, producing and fully participating in the 26th Annual Lionel Hampton-Chevron Jazz Festival.

Notes

1. George T. Simon, *The Big Bands,* rev. ed., New York: Collier Books, 1974, p. 236.
2. Stanley Dance, "Sailing With Hamp," *Jazz Times,* April 1986, p. 20.
3. Burt Korall, "Hamp," included in Dedication Booklet, The Lionel Hampton School of Music, 1987, reprinted from *BMI* (Issue No. 2, 1986).
4. Orrin Keepnews and Bill Grauer, Jr., *A Pictorial History of Jazz: People and Places from New Orleans to Modern Jazz,* rev. ed., New York: Crown Publishers, 1966, p. 165.
5. Burt Korall, *op. cit.*
6. *Ibid.*
7. Maynard Good Stoddard, "Living Legend Lionel Hampton," *Saturday Evening Post,* March 1990, p. 48.
8. Dedication Booklet, The Lionel Hampton School of Music, University of Idaho, February 28, 1987.
9. *Ibid.*
10. *Ibid.*
11. Press Release, National Endowment for the Arts, January 1, 1988.
12. Lionel Hampton (with James Haskins), *Hamp: An Autobiography,* New York: Warner Books, 1989.
13. A. S. "Doc" Young, "Lionel Hampton's Wife Gladys Was Buried in L.A.," *Chicago Defender,* May 15–21, 1971, p. 16.
14. *Ibid.*

Margaret Rosiezarian Harris

MARGARET ROSIEZARIAN HARRIS

BIRTHDATE/PLACE: September 15, 1943; Chicago, Illinois.

EDUCATION: Curtis Institute of Music; B.S. (1964) and M.S. (1965), Juilliard School of Music.

MAJOR APPOINTMENTS: 1960s–1970s, Musical Director, Negro Ensemble Company; New York Ensemble Company; New York Shakespeare Festival; Faculty, Dorothy Maynor School of Performing Arts (Harlem) (currently Harlem School of the Arts).

MUSIC/ARTISTIC CONSULTANT: New York City Board of Education, District 17; Newark, New Jersey, Public School System; University of Delaware; University of Illinois; Illinois Central College; Malcolm X College; Illinois Institute of Technology; Howard University; Bennett and Voorhees Colleges; Hillsborough Community College (Tampa, Florida); University of West Florida (Pensacola), Distinguished Visiting Professor.

ADMINISTRATOR: Harlem School of the Arts, Newark Boys Choir.

CONDUCTOR/BROADWAY: "Hair" (1970), "Two Gentlemen of Verona" (1971), "Raisin" (1973), "Guys and Dolls," "Amen Corner."

CONDUCTOR/NATIONAL: "Hair," ten touring companies, "Two Gentlemen of Verona," "Raisin."

CONDUCTOR/INTERNATIONAL: "I Love New York," France, Italy, and Spain; "My Heart Belongs to Broadway," Israel; "Black New World Ballet" (Conductor and Pianist), 11 European and Scandinavian countries.

CONDUCTOR/ORCHESTRAS and OPERA COMPANIES: Chicago, Detroit, St. Louis, Minnesota, San Diego, American, Grant Park, Wolf Trap, Los Angeles Philharmonic (Hollywood Bowl), and Winston Salem Symphony Orchestras; Dayton Philharmonic; Bronx Arts Ensemble; Opera South (Jackson, Mississippi) and Opera Ebony (New York and Philadelphia).

CONDUCTOR/ARRANGER: Album—"Sing Ye the Praises of the Lord," CBS-TV Emmy Award-Winning Series "Razzmatazz," CBS-TV Special—"The Shape of Things," CBS-TV National Football League Theme.

TELEVISION APPEARANCES: "The Today Show," "The David Frost Show," "The Joe Franklin Show," "The Will Rogers, Jr. Show," "Like It Is" (New York).

LISTINGS: Who's Who in the World, Who's Who in the East, Who's Who Among Black Americans, Who's Who in Entertainment, Musical Prodi-

gies, Dictionary of International Biography, Notable Americans of the Bicentennial Era.
AWARDS/HONORS: National Association of Negro Musicians (1972); Dame of Honour and Merit, Order of St. John, Knights of Malta (1987).

REFLECTING ON THE 1970–71 RETURN to America (for guest appearances) of pioneering black symphonic conductor Dean Dixon,* black journalist Earl Calloway (*Chicago Defender*) appealed for greater opportunities and recognition of all black conductors. Wrote Calloway:

> When a brother makes it through those dismal clouds, let everybody say "Amen," "Right on Brother".... Realizing that it is difficult for American-born whites, then the situation has been almost impossible for blacks.

Titling the article "Black Conductors Making Progress," the journalist recognized the achievements of nine black conductors, including in the list one female, Margaret Harris.[1]

Three years later, Calloway did a feature story on Harris, headed "A Woman Full of 'Firsts'," pointing out that Harris was "the first black woman to conduct a Broadway show" (actually Joyce Brown was first) and "the first black woman to have conducted more than 10 major American orchestras . . ."[2] Harris was then in her third year as conductor of the Broadway musical "Hair."

It was "Hair" that brought Harris to national prominence as a conductor. The 1968 production that brought rock, nudity, and youth to Broadway, brought along black Margaret Harris, "vivacious, young enough to be in the 'Hair' generation," as the production's musical director in 1970.[3]

In an article prepared for *Musical America* on the subject of women maestros, musician/writer Catherine Contos included two black women, Joyce Brown and Margaret Harris. Wrote Contos:

> . . . Joyce Brown made musical history in March 1970 when she became the first black woman to conduct a Broadway opening. However, a man is still billed over her as "musical supervisor."

Contos added:

> At "Hair," Margaret Harris has top billing as musical director and is probably the highest paid musician on Broadway. A sure sign of her

success is that acquaintances are beginning to ask her mother whether Margaret, also a concert pianist, is not "prostituting her art." Her mother's reply: "With her salary, she can donate to any symphony orchestra."[4]

The close musical relationship between professional seamstress mother Clara Lee Townsend Harris and her only child Margaret Rosiezarian began early in her daughter's life. The mother played piano and sang daily to her beautiful child, whom she placed on the piano beside her once she was able to sit up unaided. At age two and a half, Margaret began making her own music; by age three, she had given her first public recital. Margaret Harris recalled almost four decades later:

> Mother is a very religious person, and I was taught that the talent I had was loaned to me while I'm on earth, that it was passing through me to others, and that while I'm here, I should use it to the best of my ability and it would not die with me but be passed on like a torch in the Olympics. It may sound strange, but that's what I believe. And when my playing and compositions make people happy, I feel in some way like a missionary, which is what my mother had wanted me to be.[5]

Under the heading "Child Pianist Has 75 Concert Dates," the following appeared in the *Afro-American* newspaper on October 11, 1947:

> Margaret Harris, four-year-old piano prodigy, through her discoverer Leo Salkin, already has more than 75 concert dates booked. Judge Waugh of the probate court approved the contracts.
>
> With a classical repertoire of 14 pieces, little Margaret will play two concerts weekly, with the first as guest star with a symphony orchestra in St. Louis.[6]

When she was ten, she performed as soloist with the Chicago Symphony Orchestra. Following study at the Curtis Institute of Music, two degrees from The Juilliard School of Music (1964 and 1965), and several years of teaching at the Dorothy Maynor School of the Performing Arts (now Harlem School of the Arts), Harris made her Town Hall debut (as a concert pianist) in 1970. The program included several of her own compositions.

Harris had earlier appeared at Radio City Music Hall (New York City) as one of the soloists in a solo-piano arrangement of Tchaikovsky's Piano Concerto in B flat minor. Before reaching the age of thirty, Harris had acquired recognition as a pianist, a composer, and a conductor.

There were other significant accomplishments. In 1967, at twenty-four, she toured Europe and Scandinavia (eleven countries) as musical director and pianist with the ballet "Black New World." She returned to the States to assume the duties of pianist with the Negro Ensemble Company's first production, "The Song of the Lusitanian Bogey." This led to a long affiliation with the New York City Shakespeare Festival.

Her first assignment as pianist/conductor with the Shakespeare Festival was for "Sambo," followed by "Two Gentlemen of Verona." But it was her musical leadership of the musical "Hair" that brought Harris to national prominence as a conductor. She commented on the experience in an interview with *Record World*.

> It's really a new experience for me. I'm a classical pianist, but I'm glad I was able to bridge the gap; I like both kinds of music, and I think I'll be getting more into commercial sounds.[7]

Harris served as musical director of "Hair" for the Broadway production as well as ten touring companies.

She includes many successful productions in her personal "career highlights," in addition to those previously mentioned: "Raisin," "Guys and Dolls," "Amen Corner," "I Love New York" (France, Italy, and Spain), and "My Heart Belongs to Broadway" (Israel). As conductor/arranger, her career highlights include "Razzmatazz," a CBS-TV Emmy Award–winning series; "The Shape of Things," a CBS-TV special; the National Football League theme for CBS-TV; roles as musical director, producer, and pianist at La Romme Hotel in Eilat, Israel; as well as television and radio shows throughout the United States, Canada, Europe, and Israel.

Harris was featured on "The Today Show" (Los Angeles); "The David Frost Show," "The Joe Franklin Show," "The Will Rogers, Jr. Show," and "Like It Is" (New York City). For Opera South in Jackson, Mississippi, she conducted the first productions of two works by black composers in 1972 (Ulysses Kay's "The Juggler of Our Lady" and William Grant Still's "Highway 1, U.S.A.") and was

a co-founder of Opera Ebony (New York City/Philadelphia), which
she served initially as general director.[8]

Multi-talented Margaret Harris is a much sought-after music
consultant, lecturer, choral coach, and artistic demonstrator. Her
skills and musical "know-how" have been utilized by the National
Endowment for the Arts, the National Opera Institute, Affiliate
Artists, the New York City Board of Education, the Newark (New
Jersey) Public School System, and New York City Boys Choir, the
University of Delaware (Dover/Wilmington), University of Illinois
and Illinois Institute of Technology, Illinois Central College (Peo-
ria), Howard University (District of Columbia), Bennett College
(Greensboro, North Carolina), Voorhees College (Denmark, South
Carolina), Hillsborough Community College (Tampa, Florida), and
the University of West Florida (Pensacola).

For the children's book *Time and Tigers* (1980), Harris wrote of her
proudest achievement:

> I'm most proud of . . . being able to conduct a major American
> symphony orchestra. Frankly, I think that fifteen years ago it would
> never have happened. We've had black conductors, but they've all
> been men. To be the first black woman conductor is an experience I
> value. Since my U.S. debut with the Chicago Symphony Orchestra
> [1971], I've been a guest conductor with the Los Angeles Philhar-
> monic and soon will conduct the St. Louis, Minneapolis, and San
> Diego symphonies as guest conductor.[9]

Harris reiterated this fact in 1989 when the author inquired of the
"most significant milestone(s)" in her conducting career. Of her most
significant achievements, other than conducting, she listed her debut
at age three and her having had the distinction Dame of Honour and
Merit, Order of St. John, Knights of Malta, bestowed upon her in
1987.[10]

As to her personal conducting identity, Harris emphatically and
proudly wrote, "I am an American Black Female Conductor." She
listed Zubin Mehta and Abraham Kaplan as two conductors who
served as sources of encouragement and inspiration. Her advice to
aspiring black conductors, both male and female, was "Be good at
your craft; learn as much as you can, and have faith."[11]

In a *U.S. News & World Report* interview, Harris commented that she
has found "being a black woman no handicap in a field that is largely
dominated by white males." Quoting Harris, the article continued:

When they first see me, the orchestra players sometimes do a low wolf whistle. . . . Then they say: What a relief! We thought you were going to look like a Mack truck driver.[12]

In the late 1980s Harris established Margaret Harris Enterprises, stating that the time had come "to pass the torch to someone else." She explained to journalist Alice Crann:

I'm starting a consulting firm for students in the arts, students who just graduated from college . . . There are too many agents out there saying "Yes, I can make you a star."

Any student, not just black students, need[s] to be aware that you have to work hard. You have to hone your talent and be the best you can be. You have to be positive and keep on going.[13]

Moving into the 1990s, Program Corporation of America announced the availability of Harris for lecture/demonstrations, piano recitals, master classes in piano and choral literature, and as an artist-in-residence. Her lecture topics included "The Business of Being An Artist," "The Survival of a Musical Artist In a Competitive Society," "Overcoming Obstacles In Life and Career," "The Responsibilities and Obligations of an Artist to Society," "The Arts in the United States: The Government and Artist," "Bringing A Production to the Public: From Idea to Opening," "The Black and Minority Artists in the United States," "Affirmative Action: Friend Or Foe to the Black/Minority Artist," "Discrimination in the Arts," "The Economics of the Arts and Artists in America," "Outside Influence On the Artist," "Marketing and the Arts," and "Women in the Arts."

From all indications (including training and experience), Harris is fully qualified to properly inform her audiences on all of these topics (and perhaps many more). States her publicist,

Dialogue is the best means of gleaning information, and "meetings" such as the one described herein can extend the vast universe of knowledge which each of us seeks and savors.[14]

Press Comments

"Margaret Harris, who has conducted on Broadway and with major symphonies, is about as attractive a young leader as any orchestra is apt to find. Yet with all her

obvious charm, she does not play to the audience at all. Except for the brief formal bows, she paid strict attention to the orchestra."

        Detroit Free Press

"{T}he singers were given excellent support by the American Symphony under Miss Harris's direction."

        New York Amsterdam News

". . . brilliant, sparkling, with enthusiasm and intensity as Miss Harris permitted the full sonorities of the orchestra to exert itself . . ."

        Chicago Defender

"Outstanding performances and a superb orchestra in Margaret Harris's strong hands. . ."

        Jackson Daily News

"Margaret Harris, the lovely and charming young conductor . . . directed musicians and singers with clarity and sureness . . ."

        Clarion Herald

"The success of the evening owed much to Margaret Harris, who conducted . . . with an effective blend of spirit and control. . . ."

        Opera News

"For the first time in its 69 years, the Minnesota Orchestra (formerly the Minneapolis Symphony) was conducted by a woman—Margaret Harris. . . . Beethoven was clean, no-nonsense, never strained. . . . {Her} conducting has both grace and precision."

        Minneapolis Tribune

"{T}he real discovery at Friday's Dayton Philharmonic Pops concert . . . was conductor/pianist Margaret Harris."

        Dayton Daily News

"Harris, a thorough musician with a clean beat and strong musical convictions. . ."

        Dayton Daily News

Notes

1. Earl Calloway, "Black Conductors Making Progress, *Chicago Daily Defender,* January 8–14, 1972, p. 36. Note: The other eight black conductors were Dean Dixon, James Frazier, Paul Freeman, Isaiah

Jackson, Primous Fountain (primarily a composer), Henry Lewis, James DePreist, and Everett Lee.

2. ———, "A Woman Full of 'Firsts'," *Chicago Defender,* September 6, 1975, Accent Section, p. 3.

3. Mary Campbell, "A 'Hair' Raising Conductor," *News and Observer,* June 13, 1971, p. 4.

4. Catherine Contos, "Brava, Maestra," *High Fidelity/Musical America,* May 1971, p. 7.

5. Margaret Harris, "A Life of Music," as told to Suzanne Seed, in *Time and Tigers,* New York: Harper and Row, 1980, p. 101.

6. "Child Pianist Has 75 Concert Dates," *Afro-American,* October 11, 1947, p. 6.

7. Mike Sigman, "Multi-Talented Margaret," *Record World,* January 1, 1972, p. 24.

8. Opera South was founded in 1970 in Jackson, Mississippi, by Sister Mary Elise of the Sisters of the Sacrament, under sponsorship of three black colleges (Jackson State University, Utica Junior College, and Tougaloo College). Sister Elise founded Opera Ebony in Philadelphia, Pennsylvania in 1974 (as a regional company, including Philadelphia and New York City), along with co-founders Benjamin Matthews (bass-baritone), Wayne Sanders (pianist), and Margaret Harris.

9. Harris, *Time and Tigers,* op. cit., p. 102.

10. Questionnaire, January 21, 1989.

11. *Ibid.*

12. "Margaret Harris: Composer, Conductor, Pianist," *U.S. News & World Report,* May 19, 1975, p. 60.

13. Alice Crann, "The First Hopes She's Not the Last," *News Journal,* February 7, 1989, p. 6D.

14. Flier, Program Corporation of America (White Plains, New York), 1991.

Raymond Curtis Harvey

RAYMOND CURTIS HARVEY

BIRTHDATE/PLACE: December 9, 1950; New York, N.Y.

EDUCATION: B. Mus. and M. Mus., Oberlin College Conservatory of Music (Majors: undergraduate, Music Education; graduate, Choral Conducting); M.M.A. and D.M.A., Yale School of Music (Orchestral Conducting).

MAJOR INSTRUCTORS: Joseph Schwartz, Piano and Otto-Werner Mueller, Conducting.

MAJOR APPOINTMENTS: Music Director, Texas Opera Theater, 1978–80; Associate Conductor, Des Moines Metro Opera; Exxon/Affiliate Artists/ Arts Endowment Conductor, Indianapolis Symphony, 1980–83; Music Director, Marion (Indiana) Philharmonic Orchestra, 1982–83; Associate Conductor, Buffalo Philharmonic, 1983–86; Music Director, Springfield (Massachusetts) Symphony Orchestra, 1986–94; Music Director, Fresno Philharmonic, 1993—.

GUEST CONDUCTOR: Texas Chamber Orchestra; Cleveland Orchestra; New York, Los Angeles, and Rochester Philharmonics; Denver, National, Detroit, Tucson, American, Lincoln (Nebraska), San Antonio, Virginia, Richmond (Virginia), Minnesota, Louisville, and Indianapolis Symphony Orchestras; Boston Pops Orchestra; Berkshire Choral Institute; Houston Grand Opera and the Indianapolis Opera; Goldman's Radio City Music Hall production of "Porgy and Bess," Boston, Toronto, and Florence.

RAYMOND HARVEY CONSIDERS HIS SUMMER 1987 appearance with the New York Philharmonic to be a most significant milestone in his career as a conductor.[1] The personal assessment is understandable—a unique experience, before a highly select audience, on a most auspicious occasion, leading a world-class orchestra (the nation's oldest) at Avery Fisher Hall, Lincoln Center for the Performing Arts, in New York City.

Delegates to the American Symphony Orchestra League's Forty-Second National Conference in New York City (June 1987) shared in a new League project, the American Conductors Program. This program was established "to bring recognition to gifted conductors whose work has had a notable impact on American Orchestras and

222

the communities in which they perform."[2] Four gifted American conductors, chosen from a rigorous application and selection process from 124 applicants, directed the New York Philharmonic in two special concerts: a New Music Project Reading Session (June 10, 1987) and the American Conductors Program (June 11, 1987).

One of the four conductors was Raymond Harvey, who had just completed his first season as Music Director of the Springfield Symphony Orchestra in Springfield, Massachusetts. *New York Times* critic John Rockwell offered an assessment of the four conductors' performance and had the following to say of Harvey's leadership of Elgar's "In the South" Concert Overture:

> Mr. Harvey . . . elicited really polished playing from the Philharmonic both corporately and individually.[3]

Harvey had prepared well for this opportunity. A native of New York City, he began studying piano at the age of eight and won his first music contest while in the fifth grade. His mother, Doris Walwin Harvey, an amateur singer and pianist, served as his first instructor. Showing rapid progress, he was soon enrolled at the Brooklyn Conservatory of Music, studying piano and music theory. With steady support from family, teachers, and friends, Harvey was soon giving recitals, accompanying singers and school choruses, and participating in musical shows. Along the way, he played French horn and assisted his high school music director in musical theater productions.

As he recalled the formative years:

> I was never discouraged from pursuing a career in classical music, although some thought it was risky to try to make a living as a conductor. Though I was a very talented pianist, I was drawn to conducting because of the opportunity to work with other people. I was first inspired by choral music. There is a great challenge involved in thoroughly studying a score and then sharing your feelings for the composition with other musicians.[4]

As early as age 10, his weekends were consumed with studying opera scores secured from the Lincoln Center Library.

> [A]ll Saturday afternoon [I'd] sit there at the piano and play everything, singing all the parts and making up the Italian pronunciations. I suppose I had a fertile little imagination.[5]

After graduation from high school, Harvey attended Oberlin College Conservatory (1968–73), where he obtained the B. Mus. in music education and the M. Mus. in choral conducting. Between 1973 and 1976, he served as director of choral music at the Northfield Mt. Hermon School in Western Massachusetts. Under his leadership, the choir completed a successful two-week tour of Rumania under auspices of Friendship Ambassadors, Inc.

Harvey returned to the classroom in 1976, entering the Yale School of Music and subsequently receiving the M.M.A. and D.M.A. in orchestral conducting. Between the M.M.A. and the D.M.A., Harvey was employed by the Texas Opera Theater, an affiliate of the Houston Grand Opera, and eventually assumed the post of music director. Additionally, he served as associate conductor of the Des Moines (Iowa) Metro Opera. With both companies he conducted performances of such standard masterworks as Puccini's "Madame Butterfly," Mozart's "Così Fan Tutte," Strauss's "Ariadne auf Naxos," Verdi's "Il Trovatore" and "Rigoletto," and Donizetti's "Don Pasquale."

Perhaps the most significant boost to Harvey's career advancement as a conductor occurred in 1980, when Affiliate Artists and the Indianapolis Symphony Orchestra selected him to be a participant in the Exxon/Affiliate Artists/National Endowment for the Arts Conductors Program. The stated criteria for selection were "exceptional musical literacy, significant leadership potential, and a genuine commitment to community service."[6] Harvey met each of these specifications.

The Indianapolis years were rewarding ones. During his final year, Harvey was initiated as a National Arts Associate by the Indianapolis Alumnae Chapter of the national music society Sigma Alpha Iota.[7] In 1983, he was selected as associate conductor of the Buffalo Philharmonic Orchestra (also as an Exxon/Affiliate Artists/Arts Endowment conductor), where he remained for three seasons.

In mid-November 1985, the following articles appeared in Springfield, Massachusetts, area newspapers: "Symphony Announces 4 Finalists for Conductors" (*Springfield Union*) and "Audience to Choose New Music Director" (*Holyoke Transcript Telegram*). The Springfield Orchestra Association's search for a new artistic director/conductor had been narrowed from thirty to four: (1) the associate music director of the Australian Ballet Company, (2) the principal conductor of the Hong Kong Philharmonic, (3) the associate conductor of the National Symphony Orchestra, and (4) the associate conductor of the Buffalo Philharmonic. Each would conduct the orchestra, with Harvey making his appearance on February 25, 1986, as the final contender.

Evaluation forms were distributed to concert-goers, whose response to each conductor was weighted heavily in the Board's (and orchestra members') final decision. The announcement of Harvey's appointment was made on March 11, 1986; his tenure began September 1.

Harvey deemed the appointment as music director of one of the nation's premiere regional orchestras as another significant milestone in his steadily developing conducting career. His arrival coincided with the departure of executive director Wayne S. Brown, another black American.[8] Said Brown of the appointment:

> I am delighted at the selection of Raymond Harvey as the new Music Director of the Springfield Symphony Orchestra. His vision, experience, and artistic insights will undoubtedly lead this organization into a new era of prosperity.[9]

Commented President of the Board of Directors Janee Friedman,

> Let it be said that after seeing each of the four conductors work with our orchestra, we on the Committee and on the Board of Directors saw an extra something special in the way that Raymond Harvey performed in rehearsal, in interviews and on the podium. We truly believe that this man is the best person that we could have as our Music Director. We look forward to his insight, his warmth and most of all, his beautiful music.[10]

The orchestra's theme for the 1986–87 Season was "A New Brilliance." Wrote Harvey for the orchestra's brochure:

> As I have already been so warmly welcomed to the Springfield community, I wish to welcome all of you to our 1986–87 season, a season of New Brilliance. . . . The Springfield Symphony Orchestra's 43rd season will bring you some of the world's finest artists and greatest music . . . . I eagerly look forward to working with our fine Springfield Symphony Orchestra. . . .[11]

Throughout the Orchestra's attractive brochure, introduction of the magical musical collaboration of Raymond Harvey and the

Springfield Symphony Orchestra was stressed: The Great Performers/ Classical Sampler Series, Pops Series, Special Events Series (including a Martin Luther King Celebration Concert), and a Chamber Music Series, with Harvey as host—all reflecting imaginative, but safe, programming.

The brochure announcing the Orchestra's 1987–88 Season read:

> Maestro Harvey's contributions to the city of Springfield have been impressive since his arrival. His dynamic presence and commitment to making the Springfield Symphony Orchestra an integral part of the fabric of life in the Pioneer Valley insures many exciting moments to come in Symphony Hall and throughout our region.[12]

The Chamber Music Series, with Raymond Harvey as host, was now designated "The Harvey and Friends Series."

Prior to his New York Philharmonic debut in 1987, Harvey's guest appearances were frequent, including the Los Angeles and Rochester Philharmonics, Cleveland, National, Denver, Detroit, and American Symphony Orchestras, as well as the Texas Chamber Orchestra. He had guest-conducted the Houston Grand Opera and the Sherwin M. Goldman's Radio City Music Hall production of "Porgy and Bess" in Boston, Toronto, and Florence.

The thirty-five-year-old conductor was well on his way to making a most significant contribution to continued orchestral excellence in America. His achievements have an additional meaning. On the subject of role modeling for young Blacks, a Harvey quote appeared in *Jet* Magazine's "Words of the Week":

> I think many minority kids don't get into classical music because they don't see anyone else doing it. And that's not a good precedent.[13]

Harvey recalled, for journalist Shelly Branch, an outdoor concert that he conducted in Buffalo. Two black youths approached him and asked what instrument he played. When he replied that he did not play an instrument, "he was the conductor," both children were amazed; one stated, "I didn't know they allowed black people to do that."[14]

In March 1988, the Springfield Orchestra Association announced that its maestro was currently engaged in a national guest conducting tour, including the Tucson and Detroit Symphony Orchestras (a return engagement for the latter), and the Boston Pro Arte Chamber

Orchestra. The tour ended two months later with a performance at the helm of the Hartt School of Music Orchestra. He had earlier in the year made his conducting debut at the Berkshire Choral Institute.

The Orchestra's 1988/89 season brochure included the following about Harvey, as he entered his third season:

> [S]ince his gala debut, Springfield audiences have experienced the dramatic and breathtaking responses of the Springfield Symphony Orchestra to the Maestro's baton. . . . [T]he Maestro's innovative programming, informal talks and new docent program are making the symphonic experience more accessible and enjoyable to Springfield audiences.[15]

Symphony, an American Symphony Orchestra League publication, featured Raymond Harvey in its Summer 1989 issue. The entry was appropriately titled "Reaching Out, Not Down." Of particular interest were his comments related to the issues of black conductors and symphony orchestras, Martin Luther King/Black History Month concerts, and increasing minority audience participation:

> I've made it a very strong point to not do a Martin Luther King concert for my first appearance with an orchestra. That's like an Oriental soprano doing only "Madama Butterfly," no matter what else she can sing. . . . Managers sometimes make the mistake of thinking that if they have a Black conductor or artist they will automatically have more Blacks in the audience. Sometimes yes, sometimes no.
>
> Managements are frequently just throwing little things out there in an effort to appeal to more minority groups. An orchestra says, "We do a special concert." Fine. But when will they do another? . . . .Why isn't there a "plan" for minority audiences?
>
> [D]on't water down the music or play pieces that aren't suited to the orchestra. Reach out, but never down.[16]

This author inquired of Harvey, "What advice would you offer to aspiring black conductors?" His response:

> Be extremely secure in their musical training. They will be challenged (in many ways) and will need a solid musical background on which to stand. I would also emphasize to them that wealth of

great music transcends all color barriers. Conductors are called upon to be masters of many styles and nationalities. Therefore, the black conductor should strive to be a master of music. The fact of his color may be important to those who watch him, those who would hold him up as a role model; but it has no bearing on the extent to which he can communicate as a musician.[17]

As of August 1994, Mr. Harvey will terminate his relationship with the Springfield (MA) Symphony Orchestra, to pursue new opportunities for artistic growth. He will continue as Music Director of the Fresno Philharmonic.

Press Comments

"We may have to change the standards by which we judge the Springfield Symphony."

Union News

". . . an intelligent and stylish musician."

Detroit Free Press

Harvey's manner "was deftly purposeful and frugally circumspect, and the music he controlled was unusually clearly defined."

Springfield Daily News

". . . both refined and energetic, an unusual combination of talents."

New York Times

"There was grace, raw power and almost ominous energy . . . Raymond Harvey was the toast of the town."

Springfield Daily News

"Under the ebullient direction of Raymond Harvey, The SSO performed . . . with verve and effervescence.

Jewish Weekly News

Notes

1. Correspondence, Harvey/Handy, September 13, 1987.
2. Flyer, American Conductors Program, Performance, June 11, 1987.

3. John Rockwell, "Philharmonic: Regional Conductors," *New York Times,* June 13, 1987, p. 9.

4. Correspondence, *op. cit.*

5. Shelly J. Branch, "On the Upbeat: Two Young Conductors," *American Vision,* August 1989, p. 25.

6. Publicity material, Affiliate Artists, Inc.

7. "New National Arts Associates," *Pan Pipes of Sigma Alpha Iota,* Summer 1983, pp. 10–11.

8. Harvey arrived as Wayne Brown departed for the Louisville Symphony Orchestra, where he assumed the duties of executive director during the 1986–87 Season.

9. Press release, Springfield Orchestra Association, April 16, 1986.

10. *Ibid.*

11. Springfield Symphony Orchestra's 1986/87 brochure.

12. Springfield Symphony Orchestra's 1987/88 brochure.

13. "Words of the Week," *Jet,* March 17, 1986, p. 40.

14. Branch, *op. cit.,* p. 26.

15. Springfield Symphony Orchestra's 1988/89 Brochure.

16. Nancy S. Grant, "Reaching Out, Not Down," *Symphony,* July/August 1989, p. 92.

17. Correspondence, Harvey/Handy, *op. cit.*

Fletcher ("Smack") Henderson (at piano) and his 1936 Band (Courtesy: Frank Driggs Collection)

(JAMES) FLETCHER HAMILTON HENDERSON, JR. ("SMACK")

BIRTHDATE/PLACE: December 18, 1897; Cuthbert, Georgia.
DEATH DATE/PLACE: December 28, 1952; New York, New York.
EDUCATION: B.S. (mathematics and chemistry), Atlanta University, 1920.
BAND/ORCHESTRA LEADER: Black Swan Jazz Masters, early 1920s; Fletcher Henderson Bands and Orchestras (most notably at the Club Alabam and Roseland in New York; Grand Terrace in Chicago), 1924–39; late 1941–49.
ARRANGER: For his own bands and orchestras, Benny Goodman, Isham Jones, Glen Gray, Teddy Hill, Will Bradley, Jack Hylton, Jimmy and Tommy Dorsey.
BEST KNOWN ARRANGEMENTS: "Sometimes I'm Happy," "When Buddha Smiles," "King Porter Stomp," "Blue Skies," "Sweet and Lovely," "Stealin' Apples," "Spring Song," "Night and Day," "Taking A Chance on Love," "Back in Your Own Back Yard," "On A Slow Boat to China," "South of the Border."
COMPOSITIONS: "Down South Camp Meeting," "Wrapping It Up," "Stampede," "Bumble Bee Stomp," "No, Baby, No," "It's Wearing Me Down," "Hotter Than 'El!."

FLETCHER HAMILTON HENDERSON, JR., CALLED BY HIS FRIEND JOHN HAMMOND, "the greatest orchestra leader of the '20's, supreme arranger of the '30's, and a man who launched the careers of scores of our greatest soloists," was probably born James Fletcher Henderson.[1] He was born into a musical family; both his parents played the piano, and his brother Horace became a professional musician (jazz pianist and arranger). However, Fletcher Henderson, Sr., was very strict in his attitudes about music. Even after his sons achieved fame, playing jazz in his house was forbidden.[2]

Fletcher studied piano from age six (first with his mother, and then with other teachers) until age thirteen (because his father insisted) and then continued his musical education at a local private school where his father was a teacher. After studying at the

231

preparatory school of Atlanta University (1911–16), Fletcher enrolled there as an undergraduate and majored in mathematics and chemistry. Henderson excelled in both football and baseball and involved himself far less in music than his early training might have suggested he would. However, he did write about music in the college paper, play piano jobs occasionally, and reportedly continue to study the organ.[3]

During his college years, Henderson played for productions directed by black violinist Kemper Harreld, and in the summers he played piano at Woods Hole (a "whites only" resort in Massachusetts). After graduating from Atlanta University in 1920, Henderson went to New York, intending to pursue graduate studies in chemistry at Columbia University. However, the direction of his life changed course when Henderson substituted for his ailing roommate as pianist on a Hudson River pleasure boat and, after several weeks, was asked to become a regular.

Sometime in the fall of 1920, Henderson became a song demonstrator with the Pace and Handy Music Company. Later he was employed with the Pace Phonograph Corporation (after Pace left Handy) as musical director, accompanist, and bandleader for the company's Black Swan Jazz Masters. During that period he accompanied such blues and jazz singers as Mamie Smith and Ethel Waters. (Waters is credited with having coached Henderson in the "down home" blues style for her recordings.[4])

Henderson made his actual recording debut in 1921, as pianist for the male balladeer C. Carroll Clark.[5] For the next three years he regularly led fully staffed recording orchestras, prior to regularly leading orchestras before audiences. The roster of singers whose recording bands he assembled and led included Bessie Smith, Ida Cox, Clara Smith, Trixie Smith, Alberta Hunter, Ma Rainey, Rosa Henderson, and Viola McCoy. It is reasonable to suppose that his putting together groups to accompany the singers for the Black Swan Jazz Masters recordings contributed to Henderson's developing a career as a bandleader.

In the spring of 1923, Henderson departed briefly from his role as a bandleader. He toured for several weeks as pianist with Will Marion Cook's twenty-five–piece Clef Club Orchestra, which stopped in Philadelphia, Baltimore, and finally at the Lafayette Theater in New York. Following that engagement, Henderson began to organize his first big band, using as the nucleus musicians he had assembled for recordings. The band made its debut at a cellar club on West 44th Street, the Club Alabam (the date is variously reported as 1922, 1923, or 1924), and almost immediately was hired as the house band. Later in 1924 Henderson was offered the position as leader of the house band at Roseland (which later became the best-known dance hall in New York City). His tenure at Roseland lasted until the mid-1930's.

According to British band leader and radio personality Humphrey Lyttleton:

At the Roseland [a whites-only establishment], Henderson played opposite the best white bands of the day, and in terms of the music which he offered the dancers, he had to conform to their standards. . . . It set the pattern which all big bands, sweet or swing, would follow to the present day.[6]

Early in the Roseland years, Henderson's band was probably just another good dance band. It had not begun to exploit the blues, spirituals, and work songs, and the "new jazz" emerging from the South. Henderson himself was a product of middle-class orientation, and only in the early 1920s had he begun to develop as a jazz pianist. But he was sensitive to the influences around him and was aware of musicians playing in new styles. Among them was Louis Armstrong, who at the time was playing with "King" Oliver's band in Chicago. Henderson convinced Armstrong to join his band in September 1924, and Armstrong remained until November 1925. Armstrong was brought in as a jazz specialist; however, the inventiveness of his propulsive swing style quickly began to influence not only the players in Henderson's band but also other New York musicians as well.

The changes in the band's style can be attributed in part to Armstrong's playing style. However, the greater effect resulted from the arrangements of Don Redman. To Redman is credited the development of the interplay between brass and reed sections, sometimes in the call-and-response style of the southern black singing tradition and at other times with one section backing the other, playing riffs. No matter which style was used, solos were always interspersed between arranged sections.

Though Armstrong left in 1925, the band continued to develop the propulsive jazz style he had introduced. By 1927, the band as a whole had mastered the form and the individual musicians had developed Armstrong's solo style. In that year, Redman, who had probably created most of the band's arrangements, left to join McKinney's Cotton Pickers, compelling Henderson to create the arrangements himself—a task at which he proved to be exceptionally good.

Toward the late 1920s, Henderson's interest in his band seems to have waned somewhat. He recorded less in 1929 and 1930, and bookings in the Depression years decreased. According to music journalist and "catalytic agent" John Hammond, "the band spent more time laying off than working."[7] Henderson lacked the skills and ability to promote his band, and he could not control his often unruly musicians, many of whom were coaxed away by other bandleaders. His ineptness as a manager led to the disbanding of the group on several occasions. After a time, the band did land successful engagements at Connie's Inn in Harlem and other ballrooms and theaters, which stimulated its recording activities.

In the early 1930s, Fletcher engaged his brother Horace as pianist and began a round of touring, with varying success. The roster of his touring personnel included, at times: trumpeters Red Allen, Joe Thomas, Roy Eldridge, Dick Vance, and Emmett Berry; trombonists Claude Jones, Keg Johnson, Fernando Arbelo, J. C. Higginbotham, Dickie Wells, and Benny Morton; alto saxophonists Edgar Sampson, Russell Procope, and Hilton Jefferson; tenor saxophonists Ben Webster and Chu Berry; guitarists Clarence Holiday and Lawrence Lucie; bassists John Kirby and Israel Crosby; drummers Walter Johnson and Sid Catlett.[8]

Henderson the arranger achieved considerable prominence during the early 1930s, and he provided his services for other bands, including those of Isham Jones and Jimmy and Tommy Dorsey. In 1934, serious financial difficulties forced him to sell many of his best arrangements to Benny Goodman, who was just starting his band. Henderson achieved his greatest recognition for such arrangements as "Sometimes I'm Happy," "King Porter Stomp," "Blue Skies," and "Wrapping It Up" for Benny Goodman. These arrangements were undoubtedly responsible, at least in part, for the enormous success of swing bands between 1935 and 1945.

Henderson continued to lead his own bands until 1939, when he joined the Goodman band as full-time arranger and pianist. In 1941 he returned to leading bands intermittently (including engagements at the Savoy Ballroom in Harlem and Chicago's DeLisa Club) and continued doing arrangements. By 1945 Henderson was to be found mostly in Chicago, where his group disbanded again in 1947. During 1948 and 1949, he toured as pianist with Ethel Waters. In 1950, Henderson was hired to assemble a band for the revue "Jazz Train," for which he had written the music. Just before Christmas of that year, he suffered a stroke while leading the Jazz Train Sextet at New York's Cafe Society. That stroke left him partially paralyzed and ended his active career. Though he made several arrangements for Benny Goodman in the early 1950s, he was bedridden for the rest of his life.

In his writings about seminal jazz musicians of the 1920s, Richard Hadlock wrote, "Few men in the annals of jazz have given rise to as disorderly a lot of historical misconceptions as has Fletcher Henderson."[9] His birth and death dates, band personnel for recordings and jobs, dates for important engagements at clubs and dance halls, even his name continue to be disputed by jazz scholars, music historians and members of his family. However, his significance in the development of big band, arranged jazz is clear:

> Fletcher's rightful place in jazz can best be appreciated, perhaps, by regarding him as the focal point in a musical movement that involved a number of important allied contributors. Henderson's was the role of musical catalyst, patriarch, straight man, and sometimes fall guy in the story of the evolution of big-band jazz.[10]

Big band historian George T. Simon wrote that Henderson's early bands "served to start the entire swing band cycle. . . . [S]uccessful swing bands of the future . . . based their styles on Fletcher's."[11] Duke Ellington himself offered that Fletcher Henderson's was the band he attempted to emulate.[12]

In his assessment of those qualities that made Henderson and his music so remarkable, writer Orrin Keepnews observed:

> It cannot be said that Henderson deliberately and specifically set out to create something called "big band jazz". . . . But it can be put pretty much like this: Henderson, by applying his own talents and those of his sidemen to the problem of creating good dance music with the satisfying lift and beat to it, came up with the best and most workable formula for making upwards of ten men *swing* together. Although not necessarily the first and of course not the only leader to use these techniques, he was in a very real sense the trail-blazer.[13]

And, in a tribute to Fletcher Henderson a few weeks after his death, jazz scholar and author Wilder Hobson wrote:

> Fletcher never seemed to be leading a band so much as moderating, quietly, at a very eruptive symposium.[14]

Notes

1. John Hammond, "Salute to Fletch", *Negro Digest,* August, 1951, p. 95. Considerable controversy has surrounded Henderson's name. Leonard Feather in the 1955 edition of his *Encyclopedia of Jazz* gives the first name as "James." That contention is supported by early public school records, documents at Atlanta University, and an article in the *Pittsburgh Courier* (January 25, 1936). However, other Atlanta University records, ASCAP's 1966 listing (though not its 1952 edition), and an interview by Jeff Tarrer with his sister Irma in the 1960s refute that assertion. Since no birth records are extant, the issue remains in dispute.
2. Walter C. Allen, *Hendersonia: The Music of Fletcher Henderson and His Musicians,* monograph published by Walter C. Allen, Highland Park, New Jersey, July 1973, p. 3.
3. *Ibid.,* p. 4.
4. *Ibid.,* p. 17.
5. *Ibid.,* p. 11.
6. Humphrey Lyttleton, "Fletcher Henderson", *The Best of Jazz: Basin Street to Harlem, 1917–1930,* New York: Taplinger Publishing Company, Inc., 1982, pp. 114–115.
7. Hammond, *op. cit.*
8. Leonard Feather, *The Encyclopedia of Jazz,* New York: Bonanza Book, 1960, p. 250.
9. Richard Hadlock, "Fletcher Henderson and Don Redman", *Jazz Masters of the Twenties,* New York: Collier Books, 1965, p. 194.
10. *Ibid.*
11. George T. Simon, *The Big Bands,* rev. ed., New York: Collier Books, 1974, pp. 243–244.
12. Edward Kennedy Ellington, *Music Is My Mistress,* Garden City, New York: Doubleday and Company, Inc., pp. 49–50.
13. Orrin Keepnews, liner notes, "Fletcher Henderson". Jazz Archives Series. Riverside Records, New York, RLP 1055.
14. Wilder Hobson, "Farewell to Fletcher", *Saturday Review,* January 31, 1953, p. 48.

Luther Henderson, Jr.

LUTHER LINCOLN HENDERSON, Jr.

BIRTHDATE/PLACE: March 14, 1919; Kansas City, Missouri.

EDUCATION: College of the City of New York (Mathematics), 1935–38; B.S., Juilliard School of Music, 1942; New York University, 1946–47.

MAJOR INSTRUCTORS/COACHES: Sonoma Talley (Piano); Rudolph Schramm (Shillinger System).

ASSIGNMENTS: Pianist with Leonard Ware, 1939–44; Staff Orchestrator, U.S. Navy School of Music, Washington, D.C., 1944–46.

MUSIC DIRECTOR/CONDUCTOR: Luther Henderson Orchestra; Broadway (partial)—"Ain't Misbehavin'," "Hallelujah, Baby," "Black and Blue," "Jelly's Last Jam"; television (partial)—"The Helen Morgan Story," first and second Victor Borge Specials, "The Bachelor," "The Polly Bergen Show," "Polly and Me," "Summer in New York" (Phil Silvers TV Special), "Carol Lawrence TV Special"; "Eliza" (television movie for Public Television-WNET); night club acts—Lena Horne, Polly Bergen, Carol Haney, Anita Ellis, Carol Lawrence, Nancy Wilson, Teresa Brewer, Dinah Shore, Diahann Carroll, Leslie Uggams, Florence Henderson, Liza Minnelli, Robert Goulet and Carol Lawrence; Lincoln Center Specials—Salutes to Harold Arlen and ASCAP; Movies—"Recess," "The Slams" (with Jim Brown).

MUSIC CONSULTANT/SUPERVISOR/ARRANGER/ORCHESTRATOR/ or COMPOSER: Broadway—"Jelly's Last Jam," "Black and Blue," "Lena Horne: The Lady and Her Music," "Three Black Kings" (ballet by Duke Ellington, commissioned by Dance Theatre of Harlem), "Flower Drum Song," "Do Re Mi," "Funny Girl," "Purlie," "No, No Nanette," "Katherine Dunham's Tropical Revue," "I Had a Ball"; off-Broadway and regional theater—"The All Night Strut," "Jazzbo Brown"; television—"Miss Teen U.S.A. Pageant" (1983), "The Entertainers" (Carol Burnett series), Specials: Gary Moore, Carol Burnett, Ed Sullivan, Andy Williams, Red Skelton, Dean Martin, Bob Hope, Ann-Margret, "Home for the Holidays" (NBC), "Bell Telephone Hour," "Maude," "Hollywood Palace."

AWARDS/HONORS: Winner (with his trio), Amateur Hour Competition, Apollo Theatre (1934); Emmy Award (with Polly Bergen).

IT SEEMS ALTOGETHER FITTING AND NATURAL that Luther Henderson, Jr., should observe his seventy-third birthday on the rehearsal set of

"Jelly's Last Jam." As composer, arranger, and orchestrator for that Broadway-bound musical (which was to win three 1992 Tony awards) based on the life of pianist/composer Jelly Roll Morton, Henderson was simply continuing in his own legendary tradition as conductor and guiding musical force behind countless Broadway and off-Broadway shows (including "Purlie," "Lena Horne: The Lady and Her Music," "Ain't Misbehavin'," "Funny Girl"), television shows (among other assignments, the "Shows" of Bob Hope, Carol Burnett, Ed Sullivan, Andy Williams), recordings (cast album of "Ain't Misbehavin'," and albums featuring Nancy Wilson, Carmen McRae, and Eileen Farrell), and night club shows (including those of Diahann Carroll, Leslie Uggams, Eartha Kitt, and Liza Minnelli). Though his contributions to the music of "Ain't Misbehavin' " (in which he played piano on stage) and "Black and Blue" were prominent, "Jelly's Last Jam" offered an even greater opportunity for him to effect the production: "This time I've been given more room to compose instead of recomposing. Along with Jelly's great tunes, I will offer some of my original music."[1] In addition to his other prodigious talents, Luther Henderson, Jr. is also a composer, having produced scores for musical plays and musical comedies, and written such pop standards as "Ten Good Years," composed with Martin Charnin, and recorded by Nancy Wilson on her "Coconut Grove" album.

Luther Henderson, Jr., was born in Kansas City, Missouri, but to further his own career on the stage, Luther Sr. moved the family to New York City when Luther Jr. was four years old. Luther Jr. began piano study when he was a small child. He recalled: "Music and the piano came natural to me. I never found it a chore and, unlike most child musicians, my parents never had to pull me away from the ball games to practice."[2]

Henderson credits the tutelage of Sonoma Talley and his close friendships with Mercer Ellington and his father, "The Duke," as guiding forces in his pursuit of a musical career:

> Duke Ellington's son, Mercer, and I were really tight buddies. . . . We'd say we were on the same block gang. We were in high school, and I got to go with Mercer every once in a while to hear his father in some clubs. I remember going to a place called Reuben's, where the musicians would come after hours. It was on 132nd or 133rd Street in Harlem, in the basement of a brownstone. Art Tatum, Coleman Hawkins—they would all come in to play and booze it up a little.[3]

Despite the friendship and influence of the Ellingtons, music as a career for Henderson was almost nullified by the results of the New York Regents' examination (required by high school seniors for graduation):

> To the complete amazement of my teachers [at Evander Childs High School in the Bronx], parents and myself, I scored 100% on the mathematical section. . . . This meant that I must enter college and become a math major.[4]

Hence, Henderson enrolled at the City College of New York, concentrating in mathematics. However, after two years, he concluded that, math aptitude notwithstanding, music was the only career for him. With the encouragement of the Ellingtons, he enrolled at the Juilliard School of Music (then known as the Institute of Musical Arts). He received his bachelor of science degree in 1942. At Juilliard, Henderson's training was totally "classical." "When I was there, jazz was not part of the curriculum. . . . And if you were caught playing the blues, you could be expelled."[5]

After Juilliard, Henderson joined the U.S. Navy and was stationed with the all-black musical units at the Great Lakes Naval Training Center at Carbondale, Illinois (near Chicago). At Great Lakes, Henderson's musical colleagues included jazz trumpeters Clark Terry and Jimmy Nottingham; trumpeter, band leader, and composer Gerald Wilson; bassist Major Holley; symphony cellist Donald White; and hundreds of other musicians. (More than 5,000 instrumentalists, and a great number of vocalists, were stationed at Great Lakes during the period 1942–45.) The men of the Great Lakes bands were hardly novices: many had played previously with such esteemed musical organizations as the Carolina Cotton Pickers and the bands of Chick Webb, Fate Marable, Jimmie Lunceford, Charlie Spivak, Duke Ellington, Earl Hines, Fletcher Henderson, Jeter-Pillars, and Jay McShann. Many of those former Navy bandsmen later continued, or embarked upon, careers as jazzmen, studio musicians, and solo and ensemble performers of "classical" music. Others became college professors, college presidents, lawyers, and judges.[6] In addition to performing, Henderson's responsibilities included making arrangements for the bands.

After Great Lakes and the end of the war, Henderson returned to New York and began to make his mark in the world of entertainment. His first significant job was the scoring of a musical, "Beggar's Holiday," in collaboration with Billy Strayhorn.[7] For a while he was pianist with Mercer Ellington. In 1947, he joined forces with Lena Horne as her pianist and music director and continued with her for three years.

Throughout the 1950s and early 1960s, Henderson worked as arranger and conductor on Broadway, adding to his credits such shows as Rodgers and Hammerstein's "Flower Drum Song" and Styne, Comden, and Green's "Do Re Mi." At the same time, Henderson was extremely active in television and recordings. In the mid-1950s, he was contracted by NBC for a series of television specials and regular shows, including "The Bachelor" and the Emmy-award-winning "The Helen Morgan Story," starring Polly Bergen. The association with Bergen included work on several albums, a TV special, and then the regular Polly Bergen Show. Other specials and shows followed, including those with Victor Borge, Phil Silvers, Carol Lawrence, Gary Moore, Dean Martin, and Ann-Margret.

His recording career has been equally broad. He has recorded with his own orchestras, cast albums and compilations of Broadway songs, and (as conductor) the orchestras of Duke Ellington and Andre Kostelanetz. He has participated (as some combination of arranger, orchestrator, performer, advisor) in recordings of such disparate singers as Anna Maria Alberghetti, Tammy Grimes, Theresa Brewer, and Anita Ellis.

In an interview conducted in the 1950's, Luther Henderson, Jr. was asked what he wanted ultimately to do. His reply was, "Just be a good musician. That's all I ever want to be. Just be a good musician."[8] His career speaks persuasively to the realization of his ambition.

Notes

1. Herb Boyd, "Luther Henderson," *EMERGE: Our Voice in Today's World,* June 1992, p. 54.
2. Louis E. Lomax, "The Polly Bergen Show's Musical Director," *Afro-American Magazine Section,* February 1, 1958, p. 1.
3. Kyle Kevorkian, "'Ain't Misbehavin': Luther Henderson On Fats Waller & The Spirit of Stride Piano," *Keyboard,* December 1988, p. 34.
4. *Ibid.*
5. Boyd, *op. cit.*
6. Samuel A. Floyd, Jr., "The Great Lakes Experience: 1942–45." *Black Perspective in Music,* Vol. 3, No. 1, p. 17–19.
7. Lomax, *op. cit.*
8. *Ibid.*

Luther Henderson, III.

LUTHER LINCOLN HENDERSON, III

BIRTHDATE/PLACE: March 19, 1949; New York, New York.

EDUCATION: B. Mus. and M. Mus., Eastman School of Music, 1971, 1973 (Music Education); DMA, The University of Texas at Austin, 1980 (Conducting).

MAJOR INSTRUCTORS: Eugene List and Maria Faini (Piano); William Osseck (Saxophone); Samuel Adler and Warren Benson (Composition); D. Thomas Lee (Band Literature); Rayburn Wright (Arranging, Jazz Studies, and Contemporary Media); Chuck Mangione (Jazz Ensemble); Milfred Fargo (Choral Music); Walter Hendl (Orchestra); Donald Hunsberger, Jonathan Sternberg, A. Clyde Roller, and Cornelius Eberhardt (Conducting).

TEACHING POSITIONS: Director of Instrumental Music, Mount Vernon Jr. High School, Los Angeles, 1973–74; Instructor of Music Theory, Pasadena City College, Pasadena, California, 1974–75; Director of Instrumental Music, Beverly Hills High School, 1974–78; Associate Professor of Music and Humanities and Chairman, Department of Music, Los Angeles Mission College, San Fernando, California, 1981–84; Associate Professor of Music and Humanities, Los Angeles City College, Los Angeles, California, 1984—.

CONDUCTING ASSIGNMENTS: Conductor/Pianist, Freda Payne, 1974; The University of Texas at Austin Symphony Orchestra and Chamber Ensembles, 1978–80; Duke Ellington's "Sophisticated Ladies," Los Angeles Production, 1982; Grammy Awards Television Show (CBS), 1982; Easter Seal Telethon with Pat Boone, 1982; Associate Conductor/Director of Educational Activities, The Foundation for New American Music, Inc. (Beverly Hills, California) and Music Director, the Studio Workshop Institute Orchestra (training arm for minority musicians of The Foundation for New American Music, Inc.), 1982–84; Music Director/Conductor, Southeast Symphony Orchestra (Los Angeles), 1987–89.

GUEST CONDUCTOR: Southeast Symphony Orchestra, 1980, 1983, 1985, 1987; The Merv Griffin Show, 1982, 1985, 1986; The Dance Theatre of Harlem—Los Angeles Olympic Arts Festival and company's three-week performance in London (London Gala Orchestra), Brooklyn (members of the Brooklyn Philharmonic Orchestra), and San Diego, California (members of the San Diego Symphony), 1984.

243

LUTHER HENDERSON III'S ADMIRATION for his father, Luther, Jr., is tremendous. As "Luther the Younger" recalls:

> During the first seven years of my life, my father . . . would play the piano for me. He would compose songs for me and I enjoyed listening to his music-making. He would take me to his rehearsals with various personalities.[1]

On one such outing, father and son went to see Arturo Toscanini conduct the NBC Symphony Orchestra. The trip made a lasting impression on Luther III, for it was at that moment that he made a life's career choice—before he was eight years old. "I'll be a conductor," announced the young one.

When his parents divorced in 1957, young Henderson was sent to Los Angeles to live with his maternal grandmother. An unused piano in the home contributed to the decision that Luther III would begin taking piano lessons and that a minimum of thirty minutes practice per day would be required. Shortly thereafter, he made his solo debut at a cub scout meeting. "It was a success."

After six months, mother and brother followed Luther III to Los Angeles. For the next decade, his father visited regularly from New York City, or father and son visited together in the East. Musical support came from his grandmother, mother, and father, as well as junior and senior high school instructors Peter Gregg, Donald Simpson, and Albert J. McNeil (the black founder-director of the Albert McNeil Jubilee Singers, who was then an instructor at Susan Miller Dorsey High School). According to Henderson, it was McNeil who made him aware of such black musical achievers as composers William Dawson and William Grant Still and conductors Dean Dixon and Henry Lewis (also a Dorsey High School graduate). It was Simpson, currently Henderson's colleague on the Los Angeles City College music faculty, who gave him the opportunity to join the Dorsey High School band as a trumpet player. All encouraged him as a composer.[2]

Upon graduation from high school, Henderson was accepted by Eugene List as a piano student at the Eastman School of Music. Because of the positive influence of Everett Gates, chairman of the Music Education Department, he changed his major from piano to music education:

> The Eastman philosophy of music education was one of "can do."
> Music education majors were expected to be outstanding performers
> on their instruments as well as excellent teachers. Gates opened the
> doors of the entire school to me. I was taught all the orchestral
> instruments by the major professors of those instruments . . . My years
> at Eastman were some of the best educational experiences of my life.[3]

Henderson studied at the Eastman School of Music from 1967 to
1973, earning both the B.Mus. and M.Mus degrees in Music
Education. During the summers, he shared his talents with the Manna
House Workshop in New York City (1971) and the Arts Council's Free
Street Theatre in Chicago (1972). One of his first professional
assignments after graduation was music director/pianist for singer
Freda Payne.

Henderson returned to Los Angeles in 1973 to work for five years
as a music educator for secondary schools in Los Angeles and Beverly
Hills. His interest in developing the skills of less-advantaged
inner-city students remained consistent and strong. During the
academic year 1974–75, he doubled as a music theory instructor at
Pasadena City College.

Henderson enrolled at The University of Texas at Austin in 1978
to pursue the Doctor of Musical Arts degree with a major in
conducting—the next step toward fulfilling his childhood dream of
becoming a recognized and respected conductor. While enrolled, he
guest conducted the University's symphony orchestra and various
chamber ensembles.

He received the DMA in 1980, the same year that he accompanied
(as pianist) singers Barry White, Patti LaBelle, Rocky Robbins, and
The Temptations in a Brotherhood Crusade concert in Los Angeles.
During his final year at the University, he participated as pianist in
three "Monster Concerts" honoring the 150th anniversary of Louis
Moreau Gottschalk and the 126th year of Steinway and Sons, with
his former piano instructor Eugene List as artistic director. With
performances at the White House, Carnegie Hall, and Royce Hall
(University of California at Los Angeles), these concerts featured "40
pianists, 400 fingers, 10 pianos, and 880 piano keys."

The 1980s proved to be rewarding years, bringing him closer to
realizing another lifelong ambition. Between 1981 and 1984,
Henderson served as associate professor of music and humanities and
chairman of the Department of Music at Los Angeles Mission College

in San Fernando, California. In 1984 he assumed the duties of associate professor of music and humanities at Los Angeles City College, a position he currently holds.

His abilities were beginning to attract a sizeable following. One interested person desirous of "spreading the word" was Carla Simone who did a feature article ("Henderson Knows the Score") for *Right On!* in May 1984. As Simone indicated, "Be it finger popping, foot stomping, or an easy jazz melody, Luther Henderson III can conduct them all."[4] During the course of the interview, Simone inquired of Henderson's future plans. Answered Henderson:

> My main concern is putting together a musical career. Ultimately, I want to have the opportunity to write music for motion pictures, do arranging for records and conduct a major orchestra.[5]

He first guest conducted the Southeast Symphony Orchestra of Los Angeles in 1980, with additional opportunities in 1983, 1985, and 1987 (the year he was selected to serve as the organization's music director and conductor). On several occasions, he appeared as the orchestra's guest pianist as well.

As leader of the Southeast Orchestra, his commitment to the music of black composers was readily evident, as was his commitment to promoting black artists as soloists in various genres. He featured such artists as vocalists Nancy Wilson, Brenda Wimberly, and John Patton; saxophonist Grover Washington; flutists Hubert Laws and Kent Jordan; trumpeter Marlon Jordan; and pianist Althea Waites. His concern for emerging black musical talent was apparent as he featured orchestral "Spotlights on Youth" (violinist Ronald Clark, cellist Margot McCoy, sopranos Felicia Ford and Sheila Tate, and bass-baritone Michael Smith).

The Southeast Orchestra, organized in 1948, "grew out of a predominantly minority neighborhood" and presents all concerts (five per season) free of charge to the public. The orchestra is committed to "elevating the cultural consciousness of the community by making the arts accessible to all." It is worth noting that the Southeast Orchestra was once conducted by the late Leon Everette Thompson,* one of Henderson's idols.[6]

When the Beverly Hills–based New American Orchestra (NAO) wrestled with complaints about the shortage of minority musicians,

Luther Henderson III offered a workable solution. He was well aware of Dr. Thompson's work with the New York Philharmonic (1970–1980), as a result of his doctoral dissertation, "The Role of the New York Philharmonic's Director of Educational Activities: A New Dimension for the Conductor."

As NAO's music director and co-founder Jack Elliott recalled,

> Luther showed me the treatise he'd written. . . . We brainstormed for a long while and Luther saw that although we didn't have the New York Philharmonic's budget, what we were doing was more relevant, because the NAO was performing music most people can readily understand.

This young orchestra (founded in 1979) specializes in a wide range of musics:

> pop, jazz, fusion, Brazilian, movie scores, [and] modern classical compositions. . . . But [t]here was no program offering qualified musicians the necessary workshop experience in the studio environment, and no clearing house to provide contractors with lists of suitable minority musicians.[7]

When Luther III visited Elliott's office, his purpose was to convince him to consider performing one of his compositions. The conversation instead led to his being invited to serve as director of educational activities for the Foundation for New American Music and associate conductor of the Foundation's performing arm, the New American Orchestra. Of his service there from 1982 to 1984, Henderson wrote:

> In these capacities, I developed and implemented the Foundation's educational program—The Studio Workshop Institute. The SWI provided training and experience to qualified professional level minority musicians who were actively pursuing careers in the motion picture, television, and recording industries in Los Angeles. This program placed SWI members in motion picture scoring sessions and the 1984 Grammy Award Show Orchestra. Musicians were auditioned by a selected Educational Committee and rehearsed at the KABC-TV Studios, often with contractors from major motion picture studios in attendance.[8]

Jazz journalist Leonard Feather stated, "The venture with Luther Henderson is a commendable attempt to right some wrongs in the generally cynical and cliquish Hollywood music industry."[9] Unfortunately, the program was suspended in 1984 due to budget restraints.

Other gratifying conducting experiences in the decade of the 1980s included the Los Angeles production of Duke Ellington's "Sophisticated Ladies." The list of guest conducting appearances included the Grammy Awards Television Show (CBS), the Tonight Show (NBC), the Merv Griffin Show, and an Easter Seal Telethon with singer Pat Boone. He was also orchestrator/arranger for several Emmy Awards television productions and performed as music director, pianist, and arranger for the Bi-Lingual Foundation of the Arts production "Wanted: Experienced Operators," staged at the Inner-City Cultural Center in Los Angeles. Not to be forgotten is Henderson's 1984 conducting tour with Dance Theatre of Harlem in Los Angeles and San Diego, California; Brooklyn, New York; and three weeks of performances in London.

Between 1985 and 1987, the energetic Henderson also conducted the Cathedral Choir at the First African Methodist Episcopal Church of Los Angeles. Moving into the 1990s, he remains active as a free-lance pianist, arranger, and conductor in the Los Angeles area. He continues to lead the wind ensemble at Los Angeles City College. His stated objective remained "a challenging and responsible position as a Conductor/Music Director of Professional and University Orchestras," though we are certain that the desire to "write music for motion pictures and do arrangements for records" still exist.

Press Comments

"Henderson proved himself throughout the evening to be a musician of exceptional talent and perception, and further, a conductor of the first rank."

Los Angeles Sentinel

"To the orchestra and performers at the Shubert Theater, Henderson brings style, experience and a deep-seated knowledge of music."

The Valley Experience

Notes

1. Correspondence, Luther Henderson, III/Handy, December 18, 1988.
2. *Ibid.*
3. *Ibid.*
4. Carla Simone, "Henderson Knows the Score," *Right On!,* May 1984, pp. 21–23, 62.
5. *Ibid.,* p. 62.
6. Program Bulletins, 1987–88, The Southeast Symphony Association.
7. Leonard Feather, "New American Orchestra—Past and Future Struggles," *Los Angeles Times/Calendar,* April 22, 1984, p. 80.
8. Correspondence, *op. cit.*
9. Feather, *op. cit.*

Earl ("Fatha") Hines, performing at the District Building, Washington, D.C., 1979. (Copyright, *Washington Post,* Reprinted by permission of D.C. Public Library.)

EARL (KENNETH) "FATHA" HINES

BIRTHDATE/PLACE: December 28, 1905; Duquesne, Pennsylvania.
DEATH DATE/PLACE: April 22, 1983; Oakland, California.
EDUCATION: Schenley High School (Pittsburgh).
MAJOR INSTRUCTOR: Emma D. Young (Piano).
CAREER HIGHLIGHTS: church organist; pianist with bands led by Lois Deppe (Pittsburgh), Louis Armstrong, Sammy Stewart, Erskine Tate, Carroll Dickerson, and Jimmy Noone (Chicago); led Earl Hines Big Band (1928–48); piano soloist/leader, small combos; United States Department of State tour to Russia, 1966; television appearances—Johnny Carson, Merv Griffin, Mike Douglas, and David Frost Shows; important venues—Grand Terrace (Chicago); Carnegie Hall, Town Hall, Avery Fisher Hall (New York); Wolf Trap (Virginia), 1976; White House (Duke Ellington's Seventieth Birthday Party), 1976.
HONORS: Esquire Award, 1944; Down Beat's International Critics' Hall of Fame, 1966; Newport Hall of Fame, 1975.

EARL HINES LED HIS OWN BIG BAND for two decades (1928–48). Home base was Chicago's Grand Terrace Ballroom, a club that granted him a lifetime contract. His reputation as a band leader was built there, just as Duke Ellington's was built at New York City's Cotton Club. Hines was one of the rare breed of jazz pianists/leaders who operated successfully almost entirely outside of the Big Apple.[1]

He was born in Duquesne, Pennsylvania, then a suburb of Pittsburgh. His father was a crane foreman on the coal docks, as well as a cornetist and leader of a brass band. His stepmother was an organist. Before reaching his teens, the younger Hines's musical roles included church organist and piano recitalist. He also competed successfully in various local competitions. Though he early aspired to become a concert pianist, exposure to such pioneers as Eubie Blake, Noble Sissle, and Charles "Luckey" Roberts (frequent visitors at his aunt's residence) prompted movement in another direction.

Hines's designation as a leader was determined while he was still in high school. During these years he was in charge of most school

251

and community entertainment activities and was generally available as a "more than adequate" pianist. Such abilities were detected by baritone Lois Deppe, himself trained as a concert artist.

Deppe selected Hines to be his accompanist when Hines was only seventeen. As Deppe recalled for British jazz critic and author Stanley Dance (and Hines's biographer):

> [Prior to September 1918], I'd heard a couple of kids playing at a rent party. They were in bloomer pants, like they wore in those days. A little boy named Harry Williams was beating on the drums, and the other was a tall, lanky kid from Duquesne named Hines. Those two, with Emmett Jordan on violin, were known as Earl Hines's Melody Lads.[2]

Continuing, Deppe recalled:

> In 1921, Earl and I created a little excitement as a duo at Loew's Vaudeville Theatre. We were going over like a house on fire there. . . . He was very exuberant about making his first stage appearances, . . .[3]

When in 1922 Deppe formed a big band (Deppe and His Serenaders), Hines was the designated pianist. He toured with the band, appeared on radio, and recorded for Gennett. But the experience was short-lived. For the next few years, Hines played solo in several different Pittsburgh nightclubs and fronted ensembles of varying size.

Hines left Pittsburgh in 1924. Arriving in Chicago, he secured his first job playing with a small group at the Elite No. 2 nightclub. He soon began working with such established bands as Sammy Stewart's, Erskine Tate's, and Carroll Dickerson's. With Dickerson's Syncopators, Hines completed a forty-two–week tour on the Pantages Circuit.

The Dickerson band, including trumpeter Louis Armstrong, was led by Hines in 1927. He then worked with Louis Armstrong's Stompers at the Sunset Cafe. When Armstrong returned to Dickerson's band, Hines joined Jimmie Noone's band at the Apex Club. According to Richard Hadlock, Hines began rehearsing with a group of friends in the fall of 1928, with no plans or contracts for performance. There was only group satisfaction and establishment of a library. When Hines was called on to lead a band at the Grand

Terrace Ballroom, upon the recommendation of band leader Lucky Millender, he gathered together his rehearsal group.

> Earl's knowledge of showmanship, staging, and musical directing put the fast-moving Grand Terrace show on a par with the reviews at the Sunset and the Savoy.[4]

On Hines's twenty-third birthday, December 28, 1928, he introduced his own band at the Grand Terrace. Hines recalled:

> It got so the Grand Terrace was no Grand Terrace without us, because we were there so long [ten years]. When people came to Chicago and the club was mentioned, they naturally thought of us.[5]

The band toured and broadcast from the Grand Terrace, first on a local station, then on NBC to New York, California, and Canada. As biographer Dance wrote:

> Chicago, . . . was an influential and powerful broadcasting centre, and radio was a far stronger force than records in the '30s, stronger even than television today so far as music was concerned.[6]

The presence of emerging young bop musicians in his 1940–43 band, and Hines's receptiveness to the idea of broadening the band's style, established it as an "important early chapter in the story of modern jazz." The Hines band of this period is considered by many as "a bop incubator." The harmonic and rhythmic innovations were brought on by the presence of such sidemen as John Birks "Dizzy" Gillespie, William "Billy" Eckstine, Albert "Budd" Johnson, Charlie "Yardbird" Parker, and singer/second pianist Sarah Vaughan. Unfortunately, the American Federation of Musicians' temporary ban on recordings at just that time prevented these innovations from being documented.

The Hines band continued long after its Grand Terrace residency, touring widely and completing residences in other cities throughout the country. In 1943 he augmented his band with an all-woman string section: Lavella Tullas, harp; Lucille Dixon, bass; Roxanna Lucas, guitar; Ardine Loving, cello; and Angel Creasy, Helen Way, Sylvia Medford, and Lolita Valdez, violins. The experiment was of short duration. The venture, of course, grew out of an anomalous ambition he had nurtured a long time: to front a huge stage orchestra built along Paul Whiteman lines, complete with a string section. By mid-1944, Earl was back to seventeen men.[7]

In late 1944, more problems were apparent. According to jazz historian Hadlock:

Most of the trouble, or course, came from Earl himself. He was not a good businessman and always seemed to make the right move at the wrong time. . . . Though its [the band's] fortunes rose and fell on the waves of mismanagement, the Hines band [throughout its history] was still a musically rewarding outfit to hear.[8]

Having given up the idea of leading a big band, Hines joined Armstrong's All-Star Sextet, remaining until 1951. "It was not a good musical solution to Earl's dilemma, but the pay was good and the headaches few."[9]

Leading small groups, he then began touring widely throughout the world, including Europe, Japan, Australia, Latin America, and Russia. He settled in Oakland, California in 1960 and continued to perform as a solo pianist and leader until his death in 1983.

Lamenting Hines's absence from the big band scene, former band member Wallace Bishop remarked in the mid 1970s:

I think Earl should have a big band again, because he really knows how to direct a band and get things out of men. He's a good leader. He was head of the band, but he never said, "I'm the boss!" He'd tell you what you had to do, and he'd be polite about it, and everybody would cooperate. He's the greatest as a leader and a pianist. . . . Earl's the swingingest cat I know.[10]

It is often suggested that Hines's style of piano playing was strongly influenced by Louis Armstrong's trumpet playing—horn-like phrases, with an eccentric bass playing between the beats. Pianist Teddy Wilson said that "You could write backgrounds behind him just as you would for a trumpet or tenor sax."[11] Encyclopedist, critic, and record producer Leonard Feather wrote:

After the ragtime archetypes and the stride pioneers, the next giant, emphatic both in his influence and in the vigorous, flamboyantly

rhythmic nature of his approach, was Earl "Fatha" Hines. . . . Though
"The Houdini of jazz piano" might have been a more fitting name,
he was often called "the trumpet style pianist," because the octaves on
single note lines in the right hand, in contrast with the emphasis on
chords that had predominated among the ragtimers and early stride
pianist, lent the solos a bright and brassy quality that brought to
mind the impact of a horn.[12]

Of his band, Feather wrote, "Earl Hines, from 1928 until 1948,
led a band that was important for the gifted sidemen that it produced
rather than for any individual style." In addition to the sidemen
previously mentioned, the Hines roster included Benny Carter,
Shirley Clay, Ray Nance, Trummy Young, Jimmy Mundy, Herb
Jeffries, Benny Green, Walter Fuller, and Omer Simeon.[13]

Notes

1. Richard Hadlock, *Jazz Masters of the Twenties,* New York: Collier Books, 1965, p. 50.
2. Stanley Dance, *The World of Earl Hines,* New York: Scribner, 1977, p. 132.
3. *Ibid.,* p. 134.
4. Hadlock, *op. cit.,* pp. 59, 62.
5. Dance, *op. cit.,* p. 72.
6. *Ibid.,* p. 2.
7. Hadlock, *op. cit.,* p. 68.
8. *Ibid.,* p. 65.
9. *Ibid.,* p. 70.
10. Dance, *op. cit.,* p. 176.
11. *Ibid.,* p. 184.
12. Leonard Feather, *The Book of Jazz: From Then Till Now,* New York: Dell Publishing Co., Inc. (rev. ed.), 1976, pp. 74–75.
13. *Ibid.,* p. 199.

Darrold Victor Hunt

DARROLD VICTOR HUNT

BIRTHDATE/PLACE: June 29, 1941; New Bedford, Massachusetts.
EDUCATION: New Bedford Institute of Technology, Southeastern Massachusetts University (Electrical Engineering), 1959–63; Conducting Fellow, Berkshire Music Center (Tanglewood), 1963; B.S., the Juilliard School of Music (Choral Conducting), 1970; M.S., the Juilliard School of Music (Choral Conducting), 1971; Conducting Fellow, National Orchestral Association, 1969–72; Conducting Fellow, Aspen Music Festival, 1973; Courses at the University of California at Los Angeles (UCLA) and Columbia University.
MAJOR INSTRUCTORS: Abraham Kaplan (Choral Conducting); Leon Barzin and Jorge Mester (Orchestral Conducting).
MAJOR APPOINTMENTS: Conductor of Men's Glee Club, New Bedford Institute of Technology, 1961–63; chorister, Norman Luboff Choir, 1963; Instructor, Cooperative College Center in Mt. Vernon, State University of New York, 1969–70; music director and conductor, Harlem Youth Philharmonic Orchestra, 1970; instructor/assistant professor of aesthetics and philosophy, Brooklyn College School of Contemporary Studies, 1971–73; apprentice conductor (1973–74)/assistant conductor (1974–77), Baltimore Symphony Orchestra; music director and conductor, Brooklyn College (CUNY) School of Performing Arts Symphony Orchestra, 1977–80; *FOUNDER/MUSIC DIRECTOR and CONDUCTOR,* Urban Philharmonic Society, 1970—; Washington Philharmonic Orchestra, New Columbia Concert Series, Young Virtuosi (Urban Philharmonic Society), 1978—.
GUEST CONDUCTOR: New York Choral Society, New York Housing Authority Orchestra, National and Detroit Symphony Orchestras.

ESTABLISHMENT OF THE URBAN PHILHARMONIC represented the fulfillment of Darrold Hunt's dreams. Hunt firmly believed that it was possible "to create a full[y] professional orchestra which would perform in minority and other underserved communities."[1] Founded in 1970, the fully integrated organization was based in New York City for the first seven years, performing at various locales in Harlem, Town Hall, the Academy of Arts and Letters, St. Peter's Church, and Lincoln Center, as well as the Lyric Theatre and Johns Hopkins Plaza in Baltimore, Maryland.

But Washington, D.C. seemed to be a particularly attractive place for the kind of orchestra that Hunt envisioned. In 1977, the visionary and energetic conductor viewed the District of Columbia as "a cultural boom town." Said Hunt:

> There's cultural excitement here, and what the Urban [Philharmonic] can do is involve that part of the community that hasn't been involved in the excitement of the arts—open it up, bring the black community out into the mainstream.[2]

Bringing Blacks into the cultural mainstream was at the same time a concern of Roger L. Stevens, Chairman of the Kennedy Center for the Performing Arts in Washington, D.C. An eighteen-member commission was established to investigate the situation and propose remedies. The timing was right for both Kennedy Center's Commission on Cultural Diversity and dreamer Darrold Hunt.

One of the Commissions's first efforts was to present the Urban Philharmonic. With funds from the Kennedy Center and a small grant from the D.C. Commission on the Arts and Humanities, Hunt and his Urban Philharmonic made their D.C. debut on May 7, 1978. Trans World Airlines (TWA) was the orchestra's first D.C. sponsor, supplying funds to transport five hundred school children to the concert at the Kennedy Center.

Wrote *Washington Post* music critic Paul Hume of the orchestra "organized to give special emphasis to black players in symphony orchestras":

> In Beethoven's Coriolan Overture, the Mozart A Major Violin Concerto, and the Symphony No. 8 by Dvorak, the orchestra demonstrated a highly professional ensemble. . . . The program also was enhanced by two works by black composers, the familiar "Night Music" by Howard Swanson . . . and "Lyric for Strings" . . . by George Walker.[3]

Soloist for the Mozart Concerto was the New York-based black violinist Sanford Allen, formerly of the New York Philharmonic. Hume wrote of the audience, "highly enthusiastic," but disappointing in size. "By the next concert perhaps the word will have spread."[4]

Critic Irving Lowens of the now defunct *Washington Star* wrote of the group's Washington debut:

If you were to use excellence as the yardstick of success, the Urban Philharmonic had a most successful local debut. It is to be hoped that the orchestra will indeed succeed in finding a welcome and a home here; it would be an adornment to the cultural life of any city in the country.[5]

Hunt indicated that he was settling into the capital "for a long-haul project—to make an orchestra called the Urban Philharmonic a basic, permanent fixture of Washington's musical life." He added:

We have our track record in terms of performances and they have all been professional performances and quality performances. . . . We won't have the kind of sound that you get from a resident orchestra that sits and plays together for years, but we have a sound that is professional and exciting.[6]

The May 1978 concert was both the beginning and the end of the Urban Philharmonic/Kennedy Center relationship. Though the projected residency of Hunt's orchestra did not materialize, Hunt's dream orchestra continued. The name of Leonard Bernstein as sponsor and that of Billy Taylor as music advisor appeared on the Society's stationery. Support came from The Juilliard String Quartet in the form of a black-tie reception at the Corcoran Gallery. Wrote Joseph McLellan of *The Washington Post:*

The Juilliard, one of the world's most prestigious organizations . . . played for the benefit of the Urban Philharmonic Orchestra, a worthy group that has been struggling slowly uphill for 10 years and seems about to make a breakthrough with a summer program at Carter Barron (under auspices of the Department of Interior). . . . [L]ast night's crowd had a sprinkling of congressmen and sub-cabinet government officials, all obviously enjoying the concert and reception.[7]

Sponsor Leonard Bernstein, unable to attend the benefit performance, sent a telegram: "My heart is with you all."

A name-change took place, resulting from Hunt's desire both to give the orchestra a clearer community identity and to distinguish the organization from the various programs it would begin sponsoring. In October 1984, a lengthy article in *The Washington Post* carried the title "Happy Baton—Washington Conductor Darrold Hunt, Using Music for His Community." The article served to inform *The Washington Post* readership of the D.C. residency of a persistent maestro, citing both current and previous activities and announcing a performance by Hunt's newly renamed Washington Philharmonic Orchestra.

The Washington Philharmonic Orchestra, formerly the Urban Philharmonic, had become one of three programs under the Urban Philharmonic Society (UPS) rubric. Other programs of the Society now included the New Columbia Concert Series (featuring some of the nation's gifted but underexposed solo recitalists) and the Young Virtuosi (an ensemble of highly gifted, young pre-professional composer-performers, bringing concerts to the elderly in all parts of the District).

The *Post* article recalled Hunt's professional involvements of a few years earlier and gave a personal and professional status report on Hunt in 1984. The writer reported:

> Darrold Hunt has no steady income; he lives as a permanent guest in a home in Logan Circle, which is part of his base of operations. He eats a lot of his lunches free at the Metropolitan AME Church on M Street NW, another base of operations. His small personal expenses are covered by occasional checks from his brother Errol [a Rhode Island minister and President of the Providence Urban League]. . . .[8]

The writer indicated however that Hunt seemed to be "one of the happiest people in Washington," for despite any personal deprivations, the idea of rooting "community-based programs of classical music" in the nation's capital was catching on. Then forty-three-year-old Darrold Hunt believed his dream was progressively moving into the realm of actuality; his orchestra was "drawing audiences from Washington and the suburbs." Said Hunt:

> There is excitement in bringing people together for music and to celebrate. . . . There's no salary, but this is obviously more than a full-time job. . . . I have my personal agenda . . . I want to conduct an orchestra of people that I know and have grown with over the years. . . . There is a great deal to be said for staying, teaching and growing in one place, so that the community sees you as a vital part of itself. You don't become plastic.[9]

Washington Post critic McLellan raised a valid question:

> In 1977, Darrold Hunt seemed to have everything he could want. He
> had been for four years the assistant conductor of the Baltimore
> Symphony Orchestra. And he was an associate professor of music at
> Brooklyn College, where he had his own orchestra to conduct. . . .
> What happened? In 1977, Hunt decided to give up a career and
> pursue a dream.[10]

In his own assessment however, Hunt did not consider that he had
sacrificed one at the expense of the other. Only by reviewing his past
can one begin to understand Darrold Hunt, in pursuit of both career
and a dream.

Hunt's association with music began with membership in the
family singing group "The Rays," consisting of his late father
Edward (guitarist, pianist, and singer), his mother and three
brothers. The Rays, specializing in the singing of spirituals, toured
throughout New England during the 1940s and 1950s. With a
piano and clarinet background and a beautiful tenor voice, Hunt
began conducting various choirs while still enrolled in high school.
But only after several years of studying electrical engineering did he
elect to make music his life's career. While at the New Bedford
Institute of Technology/Southeastern Massachusetts University, he
directed a men's glee club.

Hunt was selected as a conducting fellow at the Berkshire Music
Center at Tanglewood in 1963 and subsequently toured with the
Norman Luboff Choir. Settling briefly on the West Coast, he studied
and worked with such choral luminaries as Gregg Smith and Roger
Wagner.

Hunt entered The Juilliard School in 1965 and received the B.S.
degree in 1970 and M.S. degree in 1971, both in choral conducting.
Concurrently, he was a conducting fellow with the National
Orchestral Association, working under the guidance of maestro Leon
Barzin.

Between the years 1970 and 1972, Hunt (then based in New York
City) was conductor of the Harlem Youth Philharmonic Society,
conductor of the Afro-American Singing Theater at City Center, and
music director of both the North Shore Unitarian Society Church on
Long Island and the Harlem Chorale.

During the Summer of 1973, Hunt received a conducting
fellowship to the Aspen Music Festival. He joined the conducting
staff of the Baltimore Symphony Orchestra for the 1973–74 season.
Following one season as apprentice conductor, Hunt was elevated to

the position of assistant conductor. There he remained through the 1976–77 season. Hunt acquired professional academic experience first at the Brooklyn College School of Contemporary Studies where he taught aesthetics and philosophy (1971–73), then as associate professor and music director of the orchestra at the Brooklyn College School of Performing Arts (1977–80).

In 1980 Hunt completed the move to the District of Columbia, a move that he made only partially in 1977. Explained Hunt:

> I knew it would take as much work to pursue traditional conducting slots politically as it would to direct the kind of society the Philharmonic now is, . . . I had to ask myself where my commitment was ultimately. The only answer I could come up with was that success without vision is degenerate. I have seen it from the inside and that kind of success is not the life I am going to live.[11]

The D.C. Community Humanities Council recognized Hunt's musical insights when it invited him in February 1985 to join the Council for a term of three years. The following year he was asked to serve as a panelist for the D.C. Arts Council. During fiscal year 1987, Hunt and his Urban Philharmonic Society received their first grant from the National Endowment for the Arts, the same year that Hunt guest conducted the Detroit Symphony.

A special grant from the D.C. Commission on the Arts and Humanities enabled the Society to present three admission-free concerts during the month of August 1988 in the nation's capital. Designated "A Summer Music Festival," two concerts featured the strings of the Washington Philharmonic and a third the Wesley Boyd Gospel Ensemble and the Young Virtuosi. The well-established presenting organization District Curators sponsored Hunt and nine musicians from the Washington Philharmonic in Igor Stravinsky's "L'Histoire du Soldat" during "Add Arts '88."

In July 1991, an informative article appeared in the D.C. monthly "free" publication *In Towner*. "Urban Philharmonic On the Right Track" alerted the city to the following:

> Most musicians who also administrate, publicize and fund raise burn out in a few years. Darrold Hunt almost did. For a few years, he closed shop at the Urban Philharmonic Society, shelving his dream of a community-based orchestra . . . But the force of idealism—not to mention Haydn, Mozart and Brahms—proved a powerful match for

Hunt's fatigue, summoning him back to the podium and to a one-person office on F Street.[12]

These were the lead sentences of an article by Marion S. Jacobson, a review of a June 9 appearance of the Washington Philharmonic concert at the National City Christian Church, a downtown edifice. In terms of Hunt's performance, Jacobson wrote, "Everything he does seems to be a high-wire act, and the June 9 concert was no exception."[13]

At the commencement of the century's last decade, Hunt and the Urban Philharmonic Society continued to arouse the interests of the D.C. community and the local press, as well as the continued support of People's Congregational and Metropolitan African Methodist Episcopal Churches. Scattered concerts continued, featuring music from the standard orchestral repertoire as well as music of black composers. Consistent with the mission and commitment of the Urban Philharmonic Society (and its conductor), the roster of featured soloists included emerging black talents, in addition to major artists. Universally acknowledged is Hunt's ability as an impresario, always with "an eye for young talent on the rise." Hunt would find a way to get them before the public and to sustain his ambitions as a productive music director and conductor.

Still recognizing the importance of Hunt's artistic efforts and vision, *The Washington Post* covered a late May 1992 Washington Philharmonic Orchestra concert at St. Paul's Lutheran Church and reviewed the event under the heading "Philharmonic: Undiscovered Treasure." Wrote music critic Mark Carrington:

> The truth is, conductor Darrold Hunt has hit a seam of gold with the Washington Philharmonic Orchestra. He has an ensemble that plays splendidly together, that ekes beauty out of the familiar, and does it all on the strength of one rehearsal because that's all it can afford. . . . The Washington Philharmonic might be one of the capital's best secrets. On the strength of this performance, let's hope it's not a secret for much longer.[14]

The Urban Philharmonic Society's 1992–93 season brochure, projected five orchestral concerts by the Washington Philharmonic and eight events in the New Columbia Concert Series. A Paul Robeson Vocal Competition had been added and the Washington Philharmonic Chorale had been created. The latter ensemble made its debut in a performance of Beethoven's "Mass in C" at the orchestra's May 14, 1993 concert.

Press Comments

"{Hunt,} a conductor of restraint who shapes the air as a sculptor shapes his marble, coaxed the maximum out of the Baltimore Symphony Orchestra and the evening emerged as an intense musical experience."

Baltimore Sun

"Hunt led his players throughout the afternoon with solid musicianly taste, animated by a fine vitality and keen feeling for the lyric line."

Washington Post

"Beethoven's Seventh Symphony sprang from the baton of Darrold Hunt yesterday afternoon as fresh and new as it must have been at its first performance 172 years ago. . . . {The Urban Philharmonic} engaged{d} in intense, precise communication at a level of excellence."

Washington Post

"Hunt's interpretation gave the music a classic poise without distracting from a special air of spontaneity—almost as though the symphony were happening for the first time."

Washington Post

"Hunt's forceful moves proved both visually and aurally pleasing."

Washington Post

Notes

1. 1986 biographical statement, prepared by the Urban Philharmonic Society.
2. Joseph McLellan, "The Making of a Musical Fixture," *Washington Post,* May 7, 1978, p. L8.
3. Paul Hume, "Urban Philharmonic," *Washington Post,* May 8, 1978, p. B 13.
4. *Ibid.*
5. Irving Lowens, "Urban Philharmonic Does Itself Proud," *Washington Star,* May 9, 1978, p. D4.
6. Joseph McLellan, *op. cit.,* pp. L1, L8.

7. ———, "Black Tie and Brahms," *Washington Post,* March 26, 1981, p. D6.

8. ———, *"Happy Baton—Washington Conductor Darrold Hunt, Using Music for His Community,"* Washington Post, October 28, 1984, p. H1.

9. *Ibid.,* p. H1, 8.

10. *Ibid.,* p. H1.

11. *Ibid.,* p. H8.

12. Marion S. Jacobson, "Urban Philharmonic On the Right Track," *In Towner,* July 1991, p. 16.

13. *Ibid.*

14. Mark Carrington, "Philharmonic: Undiscovered Treasure," *Washington Post,* May 23, 1992, p. D3.

Leroy E. Hurte

LEROY E. HURTE

BIRTHDATE/PLACE: May 2, 1915; Muskogee, Oklahoma.
EDUCATION: Wilkins Piano Academy, Los Angeles City College, University of Southern California, University of California at Los Angeles, Juilliard School of Music, Tanglewood Music Workshop, National Orchestral Association, New York.
MAJOR INSTRUCTORS: Lucien Calliet, Darryl Calker, Leon Barzin, Leonard Bernstein, Felix Prohuska, Seymour Lipkin, and Everett Lee.
MAJOR APPOINTMENTS: Music Director, Angel Symphony Society (Los Angeles) 1957–1967; Music Director and Business Manager, Inglewood Philharmonic Association (Inglewood, California), 1972–81; Music Director and Conductor, Inglewood Philharmonic Association, 1981—.
GUEST CONDUCTOR: Los Angeles Community Orchestra, Southeast Symphony, California Junior Symphony, Kings County Symphony, and Fresno Philharmonic.
BOARD MEMBERSHIP: Young Audiences and Association of California Symphony Orchestras.
AWARD/HONORS: Rotary Club Achievement Award, Ten Thousand Men of Achievement, Outstanding Achievement in Music Awards—City of Los Angeles and Los Angeles County, National Association of Media Women, Inc.

AS A YOUNGSTER, LEROY HURTE DEVELOPED a love for the music of Beethoven and took advantage of every opportunity to listen to symphonic music. The sound of an orchestra was most fascinating, as he sat transfixed before the family radio, listening to the local classical music station.

Though his parents had little understanding of their son's interest, they made certain that he received piano lessons from the neighborhood piano teacher. Regular study and hours of practice continued through high school. With an interest in orchestration and conducting (which he perceived as the art of transmitting to an audience that which exists on the printed page), Hurte engaged in additional study on both the East and West Coasts. Using those skills that he had acquired was his next objective.

Hurte's career direction developed from his involvement with the Hollywood film industry:

> As part of the vocal quartet "The Four Blackbirds," I performed in Irving Cobb's "Paducah Plantation," played at Frank Sebastian's Cotton Club, and appeared with Bing Crosby and Eddie Cantor. . . . However, our appearance on "California Melodies," a local radio program, was of special importance to me. For the first time, we performed with a symphonic orchestra. The experience produced in me an overwhelming desire to become a classical conductor.[1]

Following the East Coast years of study, Hurte returned to California where opportunities were few. He often heard, "You need more experience in actual conducting." Consequently, Hurte fondly recalled his guest conducting experiences with the Los Angeles Community Orchestra, the Southeast Symphony, the California Junior Symphony, the Kings County Symphony, and the Fresno Philharmonic.

In 1957, with assistance from a local music contractor, the president of the local musician's union, professional colleagues and friends, Leroy Hurte organized the Angel Symphony Society based in Los Angeles. As music director, Hurte explained the Society's creation:

> [S]ome of us, both Negro and white, who had been trying for years with little or moderate success to secure positions with symphonic orchestras in the Southern California area decided that rather than trying to crack what seemed to be the impossible, our best bet was to form an orchestra of our own through which we could not only gain the experience necessary to gain employment with a major orchestra but also to offer opportunities to young people who would never be able to demonstrate their abilities without a group of our kind. We opened our membership at the very beginning to instrumentalists, composers, and conductors without regard to race, creed or color.[2]

Though integration of Blacks into the mainstream of American culture was of keen interest during the early 1960s, such interest rarely extended to the world of symphonic music-making. At least one black publication (*Sepia*) devoted an entire article to the events taking place on the West Coast.[3] Covering a Fall 1964 concert, the article began:

> Onto the stage of the prestigeous [*sic*] Wilshire Ebell Theatre in Los
> Angeles one dreary Sunday afternoon last fall strode a lean, immacu-
> late young man, as graceful as a gazelle and with the rhythmic body
> motion of a new metronome. When he reached the center of the
> curving expanse of space, bowed to the sizeable audience which
> partially filled the balconied hall, Leroy Hurte turned to the poised
> orchestra of some sixty-five pieces in front of him, and, in time-
> honored tradition of symphony conductors the world over, gave a
> swirling downbeat as the cue for the musicians to launch into the first
> few melodic strains of Beethoven's "Eroica" Symphony. . . . Leroy
> Hurte and his orchestra are subjects which will not be easily
> duplicated anywhere in this country. They inhibit a small domain
> which is a real rarity.[4]

Made up of some of the city's best musicians, the Angel City
Symphony had the support of the Los Angeles County Music
Commission, as well as the local business and industrial communi-
ties. This unique orchestra existed through ten four-concert seasons.
Hurte later indicated that, during these ten years,

> the elements of conducting finally began to fall into place. I felt ready
> for a Philharmonic, but was surprised by the competitive nature of
> the profession, as well as the prejudice in favor of European
> conductors, and against America's own rising talents.[5]

Unable to make a satisfactory living from conducting alone,
Maestro Hurte supplemented his income by running a music store,
a small music-publishing company, and directing several church
choirs. Such involvements continued, though in 1972 Hurte was
invited to become conductor and music director of the Inglewood
Philharmonic Association, which had been founded some 22 years
earlier. Hurte was charged with the responsibility of rebuilding the
Inglewood Philharmonic which had fallen on hard times three years
earlier. The process was a slow one; a full-fledged orchestra was not
again presented to the general public until October 1981. Support
came from city officials, civic leaders, and the local community.

The orchestra's first concert included Glinka's "Ruslan and
Ludmilla" Overture, Beethoven's "Emperor" Concerto,
Tchaikovsky's Fourth Symphony, and William Grant Still's "Sum-
merland." The brilliant young black pianist Janise McRae was
soloist in the Beethoven Concerto. Introducing the music of black

composers such as Still and exposing emerging musical talent to the general public were two of Hurte's basic goals. As he explained, "I want the community to realize that America has composers whose music can compete with that of the world's greats."[6] Consistent with another Hurte objective, the Inglewood Philharmonic's composition was approximately one-third black, one-third other minorities, and one-third white.

Following the orchestra's second concert in February 1982, the *Los Angeles Times* reported:

> As a leader of a community orchestra, [Hurte] is one of a handful of black conductors plying his trade in a tradition that is essentially European. Like most community orchestras, his has no ongoing personnel and must draw talent from surrounding orchestras, as well as from a large pool of non-union musicians. Only 60% to 70% are able to play with the orchestra consistently.[7]

Nevertheless, Hurte persisted. He explained to a *Times* journalist:

> I would like to see it become the featured orchestra for the city. I would like to see it do the same things for the city of Inglewood that the Los Angeles Philharmonic does for Los Angeles.[8]

By 1986, the season consisted of five concerts. Hurte was offering a varied fare, was wooing back its original audience, and was attracting new music lovers and general supporters. Realizing the importance of educating school children to symphonic music beyond the five-concert season, the orchestra was holding annual Concerts for Youth in conjunction with the Inglewood Unified School District.

With the awareness that few people were familiar with the orchestral writings of black American composers, Hurte stated that

> part of [his] job was to make this music more available, especially to young people; to make them aware that musical culture extends beyond jazz or rock, and that by being aware of our vast musical heritage, they too become enriched, and can strive to excel as did Anderson, Maynor, Dixon, or Still.[9]

Such a commitment was evident in both Angel City Symphony and Inglewood Philharmonic programming.

Press Comments

"{A} musical personality of extreme depth and versatility."

Sepia

{First concert, reorganized Inglewood Philharmonic}; "A core of professional players, familiar in face and name, gives the group its basic musical thrust. Add Hurte's solid leadership, and the total sound promises bonafide future music-making."

Los Angeles Times

"Inglewood's own version of Don Quixote."

Los Angeles Times

Notes

1. Inglewood Philharmonic Association's 1986–87 Program Booklet, p. 2.
2. "Angel City Symphony Orchestra," *Sepia,* May 1965, pp. 22–23.
3. In November 1966, *Ebony Magazine* covered a similar orchestra on the East Coast that came into existence in New York City in 1965, the Symphony of the New World.
4. "Angel City Symphony Orchestra," *op. cit.,* p. 20.
5. Inglewood . . . Program Booklet, p. 3.
6. Questionnaire, June 1987.
7. Stanley O. Williford, "Inglewood's Upbeat Maestro," *Los Angeles Times,* February 24, 1982, p. 6.
8. *Ibid.*
9. Inglewood . . . Program Booklet, p. 3.

PART III: CONDUCTOR PROFILES, J–W

Isaiah Allen Jackson, III. (Photo: Roy Jones; Courtesy: Dayton Philharmonic Orchestra.)

ISAIAH ALLEN JACKSON, III

BIRTHDATE/PLACE: January 22, 1945; Richmond, Virginia.

EDUCATION: B.A., Harvard University (Russian Studies), 1966; M.A. Stanford University, 1967; M.S., Juilliard School of Music (Conducting), 1969; D.M.A., Juilliard School of Music (Conducting), 1973.

ADDITIONAL STUDY: American Conservatory at Fontainebleau, 1967; Aspen School of Music, 1969; Conducting Fellowship Program, Berkshire Music Center at Tanglewood, 1970.

MAJOR INSTRUCTORS/COACHES: Audrey Bradford Robinson, Ann Burrell, Piano; Joseph Kennedy, Norwood Hinkel, Clarinet; John Ferris, Shondo Shago, Suzanne Bloch, Edgar Schenkmann, Jean Morel, Leonard Bernstein, Leon Barzin, Conducting.

MAJOR APPOINTMENTS: Musical Director, Youth Symphony of New York, 1969–73; Assistant to Leopold Stokowski, American Symphony Orchestra, 1970–73; Assistant Conductor, Baltimore Symphony Orchestra, 1970–73; Associate Conductor, Rochester Philharmonic Orchestra, 1973–86; Music Director, Flint (Michigan) Symphony Orchestra, 1983–86; Music Director, Anchorage (Alaska) Symphony Orchestra, 1983–84; Principal Conductor, Royal Ballet, Covent Garden, 1986–90; Music Director, Royal Ballet, Covent Garden, 1987–90; Music Director, Dayton Philharmonic Orchestra, 1987—; Principal Guest Conductor, Queensland Symphony Orchestra (Australia), 1993—.

GUEST CONDUCTOR: Alabama, American, Berlin, Dallas, Hartford, Indianapolis, Long Beach, National, Richmond, San Diego, San Francisco, Youngstown, Toronto, Vienna Symphony Orchestras; Buffalo, Helsinki, Los Angeles, New York, and Rochester Philharmonics; B.B.C. Concert, Cleveland, R.A.I., and Royal Ballet Orchestras; Baltimore, Detroit, Gaevleborgs, Oakland, Adelaide, Brisbane, Hobart, Melbourne, Queensland, Perth, Sydney, Tasmanian, West Australian Symphony Orchestras; New Orleans Philharmonic Society; L'Orchestre de la Suisse Romande; Asian Youth Orchestra; Spoleto Festival; Boston Pops; Boston Pops Esplanade Orchestra; Grant Park; Eliot Feld and Dance Theatre of Harlem Ballet Companies.

AWARDS/HONORS: Cum laude graduate, Harvard University, 1966; Recipient of First Governor's Award for the Arts in Virginia, 1979; Special Commendation, Senate Joint Resolution No. 27, Virginia General Assembly, 1988; Medal for Achievement in the Arts, Signet Society of Harvard University, April, 1991.

HEADLINE IN THE FEBRUARY 4, 1987 edition of the *Richmond Times-Dispatch* read, "Isaiah Jackson named to post at Royal Ballet."[1] Jackson, the first American and the first black to be appointed to the position, was concurrently one of six finalists for the post of music director of his hometown Richmond Symphony. He was, at the time of the news article, just weeks away from his final appearances with the Symphony and its chamber orchestra (the Richmond Sinfonia) prior to the board's making its selection. The article quoted Jackson as saying, "I'm still very much a candidate for the Richmond appointment . . . and looking forward to being home again."[2] Two weeks later, expressing a keen loss, Jackson announced his withdrawal from consideration, citing the combination of his Royal Ballet schedule and his duties, beginning fall 1987, as music director of the Dayton Philharmonic as not allowing him the time to do Richmond justice.[3]

These two events of February, 1987—Jackson's appointment as Music Director for an internationally celebrated ballet company in one of the world's most prestigious houses and his withdrawal from consideration for the Richmond post—represented in a significant way his steady progress through the important and necessary ranks of assistant and associate conductor (vested with responsibility for those children's concerts, community outreach programs, and other special events that are often the domain of apprentices) to posts that command the leadership that only conductors of world-class stature capture.

Jackson grew up in Richmond, Virginia, in a family of medical doctors. For a time, he thought he might follow in the footsteps of his father, a surgeon. Significantly, Jackson's musical development might be attributed to a medical misfortune; when he was eighteen months old, he fell on a milk bottle and severed the tendons in his left hand. The piano lessons he started at age four as therapy for the hand perhaps sparked the interest in music that Jackson describes as "insatiable." He recalls that his mother often had to practically pull him from the piano bench and send him outdoors to play.[4]

Jackson attended Baker Elementary, Benjamin A. Graves Jr. High, and Maggie L. Walker High Schools in Richmond. Among those he considers to have exerted the greatest influence on his musical development are Audrey B. Robinson, an early piano teacher, and Joseph J. Kennedy, Jr., his high school band instructor.

Jackson remembers that a small group of like-minded friends, a "charmed circle," was an important force in his growing up. With those associates—who studied piano and played recitals, who studied voice and sang art songs—he shared what he believes they felt to be

> their birthright as educated boys and girls . . . who read Shakespeare, listened to and played Mozart. I didn't feel like an oddball. I had company. We didn't fit into the mainstream, but we were tolerated, appreciated, and respected.[5]

After his first year in high school, Jackson enrolled at the Putney School in Vermont, which boasted a strong music program. At Putney, he continued studying the piano and the clarinet, and participated in the orchestra, the chorus, and the compulsory School Friday Night Sing, which included not only madrigals and rounds but also choruses from Bach's B-Minor Mass, and both the Mozart and the Brahms Requiems.

Jackson entered Harvard University in the fall of 1962 and graduated with a major in Russian studies in 1966. Early in his life there, he sang in the all-university choir and the glee club, and began to study conducting. His ambition to become conductor of the Bach Society Orchestra—a prestigious post always held by an undergraduate—led him to establish the Leverett House Opera Society as a means of gaining exposure, experience, and recognition. This new organization, which Jackson created with the encouragement and backing of Archie Epps, tutor at Leverett House, performed both "Cosi Fan Tutte" and "Don Giovanni" in its first season and helped gain for Jackson the directorship of the Bach Society Orchestra. Epps, who was also assistant dean of students, encouraged Jackson to pursue conducting, rather than teaching Russian, as a career, and to undertake graduate and conservatory degree programs to advance that goal.

The decision to become a conductor was a perilous one for Jackson in 1966. Though a few black conductors were making their way, the future was uncertain at best. However, despite the legitimate and understandable concern of his parents, Jackson was compelled by his own inclinations and the Yankee philosophy that undergirded his undergraduate training: "I felt it was possible because you know at

Harvard they teach you that all you have to do is to put your right foot in front of your left foot."[6] And he was inspired by the successes of Henry Lewis* (who by that time had enjoyed some conducting success with the Los Angeles Philharmonic). "If it can happen for Henry Lewis, it can happen for me."[7]

Jackson enrolled in a graduate program at Stanford University in the fall of 1966 and received a master's degree in 1967. At Stanford, Jackson was head coach of the Stanford Opera Workshop. He studied with Shondo Shago, whose advice to go to Paris to study with Nadia Boulanger he accepted. In Boulanger's studio, Jackson met several students from the Juilliard School of Music, who encouraged him to enroll there to continue his preparations for a conducting career. Boulanger recommended that he also study privately with Suzanne Bloch, daughter of composer Ernest Bloch. And so, working with Suzanne Bloch, James Wyner for theory, and Edgar Schenkmann (at that time conductor of the Richmond Symphony), Jackson prepared for the Juilliard auditions.

In June, 1969, Jackson earned a master's degree in conducting from Juilliard. During the 1968–69 season, he founded the New Amsterdam Chamber Orchestra in New York City. This ensemble of fifteen to twenty musicians rehearsed weekly, rotating among the spacious apartments that sympathetic supporters in New York made available for its use. The ensemble played four concerts each year and ended its 1968–69 season with a performance on the bandstand in Central Park. At that concert, the orchestra committee from the Youth Symphony of New York saw Jackson conduct.[8]

The orchestra committee, which was looking for a new conductor, had been advised by Jean Morel, who was Jackson's teacher at Juilliard and whose recommendation they had always sought in the selection of a conductor, that Jackson was the best candidate for the post. When they discovered Jackson was black, the committee returned to Morel to solicit another recommendation. Morel refused to honor their second request and promised that he would never again provide a recommendation if he ever learned that Jackson had been rejected because of his race. Jackson spent the summer of 1969 studying at the Aspen School of Music, and, in the fall of 1969, as he began his doctoral program, was appointed conductor and musical director of the Youth Symphony of New York, a position he held until 1973.

In the summer of 1970, Jackson participated in the Berkshire

Music Center's Conducting Fellowship Program, studying with Leon Barzin and attracting the attention of Leonard Bernstein.[9] It was Bernstein who recommended Jackson as Artistic Director of Vienna's Youth Festival in the summer of 1973, when he conducted an international orchestra of top youth instrumentalists.

During the 1970–71 season (his second year in the Juilliard doctoral program), Jackson served as assistant to Leopold Stokowski at the American Symphony Orchestra and conductor for the Feld Ballet. Also in 1970, Jackson was introduced by Stuart Warkow of Carnegie Hall to Sergiu Comissiona (Music Director of the Baltimore Symphony Orchestra), who was looking for conductors for young people's concerts.

Several successful guest engagements with the Baltimore Symphony led to the offer of an assistant conductor's position, which Jackson began in 1970, simultaneous with full-time studies at Juilliard, assisting Stokowski, and conducting for the Feld Ballet. He maintained the post at Baltimore until 1973. Though in Baltimore Jackson was primarily responsible for planning and executing children's concerts and for conducting in-school classroom residency programs, the association provided him the opportunity to experience the entire spectrum of conducting activities.

During the 1972–73 season, Jackson attracted national attention when he conducted a series of performances of Humperdinck's "Hansel and Gretel" around the country. These performances were distinguished by Jackson's use of local school children in the finale. The fourteen performances, organized under the auspices of the Berkshire Boy Choir (a youth choral group organized at Amherst College) not only employed the youth but also featured six young professional opera singers and an orchestra drawn from the Syracuse Symphony.[10] The tour sites included Jackson's home town, Richmond, Virginia.

In the early 1970s, Jackson was offered his first professional guest conducting opportunities. He performed three engagements with the National Symphony in Washington and conducted the Dallas and Vienna Symphony Orchestras, and the Rochester Philharmonic. In 1973, Jackson added to his growing list of conducting posts the associate conductor slot at the Rochester Philharmonic. He was appointed at the time David Zinman was hired as music director. According to Jackson,

Zinman was the players' choice for conductor and the board acceded to their wishes in order to show good faith in repairing a potentially fatal situation in Rochester . . . Zinman was only available six weeks this past [1973–74] season, so guests were hired and I was given the tours, the shopping centers and some subscription concerts. This year, he is conducting more, but I still have the tour, children's concerts and more subscription concerts.[11]

On March 30, 1974, Jackson's touring with the Rochester Philharmonic brought the conductor and orchestra to Virginia State University (then Virginia State College), twenty-five miles from Richmond. On that occasion, a local newspaper critic made the following observations:

> The Rochester Philharmonic Orchestra came to Virginia State College Saturday night and demonstrated some of the most professional orchestral playing seen in these parts. . . . It was an evening of standard works including Berlioz, Debussy, Liszt, and Bartok, but under Isaiah Jackson's leadership the orchestra proved itself capable of both a warm and sensuous sound and stunning virtuosity. . . . The Bartok *Concerto for Orchestra* (to be played soon by the Richmond Symphony) was the event of the evening. Though the orchestra tours somewhat under strength in strings, it did not lack for intensity of depth and tone. The communication between conductor and players was instantaneous and omnipresent. Matching tone across sections . . . was on a level seldom achieved by our [Richmond Symphony] orchestra.[12]

Jackson viewed the Rochester appointment as an important opportunity to prepare himself for the time that he would be appointed to the music directorship of his own orchestra.[13]

In the spring of 1981, Jackson was asked by Arthur Mitchell, executive director of the prestigious Dance Theatre of Harlem, to conduct for the company's first season at the Royal Opera House, Covent Garden. The invitation, which Jackson accepted, represented his debut at Covent Garden, in London, and with the Royal Opera Orchestra. The season led to Jackson's being invited to conduct at Covent Garden during the Royal Ballet's 1984–85 season, and subsequently to his appointments as principal conductor in 1986 and music director in 1987.

Since the early 1980s, recognition of Jackson's growing stature as a conductor has led to an impressive list of engagements. In 1983, he was named music director of both the Flint (Michigan) symphony and the Anchorage (Alaska) symphony. During the 1983–84 season, in addition to his regular conducting assignments with the Rochester, Flint, and Anchorage Symphony Orchestras, Jackson made debuts with the Cleveland Orchestra, the Detroit Symphony Orchestra, and the New Orleans Philharmonic Society.

In the summer of 1984, Jackson conducted the San Francisco and Long Beach Symphony Orchestras and the Cleveland Orchestra at the Blossom Music Center. All engagements were debuts. The 1984–85 season brought debut engagements on the subscription series of the Symphony Orchestras of Detroit, Baltimore, Toronto, Oakland, and San Diego, and a return engagement with The Royal Ballet. Jackson made his first appearance with the Orchestre de la Suisse Romande (Geneva) in December 1985, adding to the list of European orchestras he had conducted that already included the R.A.I. Orchestra in Rome and the Spoleto Festival in Italy.

Jackson's inaugural season as principal conductor of The Royal Ballet (1986–87) included performances in two London seasons, as well as touring to the Netherlands and the Soviet Union. In the summer of 1987, he made his debut at the Promenade Concerts, Royal Albert Hall (London) and with the Helsinski Philharmonic at the Helsinki Festival. During the 1987–88 season, Jackson made his first German appearance with the Royal Ballet, and in January 1989, he made his German orchestral debut with the Berlin Symphony.

Throughout the 1980s and into the 1990s, Jackson's growing prominence garnered for him increasingly more prestigious assignments in the United States, Europe, Asia, and Australia. However, he firmly maintained his ties to his home town, and those who had known him during his Richmond years returned the affection and regard he felt for them. On December 13, 1988, the Richmond Public School System, Philip Morris USA, and the Richmond Delegation to the Virginia General Assembly sponsored a reception at the Virginia Museum of Fine Arts in Jackson's honor. On that occasion, surrounded by family, former teachers, friends, and a representative from the Music Program of the National Endowment for the Arts, he was presented the Virginia General Assembly Senate Joint Resolution No. 27, lauding Jackson as ". . . a creative and dynamic force in music in the Commonwealth and internationally."[14]

Jackson's May–September 1992 itinerary included his debut with Chicago's Grant Park Orchestra and a return visit to Australia to lead the Orchestras of Sydney, Brisbane, and Melbourne. He would return to Symphony Hall in Boston for a series of concerts with the Boston Pops and the Boston Pops Esplanade Orchestra. He would conduct "A Celebration of African-American Music" with the Youngstown Symphony and inaugurate his Dayton Philharmonic's first summer season.

When Jackson is asked about those black musicians, in addition to teachers, who have played special roles in the development of his career, or who have inspired him to success, he produces a diverse list:

- the late clarinetist F. Nathaniel Gatlin* (former professor of music at Virginia State University in Petersburg and music director of the Petersburg Symphony), who fought for the acceptance of blacks into the Richmond Symphony;

- Leontyne Price, who was the first person to call him "maestro" (during preparation for the opening of the new home of the Juilliard School of Music at Lincoln Center);

- Dean Dixon,* the "Dean of Black American Conductors," whom Jackson met while a student at Juilliard when, in a rare appearance in this country, Dixon conducted the New York Philharmonic;

- the late Leon Thompson,* conductor, fellow Richmonder, and former director of educational activities for the New York Philharmonic, who not only encouraged Jackson in his pursuit of a conducting career, but also helped his parents understand the challenges and rewards of the profession, and the support their son would need from them; Pianist Andre Watts, with whom he has worked, and with whom he continues to maintain a friendship; and Henry Lewis,* with whom he can share the joys and challenges of making one's way in the world of conducting.

Jackson is unambiguous about his increasing responsibility to the music of black composers, and the joy he derives from programming and conducting this music:

> It is *our* music . . . it's our job to promote *our* music. These are the people who speak with *our* voice . . . . After so many years of learning from Germans how to do German music, and learning from the English how English music should sound, from the French how to do French music, this is *my* music. And I don't have to take lessons on

this. . . . I went down to Greater St. Stephens, and I *know* how gospel music sounds. . . . Doing this feels like nothing else.[15]

He is similarly positive about the role music created by black people has played in the continuing development of his career. Jackson attributes the offers of concerts in the 1980s, which he considers to be his second round of guest conducting, to the yearly programs featuring the music of black composers given by many of the country's major orchestras: the Cleveland Orchestra's "Martin Luther King Celebration Concert"; the Detroit Symphony Orchestra's "Classical Roots"; the New Orleans Philharmonic Symphony's "Concerts in Black". The successes of those concerts prompted orchestras to invite him back to conduct, in some instances, more prestigious subscription concerts.

Jackson is quick to add that often those initial invitations resulted from the stimulation and encouragement of people within black communities in those major cities, who made known to orchestra management their interest in hearing music of black composers and even their awareness of Jackson as an important black conductor who might be invited to conduct. Jackson views this specific activity as reflective of what he has discovered to be a larger and more universal disposition: black people are proud of black musicians, are interested in their advancement, and will work to assist their progress.

Jackson advises aspiring black conductors to prepare themselves well musically; to study solfeggio and ear training, which are especially important for a conductor; to maintain a sound body and mind; and, above all, to "follow your star. Each of us is unique and each of us brings something to the artistic experience that no one else would bring . . . Be true to yourself."[16]

Press Comments

"His gifts are manifold and his manner natural and engaging."

Washington Post

"Isaiah Jackson revealed an impressive command of the Wagner style as he and soprano Eileen Farrell combined for a moving performance of 'Bruennhilda's Immolation Scene' from 'Die Goetterdaemmerung.' "

Rochester Democrat & Chronicle

"The orchestra sounded unusually well under Isaiah Jackson, whom I remember from this summer's Tanglewood contemporary concerts."

Chicago Tribune

"The orchestra obviously included many fine players, but the lion's share of the credit for their achievements must belong to Isaiah Jackson, the music director and conductor, whose efficiency, energy and interpretive authority were in evidence at all points."

New York Times

"Guest conductor Isaiah Jackson made glorious music out of some warhorses. Jackson's Tchaikovsky was elegant and sleek. Jackson avoided every bit of vulgarity. No matter how familiar the theme, he graced it with the most attentive interpretation. . . . For all his refinement, however, there was nothing fussy or pedagogic about his approach."

Los Angeles Times

"{S}ince he made his presence felt from the first bars of music, compliments to the guest conductor, Isaiah Jackson. Remembered from an earlier visit to Covent Garden with Dance Theatre of Harlem, he made his Royal Ballet debut with a notably dramatic and lyrical account of Minkus's music for 'La Bayadere'."

The Times (London)

"In Liszt's 'Les Preludes', Jackson showed a fine sense of line and proportion. . . . Overall he brought the tired old symphonic poem a feeling of freshness and an appreciation for its inherent drama."

Cleveland Plain Dealer

"What Jackson does on the podium seems to have a musical purpose. . . . One feels he is there to serve the music and musicians rather than an inflated ego. . . . Clarity and precision were present. Climaxes were built surely, carefully. This timeworn overture {Rossini's 'Semiramide'} possessed what seemed like new-found freshness."

Richmond News Leader

"Isaiah Jackson, a superb and elegant conductor . . . delineated the music with supple and dancing gestures, conducting the orchestra (de la Suisse Romande) with an infinite amount of craft and musicality."

Lausanne Journal "24 Heures"

"As an orchestral interpreter, especially in the string sound he obtains, Jackson has often been likened to Leopold Stokowski."

Richmond Times-Dispatch

"The most notable performance in the Royal Ballet's all-Ashton programme at Covent Garden on Saturday evening came from the pit where the orchestra, under the direction of newly appointed principal conductor Isaiah Jackson, played with unusual expressiveness. . . . Jackson has worked a musical miracle in a short while and his solo curtain call was warmly applauded."

(London) Evening Standard

"Jackson showed that he was a splendidly talented young conductor with ideas of his own and . . . not afraid to express himself musically. It was committed music-making on his part, rather than antiseptic baton work."

Cleveland Plain Dealer

"{H}e proceeded to show off his stuff with Britten's 'The Young People's Guide to the Orchestra' in an interpretation of exceptional finesse and polish. His ability to catch the pointed edge of a rhythm or the delicate curve of a melody revealed the score's many subtleties."

Washington Post

"Pops concerts aren't normally where auspicious conducting debuts are made, but if this particular Pops concert was a fair indication, we will be hearing a great deal more of Isaiah Jackson. . . . It wasn't just good Pops conducting; it was good conducting period. Frankly, your reviewer was blown away."

Boston Globe

"In the Royal Ballet's all-Ashton triple bill, honours go to the conductor Isaiah Jackson whose renderings of Mendelssohn, Franck and Chopin consistently charmed the ear."

London Weekly Diary

"Isaiah Jackson produced a performance that was ultimately intoxicating."

The West Australian

"The genial stage presence of visiting American conductor Isaiah Jackson dominated proceedings at Saturday's Queensland Symphony Orchestra concert."

Courier-Mail (Brisbane, Australia)

"The highly talented conductor, Isaiah Jackson, who has already made numerous impressive appearances with the Berlin Symphony Orchestra, overwhelmed the audience with an unusually deeply-felt and sensitive interpretation of the 'Siegfried Idyll'. Maestro Jackson's broad tempo allowed the themes to unfold with an inner peace. . . ."

Berliner Morgenpost

Notes

1. Clarke Bustard, "Isaiah Jackson named to post at Royal Ballet," *Richmond Times-Dispatch,* February 4, 1987, p. A–1.
2. *Ibid.*
3. Deborah George, "For Isaiah Jackson, Richmond means memories, mostly good," *Richmond News Leader,* February 19, 1987, p. 23.
4. Marie H. Beach, "Isaiah Jackson's Conducting Career Followed Early Childhood Accident." *Richmond Times-Dispatch,* December 17, 1972, p. J–1.
5. Interview, William E. Terry with Jackson, December 4, 1986, Norfolk, Virginia.
6. *Ibid.*
7. *Ibid.*
8. *Ibid.* The Youth Symphony of New York was founded in 1963 to give youth between the ages of 12 and 20, selected by audition from throughout the metropolitan area, the opportunity to perform under professional leadership, and to perform for their peers in free concerts in major halls.
9. *Ibid.*
10. "Babes in Opera Land," *Newsweek,* January 1, 1973, p. 40.
11. Ira Lieberman, "Virginian Isaiah Jackson Conducts at Massanetta," *Richmond Times-Dispatch,* June 30, 1974, p. H–4.
12. ———, "Music," *Richmond Times-Dispatch,* April 1, 1974, p. A–14.
13. ———, "Massanetta," *Richmond Times-Dispatch,* June 30, 1974, p. H–4.
14. Clarke Bustard, "Growing up here gives you a wonderful vantage." *Richmond Times-Dispatch,* December 16, 1988, p. D–10.
15. Interview, *op. cit.*
16. *Ibid.*

Francis ("Frank") Johnson (Courtesy: *The Black Perspective in Music.*)

FRANCIS (FRANK) JOHNSON

BIRTHDATE/PLACE: 1792; Martinique, West Indies.†
DEATH DATE/PLACE: April 6, 1844; Philadelphia, Pennsylvania.
CONDUCTOR, composer, performer on the keyed bugle and violin, leader of military ensembles, dance and concert orchestras.
MASTER TEACHER (music studio in Philadelphia);
CAREER HIGHLIGHTS (1815–1844): Composer of over 200 published compositions (salon music, cotillions, quadrilles, marches, galops, patriotic songs, sentimental ballads, and arrangements of operatic airs); Johnson (and his band/orchestra), among the leading performers of the pre–Civil War period; developed a "school" of black musicians; provided music for aristocracy; long associated with the distinguished State Fencibles Regiment (beginning 1821); first American (black or white) to take a musical ensemble to Europe (1837); introduced the "Concerts à la Musard" (Promenade Concerts) to America (1838).
GIFT and HONOR: Silver bugle from Queen Victoria (1838); Honorary Membership in the Artillery Corps Washington Grays at Philadelphia, 1980 (posthumously); "Commemoration of a Musical Master" on the occasion of the 200th anniversary of his birth, entered into the Congressional Record, 102nd Congress (July 22, 1992).

THOUGH HE WAS ONE OF THE MOST CELEBRATED composers of the first half of the nineteenth century, Frank Johnson also distinguished himself as an outstanding band and orchestra leader. And according to musicologist Eileen Southern, his accomplishments extended even further:

> Frank Johnson stood tall in the center of a Philadelphia School that included William Appo, William Brady, Aaron J. Connor, Isaac Hazzard, and James Hemmenway [all Black]. . . . [He was] a role model for his contemporaries to emulate, white as well as black. It was Johnson who began to publish music as early as 1818 . . .; who

---

†According to biographers Charles K. Jones and Lorenzo K. Greenwich II, Francis Johnson was born in Philadelphia.

periodically imported new music from Europe . . .; who introduced new instruments to the city . . . ; who developed the skills of his musicians so that they could provide military, dance, and sacred-concert music for Philadelphia and other cities of the nation; who took his group to Europe to perform, apparently the first American to do so; and who finally lifted his dance music onto the concert stage with promenade concerts.[1]

Frank Johnson is believed to have settled in Philadelphia around 1809, establishing himself as a premier composer (salon music, marches, quadrilles, galops, cotillions, sentimental ballads, and other dance forms), a distinguished performer on the recently popularized keyed bugle and violin, and a celebrated bandmaster. The actual source of Johnson's early musical training is unknown. It is speculated that he played in a band led by a local black bandleader and studied with him. It has been suggested that he also studied with Richard Willis, director of the West Point Military Band of the United States Army.[2]

As early as 1819, he was identified by one writer as "leader of a band at all balls, public and private; sole director of all serenades . . . inventor-general of cotillions. . . ."[3] Johnson's bands played for the city's highest society at balls, private parties, parades, and dance schools. His reputation as a composer was firmly established as early as 1818, when G. Willig published his "Six Setts of Cotillions." Favorable press coverage followed.

Frank Johnson figured prominently in black music historian James Monroe Trotter's book *Music and Some Highly Musical People* (1878).[4] His career was carefully treated in Eileen Southern's *The Music of Black Americans: A History* (1971, rev. 1983)[5] and has been the subject of several articles in the journal *The Black Perspective in Music,* edited by Southern.

In recent years, the music of Frank Johnson began attracting the attention of solo and ensemble performers, and stimulated the curiosities of "black music" scholars and students alike. Between 1975 and 1984, the Trio Pro Viva (flute, cello, and piano) regularly performed music of Johnson, featuring works originally scored for pianoforte with flute obbligato. Dr. Southern presented a paper on "Johnson and His Promenade Concerts" at the Annual Meeting of the American Musicological Society, November 1976, in Washington, D.C.[6] Two Johnson compositions (a galop and a quadrille) were included in the *Recorded Anthology of American Music* by New World

Records, 1978.[7] His sentimental ballad "A Place in Thy Memory Dearest" (soprano with piano accompaniment) was included on a Smithsonian Institution concert in the nation's capital on May 3, 1987. Johnson compositions (orchestrated by black composer Hale Smith) appeared on the world premiere performance of the Chicago-based Black Music Repertory Ensemble on March 25, 1988. Based on the ensemble's mission, one may be certain that Frank Johnson compositions would continue to be programmed by this group.

To celebrate the 1983 release of Charles K. Jones and Lorenzo K. Greenwich II's book *A Choice Collection of the Works of Francis Johnson,* the First Troop Philadelphia City Cavalry hosted a reception in February 1984. Johnson musical selections were performed by The United States Military Academy Band from West Point. As assessed by Jones and Greenwich:

> Francis "Frank" Johnson became the pivotal force in the development of what is known as the musical culture of America today. . . . [T]he music and legacy of Francis Johnson is one of America's most valuable cultural assets.[8]

Parallelodrome, Ltd., a non-profit educational private foundation established by Jones and Greenwich "to broaden the awareness, increase the knowledge, [and] stimulate and heighten the interest of an already curious public," released Volume I of *Francis Johnson's American Cotillions* in 1989, performed by a native black Philadelphian, pianist David Anthony Lofton.[9] This recording release was a prelude to the Jones and Greenwich-guided 1992 Commemoration of the Bicentennial of the Birth of Francis Johnson. The purpose of the commemorative events

> was to focus greater public attention upon the lifework and contribution made by him toward the development of early American music and the musical culture of our nation; to, perhaps, create . . . a methodology that might become a prototype toward a stimulation of the interest of our youngsters, from grades one through six, in the life and music of this great early American.[10]

The year-long tribute of commemorative events would include a series of exhibits, and special events, including a parade, the erection of a State/City (Philadelphia, Pennsylvania) Historical Marker at the site of Johnson's residence, and a Grand Concert of his music. These activities would be undertaken in concert with the Division of Music Education of the School District of Philadelphia. The United States Military Academy Band would record a collection of Johnson's most celebrated grand marches.

The mayor of Saratoga Springs, New York, proclaimed 1992 "to be officially recognized as the Bicentennial of Francis Johnson in the city of Saratoga Springs," in recognition of Johnson's (and his band's) more than twenty years (1821–1843) of performing concerts in the afternoon and playing parties and balls in the evening during the months of August and September. The Mayor of Buffalo, New York, proclaimed for his city the year 1992 as "The Bicentennial of the Birth of Francis Johnson," in recognition of the band's appearances in that city between the years 1839 and 1842. Congratulatory letters were received from the Governor of Pennsylvania, the Mayor of St. Louis, the chairman of the National Endowment for the Arts, as well as the White House. Serving as Co-Chairman of the Memorial Bicentennial Committee would be the Honorable Coleman A. Young, Mayor of Detroit (where Johnson's band also performed) and the Honorable W. Wilson Goode, then Mayor of Philadelphia.[11]

February 3, 1992, was declared "Frank's Day" in Philadelphia, at which time an official historical marker was unveiled on Pine Street, between 5th and 6th streets, in front of Frank Johnson's place of residence for many years. Music (Frank Johnson's) was provided by The United States Military Academy Band.

Johnson's military band leadership was the focus of an article written by John W. Cromwell (*People's Advocate* editor, black scholar, and lawyer) in 1900 and published in the *Southern Workman*. The article was reprinted in *The Black Perspective in Music* Bicentennial Issue, July 1976. Cromwell noted that Johnson early "enjoyed the patronage of a popular [white] military company" of Philadelphia and that his orchestra "received that of the highest and most fashionable circles" of the same city. Wrote Cromwell:

> In the growth of the martial spirit as a sequence of the War of 1812 may be traced the moving cause and impulse that placed this organization so prominently before the public. . . . Frank Johnson . . . succeeded because he also possessed the qualities that merit success in any enterprise.[12]

It is obvious from the testimony of his peers that skillful personal performance abilities, pedagogical know-how, disciplinary mastery, and business astuteness all numbered among Johnson's distinguishing traits.

For parades, the Johnson Band consisted primarily of woodwinds, supplemented by French horn, bell harmonicon, ophicleide, cymbals, bells, triangles, and drums. For dances, string instruments were substituted for or added to the winds. The first Johnson band was organized by the Third Company of Washington Guards in Philadelphia in 1815. In 1821, Johnson was engaged as bandmaster of an elite regiment, the Philadelphia State Fencibles. For more than two decades (1821–1843), Johnson and his celebrated band entertained villagers and visitors during the summer months at Saratoga Springs, with performances at Congress Hall, the United States Hotel, and Congress Park. Also during the summer months, he and his band often performed in Cape May, New Jersey, and White Sulphur Springs in Virginia.

Johnson was trumpeter with the First Troop Philadelphia City Calvary, now known as Troop A, 1st Squadron, 104th Calvary, 28th Infantry Division, Pennsylvania Army National Guard—the oldest military unit in continuous service in the annals of the nation—from 1822 to 1829. The First Troop served as escort of presidents and visiting heads of state.

In addition to his service as trumpeter with the First Troop, Johnson led a cotillion band, "a long standing favorite among the fashionables and the gentry of Philadelphia [and] a featured attraction of the convivial activities of the First Troop." When in 1824 General Lafayette arrived in Philadelphia, Johnson's military band participated in the great parade. For the evening's Grand Concert and Civic Ball, his cotillion band (enlarged with strings) provided the music.[13]

The band toured the principal cities of the North and East, as well as Canada. Performances also took place at Mt. Vernon and Washington. But Johnson's most ambitious trip took place in 1837, when he and four of his bandsmen traveled to England. Eileen Southern reminded us that perhaps Johnson was inspired by the successful British journey of black actors Ira Aldridge and James Hewlett only a few years prior (1824 and 1826 respectively).[14] Bandsman Johnson's express purposes for the visit were "to improve his musical knowledge, to cultivate his musical taste, and learn airs still more délightful and pleasing."

Philippe Musard's Promenade Concerts were introduced to Paris in November 1833. These musical events took place in London during Johnson's residency, inspiring Johnson to journey to Paris to meet personally with Musard. Upon his return to London, Johnson also witnessed the "lighter musical events" presented by Johann Strauss (the elder), who was in Britain for celebrations of Queen Victoria's coronation.

Philadelphia (and all of America) was introduced to Promenade Concerts in December 1838. The presenter was Frank Johnson with his celebrated band, recently returned from abroad. The trip had been extremely successful and most enlightening. Johnson's band, believed to be the first such American group to give concerts in England, included in its British itinerary performances in London, other large British cities, and a command performance for the Queen and her mother, the Duchess of Kent. As an expression of her appreciation, Queen Victoria presented Johnson with a silver bugle. Wrote Cromwell in 1900:

> [O]n his return his successes were greater than ever; he was as great as Dodworth, Gilmore, or Theodore Thomas a generation later, or as is Sousa today.[15]

Just three years prior to his death, Johnson and his musicians accompanied a chorus of more than 100 voices (directed by Morris Brown) in a performance of Haydn's oratorio "The Creation," first for "the colored people of Philadelphia," followed by a performance for a white audience.

Following his death on April 6, 1844, the editor of the *Public Ledger* observed,

> This worthy and respected colored man was buried yesterday afternoon in the graveyard of St. Thomas' (African) Church, ... The procession was one of the most solemn we have ever witnessed. . . . One of the most touching parts of the whole ceremony was the far-famed brass band, following their deceased leader, with instruments shrouded in mourning and playing a parting dirge over his grave.

> Frank was one of the most celebrated personages of Philadelphia. His talents as a musician rendered him famous all over the Union. . . . It will be a long time before his place can be similarly filled.[16]

Fifty-six years later, John Cromwell wrote of the band's continuation and summarized its leader's importance in American musical history:

> [He] had so thoroughly imbued his colleagues with the principles of music, self respect, and confidence that . . . the organization [under the leadership of Joseph G. Anderson] continued. . . . [The creation and existence of the Frank Johnson Brass and String Band] is a part of the musical history of the great city of Philadelphia, and whose artistic achievements are a part of the trophies of American art.[17]

Notes

1. Eileen Southern, "The Philadelphia Afro-American School," *Black Perspective in Music,* July 1976, p. 238.
2. "Francis (Frank) Johnson," in *Biographical Dictionary of Afro-American and African Musicians,* compiled and edited by Eileen Southern, Westport, Connecticut: Greenwood Press, 1983, p. 206.
3. Robert Waln, *The Hermit in America,* chapter titled "The Cotillion Party," reprinted in *Readings In Black American Music,* compiled and edited by Eileen Southern, New York: W.W. Norton and Company, Inc., 1971, pp. 123–124.
4. James Monroe Trotter, *Music and Some Highly Musical People,* Boston: Lee and Shepard, 1878. (Reprint, New York: Johnson Reprint Corp., 1968.)
5. Eileen Southern, *The Music of Black Americans: A History,* 2nd Edition, New York: W. W. Norton, 1983.
6. ———, "Frank Johnson of Philadelphia and His Promenade Concerts," *Black Perspective in Music,* Spring 1977, pp. 3–29.
7. Album, "Come and Trip It" (Instrumental Dance Music 1780s–1920s), *Recorded Anthology of American Music,* New World Records 293.
8. Charles K. Jones and Lorenzo K. Greenwich II, *A Choice Collection of the Works of Francis Johnson,* volume I, New York: Point Two Publications, 1983, p. 12.
9. Album "Francis Johnson: American Cotillions," Vol. I, Books 1 & 2 (Piano), Parallelodrome P-1001JV1L, 1989.
10. Publicity material, dated December 12, 1991.
11. *Ibid.*
12. John W. Cromwell, "Frank Johnson's Military Band," *Southern Workman* 29 (1900), pp. 532–535; reprinted in *Black Perspective in Music,* pp. 208–209.

13. Jones and Greenwich, *op. cit.,* n.p.
14. Southern, "Frank Johnson of Philadelphia and His Promenade Concerts," *op. cit.,* p. 5.
15. Cromwell, *op. cit.,* p. 211.
16. Southern, "Frank Johnson of Philadelphia and His Promenade Concerts," *op. cit.,* p. 16.
17. Cromwell, *op. cit.,* p. 212.

William LaRue Jones

WILLIAM LaRUE JONES

BIRTHDATE/PLACE: October 19, 1939; Roanoke, Texas.

EDUCATION: B.S. and M.A., Kansas State University, Manhattan, 1960 and 1962, respectively; MFA, University of Iowa, 1970; DMA, University of Wisconsin, Madison, 1972 (Major: Bassoon Performance; Minor: Musicology/Conducting); additional Study, North Texas State University and Juilliard School of Music.

APPOINTMENTS: Freelance/Substitute—Metropolitan Opera Touring Company Orchestra, American Ballet Theatre, Saint Paul Chamber Orchestra, Minnesota Orchestra; Membership–Topeka and Cedar Rapids Symphonies; Minnesota Opera and Ballet (Bassoon).

FACULTY—Cornell College (1967–70), Mount Vernon, Iowa;

PRINCIPAL CONDUCTOR—North Carolina School of the Arts;

CONDUCTOR—Bethel College Orchestra.

MUSIC DIRECTOR/CONDUCTOR: 3M Symphony (Saint Paul, Minnesota), 1974–87; MacPhail Center for the Arts Concerto Orchestra, 1979—.

FOUNDING MUSIC DIRECTOR/ADMINISTRATOR: Greater Twin Cities' Youth Symphonies (Minneapolis and Saint Paul, Minnesota), 1972—.

FOUNDING ARTISTIC DIRECTOR/ADMINISTRATOR: Orchestral Institute of America, 1986—.

CLINICIAN/WORKSHOP LEADER (partial): Interlochen Arts Academy; Universities of Utah State, Iowa, Colorado, Minnesota, Oregon, Alabama, Southern Mississippi, Wisconsin, Baylor; Oberlin Conservatory; American Symphony Orchestra League.

GUEST CONDUCTOR: Minnesota Orchestra; Saint Paul Chamber Orchestra; Minneapolis Chamber Symphony; Minneapolis Pops Orchestra; South Dakota, Hershey, Rochester, Bloomington, and Mankato Symphony Orchestras; All-State and Festival Orchestras (in over 40 states and Canada); MENC All-Eastern and All-Northwest Orchestras; Sinfonie Orchester AML (Lucerne, Switzerland); International String Orchestra, Graz, Austria (1989); Calgary, Alberta (1990), Lausanne, Switzerland (1991).

AWARDS/HONORS: American String Teachers Association, Exceptional Leadership and Merit Award; Twin Cities Mayors' Public Art Award; Sigma Alpha Iota, Musician-of-the-Year Award.

FOUNDER, DIRECTOR, LEAD CONDUCTOR, and administrator of the Greater Twin Cities' Youth Symphonies (GTCYS), William LaRue Jones has since 1972 been

. . . influenc[ing] the musical outlook of a generation of classical musicians. Through the hiring and management of GTCYS's seven assistant conductors, he shapes the musical philosophy of eight orchestras, involving a thousand youngsters, that give 60 concerts a year in Minnesota and surrounding states. Former GTCYS players are now performing in major orchestras, from the Boston Symphony to The Saint Paul Chamber Orchestra.[1]

It is easy to understand the concern for the development of young talent, in view of the fact that Jones was in college before he heard or saw his first orchestral concert.

A Roanoke, Texas native, Jones played clarinet in high school. Following a brief period at North Texas State University in Denton, he enrolled at Kansas State University in Manhattan. It was there that he began studying the bassoon, becoming sufficiently proficient to play in the university orchestra and the Topeka Symphony. Both the bachelor's and master's degrees were in bassoon performance, as was his master of fine arts degree from the University of Iowa. Throughout, he minored in musicology and conducting.

Jones became serious about conducting when he joined the faculty of Cornell College at Mount Vernon, Iowa, in 1967. At Cornell he was conductor of the college orchestra and assistant professor of theory, analysis, and double reeds. He fulfilled these assignments through academic year 1969–70.

Prior to the move to Iowa and following his residency in Kansas, he matriculated at the Juilliard School of Music, where he continued to study the bassoon and, as a free-lance musician, substituted with the Metropolitan Opera Touring Company Orchestra, the American Ballet Theatre, and the New York Philharmonic.

While studying at the University of Iowa, where he obtained his master of fine arts in 1970, he performed with the Cedar Rapids Symphony. Two years later, he received the doctor of musical arts degree from the University of Wisconsin at Madison and soon thereafter moved to Minneapolis.

Also in 1972, he founded the Greater Twin Cities' [Minneapolis and St. Paul] Youth Symphonies. After two decades, his duties include artistic advising for seven assistants, recruitment, auditions, repertory selection, rehearsal procedures, publicity and public relations, community outreach, fundraising (a $400,000 annual budget), and long-range planning. The latter two assignments are carried out in collaboration with a thirty-member Board of Directors.

Between 1974 and 1987, Jones served as music director of the 3M Symphony in St. Paul, a sixty-five–piece community orchestra comprised of amateurs and professionals. In Minneapolis, he has been music director of the MacPhail Center for the Arts' Chamber Orchestra, an organization comprised of professional musicians performing concerti and arias, since 1979. Guest conducting appearances have included numerous university and conservatory orchestras, all-state and festival orchestras in over 40 states and Canada, the Interlochen Arts Academy, and the following professional orchestras: Minnesota Orchestra, Saint Paul Chamber Orchestra, Minneapolis Chamber Symphony, Minneapolis Pops Orchestra, South Dakota Symphony, and the Hershey, Rochester, Bloomington, and Mankato Symphony Orchestras. Jones guest conducted the International String Orchestra in Graz, Austria (1989); Calgary, Alberta (1990); and Lausanne, Switzerland (1991).

In 1986 Jones founded the Orchestral Institute of America, a "two-week residential Institute devoted to the study and performance of the world's finest orchestral repertoire," designed for elementary through college age students. Institute activities include private instruction, master classes, visiting artists, chamber music, and full orchestra performance. A conductor's workshop, serving adults "interested in revitalizing their score study abilities, gestural skills, and rehearsal concepts," coincides with the Institute.[2]

Dr. Jones's affiliations are extensive: Minnesota School for the Arts, Minnesota Arts Education Task Force, Minnesota State Orchestra League, Minnesota Alliance for Arts in Education, Minnesota Arts Commission, Young Audiences of Minnesota, Greater Minneapolis Chamber of Commerce, Minnesota String Quartet Residency Project, International Symposium on String Education, Yamaha International Orchestral Advisory Board, Minnesota Public Radio, and Saint Paul Chamber Orchestra Education Task Force.

William LaRue Jones has been referred to as "a scholar and a musical intellect." His conducting has been described as "forceful, pressing, determined, [and] athletic." Of self, Jones indicates, "I'm not one to be as flamboyant as a Leonard Bernstein, . . ."[3] Regardless of his identifications, his musical mission is being realized; reaped benefits of his commitments will continue to enhance the musical world generally and the orchestral universe specifically.

Notes

1. Emmon Scott, "Vitae—Dr. William L. Jones," *Minnesota Monthly,* November 1989, p. 61.
2. Curriculum Vitae, William LaRue Jones.
3. Scott, *op. cit.*

Everett Astor Lee

Everett Astor Lee conducts unidentified foreign orchestra.

EVERETT ASTOR LEE

BIRTHDATE/PLACE: 1919; Wheeling, West Virginia.

EDUCATION: B.Mus., Cleveland Institute of Music, 1940 (Major, Violin); Berkshire Music School, Tanglewood, Massachusetts, 1946; Saint Cecilia Academy, Rome, 1952–54; additional study, the Juilliard School of Music and Columbia University (Opera Workshop and Conducting).

MAJOR INSTRUCTORS/COACHES: Louis Vaughn Jones, Joseph Fuchs, and Samuel Gardner (Violin); Max Rudolph, Dimitri Mitropoulos, and Boris Goldovsky (Conducting).

MAJOR APPOINTMENTS: Violinist (Concertmaster), CBS Orchestra, 1943–44; Substitute Conductor, Broadway musical "Carmen Jones"; Assistant Conductor, "On the Town," 1944; Assistant Conductor, New York City Symphony; Music Director, Munich Traveling Orchestra, 1957–62; Principal Conductor, Norrkoping Symphony Orchestra (Sweden), 1962–72; Music Director, Symphony of the New World, 1973–77; Resident Artist, Denison University, 1982–83; Titled Conductor, Bogotá Philharmonic, and Conductor, National Symphony Orchestra (Colombia) 1979—.

FOUNDER/CONDUCTOR: Cosmopolitan Little Symphony, 1947–52, NYC.

GUEST CONDUCTOR: New York Philharmonic; Detroit, Baltimore, St. Louis, Louisville, Cincinnati and Atlanta Symphony Orchestras; New York City Opera (1956), Opera Ebony and Opera North; Berlin and Munich Philharmonic Orchestras; Buenos Aires—Radio Orchestra and Teatro Colón; National Radio Orchestra of Paris; Madrid Philharmonic; Radio Orchestra of Bruxelles (Belgium).

AWARDS/HONORS: Fulbright Scholarship for study in Rome, 1952; West Germany Government Grant for study in Munich, 1957; Pro Arts Society Award (Philadelphia), 1990.

THE FOLLOWING TWO QUESTIONS, included in the author's Questionnaire (Appendix B), elicited few responses and many "no responses" collectively:

1. Do you feel that your race has affected (positively or negatively) your opportunities to conduct? If so, in what way?

303

2. What is your personal identity? Black? Black Conductor? Conductor? American (with other identifications in combination?) Other?

Everett Lee's responses were particularly interesting and are consequently included as a part of his profile. Wrote Maestro Lee:

Being identified as a person of color has hampered my USA activity, though I have appeared with several major US orchestras—The New York Philharmonic, Cleveland, Cincinnati, Dallas, Baltimore, Detroit, and New Jersey ensembles. However, it was primarily through others' intercession that I was engaged—Cincinnati, New Jersey, Dallas, and the National Symphony, with the aid of Max Rudolph and James DePreist.* Robert Shaw, of the Atlanta Symphony is an old friend, as is Sergiu Comissiona, who engaged me as guest with his Baltimore Symphony. To say that I was engaged through "normal" channels would not quite be correct.

Now to the sensitive part: I am supposed to have a paternal Greek grandfather, a maternal full-blooded American Indian great-grandmother. We are uncertain about her husband, but he must have been of African descent. On my birth certificate it states that I am "Mulatto," a person of mixed Negro and Caucasian ancestry. It also states that I am "Octaroon," a person with one Negro and seven white great grandparents or the offspring of white and a quadroon.

When Europeans inquired of my race, I would answer "Schwarz" (Black) or "Farbige" (Colored) in German. They retorted with, "What are you trying to do—cash in on some kind of publicity?" This is what I faced in Germany, France, and Scandinavia. Many Italians think that I am a Spaniard; many Spaniards think that I am Italian. In South America, they jump at the fact that my great-grandmother was Indian, saying that I am "indigena" (indigenous), one of their own, since so many down there are related to Indians. I have been called Hawaiian, Phillipino and Korean. Since my appearance has caused so much confusion, I simply say now that I am American.[1]

In the land of Everett Lee's birth, he is a black American, not always granted the rights and privileges of either a gifted, trained, talented, and ambitious master of the baton or an American citizen.

Everett Lee has often been referred to as "the perennial traveler," frequently measuring his life (and career) in terms of geography. Spanning the globe, however, has not been his personal preference. The music directorship of a major American orchestra would be the ideal and a position of which he is deserving. As late as 1972, Russell M. Davis wrote of Lee in his book *Black Americans in Cleveland, 1796–1969* (the city where young Everett grew up, but not his place of birth), "[He] may have an opportunity to become the first Negro conductor of a major symphony orchestra."[2] Dean Dixon* had made significant breakthroughs in the early and mid-1940s (as a guest conductor), and Lee himself had been called back from Europe in the early 1970s to guest conduct the Detroit, Cincinnati, Atlanta, and Baltimore Symphony Orchestras. But the distinction of becoming the first black music director of one of this nation's leading orchestras had already gone to Henry Lewis* at the New Jersey Symphony in 1968.

One of the real pioneers in orchestral conducting among black Americans, Everett Lee first attracted attention as a conductor in 1944. Then concertmaster of the CBS Orchestra, Lee substituted on short notice for the ailing conductor of the Broadway musical "Carmen Jones." He soon assumed the duties of assistant conductor. Leonard Bernstein, composer of the score for "On the Town," engaged Lee to conduct his musical and to become assistant conductor of the New York City Symphony.

So impressive were these early conducting experiences that the powerful in the conducting world, as well as the players with whom he worked, encouraged him to seek permanence on the podium rather than a chair in an orchestral violin section. So personally satisfying were these experiences that Lee himself became convinced that he had found his musical niche. History has proven that the encouragements were justified and the decision was wise.

Lee began studying the violin at nine. He had long begged for the instrument but had to wait until he was large enough to hold one; then his father ordered a violin from the Wurlitzer Company. Private lessons followed (including those with the black violinist Louis Vaughn Jones) and though all around him he heard the question "What do you think you have for a future as a violinist?", he was not deterred.[3]

In a 1976 conversation with the black music journalist Raoul Abdul, Lee reminisced about his initial ambition of becoming a concert violinist:

> Abdul: When you were a student at the Cleveland Institute, did you ever think about the fact that there were no opportunities for a black concert violinist?

Lee: It was uppermost in my mind, but, like most young people, I
thought that I could go out and conquer the world.

He even dared to envision himself as a member of the Cleveland
Orchestra, "like all the other fellows who had come out of my class."[4]

Following a brief stint in the Air Force in 1943, Lee settled in
New York City, free lancing as a violinist, discovering his conduct-
ing talents, and engaging in further study at the Berkshire Music
School, Juilliard, and Columbia University. He also married the
concert pianist and opera coach Sylvia Olden. The great maestro Max
Rudolph took over his conducting training and guidance; career
development was encouraged by conductors Leonard Bernstein and
Boris Goldovsky.

In September 1947, the following announcement appeared in the
Baltimore Afro-American newspaper:

> Through the cooperation of Musician's Union 802, Everett Lee, 28
> year-old conductor, has organized an interracial symphony orchestra,
> for the purpose of giving more young musicians experience in
> performing symphonic repertoire. The initial rehearsal was held
> Tuesday at the Masonic Temple.[5]

The following year, just prior to the orchestra's second formal New
York concert, Lee expressed his views on the subject of black
involvement, total participation, and support for his fledgling
orchestra in a *New York Times* article, under the heading "A Negro
Conductor Appeals For a New Kind of Pioneering." He acknowledged the fact that the problem for Blacks was a social one, but
added:

> I cannot help but hold further that creating new job and training
> opportunities, in the final analysis, remains . . . a personal problem.
> For many colored musicians the securing of orchestra opportunities
> should be accepted as an individual as well as group responsibility.[6]

The Cosmopolitan Little Symphony was deliberately interracial.
For this reason, Lee encountered limited receptivity from both Black
and white citizens. He wrote:

> In spite of enthusiastic appreciation of our offering by most
> concert-goers, we have had one Negro organization in Harlem refuse

us the use of their hall for practice sessions—on the grounds that the "impression had been that this was an all-colored orchestra"—just as we have, of course, had similar difficulty downtown with whites.[7]

The determined young conductor was likewise concerned over the defeatist attitude of black players "who had studied classical music seriously [but] had come to believe that there was 'no future' in achieving high standards of proficiency." More than a year into the business of orchestra building, Lee indicated that he was

all the more convinced of the demoralizing effects of widespread racial discrimination in the disintegration of too many individuals' self-faith. The question left in my mind is, no matter what the handicaps, where are today's pioneers? . . . . We plead for more Negroes, especially, who will . . . have their personal vision and grit.[8]

Lee's instrumental ensemble of thirty-eight professional musicians gave its first semipublic concert at City College of New York in early 1948 and made its formal debut at Town Hall on May 21, 1948. The following day, *The New York Times* offered these comments:

Directing his gifted group in a positive, but self-effacing manner, [Lee] made known in his excellent readings not only sound musicianship but also marked refinement and sensitivity of feeling. He was equally at home in the classic and the modern works presented, all of which were keenly understood. His tempi were well chosen and he carefully avoided any hint of distortion or overstatement.[9]

Seven months later, the Cosmopolitan Little Symphony offered another Town Hall concert, with the celebrated Todd Duncan as soloist. Wrote Noel Straus in *The New York Times:*

Mr. Lee's conducting of the talented organization was marked by dignity and refinement. His readings possessed sensibility, as well as taste, and exhibited a laudable comprehension of the style and intentions of each of the varied compositions performed.[10]

The orchestra continued for a brief period, "on a financial shoestring." In the meantime, opera had become one of Lee's special passions, largely as a result of his work with opera conductor Boris

Goldovsky and further work at Columbia University's Opera Workshop. Despite rave reviews, few conducting opportunities were in evidence. One of the few significant breaks came in 1956, when he conducted the New York City Opera Company, a first for a black conductor.[11]

Lee received a Fulbright grant for study in Rome in 1952 and a West German government grant for study in Munich in 1957. In that same year, his European conducting career was launched with his appointment as music director of the Münchener Operabühne, a traveling opera group that performed throughout West Germany. Between 1962 and 1972, Lee served as chief conductor of Scandinavia's most progressive orchestra, the Norrkoping Symphony Orchestra, Sweden.

During his American absence, there emerged in New York City the Symphony of the New World, "the first truly integrated professional orchestra in this country."[12] *New York Post* music journalist Harriett Johnson wrote, when Lee appeared with the orchestra in late 1966:

> Everett Lee, young Negro American, who hasn't appeared here since 1956 . . . was guest maestro last night. . . . Lee showed a controlled efficient beat, authority in a variety of styles and the rare gift of communication.[13]

Under the headline "Lee Triumphs," Miles Katendieck wrote for the *World Journal Tribune:*

> Mr. Lee made an excellent impression. He is talented, musically poised, and alive. Interpreting within the tradition, he fashioned nicely proportioned, sensitive performances of both the Beethoven and Dvorak. To make the orchestra sound as well as it did indicated good control (some fine pianissimos) and reflected much respect from the players, who obviously played for him.[14]

The orchestra dedicated the concert to United Nations Day and the International Year for Human Rights, and appropriately concluded the event with Dvorak's Symphony No. 9, "From the New World."

When Lee conducted the orchestra during its seventh season (1972–73), *The New York Times* wrote:

> [O]ne of the rare conductors who knows the difference between getting musicians to play and getting them to perform. . . . Mr. Lee

knows his scores intimately and gets what he wants from an orchestra.[15]

Lee's name had appeared on the roster as guest conductor almost from the orchestra's inception. Between the years 1971 (when the original conductor resigned following an internal upheaval) and 1973, the Symphony of the New World's leadership was in the hands of an administrative group of founder-players, with guest conductors at the artistic helm. The need for a music director was increasingly more apparent. By mid-August 1973, Everett Lee had been called home from Europe and named to that position, where he remained until the orchestra's demise in 1977.

During his tenure with the Symphony of New World, Lee spoke out on the subject of limited conducting opportunities and "Catch-22" considerations for black conductors: "Someone will say, 'We had Henry Lewis* last year and we're having James DePreist* this season, but maybe we can use you next year. . . .'" To Lee (and many others), the "quota system" was in full operation.[16]

In 1976 Lee made his debut as conductor of the world-famed New York Philharmonic. For his debut he chose violinist Ruggiero Ricci as soloist in the Sibelius Concerto and black American composer David Baker's "Kosbro" (an acronym for "Keep On Steppin' Brothers") as the featured composition.[17] The occasion was the birthday of the late Dr. Martin Luther King, Jr., and the Baker work was played in his memory.

The *New York Times* described Lee's debut as "brilliant." As viewed by Harold Schonberg, the paper's chief music critic:

Mr. Lee conducted a fine concert . . . [H]e directed proportioned performances; he made good music without bending over backward to impress. A Philharmonic debut can be heady stuff, but Mr. Lee stuck to the matter at hand, refusing to be drawn into the temptation to give the audience cheap thrills.[18]

The *New York Post*'s music critic Robert Kimball extolled Lee:

He is an excellent conductor of proven ability. It would be a good idea if he could have at least two weeks at the throttle the next time he heads the orchestra. These one-week quickie orchestral encounters are hardly conducive to developing the best rapport between conductor and orchestra.[19]

When Lee made his Philadelphia debut in 1976, music critic Daniel Webster of the *Philadelphia Inquirer* made note of the fact that the fifty-seven-year-old

> was one of the tenacious group of black conductors who entered the profession about a generation before there was any place for a black conductor to work in this country. You might find it as easy to speak to him in Swedish or German, since his career . . . has been spent in Europe.

Lee had come to Philadelphia to conduct the new Opera Ebony's production of "Aida," on April 1, 1976.[20] The company had been formed by Sister M. Elise of the Blessed Sacrament, to encourage black singers and to give black musicians a forum for presenting grand opera.

Reviewing the performance, Webster indicated that it brought all the problems of a company inauguration, but significantly, Everett Lee was on the podium.

> Lee brought to the performance a security and energy developed abroad. It was his debut here and he was an oak on which many elements leaned . . . [His] unshakable work with the orchestra insured order in moments that were problematical.[21]

Lee continued his relationship with Opera Ebony (since 1987, Opera North), returning to conduct performances of Mozart's "The Marriage of Figaro," Bizet's "Carmen," Verdi's "Rigoletto" and "La Traviata," and most recently, Gershwin's "Porgy and Bess." He also continued his activities as orchestral and opera conductor throughout Europe and South America.

In 1979 he became Titled Conductor of the Bogotá Philharmonic in Colombia and soon thereafter, conductor of Colombia's National Symphony Orchestra. During the 1982–83 academic year, Lee was in residence at Denison University in Granville, Ohio.

Reflecting, from his Swedish residence, on more than forty years of musical leadership, Lee considered the most significant milestones in his conducting career to be his performances at the Bordeaux Festival, the Royal Opera in Stockholm, a "Marriage of Figaro" performance with the Opera Ebony, and appearances with the Munich and New York Philharmonics. He also valued greatly his four-year tenure as musical director of the Symphony of the New World.[22]

Indeed, Everett Astor Lee was "one of the tenacious group of black conductors who entered the profession . . . before there was any place for a black conductor to work in this country." As we note the current American presence of so many talented black conductors (many having gone beyond the ranks of assistant, associate, or guest), we must recall a recent statement of the Chicago Symphony's young black assistant conductor Michael Morgan.* "Each generation of conductors paves the way for the next, . . ."[23] Certainly Lee paved the way for many.

Press Comments

"If an American orchestra could entice Everett Lee from . . . Sweden, it would be a fortunate organization."

Atlanta Journal

"The guest conductor's shining hour came after intermission, when he captained a magnificent performance of Brahms' Symphony No. 4 in E minor."

Dallas Times Herald

"Everett Lee's conducting was sprightly, racy, fiery and full of get-up-and-go."

San Francisco Examiner

"{A}n All-Mozart evening offered by the National Symphony Orchestra. . . . Lee showed exemplary mastery of Mozartian style, balancing the sound neatly and pointing up the phrasing with minute gradations of tempo and dynamics."

Washington Post

"Lee's unshakable work with the orchestra insured order in moments that were problematical . . . {H}e led the score with an unusually sensitive hand, from the finely formed prelude to the triumphal scene." {"Aida," with Opera Ebony}

Philadelphia Inquirer

"Everett Lee . . . created long, lyrical support for the singers and ample energized tone painting. He unobtrusively adjusted the orchestral weight to the singers' capacities and provided rocklike solidity when that was needed to move the ensemble." {"La Traviata" with Opera Ebony}

Philadelphia Inquirer

". . . An evening of rich musical entertainment in which a suave guest conductor lifted the big-sounding Youngstown Symphony Orchestra to a new level of excellence."
Youngstown Vindicator

"Mr. Lee knows his scores intimately and gets what he wants from an orchestra."
New York Times

"Maestro Everett Lee conducted with distinguished character and the Santa Cecilia Orchestra and Chorus were miraculous in adapting to the style."
Paese Sera (Campidoglio/Rome)

"Maestro Everett Lee radiates both geniality and elegance when he sails into Strauss' glorious overture. He promises good things from the very beginning, remembering that this overture belongs to the feared virtuoso numbers in the orchestral repertoire."
Expressen (Stockholm)

"Everett Lee conducted a performance that kept its shape and force . . ."
Philadelphia Inquirer

"Lee showed a controlled, efficient beat, authority in a variety of styles and the rare gift of communication. The music had shape, abundant vitality and the kind of color that produces entertainment to the music's benefit."
New York Post

Notes

1. Questionnaire Handy/Terry.
2. Russell H. Davis, *Black Americans in Cleveland, 1796–1969,* Washington, D.C.: The Associated Publishers, 1972, p. 350.
3. Correspondence, Lee/Handy, July 14, 1987.
4. Raoul Abdul, *Blacks in Classical Music: A Personal History,* New York: Dodd, Mead and Company, 1977, pp. 195–196.
5. "Everett Lee Starts New Symphony," *Baltimore Afro-American,* August 30, 1947, p. 6.
6. Everett Lee, "A Negro Conductor Appeals For a New Kind of Pioneering," *New York Times,* December 26, 1948, Section 2, p. 7.
7. *Ibid.*
8. *Ibid.*
9. Noel Straus, "Symphony Group in Formal Debut," *New York Times,* May 22, 1948, p. 9.
10. ———, "Everett Lee Leads Cosmopolitan Unit," *New York Times,* December 27, 1948, p. 17.

11. This is the company that made history in 1945 when it hired black baritone Todd Duncan and continued that precedent by engaging black soprano Camilla Williams in 1946 and the black timpanist Elayne Jones in 1949.

12. For more on the Symphony of the New World, see Raoul Abdul, *op. cit.,* pp. 205–207 and "In Retrospect . . . The Symphony of the New World (compiled by Clarissa and Marion Cumbo), *Black Perspective in Music,* Fall 1975, pp. 312–330.

13. Harriett Johnson, "Lee Leads Integrated Symphony," *New York Post,* October 25, 1966, p. 66.

14. Miles Katendieck, "Lee Triumphs," *World Journal Tribune,* October 25, 1966, p. 40.

15. Donal Henahan, "New World Symphony," *New York Times,* June 25, 1973, p. 47.

16. "Symphony 'Quotas' Assailed," *Richmond Times-Dispatch,* October 28, 1975, p. B16.

17. Throughout Everett Lee's conducting career, he has been firmly committed to the music of black composers.

18. Harold Schonberg, "Everett Lee Leads Philharmonic in Debut," *New York Times,* January 16, 1976, p. 18.

19. Robert Kimball, *New York Post,* January 16, 1976, p. 17.

20. Daniel Webster, "He'll Give 'Aida' That Lee Touch," *Philadelphia Inquirer,* March 28, 1976, p. 1–E.

21. ———, "Black Opera Group Opens with 'Aida'," *Philadelphia Inquirer,* April 2, 1976, p. 6D.

22. Questionnaire, Handy/Terry.

23. Dalton Narine, "The Maestros," *Ebony,* February 1989, p. 56.

Tania León.

TANIA JUSTINA LEÓN (FERRAN)-TANIA LEÓN

BIRTHDATE/PLACE: May 14, 1943; Havana, Cuba.

EDUCATION: B.A. (Piano and Theory), C.A. Peyrellade Conservatory, Havana, Cuba, 1963; M.A. (Music Education), National Conservatory, Havana, Cuba, 1964; B.A. (Accounting/Business Administration), Havana University, Havana, Cuba, 1965; B.S. (Music Education), New York University, 1973; M.A. (Composition), New York University, 1975; Tanglewood Conducting Program, 1978.

INSTRUCTORS/COACHES: Laszio Halasz, Leonard Bernstein, Seiji Ozawa (Conducting).

MAJOR APPOINTMENTS: Music Director, Dance Theatre of Harlem, 1968–79; Music Director, Brooklyn Philharmonic Family/Community Concert Series, 1977—; Music Director, Alvin Ailey American Dance Theatre, 1983–84; Resident Composer, Lincoln Center Institute, 1985—; Associate Professor (Composition/Conducting), Brooklyn College, 1985—; Music Director, Whitney Museum Contemporary Music Concert Series, 1986; Music Director, Brooklyn College Orchestra, 1991—; Composer-in-Residence, Cabrillo (California), 1990 and Ravinia (Illinois), 1991 Music Festivals and Bellagio Center (Italy), 1992.

GUEST CONDUCTOR: Columbus, Phoenix, New World, Genova, Pasadena, Cosmopolitan, La Crosse (Wisconsin), and Puerto Rico Symphony Orchestras; Buffalo and Brooklyn Philharmonics; Cleveland Institute of Music and Juilliard School of Music Orchestras; Metropolitan, Michigan, New York Grand and John F. Kennedy Center Opera House Orchestras; Colonne, Sadler's Wells, B.B.C., Northern, and Royal Ballet Orchestras; Radio City Music Hall, Orchestra of Our Time; Lincoln Center Outdoors Festival; Festival of Two Worlds (Spoleto, Italy), Spoleto Festival (Charleston), Cabrillo Music Festival; Netherlands Wind Ensemble; RIAS Orchestra (Berlin), Beethovenhalle Symphony Orchestra (Bonn).

AWARDS/HONORS: National Endowment for the Arts Composition Award, 1975; CINTAS Award in Composition, 1976, 1979; Byrd Hoffman Foundation, 1981; Key to the City of Detroit, 1982; Queens Council on the Arts, 1983; Meet the Composer Awards, 1978–87; ASCAP Composer's Awards, 1978–87; Dean Dixon Achievement Award, 1985; Celebrate

315

Brooklyn Achievement Award, 1990; MacArthur Foundation Annual Residency for Artists (Yaddo), 1991; Academy-Institute Award in Music, American Academy and Institute of Arts and Letters, 1991.

TANIA LEÓN RESENTS AND DEFIES CATEGORIZATION as well as questions of identity and identification:

> I dislike labels. I had to learn the hard way—being called black conductor, female or woman conductor, Hispanic or Latino. Well, I had enough. I prefer to be just a musician, or a conductor, or composer. All the rest is beside the point. . . .[1]

She was one of nine expatriate musicians, all composers, asked to share their impressions of working, touring, performing, and collaborating with local artists by the editors of *EAR Magazine,* October 1989. Her response ["Cuba to the U.S."]:

> I am obsessed with integration, not separation. I don't see separation within race, gender, or place. . . . I was born in a place, I live in another place, and who knows where I will be tomorrow. . . . When I go back to my mother's place in Cuba, she always accepts me, wherever I have been.[2]

This attitude of absolutism, of being without restrictions, is inevitable for León; it reflects both her unselfconscious world view and the elements and influences in her life that cause one to consider her "universal." She is the product of several cultures (Spanish, African, Chinese, French). She is a multifaceted musician (composer, conductor, pianist, music director). Her eclectic musical tastes and her fluency in many genres reflect a myriad of musical influences— Latin, Asian, African-American; jazz and popular music; opera, dance, and other music for the theater; Western European (particularly impressionist and postimpressionist).

Her musical activities of the past twenty years bear witness to her versatility: guest conductor of the Buffalo Philharmonic, Colonne, and Sadler's Wells Orchestras and orchestras of the Kennedy Center Opera House and the Metropolitan Opera; music director for the Alvin Ailey American Dance Theatre, Dance Theatre of Harlem, and *The Wiz* (on Broadway); composer of commissioned works for the Brooklyn Philharmonia, the Whitney Museum, Lincoln Center Institute, Bay Area Women's Philharmonic, and American Composers' Orchestra; and associate professor of composition at Brooklyn College.

That her career is so varied is no longer remarkable to León. She has come to a point of comfort about herself. "In my music, I'm accepting the components that make me a person. I feel I'm speaking from an emerging point of view."[3]

The person who is still becoming Tania León began formation quite early in her life:

> Apparently I became aware of music at a very early age. My family realized that I was attracted to classical music since I loved to listen to the radio stations that would play those kinds of sounds. I was four years old at the time.[4]

Her grandmother, having lost her job scrubbing floors in a mansion because she played the piano one day, took the incident as a sign that "someone in her family would play the piano, be famous and travel."[5] She decided to take Tania to the conservatory to have her musical aptitude tested. A staff teacher recognized that León had talent but felt that she was too young to be taught. However, the grandmother persevered; Tania began studies, and gave her first public recital at age five.

León continued her conservatory study throughout her public school years. She was encouraged to pursue a career as a pianist, and though she had started to compose at age 13, never thought of herself in any other musical role than as a keyboard player. However, León was pragmatic in her approach to the future. After having earned a B.A. degree in piano and theory from the C.A. Peyrellade Conservatory (1963) and the M.A. in music education from the National Conservatory (1964), she secured a B.A. in accounting and business administration from Havana University (1965).

León left Cuba in 1967, propelled by the need to expand her musical horizons and a curiosity about other people and places. Though she was fascinated by Europe ("[When I was little] my dream was to go to Paris and live around the Eiffel Tower"[6]), she settled in New York. There she met Arthur Mitchell, founder of Dance Theatre of Harlem (DTH). The meeting was coincidental (León was substituting as DTH school pianist for a sick friend) and fortuitous: Mitchell was so impressed by León's playing that he asked her to become the company pianist. León recalls they communicated in Spanish and Portuguese since she did not speak English at the time. Shortly after her arrival, León created a music school at DTH that awarded scholarships to community students.[7]

The association with Mitchell and DTH stimulated León to compose:

> The first year or so I played with him I never played from books; I improvised everything. He would dictate a combination, and I would make a piece out of it. He persuaded me to write a ballet with him. That was my first piece, called "Tones."[8]

León also credits Mitchell with encouraging her to conduct, a musical option that had never before occurred to her. There were no role models for her; she had assumed that a woman's conducting of an orchestra was taboo. The occasion of her debut was the 1971 appearance of DTH at the Festival of Two Worlds at Spoleto, Italy. Once the company was on site, Arthur Mitchell, along with the Festival's director Gian Carlo Menotti, decided that live music would be infinitely more satisfying for the performances than taped music. Since León knew the pieces, she was drafted to conduct the Juilliard Orchestra, then in residence at the festival. That opportunity was decisive: León returned to the United States with her sights on a new goal. She quickly earned degrees in music education and composition from New York University and then began to study conducting.

For León, concern for the inclusiveness of the symphony orchestra was both as natural and as serious as the music and the institutions themselves. She believes that art should exist for all people, just as it should draw inspiration and validity from all cultures. From her earliest conducting opportunities, León always stressed music of the world's composers; she programmed music of African-American, Asian, and Latino composers alongside that of Western Europeans, and she increasingly performed contemporary works. She believed that regular concert-going audiences should be exposed to different music. And she hoped that non-traditional audiences (particularly ethnic and racial minorities) would be attracted to symphonic music if they could form an identification with the creators of the works. In 1976, León helped to create the Family/Community Concert Series at the Brooklyn Philharmonic (with which she has a continuing affiliation). The series, of which León is musical director, seeks to bring classical music to New York City's minority communities, to showcase minority musicians, and to introduce minority composers to wider audiences. Though she is proud of what the project has accomplished, she expresses some frustration:

> That series has gone on 10 years, and no one seems to move it out of what it is. . . . I thought the people it addressed would feel more comfortable coming to the concert hall because they found out they had something to do with it. But the way it has been done has perpetuated segregation. Those composers are not included in any other programs, and by not including them in a more integrated way, their communities don't come to see anything.[9]

When León has the opportunity to program, she is careful to avoid the "segregation" she observes in other situations.

> I have been conducting black composers consistently since 1974 . . . My programming reflects music of all people, old and new, conventional and nonconventional. I believe in integration.[10]

León especially champions new music and jazz. She takes pride in having premiered many jazz works by "very valuable colleagues," including Muhal Richard Abrams and Leroy Jenkins. She cites the premiere of a Noel DaCosta piece, "Primal Rites" for orchestra and drums (with Max Roach as soloist), as an unforgettably enjoyable experience.[11]

In a professional life increasingly filled with commissions (American Composers' Orchestra, DaCapo Chamber Players, National Public Radio-theme for a daily broadcast called "Latin File," Western Wind Vocal Ensemble, and Brooklyn College's 60th Anniversary), León still conducts actively. She maintains her base with the Brooklyn Philharmonic and accepts guest conducting opportunities both here and abroad. And not just with symphony orchestras. She has adopted as a goal (already partially fulfilled):

> To be considered a valid conductor among musicians all over, of all kinds of ensembles, from chamber to symphonic, from studio gigs to steel band groups—you name it![12]

Since 1992, Tania León has served as Artistic Advisor to the American Composers Orchestra's Latin American Project (having only recently served as the orchestra's Composer-in-Residence).

In early 1993, the New York Philharmonic appointed León to a two-year term as Charles H. Revson Composer Fellow.

León was on the podium, conducting the Münich Biennale Festival Orchestra, when her opera "Scourge of Hyacinths" was premiered in Münich, Germany on May 1, 1994.

Press Comments

"Olsen's 'Overture: Lulu' is a bright, sassy piece of infectious energy, and it got a fine performance as conducted by Tania León, a maestro of obvious technical and interpretive talents who really knows how to keep an orchestra in rein."

Daily News (New York)

"She is a strong musical personality who has a top-notch baton technique and a beat of utmost clarity. Moreover, the orchestra played extremely well for her."

Daily News (New York)

Notes

1. Response to author's questionnaire.
2. "An American in Paris and Other Expatriate Composers Speak Out," *EAR Magazine,* October 1989, p. 32.
3. *EAR Magazine* (New Music News), December 1986/January 1987, p. 16.
4. Questionnaire, *op. cit.*
5. Iadavaia-Cox, Angela, "The Tug Between Conducting and Composing," *Essence,* December 1976, p. 72.
6. Howard Mandel, "Tania Leon: Beyond Borders," *EAR Magazine,* December 1988/January 1989, p. 12.
7. *Ibid.*
8. *Ibid.*
9. *Ibid.,* p. 13.
10. Questionnaire, *op. cit.*
11. Mandel, "Tania Leon: Beyond Borders" p. 13.
12. Questionnaire, *op. cit.*

Henry Lewis

HENRY LEWIS

BIRTHDATE/PLACE: October 16, 1932; Los Angeles, California.
EDUCATION: University of Southern California.
MAJOR INSTRUCTORS/COACHES: Herman Reinshagen, Double Bass;
Fritz Zweig, Ingolf Dahl, Eduard van Beinum, Conducting.
MAJOR APPOINTMENTS: Music Director, Seventh Army Symphony
Orchestra, 1956; Music Director and Founder, String Society of Los Angeles
(which later became the Los Angeles Chamber Orchestra), 1959–63;
Associate Conductor, Los Angeles Philharmonic, 1962–65; Artistic Direc-
tor, Los Angeles Opera Company, 1965; Music Director, New Jersey
Symphony Orchestra, 1968–76; Chief Conductor, Dutch Radio Symphony
Orchestra, 1989–91.
GUEST CONDUCTOR: New York and Los Angeles Philharmonic Orches-
tras; Cleveland, Chicago, Philadelphia, Boston, Pittsburgh, Cincinnati,
Detroit, Baltimore, Buffalo, Rochester, San Francisco, Oakland, Milwaukee,
and American Symphony Orchestras; London Symphony; Royal Philhar-
monic; RAI in Turin, Milan, and Rome; Nouvel Orchestra Philharmonique of
France; Warsaw, Copenhagen, Monte Carlo, Japan, New Zealand, Glasgow,
and Philippines Symphony Orchestras; Metropolitan, San Francisco, Montreal,
Vancouver, Los Angeles Music Center, and New York City Opera Companies;
Opera Company of Boston and American Opera Society; Lausanne, Hamburg,
Royal Opera (Covent Garden); English National Opera; Paris, Marseilles,
Avignon, Welsh National Opera, Netherlands Opera, Venice, Scottish Opera,
La Scala (Milan), Montreal, and Rio de Janeiro Opera Companies.
AWARDS/HONORS: Key to the City, Newark, New Jersey; Grammy
(RCA, Philharmonic Orchestra and Leontyne Price).
RECORDINGS: London, RCA, EMI Records.

> Too often talented Negroes have been reluctant to compete in this
> field because they were convinced their color would be counted
> against them. One of the most important things I can do now is to
> give to other Negroes the incentive to try to win positions with
> symphonic organizations.[1]

HENRY LEWIS MADE THIS STATEMENT during an interview just before
his debut with the Los Angeles Philharmonic that made him the first

322

black conductor to lead a major symphony orchestra in a home-based, regular subscription concert. The event was a critical success and brought the twenty-eight-year-old conductor to national prominence.

Lewis had, in fact, already emerged as a trailblazer for black musicians. More than a decade earlier, at age sixteen, he auditioned successfully for a double bass position in the Los Angeles Philharmonic. Lewis was the youngest and first black musician to join the ranks of that prestigious ensemble.

In his early and mid-twenties, he was music director of the Seventh Army Symphony, founding conductor of the String Society of Los Angeles (later named the Los Angeles Chamber Orchestra), and conducted the Los Angeles Philharmonic in area tours and in a highly successful radio series of youth concerts. He went on to be the first black music director of a professional American orchestra, and the first black conductor at the Metropolitan Opera.

Born in Los Angeles, Henry Lewis was educated in parochial and public schools there. He began piano lessons at age five and went on to study various orchestra instruments before turning to the double bass. He tackled the bass "because it was the only way I could get a place in the school orchestra."[2] His interest in conducting was evident when he conducted the "Grand March" from "Aida" on his junior high school graduation day.

Lewis attributes his enthusiasm for the double bass to Herman Reinshagen, who had come to Los Angeles after many years as principal bass of the New York Philharmonic. Reinshagen guided Lewis's development as a virtuoso bass player and solo recitalist. It was the success of a full-length solo bass recital that enabled the sixteen-year-old Lewis to audition for Alfred Wallenstein and the Los Angeles Philharmonic. His youth and lack of professional experience were obstacles he overcame by renting the Wiltshire-Eben Theatre for a solo recital. The invitation to audition quickly followed.

The appointment finally convinced Lewis's father (who could not envision an orchestral career for a black musician) that his son could be successful in music after all. It also helped Lewis win a full scholarship to the University of Southern California. At the time, the University offered music degrees only in music education. But Lewis had far broader interests—languages, philosophy, and literature. Consequently, he left USC with more than enough credits to graduate, but without the necessary requirements for the music education degree.

In 1955, while still a member of the Los Angeles Philharmonic, Lewis was drafted into military service and was assigned to the Seventh Army Symphony, first as a bass player and then, in 1956, as music director. He led the orchestra in fifty-two radio broadcasts and more than one hundred live performances in Stuttgart (the orchestra's home base), and throughout Europe.[3] Lewis sees this experience as responsible for his continuing career. He was given the opportunity to develop his skills working with an ensemble of excellent musicians. They rehearsed constantly, played three or four concerts a week, and, as a Special Services unit attached directly to the General, received privileged treatment as well.[4]

When the orchestra performed in the Netherlands, Lewis caught the attention of Eduard van Beinum, then music director of Amsterdam's Concertgebouw Orchestra. Van Beinum had become music director of the Los Angeles Philharmonic by the time Lewis returned to the orchestra after his military service, and became his mentor.

In 1959, Lewis founded the String Society of Los Angeles for the pleasure of both playing and conducting chamber works. Later called the Los Angeles Chamber Orchestra, the ensemble began with some of the Philharmonic's finest players. Lewis led the Los Angeles Chamber Orchestra in concerts throughout California and, in 1963, on an extensive tour of Europe under the aegis of the State Department.

Lewis's subscription concert debut with the Los Angeles Philharmonic came in 1961 when guest conductor Igor Markevitch cancelled due to illness. The *New York Times* headline read "Negro Conducts Coast Symphony, Henry Lewis First of Race to Lead Major Orchestra in Regular Concert."[5] *Time Magazine* praised his "vigorous, sweeping" conducting and his "top-notch concert."[6] Soon thereafter, Lewis accepted an associate conductor's position with the orchestra and resigned his chair in the bass section. He remained with the Los Angeles Philharmonic until 1965.

Lewis was subsequently engaged by virtually every major American orchestra and by orchestras throughout Europe. The list includes the New York Philharmonic, Boston Symphony, Philadelphia Orchestra, Cleveland Orchestra, Chicago Symphony, the orchestras of Pittsburgh, Detroit, Cincinnati, San Francisco, Buffalo, and Baltimore; all of the major London orchestras; the RAI orchestras in Rome, Turin, and Milan; and the Nouvel Orchestra Philharmonique of France.

In February 1968, Henry Lewis was appointed music director of the New Jersey Symphony Orchestra, accepting the challenge of developing the ensemble into a major orchestra. Considering the manifestations of the civil rights movement during the 1960s, the issue of Lewis's race as a motivating factor in the selection was raised:

> When the president of the orchestra's board was asked whether Lewis' race had any bearing on his appointment, he answered, "Almost none until we came down to the final selection and realized that Mr. Lewis was the best qualified of all the candidates."[7]

Time Magazine commented:

> The orchestra insisted that it chose Lewis only because he is talented, and not because he is Negro. Still, in a city [Newark] with an estimated 55% Negro population and a recent history of racial frustration, the appointment seems astute sociologically as well as musically.[8]

Reporting that Lewis was chosen from a field of 150 candidates and observing that he thus became "the first Negro to be permanent head of a U.S. symphony orchestra," *Newsweek* added:

> The big winner in this new appointment is not Henry Lewis but the New Jersey Symphony Orchestra in securing for themselves a musician of real distinction.[9]

Lewis's eight-year tenure was remarkable: he rebuilt the orchestra from a somewhat avocational ensemble playing twenty concerts a year to a thoroughly professional contract orchestra performing more than 125 concerts a season throughout New Jersey and beyond. Carnegie Hall in New York City and the Kennedy Center in the nation's capital became regular venues. He increased audiences and attracted the nontraditional concert-goers who in larger urban areas are usually assumed to have no interest in symphonic music. And he elevated the level of playing and the orchestra's artistic standard to the point that critics began to compare it with larger, older, more prestigious ensembles.

Henry Lewis's conducting career was not limited to symphony orchestras. According to Lewis, opera has always been his first love.[10] He studied voice and vocal technique extensively. In 1961, he made his debut with the San Francisco Opera, conducting Puccini's "La Boheme." His debut at La Scala (Milan) in 1965 was conducting "Gershwiniana," a ballet-cantata based on the music of George Gershwin.

Lewis made history again in October 1972, with his conducting debut at the Metropolitan Opera. When the announcement was made in the previous spring, an article in The *New York Times* began:

> The first black conductor in the history of the Metropolitan Opera, Henry Lewis, has been engaged to make his debut with the company next season in Puccini's "La Boheme." Mr. Lewis is the 39-year-old musical director of the New Jersey Symphony.[11]

The following fall, the same newspaper reported:

> There are not many frontiers left, even if you happen to be black, but one more can be crossed off the list after Monday night's performance of "La Boheme" at the Metropolitan Opera. Just 17 years after Marian Anderson broke through as the first black singer, Henry Lewis became the first black to conduct a Met performance—and on his 40th birthday, to boot.[12]

Lewis appeared with the Metropolitan Opera in New York, on U.S. tours, and on tour to Japan. He led numerous performances of "Carmen," "Romeo and Juliette," "Un Ballo in Maschera," and "L'Italiana in Algieri." In 1977, he conducted "Le Prophète," the first Meyerbeer opera produced by the Metropolitan in more than forty years.

Despite his success with the New Jersey Symphony, when his tenure with that orchestra came to an end in 1976, Henry Lewis found only occasional guest conducting opportunities. He, like other black conductors before him, turned his attention to Europe. He achieved broad critical acclaim for his Paris Opera debut in 1982 and appeared with the Hamburg Opera, the Scottish Opera, and the opera companies of Marseilles, Avignon, Lausanne, Wales, and Venice.

Just prior to his 1986 Covent Garden debut in Rossini's *Semiramide,* journalist/music critic Andrew Clark wrote:

> [A]lthough some of the doors in his U.S. career have been closed, he has lost none of his musical gifts—the unflappable control, care for

detail and understanding of the singing voice that distinguished him as one of the rising generation of American conductors in the 1960s.[13]

American critics did not disagree. A guest appearance with the Chicago Symphony at Ravinia in 1986 prompted Robert Marsh to write, "His work was on a level that suggested we should not have to wait so long to hear him again."[14]

When Lewis was invited to conduct "Salome" for the inaugural season of the Los Angeles Music Center Opera, music critic Martin Bernheimer wrote: "he conducted with splendid sweep and urgency, with cumulative impact and where appropriate, frenzy. He also elicited brilliant playing. . . ."[15]

Henry Lewis returned as guest conductor with the New Jersey Symphony in 1985. Critic Michael Redmond wrote:

> More than any other music director in the orchestra's 63-year history, Lewis made the New Jersey Symphony what it is today . . . a first-class professional orchestra of national reputation, and an artistic entity that has set the musical standard for the entire state. . . .
>
> He left a legacy that has continued to enrich this state, even in his absence. And that is something to applaud, commemorate, and celebrate.[16]

In Europe, Henry Lewis had frequently appeared with the Dutch Radio Symphony Orchestra both at the Concertgebouw in Amsterdam and throughout Holland. From 1989 to 1991, he served as music director of this orchestra, leading a variety of symphonic programs as well as concert operas for live audiences and radio broadcast.

Lewis's discography includes works recorded for London Records' Phase Four series, recently reissued on compact disc. He has made complete opera recordings of Meyerbeer's "Le Prophète" and Massenet's "La Navarraise." In addition, he has frequently collaborated with Marilyn Horne (the former Mrs. Henry Lewis) in recordings of arias and opera excerpts. His RCA recording with the Philharmonic Orchestra (London) and Leontyne Price captured a Grammy Award. A Gershwin disc with the Royal Philharmonic (London) was issued in 1992.

In 1990, Henry Lewis accepted the invitation to collaborate with director Simon Callow in developing a London production of

"Carmen Jones," by Oscar Hammerstein II. According to *The Guardian,* Lewis agreed "because this *is* Carmen." The production opened at the Old Vic in April, 1991, and, in 1992, "Carmen Jones" captured the coveted Olivier Award for "Best Musical."

Reflecting on his current career activities, Henry Lewis commented:

> It is striking to me that an American conductor can be so successful in terms of both reviews and employment in Europe, and can be so completely ignored here. I work eight months of the year, but it's all in Europe. The only work I get here is guesting, or as a replacement for a sick conductor.[17]

Sadly, Lewis's comments reflect a condition that has been all too common for many black conductors—most notably Dean Dixon*— who are compelled to live and work outside the United States to achieve recognition and professional fulfillment. The particular irony in the case of Henry Lewis is that, unlike some of his colleagues, he has experienced a considerable degree of success with orchestras and opera companies in this country. Both guest conducting invitations and full appointments suggest that his prospects for the music directorship of a prestigious American orchestra or opera company ought to be excellent.

Press Comments

"{H}e conducted with splendid sweep and urgency, with cumulative impact and, where appropriate, frenzy. He also elicited brilliant playing. . . ."

Los Angeles Times

The Montreal Symphony responded to Henry Lewis's musical direction with some of the most tasteful and elegant playing it has produced for the opera performances. Lewis wove an enchanting spell of radiant sound with the orchestra, which securely supported but never overpowered the singers.

Opera

"{H}is work was on a level that suggested we should not have to wait so long to hear him again."

Chicago Sun Times

"Henry Lewis is, in fact, extraordinarily effective; he gave to Gounod that which Gounod lacks most—muscle!"

France-Soir (Paris)

"Henry Lewis conducted "Les Troyens." He kindled a glowing, uninhibited romantic passion . . . the orchestra's best accomplishment in a long time."

Orpheus (Hamburg)

"Mr. Lewis proved . . . that the Puccini style of broad lyricism was one he understood well and could command technically. Credit the Met with good sense in engaging him, and credit Mr. Lewis with a highly satisfactory debut."

New York Times.

"Mr. Lewis . . . led both orchestra and singers with increasing confidence and conviction."

New York Times.

"{H}is conducting has the clarity and energy that can bring the best out of people."

New York Magazine

"The quality of the New Jersey Symphony's playing, which is very near the top, attests to Mr. Lewis' sterling abilities as a trainer."

New Yorker

". . . a propulsive performance that left one impressed with the young orchestra! New Jersey Symphony!."

New York Times

"Mahler's Third Symphony was an exceptional performance, thanks to the precision of the conductor, Henry Lewis."

Netherlands

". . . conducting his first opera in Britain {"Simon Boccanegra"} . . . Lewis gave {the scenes} a musical vivacity which never allowed them to drag. He drew a warm range of expressive colour with intensity of feeling."

Music and Musicians

"Henry Lewis's experience of the work {"Les Troyens"} clearly enabled him to get the Marseilles orchestra to outdo themselves."

Opera

"{"Le Prophète"}. . . The credit belongs to Henry Lewis, a refined, experienced conductor who evidently believes in this music and enters into its spirit."

Opera

"Mr. Lewis' orchestral accompaniments {to Mahler's "Kindertotenlieder" and Wagner's "Wesendonck Lieder"} are beautifully fashioned and are executed with great authority by the Royal Philharmonic. . . . Lewis draws some remarkable playing from the orchestra. . . ." {London Records with mezzo-soprano Marilyn Horne)

Stereo Review

"The strongest musical impression was made by the playing of the Scottish Philharmonia under the baton of Henry Lewis, . . . {He} established an evidently warm rapport with the players, who responded with playing of a considerable range of expression as well as dramatic intensity. Lewis imparted vivacity to scenes {from "Simon Boccanegra"} that tend to be slow-paced, skillfully complementing both the voices and the visual effect."

Opera News

"{Carmen Jones}, . . . stylishly conducted by Henry Lewis. . . . The best musical in town."

Weekend Telegraph (London)

Notes

1. Murray Schumach, "Negro Conducts Coast Symphony," *New York Times,* February 10, 1961, p. 22.
2. Interview with Andrew Clark, *International Herald Tribune,* April 2, 1986, p. 18E.
3. "Henry Lewis," *Current Biography Yearbook,* New York, NY: The H.W. Wilson Company, 1973, p. 249.
4. Taped radio interview, George Shirley with Henry Lewis, *Classical Music and the Afro-American* (Parkway Productions, 1973).
5. Schumach, *op. cit.*
6. "Incentive to Try," *Time Magazine,* February 17, 1961, p. 48.
7. Raoul Abdul, *Blacks in Classical Music,* New York: Dodd, Mead & Company, 1977, p. 198.
8. "First Again," *Time,* February 23, 1968, p. 94.
9. "Baton Breakthrough," *Newsweek,* February 26, 1968, p. 93.
10. "Lewis, First Black on Met Podium, Leads 'Boheme'," *New York Times,* October 18, 1972, p. 36.
11. "Metropolitan Engages 1st Black Conductor," *New York Times,* April 25, 1972, p. 36.
12. "Lewis, First Black on Met Podium. . . ," *op. cit.*
13. Interview with Andrew Clark, *op. cit.*

14. Robert C. Marsh, "Horne and Lewis Bring Back Those Happy Moments," *Chicago Sun Times,* July 21, 1986, p. 37.
15. Martin Bernheimer, "Music Center Stages a Dazzling 'Salome',", *Los Angeles Times.* October 11, 1986, pp. 1, 7.
16. Michael Redmond, "Maestro Lewis Still Has His Magic Touch," *Star-Ledger* (Newark), April 1, 1985, p. 25.
17. Telephone Interview, William E. Terry with Lewis, August 1, 1989, Detroit/New York.

Walter Howard Loving (Courtesy: Moorland-Spingarn Research Center, Howard University)

Walter Loving's Philippine Constabulary Band (Courtesy: Moorland Spingarn Research Center, Howard University)

WALTER HOWARD LOVING

BIRTHDATE/PLACE: December 17, 1872; Lovingston, Virginia.
DEATH DATE/PLACE: February, 1945; Manila, Philippines.
EDUCATION: High School Diploma, M Street High School (Washington, D.C.), 1892; attended New England Conservatory of Music (Boston, Massachusetts), 1898; additional study in Germany, Italy, Vienna, and London, 1911.
MAJOR ACCOMPLISHMENT and APPOINTMENT: Organizer, Commanding Officer, and Conductor, Philippine Constabulary Band, 1902–16; 1919–23; 1937–41; Office of Intelligence (Washington, D.C.), 1917–18.
AWARDS/HONORS: Award of Merit, Philippine Government (posthumously), 1952.

UNDER THE HEADING "PERSONAL," editors of *The Journal of Negro History* registered the following in April 1945:

> One distinguished Negro left in the Philippines a more lasting impression than even some of the Americans sent there as governors. He was Major Walter Howard Loving, the director of the Philippine Constabulary Band, which he made famous throughout the civilized world.[1]

The 1922 edition of *The Negro Year Book* said of Loving, "As a band conductor . . . [he] admits no superiors and it may be said[,] few peers."[2] After all, Loving's band was the first in history to share honors with the United States Marine Band at a Presidential Inauguration (1909). His was the band that March King John Philip Sousa designated as "the finest band" appearing at the 1915 Panama Pacific Exposition. It was the only symphonic band of its size that could, within a short period of time, be converted into a full symphonic orchestra. Loving's band was the one band that critics from all parts of the world unanimously acknowledged as "excellent."

Band director and educator Claiborne T. Richardson completed an in-depth investigation of this exciting personality and his famous

334

band, and registered his findings in *The Black Perspective in Music* in 1982. He titled the article "The Filipino-American Phenomenon: The Loving Touch."[3] Richardson based his findings on material gathered through years of research in various libraries throughout the country, the National Archives in Washington, correspondence and interviews, a six-week stay in Manila (traveling with and guest conducting the Constabulary Band on its 78th Anniversary tour), and contact with Loving's widow, Edith McCary Loving. Mrs. Loving has since donated the Walter Loving Papers to the Moorland-Spingarn Research Center of Howard University.

Loving's military career began in 1893, as cornetist with the 24th Infantry Regiment, Colored,[4] at Fort Bayard, Silver City, New Mexico. He soon advanced to the solo cornetist position. With a desire "to be all that he could be," Loving studied the violin and, eventually, all the woodwind instruments. It was not unusual to find him filling in as a violinist with the 24th Infantry Orchestra.

Discharged from military service in June 1898, Loving reenlisted in August of the same year—the year of the Spanish-American War—serving as Chief Musician with the 8th Regiment, U.S. Volunteer Infantry, Colored, stationed at Fort Thomas, Kentucky. This tour of duty lasted a brief six months.

Loving soon thereafter entered the prestigious New England Conservatory of Music in Boston, Massachusetts, studying harmony, composition, conducting, and cornet. He made such a tremendous impression on his professors that his announcement of plans to leave the Conservatory to reenlist was received with regret by the faculty. Professor J. Wallace Goodrich expressed his feelings about his student in a note he wrote to Loving:

> [D]uring your course of studies in harmony and composition in this institution . . . your progress was very remarkable . . . [T]he mark that you attained as a cornet soloist has never been surpassed since this institution organized its special course for the cornet.[5]

Loving's third enlistment in September 1899 brought an assignment to the 48th Regiment Band, U.S. Volunteer Infantry, Colored. The United States' involvement was intended to end the insurrection underway in the Philippines, where the 48th Infantry was assigned. By this time, Loving had attained the position of Chief Musician and soon organized a chorus. His success was relatively assured since, in his earlier D.C. years, he had acquired experience as a church choir director and as chorister at the Fifteenth Street Presbyterian Church.

By fortunate circumstance, William Howard Taft, Secretary of the Philippine Commission, was in attendance at a 48th Regiment Chorus and Band performance. Believing that the Philippines should have a National Band equivalent to the U.S. Marine Band, Taft, when he became Governor of the Philippines, recommended that such a band be created and that Loving be the conductor. The recommendation was supported by the facts that Loving was a well-qualified musician, was fluent in the Spanish language, possessed strong leadership abilities, and had proven himself to be a good soldier.

The Philippine Constabulary Band was organized in late 1902. It was created to perform for military ceremonies and various civil and official government functions. Having attained the rank of Third Lieutenant, Loving was assigned to be the band's Commanding Officer and Conductor. With an original group of thirty, he immediately instituted a rigid physical and musical training program. Understandably, both the band's size and its reputation grew rapidly.

On March 12, 1904, the band, numbering more than eighty pieces, set sail for the United States, where it was scheduled to appear at the Louisiana Purchase Exposition in St. Louis in May. As Richardson noted:

> In attendance for the band concert were members of royalty, high officials, and dignitaries from all over the world. Added to this group of notables were the world's finest bands: the U.S. Marine Band, the John Philip Sousa Band, the Mexican National Band, the Band of the British Grenadier Guards, the Royal Italian Band, and Le Garde Republicaine Band of France.[6]

The initial performance was an overwhelming success, despite the fact that the Exposition grounds were plunged into darkness at the concert's commencement. When the lights went out, Maestro Loving simply pulled out his white handkerchief, folded it around the baton and the concert proceeded. The Filipino musicians and their black American conductor were acclaimed for their outstanding musicianship, having performed an entire program from memory.

Other major American cities were included on the band's concert itinerary. Booker T. Washington, the great educator, humanitarian, and politician, despite his firm belief that the black man could best achieve economic independence through skill in the industrial arts, also saw merit in quality artistic instruction at his now famous Tuskegee Institute [University] in Alabama. Washington directed the following letter to Taft, then Secretary of War:

> I am writing to ask whether it will be possible for you to consider the appointment of Lieutenant [sic] W.H. Loving, Philippine Constabulary, Commanding Band, Manila, P.I., to the Philippine Scout Service, and detail him to this institution, to take charge of Military Training and Band Training of our students.

The request was not honored.[7]

Taft, Governor of Ohio during the St. Louis Exposition, promised that if he were elected President, Loving and his band would be invited to perform at his inauguration. Following his victory, Taft invited the recently promoted "Captain" Loving and the Philippine Constabulary Band to escort him from the White House to the Capitol, where he would take his oath of office in March 1909. Such an honor was traditionally the possession of the United States Marine Band. For the inaugural reception, the Philippine Constabulary Band shared the platform with the Marine Band and alternated with "The President's Own" for a series of Inaugural Concerts at the Pension Building.

Additional American performances were given at such distinguished sites as Symphony Hall in Boston and the Million Dollar Pier at Atlantic City, New Jersey. En route back to the Philippines, the band performed concerts in Cincinnati; Chicago; Madison, Wisconsin; Denver; Seattle; and Honolulu.

Following an appearance at the Court Square Theater in Springfield, Missouri, the local press wrote:

> In addition to the novelty of seeing in Springfield for the first time a representative body of little brown men from our island possession in the Far East, there was genuine pleasure in the fact that they proved to be musicians well worth hearing, who played with a precision of attack and a harmony of tone that was unexpected.[8]

Such comments were typical.

Everywhere the band appeared, audiences (as well as the press) were amazed at the band's ability to double as a symphony orchestra.

Newspaper articles inquired, "Band or an Orchestra—'Little Brown Men' Switch From Brass Instruments to Strings."

In 1911, Loving took a leave of absence to study in Europe. He studied instrumentation, orchestration and music education organization in Italy, Germany, Vienna, and London. He had ideas of establishing a Philippine Conservatory of Music.

Following the band's appearance at the Seattle, Washington Exposition and the Panama Pacific Exposition (1915), failing health necessitated Loving's retirement. He took leave from the Philippines on February 20, 1916, with the rank of major.

Loving served for a brief period with the Office of Intelligence in Washington, D.C. (1917–1918), but was recalled to the Philippines in 1919 to rebuild the deteriorating Philippine Constabulary Band. With his mission accomplished and a new leader adequately trained, Loving made his second departure from the band in late 1923. He settled with his wife and son in Oakland, California, where he entered the real estate business, conducted various choral groups, and engaged in various community activities.

The "Loving Touch" was once more solicited for the Philippine Constabulary Band, now named Philippine Army Band. With the rank of lieutenant colonel in the Philippine Army and "Advisor to President Quezon," along with Douglas MacArthur and Dwight Eisenhower, Loving returned to Manila in 1937. Loving was given the specific responsibility of preparing the band for appearances at the San Francisco and New York World's Fairs in 1939. Unfortunately, the band appeared, most successfully, only at the San Francisco event, due to a shortage of funds.

When war broke out in the Philippines in December 1941, Loving and his wife were interned at the University of Santo Tamos, along with thousands of Americans and Britishers. In early February 1945, the Japanese engaged in heavy fighting in and around Santo Tomas. On February 3, 1945, the U.S. Army liberated all internees. In retaliation, the Japanese persisted in their attacks and forced the Lovings to flee from their home in Ermita. In flight, Walter Loving was wounded, and he and his wife were separated. Lacking full details of all that transpired, we can only report that Walter Howard Loving was killed by the Japanese. The body was never located.

In 1952, Mrs. Loving returned to the Philippines as guest of the people to receive a posthumous Award of Merit for her husband at a program honoring the Fiftieth Anniversary of the band.

Loving's composition "Beloved Philippines" was performed for the occasion.[9]

A notice in the Moorland-Spingarn Research Center's "Loving Papers" reveals the establishment of the Colonel Walter H. Loving Memorial Society (date unknown) and the presentation of "A Gala Memorial Concert" commemorating the Foundation Day of the Philippine Army Band on October 15, 1974. The accompanying Preamble reads:

> We, the original surviving members of the pre-war Philippine Constabulary Band, in order to perpetuate the memory of its founder, Col. Walter H. Loving, who unselfishly shared with us his sense of musical artistry and under whose direction the Philippine Constabulary Band earned plaudits from noted foreign bandmasters and critics when it played, among others, in international engagements such as the St. Louis exposition in 1904; the inauguration of William H. Taft as President of the U.S.A. in 1909; Panama Canal Exposition in 1915 and Golden Gate Exposition in 1939, thereby affording recognition to the innate musical talent of the Filipinos and bringing highest honors to the Philippines whom he loved as his own, and in pursuit of the principles and objectives hereunder stated, hereby proclaim and ordain this constitution. . . ."[10]

Notes

1. "Walter Howard Loving," *Journal of Negro History*, April, 1945, p. 244.
2. Monroe N. Work, ed., *Negro Year Book*, Tuskegee Institute, Alabama: The Negro Year Book Publishing Company, 1922, p. 288.
3. Claiborne T. Richardson, "The Filipino-American Phenomenon: The Loving Touch," *The Black Perspective in Music*, Spring 1982, pp. 3–28.
4. Status in all phases of national defense and the armed forces reflected the realities of the black man's status in American life. It was 1940 before the Selective Service Act was passed, barring racial discrimination in the military. Basically ineffective, as late as the beginning of WWII, training, combat, transportation, housing and recreation facilities were segregated. It was 1948 before President Harry S. Truman issued an Executive Order barring such segregation and 1954 before the policy of all-black units was completely abolished.
5. Letter from Professor J. Wallace Goodrich to Walter H. Loving, August 11, 1899, quoted in Richardson, *op. cit.,* p. 7.
6. Richardson, *op. cit.,* p. 10.

7. Letter from Booker T. Washington, Personal to Wm. H. Taft, Secretary of War, Washington, D.C., June 6, 1905. Copy on file, Walter Howard Loving Papers, Moorland-Spingarn Research Center, Howard University, Washington, D.C.
8. "Filipino Musicians," *The Springfield Union,* March 19, 1909.
9. Several Loving compositions can be viewed at the Moorland-Spingarn Research Center, Walter Loving Papers.
10. Flyer, A Gala Memorial Concert, sponsored by The Colonel Walter H. Loving Memorial Society, in cooperation with the Philippine Army, October 15, 1974, Little Theatre, Cultural Center of the Philippines, Manila.

James Melvin Lunceford (Courtesy: Institute of Jazz Studies)

JAMES MELVIN ("JIMMIE") LUNCEFORD

BIRTHDATE/PLACE: June 6, 1902; Fulton, Missouri.
DEATH DATE/PLACE: July 13, 1947; Seaside, Oregon.
EDUCATION: B. Mus., Fisk University, 1926; Further study, City College of New York City.
MAJOR INSTRUCTORS: Wilberforce J. Whiteman and George Morrison.
CAREER HIGHLIGHTS: Played with George Morrison's Orchestra, 1922; briefly in New York City with Wilbur Sweatman, Elmer Snowden, Fred "Deacon" Johnson, and others; music instructor, Manassa High School, Memphis (Tennessee), 1926–29; organized student band (The Chickasaw Syncopators), 1927; Nucleus of group formed a professional band, 1929.
FILM APPEARANCES (Partial): "Blues in the Night" and "Class of '44".

THOUGH LUNCEFORD WAS A MORE THAN ADEQUATE alto saxophonist and was fully capable of playing many other instruments, he was content to be a leader. Very rarely did he assume the role of player as well. He was a solidly trained musician, a master teacher, a strict disciplinarian, and a fully respected supervisor of all musical events in which his musicians were engaged. Consensus was (and is) that Jimmie Lunceford was an "orchestra leader par excellence." Reference to the Lunceford band by jazz critics, historians, and journalists alike always described the band with superlatives: "formidable jazzmen," "superb ensemble players," "one of the most important 'hot' bands of the 1930s–40s," "one of the finest orchestral units jazz has ever known," "a powerhouse crew," "an audience pleaser, both aurally and visually," "one of the most sought-after big bands in the U.S."

During the band's eighteen-year reign,[1] it included a most impressive list of members: saxophonists Willie Smith and Joe Thomas; trumpeters Eddie Tompkins, Tommy Stevenson, Gerald Wilson, and Paul Webster; guitarist Eddie Durham; trombonist James "Trummy" Young; drummer James Crawford; pianist/arranger Edwin Wilcox; and most importantly, trumpeter/arranger Melvin "Sy" Oliver. Following Oliver's years of affiliation, the band benefitted from the arranging

342

skills of Tadd Dameron and George Duvivier, and, in the earlier years, the skills of Will Hudson. It should be noted however that despite various individuals' solo capabilities, the Lunceford band was most notable for its ensemble playing and its collective "distinctive two-beat swing at medium tempo."

George T. Simon, in his definitive volume *The Big Bands,* opens his entry on Lunceford with a recollection of a dance band marathon that occurred at New York City's Manhattan Center in 1940. The event permitted twenty-eight bands each to perform a fifteen-minute set before an audience of six thousand. Included in the lineup were bands fronted by such household names as Benny Goodman, Glenn Miller, Guy Lombardo, Sammy Kaye, Count Basie,* and Jimmie Lunceford. All bands complied with the time regulation except Lunceford's. Wrote Simon:

> [T]hat one couldn't, for the simple reason that along about midnight it broke the show wide open, to such hollering and cheering and shouting for "More!" that no other band could get on stage until Jimmie Lunceford's was allowed to play some extra tunes.[2]

Lunceford fan Albert McCarthy wrote:

> [T]he Lunceford band, almost more than any other, found the secret of pleasing several audiences at once without . . . lowering musical standards. To the dancers it was a fine dance band; to the people who went to see a show it was a good theatrical spectacle; to the jazz fan it was a good jazz group. I don't think any other band succeeded so well in engaging diverse audiences.[3]

Born in Fulton, Missouri, Lunceford grew up in Denver, Colorado, where his father was a choir director. He received his high school diploma from the Denver Public Schools. The city of Denver offered Lunceford two significant experiences: studying with master teacher Wilberforce J. Whiteman (father of famous bandleader Paul Whiteman) and studying and playing with master musician George Morrison. Black violinist/bandleader Morrison related the following to composer/conductor/educator/author Gunther Schuller on the Morrison/Lunceford relationship:

> I trained him right here in this house in rehearsals, when he first started playing engagements with me. And I encouraged him to go

on to Tuskegee Institute to finish his musical education. I sent him some of my arrangements when he was organizing his band down there.[4]

The school that Lunceford attended was of course Fisk University in Nashville, Tennessee (rather than Tuskegee Institute in Alabama) and the "down there" referred to Memphis, Tennessee. He spent his college summers studying and working in New York City, playing with such outstanding jazzmen as Wilbur Sweatman, Elmer Snowden, and Fred "Deacon" Johnson.

Lunceford joined the faculty of Manassa High School in Memphis in 1926, where he formed a student jazz band. The band played regularly during the summer months and, in 1929, turned professional. The band filled local engagements and broadcasting assignments on radio station WREC in Memphis. Lunceford and his students (along with several Fisk colleagues) also filled engagements in the states of New York and Ohio, under the name Jimmy Lunceford and His Chickasaw Syncopators.

The band relocated to New York City in 1933 and had its first important engagement at the Cotton Club in 1934, now as Jimmie Lunceford and His Orchestra. During the same year, the band launched its distinguished recorded documentation with "Jazznocracy" and "White Heat." An impressive list of recordings followed: "Organ Grinder's Swing," "Rhythm Is Our Business," "Margie," "The Merry-Go-Round Broke Down," and "T'ain't What You Do," to name a few. The band also appeared in several films and shorts, including "Blues in the Night" and "Class of '44."

Lunceford and his band traveled extensively. They were on the road in Seaside, Oregon on July 13, 1947, when the "leader par excellence" suffered a fatal heart attack. Though efforts to continue the Lunceford tradition were mounted, those efforts proved ultimately futile without the "giant of a maestro" on the bandstand.

Notes

1. We are here considering the period from 1929, when the band moved into professional status, until Lunceford's death in 1947. A reorganized band continued for a brief period with Edwin Wilcox and Joe Thomas as coleaders.

2. George T. Simon, *The Big Bands,* rev. ed., New York: Collier Books, 1974, p. 328.

3. Quoted in *Jazz Panorama,* edited by Martin Williams, New York: Collier Books, 1964, p. 136.

4. Gunther Schuller, *Early Jazz: Its Roots and Musical Development,* New York: Oxford University Press, 1968. When Morrison gave this interview, he was seventy-one years of age and over forty years had elapsed.

(Georgianne) Anne Lundy

(GEORGIANNE) ANNE LUNDY

BIRTHDATE/PLACE: October 18, 1954; Houston, Texas.
EDUCATION: B.Mus. Ed. and Performance Certification, University of Texas at Austin, 1977 (Violin); M.Mus., University of Houston, 1979 (Conducting); *MAJOR CONDUCTING INSTRUCTOR:* Igor Buketoff, University of Houston.
*MASTER CONDUCTING CLASSES:*Harold Farberman, Herbert Blomstedt, Paul Vermel, Hugo Jon Huss, Elizabeth Green, Jon Robertson (Conducting Institutes, 1981–89).
ORCHESTRAL AFFILIATIONS (Violin/Viola): Austin Symphony Orchestra, San Angelo Symphony and Abilene Philharmonic.
FOUNDER/VIOLIST: William Grant Still String Quartet, 1981—;
FOUNDER/CONDUCTOR: Mountain Chamber Orchestra (Aspen, Colorado), Summer 1983; Scott Joplin Chamber Orchestra (formerly Community Music Center of Houston's Orchestra), 1983—.
OTHER MAJOR APPOINTMENTS: Executive Director, Community Music Center of Houston, 1983—; Director, Northeast Cultural Arts Council's "Arts for the Summer" (Ages 5–18), Summers of 1985 and 1986; String Instructor, Texas Southern University, 1985–87.
AWARD: Outstanding Texan, Black Caucus of the Texas House of Representatives, 1989.

A REQUEST FOR INFORMATION FROM ANNE LUNDY brought the expected response, as well as a letter expressing amazement that the author knew of her conducting activities. A second letter stated, "I am grateful for your interest in my work in Houston. It seems that people only take our work seriously if we are on the East or West Coasts."[1]

I was indeed interested in Lundy's work and in what she seemed to be developing in the very heart of Houston's black community. From Carl Cunningham's article in the *Houston Post* on October 16, 1985, it was apparent that some valuable grass roots activities were taking place:

> Just across the street from the proud old, now sadly boarded-up Almeda Theatre, a new arts enterprise has come to life. The signs over

347

a low cluster of buildings call your attention to the Community Music Center of Houston. . . .

If music is your interest, you might step inside and meet Anne Lundy, the center's executive director. She is a personable, plucky young violinist/conductor whose ambition has prompted the formation of a chamber orchestra among Houston's black musicians.[2]

The Community Music Center of Houston (CMCH), founded by Ron Scales (Black) in 1979, is a center devoted to "promoting music (through five music ensembles—orchestra, chorus, string quartet, brass quintet, and chamber singers) often overlooked" and to "exposing and involving all children in appreciating and participating in the art of music making." The Center grew out of a realization "that the minority community just wasn't being exposed to classical music on a grass roots level." Said Lundy, who joined the staff in 1983, "Our goal is to expose and involve children and adults to music. We want them to appreciate and participate in it."[3]

A real boost came to the Center in June 1984, when the steadily developing Center offered its first annual Distinguished Achievement in Music Award to violinist Jack C. Bradley. A longtime inspiration to Anne Lundy, he was retiring as Chairman of Texas Southern University's Department of Music.[4] Bradley had been a supporter of the Center since its inception, as well as a member of the orchestra and the Board of Directors. The special honor was presented at CMCH's first annual banquet, a fundraising event that generated scholarship money for the school.

Subsequent banquets honored other musicians in the community, with proceeds often being donated to music departments at historically black Texas Southern and Prairie View Universities. As Lundy explained in a 1985 interview with the *Houston Defender*:

> There aren't a lot of places where Black kids can go to get solid music lessons. . . . What they offer in the public schools is great, but they are still limited because of the large class enrollments. Private lessons give them a chance to excel and to become really good players. . . . It still distresses me that this is 1985 and there isn't a Black in the Houston Symphony or the Texas Chamber Orchestra. . . .[5]

The *Houston Post*'s Carl Cunningham further explained that Lundy had assembled the Community Music Center of Houston's Orchestra shortly after joining the CMCH staff; he quoted the young conductor:

> I just started calling up string players I knew and I found a number of people out there, teaching school, working in banks and elsewhere. Then I went to Wheeler Ave. Baptist Church, where they were planning a performance of Handel's "Messiah," and said: "Hey, how would you like to do this with an orchestra?"[6]

Black journalist and choir director Clyde Owen Jackson wrote later of the CMCH Orchestra/Wheeler Avenue Baptist Church collaboration:

> For the past four consecutive years, our church has hired her [Lundy's] orchestra each December to perform with our adult choirs. . . . Several blacks urged that I hire professionals from the Houston Symphony instead. I asked them, "If we don't provide opportunities for our struggling black musicians to play, how can they develop into the kinds of professionals hired by the Houston Symphony?"[7]

The orchestra, as a performing body, has been an interest of Lundy's since high school, when she performed as violinist with four area orchestras: R.E. Lee High School, Houston All-City, Houston Youth Symphony, and the University of Houston Symphony Orchestra. She received the B.Mus.Ed. degree from the University of Texas at Austin in 1977, along with a performance certificate in violin. During her tenure there, she conducted the University's String Project Intermediate Orchestra.

Lundy joined the Houston School System as an orchestra and general music instructor in 1977 and remained in that position until 1984. In her final two years, she conducted the Houston All-City Youth Orchestra. As Lundy explained, she was particularly proud of this affiliation, since she was carrying on a tradition begun by her older sister. "In 1965 when the orchestra was first being integrated, Jessica Lundy {a flutist and a senior at Yates High School] was the first Black to be accepted to perform with the orchestra." Young Jessica was accepted, following a challenge to the all-white status of the orchestra from the Houston Council on Human Relations.[8]

In addition to holding membership in the orchestra of the Universities of Texas and Houston, Lundy acquired performing experience as a violinist in the Austin, Abilene, and San Angelo

Symphony Orchestras. Offering private instruction in violin and viola has been a part of her regular activities since 1975.

With her conducting interest well sparked, Lundy received a M.Mus. in Conducting from the University of Houston in 1979, acquiring additional experience as rehearsal conductor of the school's symphony and chamber orchestras. Since 1980, her summers have been spent pursuing additional conducting training and experience: American String Teacher's Association Conducting Institute, Aspen Music Festival, the International Institute of Orchestral Conducting, and the Symphony School of America, studying with such conducting pedagogues as Herbert Blomstedt, Elizabeth Green, Paul Vermel, Jon Robertson, and Hugo Jon Huss. Carrying herself beyond the apprentice stage, she organized her own orchestra while enrolled in the highly competitive Aspen Music Festival conducting program. During Lundy's second year of participation (1983), the Mountain Chamber Orchestra made its debut, performing at the Aspen Community Church.

Because of her interest in research, Lundy's curiosity was aroused by her discovery of the Houston-based Ladies Chamber Orchestra, a black group established in 1915 and directed by Madame Corilla Rochon.[9] Her contact with one of the orchestra's members (whose mother also played in the ensemble) and the information she subsequently received, led to the publication of an article in 1984 titled "Conversation With Ernestine Jessie Covington Dent," in *The Black Perspective in Music.*[10] In 1987, she received a grant from the Money for Women Fund, Inc., of St. Augustine, Florida, to continue research on this history-making organization. A second article was published in *The Black Perspective in Music,* titled "Conversations With Three Symphonic Conductors: Denis de Coteau,* Tania León,* Jon Robinson* [*sic*]."[11] With an ongoing concern for the music of black composers and a desire to share her findings with others, she was successful in having published in the *American String Teacher* an article titled "Chamber Music by Black Americans."[12]

Lundy's expertise has been recognized by the Cultural Arts Council of Houston, where she has been a member of the Classical Music and Multi-Media Panel, and the Texas Commission on the Arts, where she has been a member of the Music Panel and the Committee for Cultural Diversity. For the State's November 1987 Regional Arts Conference and Showcase, Lundy served as Music Panel moderator.

In recognition of her drive, foresight, determination and know-how, she is becoming a popular guest on local radio and television talk shows. Her Still String Quartet's mid-1980s television appearance on the local PBS station has, by request, been aired on at least four additional occasions.

Lundy's (and founder Ron Scales's) Community Music Center of Houston began receiving support from the National Endowment for the Arts in 1987. With support from the Cultural Arts Council of Houston, the Texas Commission on the Arts, and the National Endowment for the Arts, the Scott Joplin Chamber Orchestra presented its first "Music of Africa" concert in November 1988 at the Shape Community Center. Orchestral works by Nigerian composers Samuel Akpabot and Fela Sowande and the black American/Nigerian-born composer Noel DaCosta were performed. The orchestra's "Discovered Treasures—Music of Black Composers" continued the idea of community outreach with an appearance at Houston's Windsor Village United Methodist Church in February 1989.

On July 1, 1989, the Scott Joplin Chamber Orchestra and the Houston Symphony united in a tributory concert to the black composer William Dawson on the occasion of the composer's approaching 90th birthday. Leading the combined orchestral forces was Maestro Anne Lundy. Joining the orchestras were the combined choirs of the Community Music Center of Houston and the Wheeler Avenue Baptist Church.[13] To be sure, Anne Lundy's Houston-based activities have reached a level of significance that merits recognition both locally and nationally.

Press Comments

"With the rising young conductor Anne Lundy at the helm, what we beheld was a glorious evening of beautiful music. . . . With a steady hand and a clear beat for which she is becoming known, Anne Lundy as usual, brought intelligence, a quiet dignity and a maturity far beyond her years to this massive, complicated and demanding work." {Handel's "Messiah"}

The Informer

"Lundy conducted . . . carefully and assuredly."

Houston Chronicle

"Lundy conducted the work {William Dawson's "Negro Folk Symphony"} alertly and capably and the combined orchestra {Scott Joplin Chamber Orchestra and the Houston Symphony} responded with an enthusiastic performance . . ."

Houston Post

Notes

1. Correspondences, Lundy/Handy, July 30, 1986; January 20, 1988, and March 15, 1989.
2. Carl Cunningham, "Sound of Music: Young Conductor's Ambition Leads to Black Chamber Orchestra, New Arts Enterprise," *Houston Post,* October 16, 1985, p. 14E.
3. Barbara Karkali, "Black Community Music Center Finds Home Where Its Heart Is," *Houston Chronicle,* October 14, 1984, p. 6.
4. Jack C. Bradley made history in 1946 when he joined the Denver Symphony Orchestra, remaining with the ensemble until 1949, when he joined the faculty of Texas Southern University.
5. "Community Music Center," *Houston Defender,* November 8–14, 1985, p. 48.
6. Cunningham, *op. cit.*
7. Clyde Owen Jackson, "Two Black Women of Courage: This Day and Age," *The Informer,* January 31, 1987, p. 3.
8. "Ann Lundy . . . Budding Conductor," *Houston Forward Times,* December 11, 1982, p. 5A. See also Mosell Boland, "All-City Symphony Accepts Negro Girl," *Houston Chronicle,* September 5, 1965, p. 14, Section 1.
9. See D. Antoinette Handy, *Black Women in American Bands & Orchestras,* Metuchen, N.J.: Scarecrow Press, 1981, pp. 38, 127.
10. Anne Lundy, "Conversation With Ernestine Jessie Covington Dent: Pioneer Concert Pianist," *Black Perspective in Music,* Fall 1984, pp. 244–265.
11. ———, "Conversations With Three Symphonic Conductors: Denis de Coteau, Tania León, Jon Robinson [*sic*]," *Black Perspective in Music,* Fall 1988, pp. 213–226.
12. ———, "Chamber Music by Black Americans," *American String Teacher,* Winter 1991, pp. 70–72.
13. Cunningham, "Combined Orchestra Pays Tribute to Prominent Composer Dawson," *The Houston Post,* July 2, 1989, p. A32.

Marsha Eve Mabrey

MARSHA EVE MABREY

BIRTHDATE/PLACE: November 7, 1949; Pittsburgh, Pennsylvania.

EDUCATION: B.Mus., University of Michigan School of Music (Major, Instrumental Music Education; Minor, Violin/Viola), 1971; M.Mus., University of Michigan School of Music (Major, Instrumental Music Education; Minor, Violin/Viola), 1972; Toward D.M.A., University of Cincinnati College Conservatory of Music (Orchestral Conducting/Viola Cognate), 1973–76.

CONDUCTING INSTRUCTORS: Elizabeth A.H. Green, Theo Alcantara, and Louis Lane.

CONDUCTING WORKSHOPS WITH: Richard Lert, Maurice Abravanel, and Otto-Werner Mueller.

MAJOR APPOINTMENTS: Instructor of Music and Music Director/ Conductor, Winona State University Orchestra, Winona State College (Winona, Minnesota), 1978–80; Instructor of Conducting, Colorado Women's College, Department of Music (Denver, Colorado), 1978; Assistant Professor of Music and Music Director/Conductor, Grand Valley State College Orchestra, Grand Valley State College (Allendale, Michigan), 1980–82; Assistant Conductor, Grand Rapids Symphony Orchestra (Grand Rapids, Michigan), 1980–81; Conductor, Summer Intermediate Division, Interlochen National Music Camp (Interlochen, Michigan), 1982; Music Director/Conductor, Emerald Chamber Orchestra (Eugene, Oregon), 1984– 89; Assistant Professor of Music and Music Director/Conductor of the University Orchestra, University of Oregon School of Music (Eugene, Oregon), 1982–89; Program Host and Interviewer, Arts Access Programs, KWAX-FM (Eugene, Oregon), 1983–85; Assistant Dean, University of Oregon School of Music, 1989–91; Vice President for Educational Affairs, Detroit Symphony Orchestra Hall, 1991—.

GUEST CONDUCTOR: Oregon Symphony Orchestra (American Symphony Orchestra League Readings of New Music), 1988; Sinfonietta Frankfurt (Germany), 1988; Savannah Symphony Orchestra, 1991; Allen Park Symphony (Allen Park, Michigan), 1992.

AS MARSHA MABREY POINTS OUT, though her instructors never discouraged her from becoming a "serious" musician, they offered little encouragement toward her pursuit of a conducting career. Most

354

recommended that she study music education and prepare herself for teaching.

Mabrey's interest in music was sparked in the fourth grade, when she was introduced to the violin. She was only a seventh-grader when she decided to become an orchestra conductor, "one who shapes the total picture rather than one who is only one element of the symphonic whole."[1] Her family was supportive, but initially had some reservations. Serious violin study was understandable, but the idea of serious conducting study seemed somewhat unrealistic. Her family doubted that she would be able to support herself.

Wrote Mabrey:

> I was aware at an early age that the conductor was an important catalyst in bringing many musicians together to create the whole picture of music. As a violinist, I was involved with just one line. Conducting came to me quite naturally and the analysis and challenge of communication with other musicians was very exciting. I enjoyed the exchange of energy between conductor, musicians, and audience in helping to convey the composer's ideas.

She added:

> As a woman, and particularly as a strong-willed black woman, things have been difficult. But I haven't let the negatives stop me. I've reframed them into positive energy, helping me to work harder toward achieving my goals.[2]

Negative experiences, but positive sights, were no doubt the primary motivators for the 1985 West Coast Women Conductor/Composer Symposium and the 1986 American Women Conductor/Composer Symposium, both of which she conceived and directed at the University of Oregon's School of Music.[3] "Positive sights" was no doubt the primary motivation behind Mabrey's return to the State of Michigan in April 1991, where she would be actively involved in the Detroit Symphony Orchestra's educational activities. Following an extensive nationwide search in 1990–91, Mabrey was hired as vice president for educational affairs of the Detroit Symphony. She would become the orchestra's primary liaison with the educational community, while of course continuing to pursue conducting opportunities.

As Mabrey's work has become better known, guest conducting invitations have been forthcoming: Greater Twin Cities Youth Philharmonia, Pennsylvania Music Educators' Association Regional High School Orchestra, All-State High School Symphony Orchestra of the Oregon Music Educators' Association Conference, Utah Music Educators' Association All-State Orchestra, University of Utah Symphony, and the Junior Division Orchestra of the Interlochen All-State Music Program. Mabrey was also a frequent West Coast clinician, adjudicator, lecturer, and popular radio and television personality.

The year 1988 proved to be a most meaningful one from the standpoint of conducting: guest conductor, Sinfonietta Frankfurt, with concerts in Frankfurt, Schwalbach, Offenbach, and Hanau, West Germany (April 26–29); and guest conductor, Oregon Symphony Orchestra (Portland), participating in the American Symphony Orchestra League's New Music Reading Program (May 27–29). Following Mabrey's appearances in Germany, Professor Hans-Dieter Resch, founder/conductor of the Sinfonietta Frankfurt and rector of the Frankfurt am Main's College of Music and Performing Arts, wrote:

> At my invitation, my colleague Marsha Mabrey was in Germany from April 18–29, 1988, and conducted four concerts. . . . The simple fact that Marsha Mabrey was the first guest conductor to whom I entrusted my orchestra . . . demonstrates the good impression about her which I brought back from my stay in Eugene. . . . [T]he orchestra adapted to Marsha Mabrey's economical, accurate conducting style and reacted precisely to her very well-prepared instructions. . . . The concerts were successful, and the reviews . . . reveal without exception, a basically positive attitude.[4]

Press Comments

"Prof. Mabrey, with empathy, left her mark on an acoustical 'Best Seller' {Vivaldi's "Four Seasons"} . . . . Without any ostentatious gesticulation, the experienced woman conductor motivated the Sinfonietta Frankfurt. . . ."
                                                          Offenbach Post (Offenbach, Germany)

"With her highly sympathetic way of conducting—no baton, no thrusting about, but instead a clear and harmonic "formulation" with both hands, Marsha Mabrey was able again and again to transmute {the composer's} intention into sound and to animate her small group so that the ensemble was excellent."
                                                          Main Echo (Hanau, Germany)

"Marsha Mabrey . . . challenged the orchestra with new and unfamiliar repertoire and was . . . successful in the ambitious endeavor."

Savannah Morning News

Notes

1. Questionnaire, December 1987.
2. *Ibid.*
3. Publicity Brochure, "West Coast Women Conductors and Composers/Video" and "American Women Conductors and Composers/Video," University of Oregon, 1985 and 1986. With a concern for "spreading the good word" further, the spirit of both symposia has been captured on video cassette and is available through the University of Oregon's Instructional Media Center. The tapes include "examination of the rewards, challenges, problems, and possible solutions for women conductors (and composers) as they move through the professional hierarchy."
4. Correspondence, Professor Hans-Dieter Resch to Marsha Mabrey, October 25, 1988.

Kermit Diton Moore

KERMIT DITON MOORE

BIRTHDATE/PLACE: March 11, 1929; Akron, Ohio.
EDUCATION: B.Mus., Cleveland Institute of Music, 1951; M.A., New York University, 1953; Artist Diploma, Paris National Conservatory, 1956; Additional Study, the Juilliard School of Music.
MAJOR INSTRUCTORS: Felix Salmond and Paul Bazelaire (Cello); Nadia Boulanger (Composition); Pierre Pasquier and Georges Enesco (Repertory).
MAJOR APPOINTMENTS: Hartt School of Music (Hartford, Connecticut), Professor of Cello and member of the resident string quartet, 1951–54; Riverside Symphony Orchestra (New York, N.Y.), Founder/Music Director, 1975; Classical Heritage Ensemble (New York, N.Y.), Founder/Music Director, 1984—.
GUEST CONDUCTOR: Symphony of the New World, Brooklyn Philharmonic, Berkeley (California), Detroit, and Birmingham (Alabama) Symphony Orchestras; Dance Theatre of Harlem, National Opera Ebony.
AWARDS/HONORS: Edgar Stillman Kelly Award (Ohio), 1944; Lili Boulanger Award, 1953; Queen Elizabeth II Medal, 1958.
RECORDING ARTIST (Cello): Orion, Musical Heritage Society, Performance, and CRI.

BY THE TIME KERMIT MOORE'S talent as a composer and conductor began to emerge, his career as a concert cellist was already established. He had made his debut as a cellist in New York City's Town Hall at age 19 and subsequently concertized throughout the United States (including appearances at Lincoln Center and Carnegie Recital Hall), Canada, Europe, Africa, and the Far East. His solo orchestral appearances included the Orchestre de la Suisse Romande, Concertgebouw Orchestra of Amsterdam, National Radio Symphony of Paris, Belgian National Orchestra, and other Dutch, French, and Scandinavian orchestras.

A 1986 concert in St. Louis, almost four decades following his Town Hall debut, presented Kermit Moore as both solo cellist and featured composer. Wrote the *St. Louis Post-Dispatch*'s critic James Wierzbicki:

359

Kermit Moore is a strong cellist, a player who digs deep into the instrument. . . . captivating from start to finish. . . . It was an exciting event, made all the more so by its inclusion of a new work commissioned by the concert's sponsor—the University of Missouri at St. Louis—in honor of the St. Louis Arts Festival.

The composer was Moore himself, and the piece was titled "Caravaggio Revisited". . . . a solid work, and very well suited to Moore's aggressive style of playing.[1]

While continuing his illustrious career as cellist and composer, Moore found conducting opportunities (many the result of his own initiative) more and more frequent. The late 1960s and early 1970s offered various occasions to conduct the Symphony of the New World, a fully professional, fully integrated New York City–based orchestra.

Under Moore's leadership, the Symphony of the New World gave the first American performance of Afro-Cuban José White's Concerto for Violin and Orchestra in 1974 at Avery Fisher Hall in Lincoln Center. First performed in 1867 (with White as solo violinist), the concerto on this occasion featured Ruggiero Ricci as soloist. Also included on the program was the orchestral piece "Tones" (1970), composed by Afro-Cuban female composer Tania León.* As assessed by *New York Times* critic John Rockwell:

The Symphony of the New World presented one of its most ambitious and impressive concerts. . . . The orchestra . . . played well for Mr. Moore, who seemed to have sensible and sensitive musical ideas about all the works on the program [White, León, Wade Marcus, William Grant Still, and Howard Swanson].[2]

Moore conducted the New York Festival Orchestra in the Great Assembly Hall of the United Nations. This concert, like many others, featured Moore's own "Many Thousand Gone" and works by 18th century black Brazilian composers. His programming on this occasion, as well as on other orchestra engagements and his own solo recitals, reflect his long-standing commitment to performance of works by black composers.

In recent years, Moore has conducted National Opera Ebony (New York City) in the performances of two works by black composers: William Grant Still's "Troubled Island" and Mark Fax's "Til Victory

Is Won." He is a frequent guest conductor of the Brooklyn Philharmonic. In September 1985 Moore led this ensemble at Damrosch Park ("Lincoln Center Out-of-Doors") in Duke Ellington's Sacred Concerts, which he had previously orchestrated on a commission from the Cleveland Orchestra.

Since 1984 Kermit Moore has annually guest conducted the Berkeley (California) Symphony Orchestra, in various San Francisco halls, in concerts often featuring distinguished soloists. In 1984 he founded the Classical Heritage Ensemble, based in New York City. The ensemble, a chamber music society, is made up of young artists of various ethnic origins, who enjoy careers as soloists and chamber players. The Classical Heritage Ensemble—performing as a chamber orchestra, string quartet, violin duo, and unaccompanied flute—was presented by the Committee of Friends of the Symphony of the New World in March 1988 at the Schomburg Center for Research in Black Culture, a division of the New York Public Library.[3]

Moore was most visible (and audible) as cellist, composer, and conductor at the Black American Music Symposium convened at the School of Music, University of Michigan, on August 9–15, 1985. He conducted the Chamber Orchestra Concert that featured works by black composers Adolphus Hailstork, Coleridge-Taylor Perkinson,* George Walker, and Ulysses Kay. His Classical Heritage String Quartet was featured in an entire program performing works by black composers Chevalier de St. Georges, Ulysses Kay, William Grant Still, and Kermit Moore (his Quintet for String Quartet and Piano). Earlier in 1985, Renaissance man Moore was featured guest conductor of the Detroit Symphony in its "Classical Roots" concert.

One of the most respected musicians in New York City, Kermit Moore's "standards of excellence" have always prevailed. He has adjudicated various competitions and, in the late 1980s, served as a panelist for the New York State Council on the Arts, Meet the Composer service organization, and the National Endowment for the Arts. As a founding member of the Society of Black Composers in 1968,[4] a founding member of, and cellist with, the Symphony of the New World, the founder/music director of the short-lived Riverside Symphony (1975), a guest conductor of the Dance Theater of Harlem and the Birmingham (Alabama) Symphony, his energy for "quality music-making" never ceases.

Press Comments

"The Symphony of the New World, conducted by Kermit Moore, presented a significant program of music by five Black composers at Avery Fisher Hall. Moore conducted with authority and conviction."

New York Post

"Kermit Moore's authoritative conducting had muscle to spare and the orchestra responded in a convincing manner. Mr. Moore is to be congratulated for selecting a demanding, difficult program and managing to enthrall the appreciative audience."

National Music Journal

". . . all forces were effectively conducted by Kermit Moore."

San Francisco Chronicle

Notes

1. James Wierzbicki, "Cellist Kermit Moore Captivating In Concert," *St. Louis Post-Dispatch,* October 28, 1986, p. 4B.
2. John Rockwell, "Moore Is Conductor of New World Unit In Music by Blacks," *The New York Times,* February 25, 1974, p. C14.
3. The historically significant Symphony of the New World terminated its existence in 1977.
4. Another founding member of the Society of Black Composers was the black composer Dorothy Rudd Moore, wife of Kermit Moore.

Michael DeVard Morgan (Courtesy: Sheldon Soffer Management)

MICHAEL DeVARD MORGAN

BIRTHDATE/PLACE: September 17, 1957; Washington, D.C.

EDUCATION: Eastern Music Festival, 1972; D.C. Youth Orchestra, 1972–75 (Student Conductor); Oberlin College Conservatory of Music (Composition/Conducting), 1975–79; Berkshire Music Center at Tanglewood, 1977 (Conducting Fellow).

MAJOR INSTRUCTORS: Richard Hoffman (Oberlin), Composition; Murry Sidlin (Baltimore Symphony's Conducting Competition), Robert Baustian (Oberlin), Seiji Ozawa and Gunther Schuller (Tanglewood), Witold Rowicki (Vienna masterclasses), all Conducting.

MAJOR APPOINTMENTS: Assistant Conductor, Schubertfest, American Symphony Orchestra, 1978; Apprentice Conductor, Buffalo Philharmonic Orchestra, 1979; Exxon/Affiliate Artists/Arts Endowment Conductor, St. Louis Symphony Orchestra, 1980; Exxon/Affiliate Artists/Arts Endowment Assistant Conductor, Chicago Symphony Orchestra and Co-Resident Conductor, Chicago Civic Orchestra, 1986–94; Music Director, Oakland East Bay Symphony Orchestra (Oakland, California), 1990—.

GUEST CONDUCTOR: Atlanta, Baltimore, Detroit, Columbus, Hartford, Houston, National, New Orleans, Seattle, St. Louis, New World, Fresno, New Jersey, Grant Park Symphony Orchestras; Brooklyn, Buffalo, New York, and Rochester Philharmonic Orchestras; Texas, Northwest, New York (92nd Street "Y"), Nebraska, and St. Paul Chamber Orchestras; Orchestra of Illinois; Lake Forest Symphony; Chicago Youth Symphony; Black Music Repertory Ensemble; D.C. Youth Graduate Orchestra; Vienna Symphony Orchestra; Warsaw Philharmonic; Aarhus By-Orkestra (Denmark); Orchestra Sinfonico di San Remo (Italy), and Vancouver Symphony (British Columbia); Chicago Opera Theater; Summer Opera Theatre (Washington, D.C.); Prince George's Civic Opera; New York City Opera (Wolf Trap, New York City, and Taiwan); Vienna State Opera; Deutsche Staatsopera (Berlin State Opera); Opera Theatre of St. Louis, Washington Opera; and Masterworks Chorale.

AWARDS/HONORS/PRIZES: Documentary "In Search of a Maestro," Baltimore Symphony's Conducting Competition (1974); Fourth Prize, Baltimore Symphony Young Conductors Competition (1973 and 1975); Prize Winner, Gino Marrinuzzi International Conductors Competition, San Remo, Italy (1975); First Prize, Hans Swarowsky International Conductors

Competition, Vienna, Austria (1980); feature—"Music Maestro Please," ABC/TV (20/20), 1987; "Musician of the Year, 1989," Chicago Music Association; "Keep Your Eye On" Recognition, *Opera News,* 1989.

> It never occurred to me that I just might not have an orchestra to conduct. . . . I figured if teachers had students to teach and doctors had patients—conductors had people to play for them.[1]

THESE ARE THE WORDS of the brilliant young conductor Michael DeVard Morgan.

In the spring of 1986, twenty-eight-year-old Michael Morgan was selected by Chicago Symphony Orchestra Music Director Sir George Solti to join his conducting staff. In Morgan's first season, 1986–87, his title was Exxon/Affiliate Artists/Arts Endowment Assistant Conductor. He would share responsibility for pops concerts, school concerts, and for conducting and developing the young musicians of the Chicago Symphony's training orchestra, the Chicago Civic.

In early September 1986, just days before his twenty-ninth birthday and before assuming his Chicago Symphony responsibilities, Michael Morgan and two other "handpicked" conductors under thirty joined Leonard Bernstein (the first native-born American to serve as music director of the New York Philharmonic) in a week of intensive coaching and rehearsals of the New York Philharmonic. The culminating activity was two evenings of appearances at Avery Fisher Hall, Lincoln Center, leading the Philharmonic, together with laureate conductor Bernstein.

Morgan's assigned composition was Richard Strauss's tone poem "Till Eulenspiegel's Merry Pranks." Wrote Bill Zakariasen of the *Daily News:*

> Morgan's assignment . . . was no doubt the most challenging . . . Morgan not only conquered every one of the pitfalls, but brought out myriad details I could swear I was hearing for the first time.[2]

A native of Washington, D.C., Michael Morgan is the elder of two children born to retired biologists; his father is a former employee of the National Cancer Institute of the National Institutes of Health, and his mother is a former employee of the National Institute of Mental Health. Morgan's musical saga began when friends of the family moved from Washington to the West Coast and elected not to transport their upright piano. The Morgans purchased the instrument for ten dollars, placed it in the basement of their home, and permitted young Michael, then about six, to make use of it. Morgan recalled:

> I began studying about two years later, though I don't remember my first piano teacher. I do remember music in the public schools. It was a class. At the time, public schools had piano teachers who went from elementary school to elementary school.[3]

When asked how the conducting interest developed, Morgan said:

> The piano interest sort of flowed into conducting. I started conducting my junior high school [McFarland] orchestra when I was 12. The orchestra teacher, Herman Suehs (who later joined the University of the District of Columbia music faculty) was the kind of teacher that, if a student came in expressing an interest in something, he would try to teach it to them. He taught me the fundamentals of score reading and transposition. I played piano in the school orchestra. At the same time, I had my own little community orchestra that operated out of People's Congregational Church. The members' ages ranged from 13 to 15. The number reached as many as 20.[4]

Morgan recalled his experience with the small community orchestra in an interview with *Washington Post* music critic Joseph McLellan, on the occasion of his professional D.C. conducting debut in 1983:

> From the time I was 12 years old, . . . I have always been able to find groups of people willing to let me conduct them—stand in front of them, ostensibly telling them what to do. I found that the District of Columbia was a good place to learn how to become a conductor.[5]

Morgan also remembered the time spent at the Dale Music Company in Silver Spring, Maryland, when he was nine or ten years old. Knowing already that he wanted to be a conductor, Morgan spent hours

> living in the miniature score section . . . David Burchuk [a musicologist and conductor], who ran the store, took an interest in me, went through some of the scores with me and gave me the run of the place. . . .[6]

Soon after, the young conductor received an open invitation to attend National Symphony Orchestra rehearsals. "[I] grew up watching [Antal] Dorati rehearse the National Symphony." In addition, his parents took him regularly to National Symphony Orchestra concerts.

Morgan seizes every opportunity to express his views on the subject of "arts in the schools," particularly the public ones. As he points out, were it not for the "arts in the public schools, . . . I would not be in my position [Chicago Symphony] today."[7]

He attended McKinley High School, D.C.'s music high school before the Duke Ellington School for the Arts was established. During these years, he also participated in the D.C. Youth Orchestra program, as a student conductor.

> I had a lot of actual time conducting, and that's the most important thing for a conductor. . . . [O]ne gets a lot of experience in that particular youth orchestra program because you get exposed to so much of the standard repertoire. That early background is very important.[8]

One McKinley High School instructor whom Morgan fondly remembers is Beatrice Gilts, his music theory instructor:

> She would stay after school to help me with four-part dictation, getting ready for conducting competitions. It was because of her that I entered [in 1973] the Baltimore Symphony Young Conductors Competition—at age sixteen.[9]

Morgan did not win this competition, but at age eighteen, he took fourth prize in the Gino Marrinuzzi International Conductors Competition at San Remo, Italy.

He enrolled at the Oberlin College Conservatory of Music in 1975, and, though Morgan left Oberlin in 1979, "a few hours short in distribution requirements for both the B.Mus. degree in composition and the M.Mus. in conducting," Oberlin claims him as one of their own. He was profiled in the Fall 1987 issue of *Oberlin Alumni Magazine*.

Assistant Editor Emily Nunn prepared the article following Morgan's numerous successes with the Chicago Symphony and the spring 1987 Morgan story that aired nationwide on ABC-TV's "20/20." Nunn reported that, during Morgan's Oberlin tenure, he organized, directed and conducted various ad hoc student recitals, "one year being devoted to Bach's music, the next to Mozart's, and others seeing the production of student musicals, chamber concerts, and solo recitals."[10]

Also during the Oberlin years, Morgan was a conducting fellow at the Berkshire Music Center at Tanglewood, where he studied with Seiji Ozawa and Gunther Schuller in 1977. During the summer of 1978, he served as assistant conductor of the American Symphony Orchestra's "Schubertfest" under Sergiu Comissiona and participated in the Vienna Master Conducting Class with Witold Rowicki.

The decision to leave Oberlin prior to graduation was totally Morgan's. First, in 1979, he had an opportunity to become apprentice conductor with the Buffalo Philharmonic Orchestra under Julius Rudel, music director, on a grant from the Martha Baird Rockefeller Fund. Second, Morgan believed that he attended an institution in order to get an education. This he had gotten. It was therefore time to move on to other opportunities and challenges.

The following year Morgan entered the prestigious International Hans Swarowsky Conducting Competition in Vienna, "not expecting to win but to broaden his experience and prepare for a less lucrative competition—the Malko in Copenhagen." As explained to Joseph McLellan:

> It was not a high-pressure situation for me. . . . It seemed safe precisely because the prize was so enormous, both monetarily and with the engagements one could get. . . . So I figured it was a pretty safe bet they weren't going to give a first prize. It was the second time they had held this competition, and they didn't give any first prize the first time, so I fully expected them not to give a first prize this time. . . . Then, almost before I knew it, I was a strong contender; the three top contestants were still holding their places but they weren't moving ahead. . . . You could score from positive 2 to negative 2, and at the end, I was the only one who had a positive score with the jury, and the next highest was negative 1.4.[11]

Morgan was declared the first prize winner. A part of Morgan's prize was the opportunity to conduct the Vienna State Opera and the Vienna Symphony. He made his debut with the former at the opera company's 1982 May Festival, conducting Mozart's "The Abduction from the Seraglio." Morgan referred to the experience as a "jump-in" with little or no rehearsal time. There were other valuable residuals:

A "jump-in" performance of Mozart's "The Magic Flute," . . . at the
East Berlin Opera, plus performances with the Vienna Symphony, the
Vienna Radio Orchestra, [and] the Warsaw Philharmonic.[12]

As Morgan later stated:

The most pretentious thing in my biography, which is full of
pretentious things, is the fact that my first opera conducting
assignment was with the Vienna State Opera.[13]

Since the Vienna experience, opera has become his consuming musical interest. On the subject of opera conducting in America, Morgan
explained to The *Houston Post*'s music editor Carl Cunningham:

America is so strange. . . . In Europe the opera conductor is considered
all-important to a production, because if he's no good, he can ruin it
for everybody. But here, people are only interested in the singers on
stage and wonder why I want to bury myself in the pit. I tell them:
"Look, I don't want to be a movie star; I want to conduct opera."[14]

Fearing too meteoric an ascent into the firmament of world-class
conductors, Morgan returned to America to begin building his career
"the hard way." He had been selected to serve as the Exxon/Affiliate
Artists/Arts Endowment conductor of the Saint Louis Symphony for
the 1980–81 season. He was chosen from a group of six finalists from
a field of 150 applicants. His roles would include "backup conductor" for Music Director Leonard Slatkin and Associate Conductor
Gerhardt Zimmerman. He would conduct children's concerts, park
concerts, and some tour programs.

Morgan remained with the Saint Louis Symphony for one season
only. In the next five years (1981–86, ages twenty-four to twenty-
nine), he made his "prize appearances" in Vienna and guest
conducted extensively both in America and abroad, including
appearances with the New Orleans, National, Hartford, and Baltimore Symphony Orchestras; the Buffalo Philharmonic; the Texas and
Northwest Chamber Orchestras; Prince George's Civic Opera;
Summer Opera Theatre in Washington, D.C; and the Aarhus
By-Orkestra in Aarhus, Denmark.

Of Morgan's July 1984 debut with his hometown orchestra—the
National Symphony—Pamela Sommers of The *Washington Post*
wrote:

[T]he audience . . . [was] clearly taken with the young man who stood at the helm of the ensemble for most of the evening.

The man was Michael Morgan, a 27-year-old, Washington-born conductor who is one of the most alert and inspiring figures on the podium today. . . . Morgan exudes a real vitality, a total comprehension of pulse and drama. . . . Morgan succeeded in summoning up fresh images and connections.[15]

Chicago Sun Times music critic Robert C. Marsh wrote a revealing article in late February 1987, captioned "Morgan Merits More Than 'Silver Lining'." The title referred to Morgan's first appearance with the Chicago Symphony Orchestra:

Michael Morgan . . . made his first appearance with the Chicago Symphony Saturday, conducting "Look for the Silver Lining" from Jerome Kern's "Sally." He deserved better. . . . The problem is that the orchestral management doesn't seem to know what to do with him—except keep him out of sight. He has waited 10 months for this debut and is not scheduled to appear in any subscription events of next season.[16]

Morgan shared that February 1987 program with the illustrious choral conductor Margaret Hillis, a medium-size group of Chicago Symphony players, soloists, and members of the Chicago Symphony Chorus (of which Hillis is the director). Marsh elaborated:

Although you can take for granted he would have preferred more serious and demanding repertory, he treated this music [Kern, Gilbert and Sullivan, and Rodgers] with respect and caught the right spirit for each composer. . . . All he needs now is an assignment that makes fuller use of his musicianship.[17]

Not an assignment, but a rare opportunity—unplanned and unexpected—presented itself only a few months later. Morgan did what assistant conductors exist to do primarily, i.e., to replace the music director, often without benefit of a rehearsal, in a program that the music director has prepared. The big break came May 26, 1987—a subscription concert appearance, two years ahead of schedule. On the program were two landmark orchestral scores: Igor Stravinsky's "The Rite of Spring" and Richard Strauss's "Ein Heldenleben." Though offered one hour of rehearsal, Morgan declined; sure of both himself and the orchestra, he would "take his chances." Undoubtedly, his confidence was boosted by his having directed the orchestra the previous afternoon in a Memorial Day Concert.

The following morning, Robert Marsh registered this report:

> In November, 1943, the 25-year-old Leonard Bernstein, then assistant conductor of the New York Philharmonic, went overnight from obscurity to fame when he substituted for an ailing senior colleague at a subscription program of that orchestra. It was the decisive moment that launched a great career.

> Morgan at 29 is a finer, more experienced musician than Bernstein was at 25. . . . What became clear Tuesday was that the promise of great talent he had offered was fully realized when tested under difficult artistic circumstances. . . . Significantly, Morgan, while drawing fully on the secure support the orchestra gave him, chose to be his own man. This was his "Heldenleben," not Solti's. If in the Stravinsky he stayed close to the Solti performance, you sensed it was because he respected Solti's interpretive ideas.[18]

It was interesting (but logical) that Marsh would draw this comparison between Bernstein and Morgan. When asked a few months later about his most positive conducting influence, Morgan, without hesitation, named Leonard Bernstein. Said Morgan:

> Bernstein was the first American conductor to have an international career. Without him, it would be even more difficult than it is for the American conductor today.[19]

His other positive conducting influences were Solti, Sergiu Comissiona, and Dean Dixon.*

The career (and plight) of black conductor Dixon had been brought to young Michael's attention by his father when he first indicated that conducting was his career choice. But as he said to *Baltimore Sun Times* music critic Stephen Wigler:

> Times have changed completely since those of Dean Dixon. . . . I almost never think about being a black conductor. . . . The only time I do . . . is when someone else's career moves faster than mine.[20]

Later in 1987, the young maestro's hometown newspaper ran a feature story titled "A Conductor's Homecoming: Michael Morgan to Conduct 'La Traviata' at Wolf Trap."[21] There would be two performances of the New York City Opera's production of Verdi's "La Traviata" at Wolf Trap's Filene Center and six additional ones in New York City later in the summer, all with the Chicago Symphony's assistant conductor at the helm.

An impressive review followed the initial Wolf Trap performance:

> [H]e proclaimed a distinctive but not eccentric musical personality from his first downbeat. He maintained a delicate balance throughout between the voices and the transparent but flavorful orchestral sound, and his balancing act became almost a virtuoso display. . . . where the orchestra remained always a cushion for the voice no matter how frenzied the dynamics became.[22]

Following his debut with the New York City Opera at the New York State Theater a few weeks later, *The New York Times* registered this report:

> Mr. Morgan kept things moving along . . . turning out a crafted, engaging version of the overture and making sure not to let his players drown out the singers.[23]

Despite Morgan's youth, there is a sense of self that has impressed many. Yet, he is unwilling to take himself too seriously. To Oberlin's Emily Nunn he said:

> It's not really for me to take myself seriously. I have been lucky in finding the thing in life that I have talent for, . . . Everyone has a talent, but few people discover theirs. I certainly can't take responsibility for such a gift; my responsibility is in working to develop it.[24]

Morgan's "off-podium" personality is often written about. One writer described his manner accordingly:

> [H]e's a bright, quick-witted fellow whose thoughts come tumbling out so fast, it's often hard to get them sorted out in your mind or set them down on paper before he's two or three thoughts ahead of you.[25]

Morgan's "off-podium" maturity, professional integrity, sound judgment, commitment to excellence, and racial pride was well-expressed in an article that he wrote for *The New York Times* in response to two black Michigan State Legislators who set out to force the Detroit Symphony Orchestra to hire more black musicians. Titled "Orchestrating A Decline in the Arts," Morgan wrote:

> My world is that of the symphony orchestra. . . . It is a special world full of extraordinary people; admission to it is certainly an honor. . . . The integrity of this world has been threatened. . . . After years of fighting by women, minorities and those seeking fairness, a procedure [auditions behind a screen] was devised to make the process more open. . . . While the conductor still makes the final decision (with many witnesses), this system does seem to have the best possible balance of fairness and artistic integrity. . . . This system is particularly important to the black musician who has perhaps spent his or her life working hard outside the mainstream of the black community. To negate our hard-won achievements and carefully developed skills by suggesting that we should now be hired by color is to render meaningless an entire life's work. No one maintains any status in this field without ego, and no ego can withstand such an affront.[26]

Morgan's "field of dreams" came when he was selected as music director of the Oakland East Bay Symphony Orchestra, signing a three-year contract on September 10, 1990. The orchestra would now perform at the Calvin Simmons Theatre, recognized for its acoustic excellence and named for the deceased black conductor of the now defunct Oakland Symphony, rather than at the Paramount Theatre.[27] One local critic commented that, in her opinion, "Morgan shares the qualities that made Simmons* so popular, and which turned him into a role model for Oakland's youth."

> Best of all, he will give the Oakland East Bay Symphony something it has sorely lacked since its resurrection two years ago: a focus, a purpose, and the solid, recognizable identity that can only come from clear guidance. . . . Morgan . . . does not believe in separating regular subscription concerts from youth concerts; there's no reason, he asserts, to segregate music according to how old you are.[28]

Three months later, in an interview with Joseph McLellan, Morgan indicated that

> In Oakland. . . . we are trying something new. An orchestra that is being run from the education department outward. We are developing the orchestra as an educational resource that gives concerts.[29]

Following the orchestra's opening concert with Morgan at the helm on January 18, 1991, *San Francisco Examiner* critic Allan Ulrich wrote:

> The concert . . . served as a harbinger of evenings to come. . . . Morgan impressed as a serious, confident musician with definite and often original ideas about the standard repertoire. His should be a welcome voice and welcome sensibility on the Bay Area music scene.[30]

At the end of Morgan's first season (and the orchestra's third), Oakland East Bay Symphony's Board President Michael A. Dean wrote to the orchestra's current and potential supporters:

> It was a proud moment for me when Michael Morgan gave the downbeat to begin his first season as Music Director of the Oakland East Bay Symphony. But the best was yet to come, as our new maestro led the orchestra through four refreshing programs bursting with energy, novelty and the glory of the concert experience at its best. . . . Just a few short months ago, Michael Morgan's inaugural season of concerts and educational outreach was a hopeful "field of dreams." By the end of the Symphony's first season with Maestro Morgan, we all have experienced what one critic has called "the grand power of a prophesy fulfilled."[31]

Press Comments

"Michael Morgan. . . . made his debut with the Brooklyn Philharmonic . . . {H}e not only left a strong impression of his own talents but has the orchestra sounding like a world-class ensemble as well."

New York Times

"{Morgan's} ability to put across his musical intentions in a clear, firmly controlled manner was never in doubt. He . . . seems to enjoy a good musical chemistry with the players."

Chicago Tribune

"{E}normously talented. . . . Morgan conducted the orchestra with his usual verve, vitality and wonderful inspiration."

Houston Post

"Mr. Morgan proved himself capable of shaping a distinctive performance with minimal rehearsal time, by leading a highly creditable performance of Beethoven's Seventh Symphony. . . . He shaped a consistent performance."

Washington Post

"Morgan makes it clear that he has secure orchestral control, admirable taste and the ability to produce a notable performance. . . . {He} got the attention, the cooperation and the quality that proves that the musicians {Chicago Symphony Orchestra} know that he knows his business."

Chicago Sun Times

"Morgan was very much in command. He . . . conducts with authority."

Washington Times

"His musical results fully justify his decisions."

Washington Post

"Zestful . . . vibrant . . . there was strong indication of excellent musical instincts and the physical capacity to convey them."

Houston Post

"In the concerto, Morgan got accompaniment brimming with style and lilt."

Houston Chronicle

"Taken together with Morgan's impressive past performance in Houston, his conducting . . . wins my vote for him as T{exas} C{hamber} O{rchestra}'s next music director, if the current powers in the organization want to have a first-class musician."

Houston Post

"Morgan got out of the orchestra {Seattle} . . . vitality and intelligence. . . . He has a keen ear for the individuality of phrases as well as building them into powerful climaxes. . . . Morgan has a highly developed sense of wit and repartee."

Seattle Post-Intelligencer

"Michael D. Morgan is one of a handful of excellent black conductors on today's podiums and he's a conductor who makes things happen. With sharp, decisive movements and an air of barely restrained energy, Morgan gets an energetic, exciting sound from the orchestra."

Seattle Times

"In the spirit of Fritz Reiner . . ."

Chicago Sun Times

"Morgan's performance was beautifully lyric without sacrificing the innate rhythmic vitality of the score. His fine ear was revealed in the skillfull way in which he balanced the voices and blended the tone colors of the ensemble."

Chicago Sun Times

"Morgan's . . . dynamic performances have earned him a position as one of the hottest young conductors in the country."

Express

"He had the orchestra sounding like a world-class ensemble."

New York Times

"Heck, I may as well admit it: If I hadn't been scribbling phrases like 'irresistable,' 'phenomenally exciting,' and 'a certified hit (four stars)' in my notebook, I would have been clapping between movements, too."

Oakland Tribune

"Fire might be his middle name."

San Francisco Examiner

Notes

1. Arrelius B. Vonleggett, Jr., "Michael Morgan: From Washington to Chicago and Beyond," *Washington View,* December/January, 1991, p. 36.
2. Bill Zakariasen, "Fledgling Maestros Sparkle," *Daily News,* September 8, 1986, p. 8.
3. Conversation, Morgan/Handy, June 22, 1987, Washington, D.C.
4. *Ibid.*
5. Joseph McLellan, "Debut In D.C.: Conductor Michael Morgan Comes Home for 'Traviata'," *Washington Post,* July 10, 1983, p. K9.
6. *Ibid.*
7. Michael Morgan, "Orchestrating a Decline in the Arts," *New York Times,* April 11, 1989, p. A11.
8. Alex Stoll, "A Conductor's Homecoming," *Washington Post,* June 21, 1987, p. G4.
9. Conversation, *op. cit.*
10. Emily Nunn, "Success According to Michael Morgan," *Oberlin Alumni Magazine,* Fall 1987, p. 17.
11. Joseph McLellan, *op. cit.,* pp. K1, K9.
12. Carl Cunningham, "Young Conductor Returns to Take Up Baton With TCO," *Houston Post,* October 26, 1984, p. E16.

13. Joseph McLellan, "Home-Grown Maestro," *Washington Post,* December 29, 1990, p. D3.

14. Cunningham, *op. cit.*

15. Pamela Sommers, "National Symphony," *Washington Post,* July 23, 1984, p. C12.

16. Robert C. Marsh, "Morgan Merits More Than 'Silver Lining'," *Chicago Sun-Times,* February 23, 1987, p. 36.

17. *Ibid.*

18. ———, "Solti Replacement Morgan Scores Big," *Chicago Sun-Times,* May 27, 1987, p. 52.

19. Conversation, *op. cit.*

20. Stephen Wigler, "Conductor's Career Prospects Are Upbeat," *Baltimore Sun-Times,* March 1, 1987, p. N1.

21. Stoll, *op. cit.*

22. Joseph McLellan, "A Robust 'Traviata': NYC's Satisfying Wolf Trap Production," *Washington Post,* June 24, 1987, p. D1.

23. Michael Kimmelman, "Music: A New Violetta in City Opera's 'Traviata'," *New York Times,* July 17, 1987, p. 22.

24. Emily Nunn, *op. cit.*

25. Carl Cunningham, *op. cit.*

26. Michael Morgan, *op. cit.*

27. For more on the 1987 demise of the Oakland Symphony, see *Autopsy of an Orchestra: An Analysis of Factors Contributing to the Bankruptcy of the Oakland Symphony Orchestra Association,* Fenton Johnson, editor (Melanie Beene & Associates), January 1988.

28. Sarah Cahill, "New Symphony, New Conductor," *Express,* September 21, 1990, pp. 3, 37.

29. McLellan, "Home-Grown Maestro," *op. cit.*

30. Allan Ulrich, "The New Leader," *San Francisco Examiner,* January 19, 1991, p. B1.

31. Letter, Board President Michael A. Dean, Oakland East Bay Symphony, June 30, 1991.

Coleridge-Taylor Perkinson

COLERIDGE-TAYLOR PERKINSON

BIRTHDATE/PLACE: June 14, 1932; New York, N.Y.
EDUCATION: High School of Music and Art, 1949; New York University, 1949–51; B.Mus., Manhattan School of Music, 1953; M.Mus., Manhattan School of Music, 1954 (Composition); Berkshire Music Center, Summer 1954 (Choral Conducting); Mozarteum (Salzburg, Austria), Summer 1960 (Orchestral Conducting); International Conductor's Course, Netherlands Radio Union in Hilversum, Summers of 1960, 1962, 1963 (Orchestral Conducting).
MAJOR INSTRUCTORS: Composition–Vittorio Gianninni, Charles Mills, Earl Kim; Conducting–Lovro Von Matacic, Jonel Perlea, Franco Ferrara, Dean Dixon.
MAJOR APPOINTMENTS: Music Director, Professional Children's School, 1952–64; Faculty Member, Manhattan School of Music 1954–59, and Brooklyn College, 1959–62; Conductor, Brooklyn Community Symphony Orchestra, 1959–62; Stuyvesant Symphony Orchestra 1960; Assistant Conductor, Dessoff Choir, 1956–57; Pianist, Max Roach Jazz Quartet, 1964–65; Co-Founder/Associate Conductor, Symphony of the New World, 1965–70; Music Director, American Theatre Lab (Jerome Robbins), 1966–67; First Composer-in-Residence, Negro Ensemble Company (founded in 1967); Music Director, Alvin Ailey American Dance Theatre, 1968–69 and 1978; Acting Music Director, Symphony of the New World, 1972–73; Music Director, Barbara McNair Show (two seasons); Interim Director, Music Program, New York State Council on the Arts, 1979; Conductor, "Lena Horne: The Lady and Her Music," 1981.
GUEST CONDUCTOR: Dallas, North Carolina, and Albany Symphony Orchestras, Orchestra Filarmonic de Bogotá; Radio Kammer Orkest, Hilversum; Brooklyn Philharmonic Orchestra; and Dance Theatre of Harlem.
AWARDS/HONORS: LaGuardia Prize in Music, 1949 (High School of Music and Art); Emmy Nomination for Outstanding Individual Achievement for Music in Documentary Programming, "Bearden On Bearden" (1985); Manhattan Borough President's Award for Public Service and Artistic Excellence in Music, 1987.

AS ONE OF TENOR GEORGE SHIRLEY'S subjects for his radio broadcast "Classical Music and the Afro-American" (1973), Coleridge-Taylor Perkinson was introduced as a young man of many musical talents, able to move with ease from concert hall to ballet and straight theater, from the Hollywood soundstage to elegant supper clubs . . . a rare breed, whose destiny was foreordained when his parents named him after the Afro-British composer Samuel Coleridge-Taylor.[1]

In summary, Perkinson is both talented and versatile, as well as a person of many accomplishments. He is one of fifteen composers profiled in the monumental 1978 publication *The Black Composer Speaks,* edited by David Baker, Lida. Belt, and Herman Hudson. Perkinson's compositional output includes orchestral, choral, chamber and solo works; music for ballet, television, and theatre; and motion picture scores.

Many of his compositions were commissioned: "Attitudes," a solo cantata for tenor, violin, cello, and piano (Ford Foundation, 1982); "Commentary," a concert piece for solo cello and orchestra (National Association of Negro Musicians, 1964); and several works for the extremely popular Dance Theatre of Harlem ("Ode to Otis," "Forces of Rhythm," "Carmen," and "Phoenix Rising") and for the Alvin Ailey American Dance Theatre ("To Bird With Love"). "Phoenix Rising" was made possible in part by a grant from The DeWitt Wallace Fund (Reader's Digest) and the New York State Council on the Arts.

He has been the recipient of several highly competitive National Endowment for the Arts Composer Fellowships and often served the Arts Endowment's Music Program as a panelist for the Jazz, Composer-Librettist, and Policy programs. He was one of two consultants contracted in the early 1980s to research needs of the jazz field and how the Endowment could most effectively assist.

Perkinson noted that the excitement of singing J. S. Bach's "Saint Matthew Passion" with the Schola Cantorum under the baton of Hugh Ross at age fifteen convinced him that music-making could be an overwhelming experience. It was membership in the Schola Cantorum that provided wide exposure to contemporary and seldom performed literature. There was also an early attraction to jazz.

A thrilling (and enlightening) experience was graduation exercises at the High School of Music and Art in 1948. The speaker was black conductor Dean Dixon.* Other early influences were Clarence Whiteman (black organist and choir director at the Church of the Master in New York City), Rev. James Robinson (Minister at the Church of the Master and Creator/Director of Crossroads Africa, "blueprint for the Peace Corps"), Hall Johnson (black composer/conductor), Clarence Cameron White (black concert violinist), Paul Boepple (director of the Dessoff Choir, specializing in early choral music), David Johnson (a black violinist who "had studied with the best teachers, . . . knew all of the literature, and . . . was capable of doing it all"), and Dimitri Mitropoulos (music director of the New York Philharmonic).[2] All assisted in helping Perkinson find his own musical voice, become conversant with various musical styles, and perfect his crafts of composing and conducting.

Training at the High School of Music and Art was excellent, according to Perkinson:

> Everything was taught to me very well in that high school; I literally learned nothing academically about music after leaving there because the training was so thorough.[3]

Following high school, he first matriculated at New York University, then at the Manhattan School of Music, where he received the B.Mus. and M.Mus. in 1953 and 1954. He majored in composition.

During the summer of 1954, the twenty-two-year-old studied choral conducting at the Berkshire Music Center (Tanglewood) and served as assistant to Hugh Ross. This experience led to his position as assistant conductor of the Dessoff Choir, 1956–57. Perkinson served intermittently on the faculty of Manhattan School of Music between 1954–59 and in 1959, joined the faculty of Brooklyn College and began conducting the Brooklyn Community Symphony Orchestra. As he recalled in *The Black Composer Speaks*:

> At that point I had had a very flourishing career . . . I had done practically everything. I had conducted orchestral and choral concerts; I had written music that had been well-received, and then all of a sudden, the bottom dropped out; whatever plateau I should have reached next simply disappeared. Thinking that perhaps I was wrong and that everyone else was right (everyone else being the social structure that I was living in), I decided to go to Europe for further study.[4]

The year was 1960.

The summers of 1962 and 1963 were also spent in Europe, working primarily with Dean Dixon. Perkinson elaborated on the excitement of working with this "master of the baton" in his interview with George Shirley:

His method of teaching and what he had to teach was simply marvelous. He never criticized you in front of the orchestra. His lessons were so simple. Many conductors were there, from all over the world.[5]

After his return to the States, Perkinson's career flourished, primarily as a composer. His work with the Negro Ensemble Company (for which he composed "Song of the Lusitanian Bogey" and "Ceremonies in Dark Old Men"), the Alvin Ailey American Dance Theatre, and the Dance Theatre of Harlem was particularly exciting. His motion picture scores (which he also conducted) included "Crossroads Africa," "Montgomery to Memphis" (a Martin Luther King, Jr. documentary), "A Warm December" (Sidney Poitier), "Amazing Grace" (Moms Mabley, Slappy White, Rosalind Cash, and Moses Gunn), and "Freedom Road" (Muhammad Ali and Kris Kristofferson). His television scores included "Room 222," the Barbara McNair Show, a Lou Rawls Special, "This Far by Faith" (the Bell System), and "A Woman Called Moses" (Cicely Tyson); his album credits included those produced by such artists as Max Roach, Donald Byrd, Leon Bibb, Marvin Gaye, Jimmy Owens, and Harry Belafonte.

Conducting opportunities also existed: music director, American Theatre Lab (1966–67), Alvin Ailey American Dance Theatre (1968–69 and 1978), and Associate Conductor and Acting Music Director of the Symphony of the New World (1965–70 and 1972–73 respectively), which he cofounded. He occasionally conducted ballet performances of his works performed by the Dance Theatre of Harlem. Other guest conducting experiences included the Dallas, North Carolina, and Albany Symphony Orchestras; the Orchestra Filarmonica de Bogotá, Radio Kammer Orkest of Hilversum, the Netherlands; and the Brooklyn Philharmonic Orchestra.

Conductor of the Broadway production "Lena Horne: The Lady and Her Music" when it opened at the Nederlander Theatre in 1981, Perkinson was designated "a man of many musical parts." He remained with the show only briefly. Other interests and new challenges kept the composer/conductor constantly moving.

For Perkinson, a choice between composing and conducting does not exist:

If I had to choose which activity I would do to the exclusion of everything else . . . if it came down to that kind of a decision, I think

I would rather compose than do anything else; however, I would not want to give up conducting because I find that when I am conducting I am actively composing, in that I work on a piece by actually recreating whatever it is that I'm dealing with. . . . I would not like to be limited just to composing. I enjoy conducting; it's the one performing medium that I like being involved in.[6]

Notes

1. George Shirley's 1973 "Classical Music and the Afro-American" radio series, Parkway Productions, aired originally on radio station WNYC. Samuel Coleridge-Taylor (1875–1912) was a distinguished turn-of-the-century Afro-British composer. He organized and conducted England's Croydon String Orchestra and conducted various British choral societies. Coleridge-Taylor toured the United States in 1904 and 1906, conducting many of his compositions. Numerous societies and other musical organizations were established in America in honor of the celebrated Trinity College music professor. See Jewel Taylor Thompson's *Samuel Coleridge-Taylor*, Metuchen, N.J.: Scarecrow Press, Inc., 1994 for more details regarding Coleridge-Taylor's life and work.
2. David N. Baker, Lida M. Belt and Herman C. Hudson, *The Black Composer Speaks*, Metuchen, N.J.: Scarecrow Press, Inc., 1978, pp. 240–242.
3. *Ibid.*, p. 242.
4. *Ibid.*
5. Shirley, *op. cit.*
6. Baker, et al., *op. cit.*, p. 264.

Karl Hampton Porter

KARL HAMPTON PORTER

BIRTHDATE/PLACE: April 25, 1939; Pittsburgh, Pennsylvania.
EDUCATION: Carnegie-Mellon University, 1958–60; Peabody Conservatory of Music, 1960–62; Juilliard School of Music, 1962–63; Berkshire Music Center at Tanglewood; Domaine School of Conducting (Hancock, Maine), 1961–63; American Symphony Orchestra League's Institute for Conductors (Orkney, Virginia), 1970.
MAJOR INSTRUCTORS/COACHES: Arthur Kubey, Sherman Walt, Elias Carmen—Bassoon; William Sebastian Hart, Leon Barzin, Laszio Halasz, Pierre Monteux, Richard Lert, Richard Burgin, Karl Kritz—Conducting.
MAJOR APPOINTMENTS: Bassoon—American Wind Symphony, 1960–61; Denver Symphony Orchestra, 1964–65; Metropolitan Opera National Company Orchestra, 1965–68; Gil Evans Jazz Band, 1967–69; American and New Jersey Symphony Orchestras; Symphony of the New World.
FOUNDER/CONDUCTOR: Harlem Youth Symphony, 1968–70; Harlem Philharmonic Orchestra, 1969–79; New York Housing Authority Orchestra, 1972–??; New Breed Brass Ensemble, Harlem String Quartet, Harlem Woodwind Quintet.
CONDUCTOR: Baltimore Symphony (Youth Concerts); Massapequa (New York) Symphony Society, 1974.
MUSIC DIRECTOR: Josephine Baker Show, 1972.
INSTRUCTOR: Newark (New Jersey) Community Arts Center, 1969–71; New York Community College of the City University of New York, 1972—; Department of Humanities, New York City Technical College, 1984—.
AWARDS/HONORS: Grants—Martha Baird Rockefeller Foundation, 1969.

One of the reasons I chose to become a conductor was because of the experiences I encountered as a pioneering black bassoonist. I thought I had the talent to change the way things were. . . . Symphony orchestras in America are still private clubs for white musicians and since the box office is not in jeopardy by not hiring more black musicians, the situation is not going to change unless more pressure is applied.[1]

SO STATED KARL HAMPTON PORTER, one who has never hesitated to express himself.

To music critic Allen Hughes, who was preparing an article on the plight of black conductors for the *New York Times* in early 1970, Porter remarked,

> I have the feeling that black conductors are going to save music in this country. . . . When a black conductor drops his guard, something happens. A new freshness enters the music.

Amazed that his Harlem Youth Philharmonic concerts in New York City's Central Park were winning critical approval, despite extremely limited financial resources, Porter pointed out that "Black people are prone to do more with very little."[2]

Karl Hampton Porter attributes his interest in music to the band of an Elks Club in his home town of Pittsburgh, Pennsylvania. When he was 9 years old, he was taken one Sunday by his grandfather to the club where the band was rehearsing for a parade. As a result of hearing that first rehearsal, Porter saved enough money from selling newspapers to buy a tenor saxophone. His grandfather intervened with the band to accept him as a member, and he soon became known as "the midget with the big horn." Soon he was playing for dances and earning enough money to pay for saxophone lessons. He continued with that instrument throughout junior high school.[3]

Carl McVicker, Porter's music teacher at Westinghouse High School, was responsible for his abandoning the tenor saxophone. McVicker asked for a volunteer to play the bassoon in the school orchestra and Porter came forward. He transferred his saxophone technique to the new instrument and, with the aid of instruction books, learned to play the bassoon. Several months later he auditioned for the all-state band and won first chair.

Rehearsals every Sunday afternoon with the Pittsburgh Youth Symphony, and later with the American Wind Symphony Orchestra, provided Porter with both the training and the discipline required for playing in an orchestra. The Youth Symphony's conductor, Marie Maazel (mother of noted conductor Lorin Maazel), gave Porter many of her early music books, encouraged him in his studies, and made certain he was able to attend concerts by the Pittsburgh Symphony. Later, he received tickets to musical events, including opera, from a blind uncle.

Porter took his musical pursuits very seriously. He never missed a rehearsal or performance of the Pittsburgh Youth Orchestra, recognizing even then the value of the training orchestra experience for an aspiring player or conductor. Later, he studied bassoon with Arthur Kubey at the Carnegie-Mellon Institute. During that time, he experienced a major disappointment because of his race:

> I thought [I was] a leading candidate for the second bassoon opening with the Pittsburgh Symphony. I was informed however, that the post couldn't go to me because I was black ("a Negro"). My addition would jeopardize this money making tour. Subsequently, Mr. Kubey groomed a white clarinettist from the Youth Orchestra for the bassoon position.[4]

Porter continued to experience subtle racism. His teacher tried to discourage him from entering a local music competition, held annually by the Pittsburgh Music Club, by telling him he wasn't ready. Porter entered without his teacher's knowledge and won first prize.

After completing high school, Porter enrolled at the Peabody Conservatory of Music in Baltimore. During his tenure there, he was assistant conductor for the opera theater and a member of the Conservatory Orchestra. After two years at Peabody, Porter went to New York and studied for a year at the Juilliard School of Music. But soon his impatience to get on with a playing career, and lack of funds to continue his studies, led him to a succession of positions as bassoonist with the Denver Symphony, various chamber groups, and the Metropolitan Opera National Company.

During his tenure with the Met National Company, an event occurred that Porter considers to be a milestone in his life. When the regular conductor failed to appear for a performance of "La Traviata" in Washington in 1967, Porter was asked to fill in. He became the hero of the company. But that appreciation was not shared by the regular conductor. "He got uptight and fired me two weeks later," said Porter.

After the Met experience, Porter returned to New York, where he freelanced as a jazz bassoonist on recording sessions and with such ensembles as Leopold Stokowski's American Symphony Orchestra. Following the death of Martin Luther King, Jr. (1968), Porter spent a brief period conducting the Baltimore Symphony in its school concerts. Also in 1968, Porter founded the Harlem Youth Symphony Orchestra, seventy-five youths, mostly black, between the ages of sixteen and twenty-five. Their inaugural concert was given in New York's Central Park May 30, 1968.

Like most fledgling arts organizations, the Harlem Youth Symphony was underfunded. After two years, and the investment of much of his own money. Hampton became discouraged about the Youth Symphony's future, and turned his attention to the formation of the Harlem Philharmonic Orchestra. This training orchestra, composed mostly of black players who were professionals or exceptional college students, was supported primarily by private contributions and modest performance fees. The Harlem Philharmonic Society continued through its tenth season, with performances in the later years being given by a chamber ensemble rather than a full orchestra.[5]

Porter was early associated with the New York Housing Authority Symphony Orchestra. Formed in 1971, the orchestra performed regularly, during the summer months, free concerts for residents of the city's public housing and in city parks. Continuing into the 1990s and functioning as one of the city's important cultural institutions, concert activities now included out-of-town venues and Alice Tully Hall (Lincoln Center).[6] The exact date of Porter's departure is unknown.

Since the early '80s, Porter has continued to appear as guest conductor with numerous orchestras throughout the metropolitan New York area and to perform as an outstanding freelancing bassoonist. Efforts to revive the Harlem Philharmonic continued.

Press Comments

"Karl Hampton Porter conducted with extraordinary aplomb."

New York Times

"Porter demonstrated a clear authoritative beat, always exhibiting innate musicality and temperament."

New York Daily News

"Mr. Porter can always be counted on for alert leadership as well as inspiring his musicians to produce sensitive, shapely performances that invariably capture the spirit of each score.

New York Times

Notes

1. Questionnaire/Correspondence, Porter to Handy/Terry, n.d. (1988).
2. Allen Hughes, "For Black Conductors, A Future? or Frustration?", *New York Times,* March 15, 1970, p. 32.
3. Questionnaire/Correspondence, *op. cit.*
4. *Ibid.*
5. *Ibid.*
6. "A Starting Place for Black Musicians," *New York Times,* December 27, 1987, p. 60.

Kay George Roberts

Kay George Roberts Guest Conducting New York City Housing Authority
Symphony Orchestra (Photo: Bert Andrews)

KAY GEORGE ROBERTS

BIRTHDATE/PLACE: September 16, 1950; Nashville, Tennessee.

EDUCATION: High School Diploma, Peabody Demonstration School, George Peabody College; B.A., Fisk University (Major, Music; Minor, Psychology), 1972; M.M., Yale University School of Music (Conducting and Violin Performance), 1975; M.M.A., Yale University School of Music (Conducting), 1976; D.M.A., Yale University School of Music (Conducting), 1986.

MAJOR INSTRUCTORS: Violin—Robert Holmes, Wilda Tinsley Moennig, Patricia Drabeck Harada, Stephen Clapp, Broadus Erle, Syoko Aki, Samuel Kissle, George Neikrug; Conducting—Otto-Werner Mueller, Margaret Hillis, Murry Sidlin, Gustav Meier.

MASTER CLASSES WITH: Seiji Ozawa, Andre Previn, Leonard Bernstein, Edo de Waart, Denis de Coteau.

MAJOR APPOINTMENTS: Associate Professor/Professor of Music and Conductor of the University Orchestra, University of Massachusetts at Lowell, 1978—; Music Director and Conductor, New Hampshire Philharmonic Orchestra (Manchester, New Hampshire), 1982–87; Music Director and Conductor, Cape Ann Symphony Orchestra (Gloucester, Massachusetts), 1986–88; Founder/Conductor, Ensemble Americana (Stuttgart, Germany), 1989—; Conductor, Artemis Ensemble, 1989–90 (Stuttgart, Germany); Co-Conductor, Black Music Repertory Ensemble (Chicago), 1990–91.

GUEST CONDUCTOR: Nashville Symphony Orchestra, 1976, 1982, and 1991; New England Women's Symphony, 1979; Nashua Symphony Orchestra, 1984; Bangkok Symphony Orchestra (Thailand), 1986 and 1987; New York Housing Authority Symphony Orchestra, 1987, 1988, 1989 and 1990; Cairo Conservatoire Orchestra (Egypt), 1988; Detroit Symphony, 1989; Women's Philharmonic (California), 1991; Haddonfield (New Jersey) Symphony and Dayton Philharmonic, 1992; Chattanooga (Tennessee), Dallas, and Cleveland Symphony Orchestras, 1993–94.

AWARDS/HONORS: National Fellowship Fund for Black Americans, Bates Junior Fellow, Jonathan Edwards College of Yale; Charles H. Ditson Scholarship, Yale University School of Music; Woman of Promise, *Good Housekeeping,* 1986; Distinguished Alumna of the Year, National Association for Equal Opportunity in Higher Education (NAFEO), 1987; Black Achievers Award, Greater Boston YMCA, 1988; Distinguished Alumna

Award, University School of Nashville (formerly Peabody Demonstration School), 1991; Outstanding Woman in the Performing Arts, League of Black Women (Chicago), 1991.

> I enjoy working with musicians and the challenge of making what's on the written page come alive. . . . It's [the orchestra] like a single large instrument you get to play.[1]

THESE ARE THE WORDS OF CONDUCTOR Kay George Roberts, as expressed to journalist Alan Bostick on the occasion of her return visit to Nashville to conduct (for the third time) the Nashville Symphony during the summer of 1991.

Two weeks later (in Stuttgart, Germany) she stated to journalist Peter Kümmel, "I have to meet high expectations. But this is not a problem, as soon as the musicians feel I have something to say musically." Commented a local observer, "This woman . . . has an incredible aura and humor. She is able instantaneously to relate without any effort to the musicians."[2]

> Just reading excerpts from Kay George Robert's appointment calendar is exhausting. June 1987, New York City: guest conductor at Lincoln Center . . . August, Lowell, Mass.: prepare to resume teaching and conducting at the University of Lowell's College of Music . . . September, Gloucester, Mass.: start second season as music director of the Cape Ann Symphony . . . October, Bangkok, Thailand: return for guest-conductor appearance with the Bangkok Symphony Orchestra . . . December, Cairo, Egypt: conduct the Cairo Conservatoire Orchestra.

> Her boundless energy alone might make Roberts stand out in her chosen profession. But she is also a black American female in a field historically dominated by white European males.[3]

So began the entry "Conducting Becomes Her" that appeared in *Newsweek On Campus,* April 1988, prepared by *Newsweek*'s associate editor Diane H. McDonald.

The writer had observed Roberts when she made her New York City debut at Damrosch Park, conducting the New York Housing Authority Symphony Orchestra, June 15, 1987. So impressed was McDonald that she instantly envisioned a story. McDonald journeyed to the University of Lowell (now The University of Massachusetts at Lowell) to observe Professor Roberts in action.

As background for the article, she researched the American orchestral conducting scene by conferring with the National Endowment for the Arts' Music Program, the American Symphony Orchestra League, and Affiliate Artists, Inc., "the nation's only program providing three-year professional [conducting] appointments." McDonald concluded her article with the following pronouncement:

> The music world can expect to hear more and more from Roberts. Whether she pursues a full-time position with a professional orchestra or devotes her major energies to teaching seems entirely her choice.[4]

Upon receipt of the Doctor of Musical Arts degree in orchestra conducting (Yale's first woman and second black recipient), Roberts became the subject of an "Alumna Profile" in her undergraduate alma mater's publication, *Fisk News*. The article recalled that she was a

> campus kid . . . remembered as a familiar shadow skipping merrily at the heels of her father, the late Dr. S. O. Roberts, founder and former chairman of the Department of Psychology, clad in a baseball cap with two healthy braids bouncing to and fro. . . .[5]

The article noted also that Roberts had recently been one of "28 Young Women of Promise" cited in a July 1986 *Good Housekeeping* article. She was one of a select group of extraordinary women "who are blazing trails now and will change our world in the future."[6]

The youngest of three girls—all recipients of terminal degrees (psychiatry, psychology, and music)—Kay George stated that outside of her conducting achievements, she was proudest of having acquired the D.M.A. At the undergraduate level, she took psychology as a minor, so that she could "get a word in edgewise at the family dinner table." Her mother was a university librarian (Tennessee State and Fisk Universities) and her maternal grandfather (George Taylor) was once president of Philander Smith College in Little Rock, Arkansas.

In a curriculum vitae from the mid-seventies, Roberts listed as her personal career goal, "to combine performance (violin) of either orchestral or chamber music with conducting and teaching on a college level." By the mid-eighties, the curriculum vitae made clear that her career goal was being accomplished. Under the caption "Kay George Roberts—Conductor," her current positions were listed: (1)

Music Director and Conductor, New Hampshire Philharmonic; (2) Associate Professor of Music and Conductor of the University Orchestra, University of Lowell, Massachusetts. Evidence of her continuing violin performance included membership in the New Haven Symphony Orchestra, 1972–80; Nashua Symphony Orchestra, 1980–84; and the Indian Hill Chamber Orchestra, 1981–85.

By the late-eighties, Roberts's resumé revealed that her professional direction was narrowing. She was by that time a full professor at the University of Lowell, was continuing as conductor of the University of Lowell's orchestra, had terminated her relationship with the New Hampshire Philharmonic, and had served as music director and conductor of the Cape Ann Symphony Orchestra (1986–88). Professional violin performance had been reduced; more guest conducting appearances were in evidence.

Meaningful ensemble performance began at age nine when Roberts began playing in the Cremona String Orchestra, organized by black music educator/conductor/composer Robert Holmes of the Nashville Public Schools (which were completely segregated at that time). Roberts elaborated on this subject when she participated on a panel devoted to "Orchestras and Minorities: Some New Perspectives" at the American Symphony Orchestra League's 42nd National Convention in New York City. Said Roberts:

> Since the Youth Symphony in Nashville was segregated, Robert Holmes formed the Cremona Strings for talented black youth. It met on Saturday mornings, at the same time as the "white" youth orchestra. Under Holmes' leadership, guidance, and enthusiasm, the Cremona Strings thrived through the 1960s and into the early '70s. In 1964, the Nashville Youth Symphony finally opened up to all musicians. Three of us from the Cremona Strings auditioned for the Youth Symphony and were accepted as regular members.[7]

While enrolled in Peabody Demonstration School of George Peabody College for secondary training (1965–68), she continued with the Nashville Youth Symphony and during her last year was invited to join the senior Nashville Symphony. Under the direction of Thor Johnson, she remained with her hometown orchestra throughout the college years and represented the ensemble as first violinist in Arthur Fiedler's World Symphony Orchestra in 1971.

As one of five Blacks, Roberts performed with approximately one hundred forty professional "musical ambassadors" representing orchestras in sixty nations, thirty-four states and the District of Columbia.[8] The unique orchestra's itinerary included three major performances: the first at Philharmonic Hall (now Avery Fisher Hall) of New York City's Lincoln Center for the Performing Arts, under sponsorship of the United Nations Association of the United States; the second at Walt Disney World in Orlando, Florida; and the third at John F. Kennedy Center for the Performing Arts in Washington, D.C.—the first orchestral performance on the stage of the Opera House of the new Center.

Roberts indicated that the M.M.A. that she received in 1976 denoted completion of predoctoral studies required for the Doctor of Musical Arts degree. The terminal degree is awarded after a period of three to six years during which time a candidate must demonstrate his or her qualifications through distinguished achievement in the profession. Toward this goal, she made her professional conducting debut in May 1976 as guest conductor of the Nashville Symphony Orchestra. In that same season she conducted two movements from Gustav Mahler's Symphony No. 1 in rehearsals with the Atlanta and Nashville Symphony Orchestras (1975–76 season). Conducting instructor Otto-Werner Mueller made a practice of carrying a student along when he made guest appearances with a major orchestra and was generous enough to share the rehearsal podium with his "sufficiently qualified" students.

The occasion of her professional debut was the Nashville Symphony Orchestra's first Centennial concert of the 1976 season, with guitarist Jorge Morel as guest soloist. Roberts chose an international program, featuring music from eight countries. Wrote *The Tennessean*'s Natilee Duning of Roberts's conducting debut (two days prior to the actual event):

> Her pursuit of a career as a conductor places Kay Roberts in that group of women who seek to cross the traditional line so long separating women from the podium. . . . The most recent American Symphony Orchestra League [survey] notes 15 women now active on the American orchestral scene.[9]

Following the event, Duning wrote:

> [A] crowd of some 2,000 listeners turned out for the occasion. . . . On the podium was Kay George Roberts. . . . in control of the music and players throughout the performance.[10]

The Nashville Banner's Werner Zepernick wrote:

> Miss Roberts had the orchestra firm in hand. She has a clear and
> steady beat and good understanding of the various styles. The
> 26-year-old conductor chose her tempi wisely, . . .[11]

When Roberts made her debut as conductor of the University of
Lowell Orchestra in 1978, the local newspaper (The *Sun*) did a
feature story. Titled "Conductor: Black Woman Musician of ULowell Succeeds in Field Dominated by Men," Dayle Zatlin wrote:

> At 28, she has just been hired to conduct the University of Lowell
> Orchestra and to teach two courses in the music school on the side.
> Although she wears the feminist symbol for female on a chain around
> her neck, Roberts plays down the fact that she is a woman, preferring
> to stress her qualifications as a musician.[12]

Continuously expanding both her training and experience, Roberts
participated during the summers of 1981–1983 in the Aspen Music
Festival Conductor's program; Conductor's Guild Workshop, West
Virginia University; and the Conductor's Seminar, Berkshire Music
Center, Tanglewood, respectively. In the spring of 1985, she partici-
pated in the American Symphony Orchestra League's Conducting
Workshop, where she was one of six selected from a group of forty
conductors to work with the San Francisco Youth Orchestra (under the
guidance of black conductor Denis de Coteau* and the San Francisco
Symphony Orchestra's conductor Edo de Waart).

Roberts gained still more experience during the years 1983–85,
when she served as Assistant Conductor of the Mystic Valley
Chamber Orchestra (1983–84) and the Greater Boston Youth
Symphony (1984–85). During this period of both teaching and
learning, Roberts accepted a few guest conducting appearances: the
New England Women's Symphony in 1979; a return Nashville
Symphony engagement in 1982; the Nashua (New Hampshire)
Symphony Orchestra in 1984; and the Greater Dallas Youth
Orchestra in 1986.

Of Miss Roberts' week as guest conductor of the 115-member
Greater Dallas Youth Orchestra, *The Dallas Morning News* wrote:

> Kay George Roberts has a certain conductivity when she works.
> When she gets fired up, she gets everyone's attention . . . [E]very
> member seemed captivated by her directing style.

Young players were quoted:

> "She works us hard, but she's good." "She's definitely good. She knows what she is talking about and her style of directing is easy to follow."[13]

Despite her many university and guest conducting assignments, Miss Roberts has always found time to work with younger musicians. In addition to her work with the Dallas organization, she has shared her conducting, coaching, and tutorial skills with members of the Summer Camp for High School Band and Orchestra Musicians of Sam Houston State University, the Rhode Island All-State High School Orchestra, the Texas Music Educators Association's All-State Philharmonic Orchestra, and the Cairo (Egypt) Conservatoire Orchestra. Her management skills were strengthened during the 1984–85 season when she served as executive director of Project STEP, a string training and educational program for minority students sponsored by the Boston Symphony Orchestra, Boston University, the Greater Boston Youth Symphony Orchestra, and the New England Conservatory.

Kay George Roberts became the New Hampshire Philharmonic Orchestra's music director and conductor during the orchestra's twenty-fifth season (1982–83). A community orchestra, in residence at St. Anselm's College in Manchester, New Hampshire, the ensemble is comprised of professional musicians, music teachers and students, and serious amateur players. At the beginning of her third season, the local press noted "vast musical improvement for the orchestra" and commented, "[I]f Saturday's concert is a signal of things to come, the citizens of Manchester are in for some first-class musical entertainment."[14]

Roberts was selected for the position of music director and conductor of the Cape Ann Symphony on the basis of board members' observation of her skills in handling the New Hampshire Philharmonic. The local critic wrote of her debut appearance with the Cape Ann Symphony Orchestra:

> A Sunday afternoon crowd . . . came to see Kay George Roberts . . . and to judge how the new conductor handles this group which is now a 35-year-old Cape Ann tradition. The consensus was, she was super. . . . Roberts' conducting style is meticulous and demanding.

From the moment she strides on stage, it is clear that this woman is in command. Her physical appearance . . . is striking. Her hand movements are precise and her facial expressions compelling. . . .

[T]he second half of the concert . . . made it clear that the Cape Ann Symphony, under Roberts, can play with great depth and feeling as well as precision and technique. . . . The Cape Ann Symphony, at 35, is a tight ship and Kay George Roberts is firmly at its helm.[15]

Roberts remained at the helm through the 1987–88 season.

The *Boston Herald* published a feature story on Roberts when she was invited to conduct the Bangkok Symphony Orchestra in Thailand during the summer of 1986. Under the heading "A Symphony of Firsts for Woman From Cambridge," the writer made note of the fact that Roberts was the first woman and first black to conduct "the 4-year old Bangkok Symphony, made up mostly of musicians from the Royal Thai Navy."[16] The orchestra is under the patronage of His Royal Highness the Crown Prince Maha Vajiralongkorn.

Roberts was invited back to conduct in Thailand, on October 12 and 13, 1987. The events organized by the Bangkok Symphony Orchestra, with sponsorship from Philip Morris International, honored His Majesty the King on his sixtieth birthday. Entitled "From Classical Favorites to Jazz," the celebration was publicized as one of the biggest cultural events of the year. Advance publicity indicated that the concert would be

phenomenal in scale and high in calibre. . . . includ[ing] five jazz artists [performing compositions by His Majesty Bhumibol Adulyadej, arranged by Benny Golson], Metropolitan opera star Isola Jones, and classical pianist William Wolfram. . .[17]

After having made her New York City debut earlier in that same year (June 1987), conducting the New York Housing Authority Symphony Orchestra in Damrosch Park, Roberts was invited back to conduct the eighteen-year-old organization at Alice Tully Hall, Lincoln Center, December 12, 1988.[18] The following year, she conducted the same orchestra in a concert in Bridgeport, Connecticut, and made her debut with a major American orchestra.

When Roberts conducted the Detroit Symphony on March 19, 1989, for the orchestra's "Celebration of African-American Sacred Music" program, she shared the podium with the black choral conductor Nathan Carter and the stage with Carter's Morgan State University Choir, and black mezzo-soprano Barbara Conrad. The *Detroit News* credited Roberts in the following manner:

> [She] opened the concert with a smartly drawn, sympathetic reading of the first two movements of William Grant Still's Sunday Morning Symphony . . .[and] returned . . . to finish the night in high gear with Frederick Tillis' rhapsodic setting of "Every Time I Feel the Spirit."[19]

When Roberts conducted a chamber ensemble in a performance of Gloria Coates's "Voices of Women in Wartime" as a part of the American Women Composers' Fourth Annual Marathon in Watertown, Massachusetts, in April 1989, *The Boston Globe* wrote, "[T]alented Kay George Roberts. . . . has been heard too little in town."[20] Shortly thereafter, Roberts departed for Germany where she would spend her sabbatical year (1989–90), during which she conducted the Artemis Ensemble (a professional group which performs and records works by women composers), received a grant from the German Academic Exchange Service for research on German women composers, and founded a new professional chamber orchestra, Ensemble Americana. Based in Stuttgart, the group made its debut November 11, 1989. The evening's theme was "The View of the New on the Old World."

Ensemble Americana is a chamber ensemble composed of American and German professional musicians living in the Stuttgart area, whose aim is to promote contemporary American music in Germany. The Roberts/Ensemble Americana relationship is ongoing.

The Black Music Repertory Ensemble, a chamber group established by the Center for Black Music Research at Columbia College in Chicago, gave its world premiere performance in March 1988. When this "first-of-its-kind" mixed ensemble—organized "to promote appreciation for the black musical heritage written between 1800 and the present"—made its New York City debut on September 10, 1990, on the podium was Kay George Roberts.[21] The Alice Tully Hall concert was followed the next day by an appearance on the NBC's "Today Show." According to the *Sun Times,* when the Black Music Repertory Ensemble appeared the following February at Chicago's Orchestra Hall, "firmly in control" was Kay George Roberts.[22]

During the summer of 1991, Miss Roberts returned to her native Nashville to again conduct the Nashville Symphony in the last of three outdoor concerts on the lawn at Cheekwood. The *Tennessean*'s staff writer Alan Bostick wrote a feature story:

> As pioneers go, Crockett and Boone have nothing on Kay George Roberts. She hasn't exactly tamed the wilderness, but she has brought a new look to a profession that traditionally began and ended with white European men.[23]

Following the July 7 concert, music critic Jerome Reed registered his reaction:

> Roberts achieved more tonal variety in this outdoor performance than one often hears in a concert hall. . . . Roberts is a fabulous conductor. I hope she comes back to Nashville soon and often.[24]

As Roberts's former instructor at the Tanglewood Music Center, Gustav Meier, recently stated:

> I was struck by the music involvement that was always evident in her conducting. . . . She's outgoing and knows how to get to the musicians, but the music is always first. It would be easy to get carried away and do your own thing. But with Kay, she has tended to put the music first. She's got the right combination of humility and assertiveness.[25]

Roberts moved on to more distinguished arenas during 1992 and 1993, as she guest conducted the Dayton Philharmonic, and Chattanooga and Cleveland Symphony Orchestras. The latter reengaged Roberts for 1994 appearances. From all indications, *Newsweek*'s Diane McDonald was totally accurate when she predicted that "the world can expect to hear more and more from Roberts."

Press Comments

"Miss Roberts . . . was in control. . . . Her signals were clear, her tempos lively and well defined."

> *Tennessean*

"The orchestra was superb, alternately vibrant and subtle when needed, with a conductor in Kay George Roberts with all of the grace of Margot Fonteyn."

> *Westford Eagle*

"Roberts developed the subtle interplay between the woodwinds and the strings; she also drew from the combined orchestral sections a full and rich sound . . . The piece was solidly directed, enthusiastically performed, and very well received."

Union Leader (Manchester, New Hampshire)

"Roberts has found her stride; she understands what pieces our audiences can receive well. And she tries to push, musicians {Cape Ann Symphony Orchestra} and audience, just a little beyond what is easy."

Gloucester Daily Times

"The concert was possibly one of the best of its kind in a long time and there was little doubt that conductor Kay George Roberts was behind the success. . . .

Bangkok Post (Thailand)

"The superstar of the evening, beyond a doubt, was the conductor Kay George Roberts. Her capable direction set the pace and from pianissimo to pizzicato, nary a string or horn beeped or squeaked out of place."

Nation (Thailand)

"Roberts . . . was firmly in control of the complexities."

Chicago Sun Times

"Kay George Roberts conducted, and drew a polished, energetic sound from the small ensemble."

New York Times

"{Roberts} led with extraordinary flair. . . ."

Newsday

"Kay George Roberts . . . was in full command of the scores and drew polished playing from the instrumentalists throughout the program."

New York Amsterdam News

". . . forceful conducting. . . . Kay George Roberts proved . . . a great musical breadth."

Stuttgarter Nachrichten

"Ms. Robert's uncanny ability to grasp the emotional center of a work was evident . . . {S}he proved herself a worthy conductor possessing great vigor and musical insight."

Chattanooga Times

"Roberts represents a triumph . . . Her ability to communicate with the Cleveland Orchestra and singers of all races and creeds from 62 church choirs wasn't lost. . . . Ms. Roberts did a beautiful job . . . The orchestra was dynamic."

Plain Dealer

Notes

1. Alan Bostick, "Breaking the Sound Barrier: The Woman Behind the Baton," *Tennessean,* July 7, 1991, p. 2 J.
2. Peter Kummel, "I Am a Minority Within a Minority," *Stuttgarter Nachrichten,* July 20, 1991, p. 16.
3. Diane H. McDonald, "Conducting Becomes Her," *Newsweek On Campus,* April 1988, p. 39.
4. *Ibid.*
5. "Kay George Roberts," *Fisk News,* Commencement 1986, p. 17.
6. "28 Young Women of Promise," *Good Housekeeping,* July 1986, p. 44.
7. Kay George Roberts, "Orchestras and Minorities: Some New Perspectives" Panel, American Symphony Orchestra League's 42nd National Conference, Waldorf Astoria, New York, N.Y., June 1987. Note: The other two Blacks who joined the Nashville Youth Orchestra were Harriette Patricia Green and William Fitzpatrick, also violinists. Green later joined the Louisville Symphony Orchestra and for a brief period, Fitzpatrick served as assistant conductor of the Nashville Symphony (late 1970s).
8. Two other black females were tympanist Elayne Jones (Kaufman), then a member of the American Symphony Orchestra, and keyboardist Patricia Prattis Jennings, a member of the Pittsburgh Symphony. See "Kay Roberts," *Nashville Banner,* October 16, 1971, pp. 1–2.
9. Natilee Duning, "Kay Roberts Returns for Conducting Debut," *Tennessean,* May 28, 1976, p. 53.
10. ———, "Outdoor Concert 'Easy Listening'," *Tennessean,* May 31, 1976, p. 20.
11. Werner Zepernick, "Nashville Symphony Opens Summer Parks Concerts," *Nashville Banner,* May 31, 1976, p. 28.
12. Dayle Zatlin, "Conductor: Black Woman Musician at ULowell Succeeds in Field Dominated by Men," *Sun,* November 9, 1978, p. 14.
13. Tonya Knight, "Guest Conductor Inspires Young Dallas Musicians," *Dallas Morning News,* June 21, 1986, p. 33 A.
14. Don W. Sieker, "NH Philharmonic Opening Musical Feast," *Union Leader,* November 14, 1985, p. 27.
15. Susan Bulba, "Symphony Makes Strong Start," *Gloucester Daily Times,* October 29, 1986, p. A 9.
16. "A Symphony of Firsts for Woman From Cambridge," *Boston Herald,* August 31, 1986, p. 5.
17. "Chulalongkorn University," *Living In Thailand,* October 1987, p. 9.
18. "A Starting Place for Black Musicians," *New York Times,* December 27, 1987, p. 60.

19. Lawrence B. Johnson, "A Spirited Celebration of Black Music," *Detroit News,* March 21, 1989, p. C 5.
20. Anthony Tommasini, "Celebration of Women Composers," *Boston Globe,* April 25, 1989, p. 22.
21. John Rockwell, "Spreading the Word On Black Classical Music," *New York Times,* September 10, 1990, p. C 16.
22. Wynne Delacoma, "Black Music Gets A Forum It Might Not Need Someday," *Chicago Sun Times,* February 7, 1991, Section 2, p. 51.
23. Bostick, *op. cit.,* p. 1 J.
24. Jerome Reed, "Spread Blanket for Fine Symphony," *Tennessean,* July 9, 1991, p. 2 D.
25. Lorrie Grant, "Good Conduct: Kay George Roberts Commands Respect in Musical Circles," *Chicago Tribune,* April 26, 1992, p. 4, Section 6.

Jon Robertson (Courtesy: Redlands Symphony)

JON ROBERTSON

BIRTHDATE/PLACE: December 3, 1942; Jamaica, West Indies.
EDUCATION: B.M., M.S., and D.M.A., the Juilliard School of Music (Piano).
MAJOR INSTRUCTORS: Beveridge Webster (Piano); Abraham Kaplan (Choral Conducting); Richard Pittman and Herbert Blomstedt (Orchestral Conducting).
MAJOR APPOINTMENTS: Music Director/Conductor, Thayer Conservatory Orchestra (Massachusetts), 1972–76; Music Director/Conductor, Kristiansand Symphony Orchestra, Norway (Sweden), 1979—; Music Director/ Conductor, Redlands (California) Symphony Orchestra, 1982—.
GUEST CONDUCTOR: New England Sinfonia (National Tour), 1975; Redlands Symphony Orchestra, Spring 1982; Norwegian Norska Opera Company, 1987; Oakland Symphony Orchestra, 1988; Beijing Central Philharmonic, 1988; Taichung (Taiwan) and Long Beach (California) Symphony Orchestras, 1989; San Francisco Symphony Orchestra, 1989 and 1990.
BOARD MEMBERSHIP: Association of California Symphony Orchestras.
FOUNDER: Atlantic Union (Massachusetts) College/Community Orchestra; Redlands Symphony Orchestra Conducting Institute.

JON ROBERTSON, A NATIVE JAMAICAN, grew up in Southern California. He made his debut as a concert pianist at New York City's Town Hall at ten. Two years later, he concertized throughout South America and the Caribbean. He earned all of his degrees (B.Mus., M.S., and D.M.A.) from the Juilliard School of Music, which he entered in 1960.

Though a piano major, Robertson studied choral conducting with Abraham Kaplan. Having decided that he should expand on his conducting interests and skills, he studied orchestral conducting with Richard Pittman and was later accepted into the master class of Herbert Blomstedt (currently music director of the San Francisco Symphony) Institute of Orchestral Conducting. Upon the invitation of Maestro Blomstedt, he spent a year in Sweden and Germany studying privately with Blomstedt, the individual Robertson credits with having changed his life. "[I]n terms of why I'm conducting today, it is Herbert Blomstedt. There's no two ways about that."[1]

The orchestral conducting interest was sparked early, when young Robertson accompanied his father regularly to Los Angeles Philharmonic concerts. He loved both the appearance and sound of the orchestra and easily envisioned himself at the Orchestra's helm. As indicated to interviewer Anne Lundy* during the Summer of 1984, he was also inspired by the presence of the Philharmonic's lone black member, bassist Henry Lewis.*[2]

For four years (1972–76), the multi-talented Robertson was music director/conductor of the Thayer Conservatory of Music Orchestra in Massachusetts and, in 1975, conducted the New England Sinfonia on a national tour. Robertson accepted the position of music director/conductor of the Kristiansand Symphony Orchestra in Kristiansand, Norway, in 1979 and currently spends roughly twelve weeks out of each season there.

The rapidly growing Redlands (California) Symphony Association invited Robertson to guest conduct the ensemble in the spring of 1982. Shortly thereafter, he was invited to accept the position of music director/conductor. The ascent of the ensemble to its current status as a quality regional orchestra took place under his leadership.

The Association's origins can be traced back to 1894, with the first efforts of the City of Redlands to provide a concert season for its citizens. In 1958 the Association began an affiliation with the University of Redlands, which by 1974 led to the coordination of the activities of the Redlands Symphony Association with the University Community Symphony. Between 1974 and 1982, the concert season included performances led by members of the University of Redlands music faculty.

The arrival of Professor Robertson in 1982 provided a kind of leadership that proved beneficial to the orchestra's expansion and artistic growth. Under Robertson's guidance, the Redlands Symphony Association incorporated, changed its name (now the Redlands Symphony Orchestra), and entered a contractual relationship with the University. Currently the orchestra boasts a sold-out season of eight concerts and an expanding youth program (concerts for fourth through sixth graders in the Redlands area).[3] In 1986, the ambitious maestro established the Redlands Symphony Orchestra Conducting Institute, which now attracts students from throughout the United States and Canada.

Redlands General Manager Mary Lou Jones said of Robertson and his relationship with the Redlands Symphony, "He really made us.

. . . It's hard to speak of Jon without superlatives. . . ." Commented Ara Guzelimian, artistic adviser of the Los Angeles Philharmonic, "That orchestra has no right to sound that good. He [Robertson] is dynamite."[4]

In the mid-1980s, the Redlands Symphony Orchestra began receiving support from the California Arts Council, based on its superior rating, and three years later, support from the National Endowment for the Arts. Robertson served on the Board of Directors of the Association of California Symphony Orchestras and was for three years a panelist for the California Arts Council. He assessed the experience as one of his life's "most rewarding" and wrote about it for the *Association of California Symphony Orchestras News* (December/ January 1988), informing readers of the review process and advising future applicants on how to improve their submissions.[5]

Robertson conducted the National Norwegian Norska Opera Company in 1987 and, during the Spring of 1988, he toured the Far East, conducting the Beijing Central Philharmonic and offering workshops in Taipei, Taiwan. The year 1988 also included a guest conducting appearance with the Oakland East Bay Symphony. At the invitation of the Ministry of Culture of the People's Republic of China, he was scheduled to conduct all four of the country's major symphony orchestras in 1989. He made his debut with the San Francisco Symphony in June 1989 at Stern Grove and in March 1990, conducted the orchestra in one of its regular season concerts.

Robertson was one of five finalists, from a pool of 250, for the position of music director of the Long Beach Symphony. Each finalist conducted the orchestra during the 1988–89 season.[6]

With a strong sense of self and a willingness to take a step-by-step route to an ultimate conducting destination, Robertson remarked:

> I feel that God gave me a talent for conducting. I feel I have a talent for communicating my ideas. I feel that my musicianship is definitely strong enough to warrant the right to conduct. I am excited about the opportunities that I have to gain the kind of experience that I feel a conductor needs before breaking into the "major ranks." . . .[B]y no means am I a household name, or may not be for many years to come, or may never be, but I do believe that in the process of the length of time that I am working that I will learn my craft.[7]

Press Comments

"Conductor Robertson and the Redlands Symphony Orchestra continue to deliver musical riches by the bushel. . . A consistently high level of performance and ambitious . . . adventurous repertory that has been a hallmark . . ."

San Bernardino Sun

"Maestro Jon Robertson stepped onto the podium . . . and gave the world a truly memorable Verdi Requiem—no easy task. It was a clear and resounding triumph for this fine conductor. . . ."

San Bernardino Sun

"Robertson's evident care for detail and his well-chosen, consistently maintained tempos were most impressive."

San Bernardino Sun

"{A}n incredible musical evening. . . . Jon Robertson's inspired conducting. . . . clearly added more laurels to those he routinely garners in Redlands, . . ."

Redlands Daily Facts

"Robertson proved himself an exceptionally sensitive and knowledgeable conductor who can achieve results without recourse to undue theatricality."

Los Angeles Times

"Jon Robertson, a conductor with authority and talent, led his forces with smart precision and a good sense of drama."

New York Times

"Robertson . . . showing considerable skill, musicianship distinctive interpretive ideas."

San Francisco Chronicle

Notes

1. Anne Lundy, "Conversations With Three Symphonic Conductors," *Black Perspective in Music,* Fall 1988, p. 222.
2. *Ibid.,* p. 221.
3. Redlands Symphony Orchestra's 30th Anniversary Season Brochure (1987–88).
4. Rodney Foo, "5 Finalists for Conductor of L.B. Symphony Named," *Press-Telegram,* April 29, 1988, p. A6.

5. Jon Robertson, "Real to Reel: High Quality Tapes Critical to CAC Review," *Association of California Symphony Orchestras News,* December/January, 1988, pp. 1–2.
6. James Chute, "Long Beach Symphony Candidates Narrowed to Five," *Press-Telegram,* April 29, 1988, p. A6.
7. Lundy, *op. cit.,* pp. 222, 224.

Calvin Simmons (Courtesy: Archives for the Performing Arts)

CALVIN SIMMONS

BIRTHDATE/PLACE: April 27, 1950; San Francisco, California.
DEATH DATE/PLACE: August 21, 1982; Lake Placid, New York.
EDUCATION: College Conservatory of Music, University of Cincinnati, 1968–70; Curtis Institute of Music, 1970–72.
MAJOR INSTRUCTORS/COACHES: Mattie Pearl Simmons, Tillie Amner, John Bigg, William Corbett-Jones, Rudolph Serkin, Piano; Madi Bacon, Max Rudolph, Zubin Mehta, Kurt Herbert Adler, Conducting.
MAJOR APPOINTMENTS: Assistant Conductor, San Francisco Merola Opera Summer Program, 1970; Associate Music Director, Western Opera Company (San Francisco); Assistant Conductor, Los Angeles Philharmonic and Conductor, Young Musicians Foundation Orchestra, 1975–78; Music Director, Oakland Symphony, 1979–82.
GUEST CONDUCTOR: London, New York, and Los Angeles Philharmonics; Oakland, Detroit, Philadelphia, National, and American Symphony Orchestras; Metropolitan, San Francisco, Glyndebourne Festival, St. Louis, New York City, Houston, San Diego, Cincinnati Opera Companies; Ojai Festival.
AWARDS/HONORS: Exxon/Arts Endowment Conductor (Los Angeles Philharmonic), 1976–78; First Winner, Stokowski Conducting Award, 1979; First San Francisco Foundation Conductor, 1979 (in first year of appointment with the Oakland Symphony).

INTERVIEWING THE TWENTY-EIGHT-YEAR-OLD conductor Calvin Simmons in 1978, Stephanie Von Buchau made the mistake of asking, "How has being black affected your career?" Simmons's response to the journalist's impertinence received the following response:

> How has being black affected my career? Well, I've never "used" it. And if anyone else cares, they sure haven't let me know about it. . . . I hate that question. Sure, I guess I was lucky to be born at the right time and the right place, but I don't sit around home wondering if I got the job because I'm black. . . . Does anyone really care?[1]

For Simmons, the question of race was a "non-issue."

412

To the extent that genetics and environment are strong determinants in the development of an individual's talents and interests, a musical career was inevitable for Calvin Simmons. His mother, Mattie Pearl Simmons, returned to her post as conductor of the choir at Mount Zion Baptist Church in San Francisco when Calvin was only six weeks old; one of the singers would hold him while she conducted. By the time he was three years old, his participation in choir practice had shifted from passive listening to actively imitating his mother's conducting, using a small stick of his own. When Simmons was six years old, his mother began teaching him the piano. He soon progressed to the point of development at which Mrs. Simmons realized other instruction was necessary; at eight, Calvin began studying with Mrs. Tillie Amner. Again, the student outpaced the teacher; about the time he completed the fifth grade, he became a student of William Corbett-Jones of San Francisco. He remained with Corbett-Jones through his teen years.[2]

His musical interests in the early years were not restricted to the piano. At age nine, he joined the San Francisco Opera Boys Chorus. According to the director, Madi Bacon, "He didn't sing very well, but oh, when he sat down at the piano . . ."[3]

Under Madi Bacon's instruction and encouragement, Simmons developed a fascination for vocal music, and the conducting of choral forces. At age eleven, Simmons was directing the chorus on occasion. And his growing love for opera found him more and more frequently at the Opera House (often dressed in his chorus uniform so he would be admitted by an unsuspecting doorman even on those nights when the chorus was not singing). Simmons often referred to the Opera House as "basically, the place where I grew up."[4] At age seventeen, Simmons became a rehearsal pianist for the Opera.

Simmons graduated from Balboa High School in 1968 and immediately entered the Cincinnati College Conservatory of Music. While in Cincinnati, just prior to beginning his studies with Max Rudolph, he performed the Grieg Piano Concerto with the Cleveland Orchestra. Said Simmons of the experience:

> There was nobody in the audience; it was the weekend of the Kent State killings. That's when I knew I wasn't going to be a pianist. Right in the middle of the performance it came to me that I couldn't express myself this way.[5]

Simmons became the protege of conductor/conducting pedagogue Max Rudolph. When in 1969 Rudolph moved to Curtis Institute in Philadelphia, Simmons soon followed. There Simmons met and worked with the noted pianist Rudolph Serkin, who, along with Max Rudolph, continued to counsel him that he was a conductor, and he should abandon the piano as a career pursuit.[6]

Simmons' Curtis years were filled with opera. He conducted the orchestra and on some occasions played a piano reduction of the orchestral score. He is fondly remembered for a performance of "Cosi Fan Tutte" in 1970, during which an electrical fuse blew, leaving the hall in the dark for an entire scene. Simmons, at the piano, continued to play.[7]

During the time Simmons was a student at the Curtis Institute Kurt Herbert Adler, then General Director of the San Francisco Opera, invited Simmons to join the conducting staff. He accepted the position, but only after he had finished school.

Following graduation from Curtis, Simmons spent four summers at the Glyndebourne Festival in England, an opera house associated especially with the music of Mozart. "I had been a Mozart freak since I was a child. So that was a great experience . . ."[8]

After those years of clearly focusing on opera conducting, Simmons made several important guest appearances as a symphony orchestra conductor. He made his debut with the Los Angeles Philharmonic in 1975 and his New York debut conducting the American Symphony Orchestra in Lincoln Center's Damrosch Park in 1976, at the age of twenty-five. In April 1978, Simmons appeared for the first time as guest conductor of the Oakland Symphony.

During the years he was guest conducting with orchestras, his engagements as an opera conductor increased considerably in prestige. On December 22, 1978, Simmons conducted the Metropolitan Opera in Humperdinck's "Hansel and Gretel." Of that performance, *New York Times* critic John Rockwell wrote that he "handled himself with distinction."[9] In that same year, Simmons conducted the San Francisco Opera in a performance of "La Boheme" at the War Memorial Opera House.

When asked by Daniel Webster of The *Philadelphia Inquirer* about having to make a choice between opera and orchestral conducting, Simmons responded:

> Symphonic music came late for me . . . but it is absolutely essential
> for me to stay in opera. I realize now that much of my orchestral
> conducting . . . is operatic. I sense great ties in the things I conduct
> and the way I conduct them.[10]

Despite Simmons' assertion that symphonic music came late for
him, the Oakland Symphony recognized early that his was a rare
talent, one that could be pivotal in raising the standard and
recognition of the orchestra. In 1979, Simmons was appointed the
orchestra's music director. Some speculated that Simmons' appointment was motivated primarily by the attraction his being black
might have to the local community (which might be encouraged to
attend Symphony performances in greater numbers) and to potential
funding sources. However, according to the president and general
manager Harold Lawrence, extraordinary musical talent was the
primary factor:

> When he was here in April [as a guest conductor] it was love at first
> sight. . . . We knew he was the man for us.[11]

Simmons approached the Oakland appointment with attitudes
about programming that were somewhat startling for a young
conductor building a career. Early on he announced his intention to
venture beyond the standard repertoire.

> Never do I want to stay always on the safer ground. . . It's not good
> for me, it's not good for the orchestra and most important it's not
> good for the public.[12]

Consistent with this philosophy, Simmons established a commissioning program that brought at least one major new work to the
orchestra each season. For the 1980–81 season, he commissioned
black composer Olly Wilson to write "Trilogy for Orchestra," which
Simmons repeated with the Detroit Symphony Orchestra on subscription concerts during the 1981–82 season.

Even as he was beginning to build the Oakland Symphony as an
ensemble contending for a more prominent position among the
nation's major ensembles, Simmons was continuing to build his own
reputation and credibility as a world-class conductor. In 1979, he
was the first winner of the newly-established Stokowski Conducting

Award. Simmons made his debut with the New York City Opera in September 1980, leading the company's new production of Bizet's "Les Pêcheurs de Perles." And, on February 26, 1982, making his debut with the Philadelphia Orchestra, he became the first black conductor to lead that ensemble in a subscription series at the Academy of Music, the orchestra's home.

In August 1982, Simmons decided to spend a weekend at Lake Placid, New York, to "soak up strength" before a return engagement with the New York City Opera (where he was to conduct Mozart's "The Magic Flute"). Simmons, an experienced canoeist and good swimmer, was standing up in a canoe on Connery Pond, posing for a photograph. Apparently Simmons lost his balance, the canoe capsized, and he tumbled into the pond, into murky water more than 20 feet deep, only 150 feet from shore. He never reappeared.[13] Volunteer divers from the local fire department, state police divers, and other volunteers dragged the pond with grappling hooks for several days. Ten days after the accident, his body was finally found in a silt bed, 30 feet below the surface of the pond. Several possible explanations were offered to account for Simmons's inability to recover from the capsizing: the several layers of heavy clothing he was wearing might have dragged him down; the differences in the water's surface temperature (65 degrees) and that 15 feet below the surface (42 degrees) might have shocked his system; Simmons might have struck his head as the canoe tipped; spasms of the larynx, which could have cut off the air supply, might have occurred after he hit the water; the shock of hitting the water could have triggered any one of a number of other bodily reactions.[14]

The music world reacted to the tragedy with shock and dismay. Simmons's close friend Beverly Sills, at that time general director of the New York City Opera, said:

> I am absolutely heartbroken at this terrible news. Calvin had so much to offer. I just can't take it all in.[15]

Robert Commanday, music critic for the *San Francisco Chronicle,* observed:

> He hadn't arrived at greatness yet . . . Perhaps he knew better than anyone how much he still had to do. But the human qualities in the man were there, integral with the musical gifts.[16]

More than 2,200 mourners attended the memorial service for Simmons at Grace Cathedral in San Francisco. The mourners were led by Kurt Herbert Adler, Simmons's mentor. The service included performances by opera star Marilyn Horne, the district chorus of Mount Zion Baptist Church (which his mother had conducted), and a string quartet from the Oakland Symphony.

Press Comments

"... *in true Mozart style, the six principals functioned smoothly as an ensemble under the unhurried baton {of Mr. Simmons}.*"

New York Times

"... *he is only 25 years old, and looks it. But he led the orchestra with plenty of confidence and authority.*"

New York Times

"*Mr. Simmons opened the program with a spirited performance of Berlioz' 'Roman Carnival' Overture.*"

New York Times

"... *{he} led a wonderfully cohesive and atmospheric performance that gave the singers their due without muting the orchestra too much in the subtlest pages.*"

New York Times

"*Humperdinck's 'Hansel and Gretel' . . . conducted with seriousness of purpose, rich musicality, a keen sense of tempo and general alertness by the debuting Calvin Simmons.*"

Opera News

Notes

1. Stephanie Von Buchau, "Born Lucky: An Interview With Calvin Simmons," *Opera News,* December 23, 1978, p. 27.
2. Jane Eshleman Conant, "Musician of the Month: Calvin Simmons," *High Fidelity/Musical America,* March, 1979, p. MA-6.
3. *Ibid.*
4. *Ibid.,* p. MA-7.
5. Von Buchau, *op. cit.*
6. Conant, *op. cit.*

7. Daniel Webster, "He's used tradition to break new ground," *Philadelphia Inquirer,* February 25, 1982, p. 1D.
8. *Ibid.,* p. 7D.
9. Edward A. Gargan, "Calvin Simmons, Oakland Symphony Leader," *New York Times,* August 24, 1982, p. B10.
10. Webster, "He's used tradition to break new ground." p. 7D.
11. Conant, op. cit.
12. *Ibid.,* p. MA-7.
13. *Obituary-* "C. Simmons, symphony conductor," *Philadelphia Inquirer,* August 24, 1982, p. 2-E.
14. Richard D. Lyons, "Police Continuing the Search For Body of Calvin Simmons," *New York Times,* August 25, 1982, p. B2.
15. Gargan, "Calvin Simmons, Oakland Symphony Leader," *op. cit.*
16. *Obituary-* "C. Simmons, symphony conductor," p. 2-E.

André Raphel Smith (Courtesy: Affiliate Artists)

ANDRÉ RAPHEL SMITH

BIRTHDATE/PLACE: September 1, 1962. Durham, North Carolina.
EDUCATION: B.Mus. (Trombone), University of Miami (Florida), 1984; M.Mus. (Trombone), Yale University, 1986; Diploma (Conducting), the Curtis Institute of Music, 1989; Advanced Certificate (Conducting), the Juilliard School, 1990.
MAJOR CONDUCTING INSTRUCTORS: David Becker (University of Miami), Otto-Werner Mueller and Arthur Weisberg (Yale University), Otto-Werner Mueller (Curtis Institute and Juilliard).
MAJOR APPOINTMENTS: Assistant Conductor, University of Miami Orchestra, 1982–84; Assistant Conductor, Yale Contemporary Ensemble and Yale Philharmonia, 1986–87; Mentor and Teaching Assistant, Harlem School for the Arts, 1989–90; Music Director and Conductor, Norwalk (Connecticut) Youth Symphony, 1990; Assistant Conductor, St. Louis Symphony Youth Orchestra, January 1991—; Affiliate Artists/National Endowment for the Arts Assistant Conductor, Saint Louis Symphony Orchestra, January 1991–94; Assistant Conductor, Philadelphia Orchestra, 1994—.
GUEST CONDUCTOR: Concerto Soloists of Philadelphia, Juilliard Symphony Orchestra, Savannah and Baltimore Symphony Orchestras.
AWARDS/FELLOWSHIPS: Lucy G. Moses Fellowship (Yale University), Bruno Walter Memorial Scholarship (Juilliard), Conducting Fellow (National Repertory Orchestra, Colorado).

ANDRÉ RAPHEL SMITH'S FORMAL MUSIC LESSONS began while he was enrolled in high school. The choice of instrument was the trombone. The youngest of four children, André Raphel had the following to say about the early years:

> I was fascinated with music from an early age. Both of my sisters had piano lessons, but unfortunately, there was not enough money for me to take lessons. At the age of 10, I began singing solos and performing in the church choir. Teachers [in the public schools] played a very important role in my development. I was fortunate to have teachers who cared about me as a person and who were dedicated

to the prospect of my intellectual growth. They instilled in me a strong work ethic and a love for my craft.[1]

Of his decision to pursue the art of conducting, Smith wrote:

> I have always felt that I had something special to say musically. I always knew that I eventually wanted to conduct, but felt that it was important to attain a certain degree of virtuosity on my principal instrument. The analysis of scores has continued to be of interest and through my work, I have been able to reach out to broader segments of the population. I chose to become a conductor because I love music and I cannot imagine doing anything else.[2]

During an interview with feature writer Sandi McDaniel of the *Savannah News-Press,* Smith recalled one person's reaction to his having introduced himself as a conductor. "Oh, you mean you work on a train?" was the response. The "conductor of orchestral music" was in Savannah, Georgia, to guest conduct the Savannah Symphony Orchestra's Black Heritage Concert, February 1990. Commented the city's "guest of honor":

> Many people simply don't realize the contributions of African-Americans to the world of classical music. . . . This is Black History month. . . . and while many famous blacks are recognized during this time, the works of noted black composers are often ignored. Their music should be performed—celebrated. . . .[3]

On this occasion, Smith programmed the works of black composers Hale Smith, William Grant Still, and Adolphus Hailstork.

The success of his first appearance warranted a second invitation. As indicated in the *Savannah Morning News,* February 7, 1992:

> Maestro André Raphel Smith, who was the BHC's guest conductor here two years ago, will return in the same capacity for this year's event. . . . Described by critics as "an American artist on the move," Smith is rapidly establishing a career as an adept and versatile conductor. . . . He is now an active and visible contributor to the artistic life of the St. Louis community.[4]

James E. Jenkins, black principal tubist with the Alabama Symphony, was the featured soloist. Included on the program were works by black composers Olly Wilson, George Walker, Ulysses Kay, and, again, Adolphus Hailstork.

Smith feels a commitment to works by composers of African descent but points out that it is very important to him that we not label artists in terms of their color. Yet, since

> their works have been neglected, I feel a strong responsibility to integrate these composers' works into the mainstream of the orchestral repertoire. This should insure the presence of more blacks at our orchestral concerts.[5]

The Savannah Symphony concerts included works by non-black composers: Brahms and Mozart in 1990, Vaughan Williams and Mozart in 1992.

Having referred to Smith as "an American artist on the move," let us trace his conducting training and experience. Though he majored in trombone at both the University of Miami and Yale University, he studied conducting with David Becker at the former and Otto-Werner Mueller and Arthur Weisburg at the latter. The emphasis was on conducting, however, when he matriculated at the Curtis Institute of Music and the Juilliard School of Music (diploma and advanced certificate respectively). The major professor at both institutions was Otto-Werner Mueller.

Much was gained from assistant conductor positions with the University of Miami Orchestra (1982–84), and the Yale Contemporary Ensemble and the Yale Philharmonia (1986–87). He guest conducted the Concerto Soloists of Philadelphia in 1987. More experience resulted from the 1988–89 opportunity to be a conducting fellow with the National Repertory Orchestra (formerly the Colorado Philharmonic).

"A valuable stepping stone" for conductors, according to journalist Valerie Cruice, became an opportunity for maestro Smith when he assumed his responsibilities with the Norwalk (Connecticut) Youth Orchestra during the fall of 1990. Composed of close to two hundred players between the ages of eight and eighteen, the orchestra is divided into three separate units (chamber, concert, and principal). All players audition, as do the three prospective conductors. Of Smith's selection as music director of the seventy-six–member Norwalk Youth Symphony's principal orchestra, the seventeen-year-old concertmistress said:

> We had three different ones for three concerts, and we auditioned others at the end of the year. André conducted our second concert. He's a lot of fun to work with and doesn't act condescending.

He takes us seriously as both musicians and young adults, which a lot of the other conductors did not do. He knows when to joke around, but he knows when to be serious. And he doesn't try to be your best friend.

Smith commented:

> I'm going to be extremely hard on them in rehearsals—nitpicky—and make them understand the composers' ideas, bringing to them a greater understanding of the piece. . . . What's not there in talent they make up with their work ethic.[6]

André Raphel Smith made his Lincoln Center debut in October 1990 and his European debut during the spring of 1991, conducting the Juilliard Symphony Orchestra on both occasions. One month following the Lincoln Center experience, his appointment as assistant conductor of the Saint Louis Symphony was announced, effective January 14, 1991. Selected as an Affiliate Artists/National Endowment for the Arts conductor, he reacted to the announcement:

> My appointment as assistant conductor of the Saint Louis Symphony Orchestra starts to fulfill a life-long dream. The opportunity to work with Maestro Slatkin and make music with an orchestra of the highest caliber will play an important role in my development. Being associated with the orchestra will foster the growth I need to become a more sensitive and mature artist.[7]

Music director and conductor Leonard Slatkin said of Smith:

> On the basis of his audition and subsequent discussion, I feel that André Smith will be a most welcome addition to our staff. He brings a high degree of youth and energy, coupled with intense musical drive and should be a great asset in reaching out to a broader segment of the community.[8]

Joseph W. Polisi, president of The Juilliard School, remarked,

> The entire Juilliard community is extraordinarily proud that André Raphel Smith has been appointed to the position of assistant conductor of the Saint Louis Symphony Orchestra, . . . Mr. Smith is an individual who has brought great creativity, energy and vision to his conducting at Juilliard. We know that he will grow through his

work with Maestro Slatkin and the exceptional musicians of the Saint Louis Symphony.[9]

Smith would conduct Young People's and Pops Concerts, engage in administrative activities, and participate in outreach into the community.

Speaking to music students at St. Louis's Visual and Performing Arts High School in April 1991, Smith said that the auditioning experience with such a great orchestra as the Saint Louis Symphony "was bliss, sheer bliss." Eight conductors "took up their batons" before this world-class orchestra, in search of the chance.

> Symphony insiders said it was no contest, that Smith was the choice of them all. He got a call saying the job was his. Smith had expected to audition in a second round. "First job on my first try," he said.[10]

According to *St. Louis Post-Dispatch*'s writer Patricia Rice, Smith's two-year stay with the Saint Louis would be like an apprenticeship. The conductor's goals were

> to gain a greater understanding of what it means to be a music director of an orchestra, including conducting, program selection, dealing with players, marketing and fund-raising. Secondly, he is determined to learn more repertory. Finally, he wants to learn how to rehearse more "effectively and efficiently" with an orchestra.[11]

His 1991–92 season with the St. Louis Symphony included Youth Orchestra Concerts, Kinder Konzerts, "Discovery" Chamber Concerts, Summer Pops Concerts, Pops Concerts, and Young People's Concerts. The schedule also called for him to conduct subscription concerts January 31, February 1 and February 2, 1992. Projected for January 2 and 3, 1993 were more orchestral subscription concerts. He would continue to engage in outreach activities for the orchestra; he would continue to secure more guest conducting appearances; and obviously he would continue to move onward in his pursuit of a vision—to become music director and conductor of a major symphony orchestra. Beginning with the 1994–1995 season, Mr. Smith would join the conducting staff of the Philadelphia Orchestra as Assistant Conductor.

Press Comments

"Dallapiccola's serene 'Piccola Musica Notturna' {was} ably conducted by Andre Smith who drew a ravishing sound from his players {the Juilliard Symphony Orchestra}."

New York Times

"For André Raphel Smith, the pressure was on. The Saint Louis Symphony's 29-year-old assistant conductor had been scheduled to share the weekend agenda with music director Leonard Slatkin {who} decided to do just the Dohnanyi and leave the rest to Smith. . . . Although under fire, Smith stayed on course; it was exciting to witness him score his success."

St. Louis Post-Dispatch

"The ensemble (Saint Louis Symphony Youth Orchestra) seemed to be in good hands. He (Smith) did very well . . . with the main themes and counter-themes, and in the concerto he was a deft accompanist. {T}he orchestra was with him all the way."

St. Louis Post-Dispatch

"Under the new conductor, André Raphel Smith, the program was an electrifying experience for players and audience. Smith, who also conducts without score, has his own energetic, positive, demanding cues for every need, and the spontaneous reaction is audibly relevant."

The Hour (Norwalk, Connecticut)

"{H}e expertly led the orchestra through a varied program that ranged from the festive exhaltations of both black composer Adolphus Hailstork and 19th century Brahms, to the intricate manipulations in Hale Smith's modern sounds, to the elegance of the Mozart concerto, to the jazz and blues idioms of William Grant Still. The audience responded warmly with applause and a standing ovation."

Savannah Tribune

"Conductor Smith got right down to business with a crisp, energetic and well-controlled performance . . ."

Savannah News-Press

Notes

1. Questionnaire, March 31, 1992.
2. *Ibid.*
3. Sandi McDaniel, "Andre Smith To Conduct Black Heritage Concert,"

Savannah News-Press (Weekend Guide to Savannah), February 9, 1990, p. 1.

4. Sterling Adams, "Black Heritage Concert Features Old Friend As Guest Conductor," *Savannah Morning News,* February 7, 1992, p. 1D.
5. Questionnaire, *op. cit.*
6. Valerie Cruice, "While Children Make Music, Conductors Make Plans," *New York Times,* October 28, 1990, p. C12.
7. Press Release, Saint Louis Symphony Orchestra, December 4, 1990.
8. "Andre Raphel Smith, Joins Symphony," *St. Louis American,* November 19–December 5, 1990, p. 1A.
9. Press Release, *op. cit.*
10. Patricia Rice, "Behind the Baton," *St. Louis Post-Dispatch,* April 8, 1991, p. D4.
11. *Ibid.*

Kirk Edward Smith

KIRK EDWARD SMITH

BIRTHDATE/PLACE: June 16, 1958; Baltimore, Maryland.

EDUCATION: B.Mus.Ed., Shenandoah Conservatory (Certification, Clarinet Performance), 1980; M.A., University of Denver (Conducting), 1983; toward D.A. in Conducting, Ball State University.

TRAINING PROGRAMS (Conducting): Aspen Music Festival, 1980; American Symphony Orchestra League Conducting Workshop, 1985; Conductor's Guild Summer Institute, 1985–87; Conductor's Guild Workshop, 1986–87; Pierre Monteux Conducting Program, 1988, 1990–92; International Workshop for Conductors (Zin, Czechoslovakia), 1992.

MAJOR INSTRUCTORS: Conducting—James Setapen, JoAnn Falletta, Harold Farberman, and Charles Bruck; Composition—Charles Wuorinen.

MAJOR APPOINTMENTS: Conductor/Music Director—Colorado Youth String Orchestra, 1984–85; Georgia State University Orchestra, 1986–89; Iowa State University Orchestra, 1989—; Fort Dodge (Iowa) Area Symphony Orchestra, 1991–92; Iowa State University Chamber Opera Ensemble, 1992—. Assistant Conductor—Colorado Youth Symphony Orchestra, 1984–85; Denver Chamber Orchestra, 1984–86; Sandy Springs Chamber Orchestra, 1988–89.

GUEST CONDUCTOR: Denver Children's Ballet, 1983; Lamont Symphony Orchestra, 1983; Golden Youth Symphony, 1986; Scott Joplin Chamber Orchestra, 1988; Montana Orchestra Festival, 1990; National Black Arts Festival, 1990; Fort Dodge (Iowa) Area Symphony Orchestra, 1990; McPhail Center (Minnesota) Chamber Orchestra, 1990; Black Music Repertory Ensemble (Chicago), 1991; Southeastern Music Center Orchestra (Georgia), 1991; Adrian Symphony Orchestra (Michigan), 1992; University of Central Florida Community Orchestra, 1992; National Taiwan Normal University Orchestra, 1992; Nashville Symphony Orchestra, 1992.

THE GEORGIA STATE UNIVERSITY SYMPHONY ORCHESTRA made an auspicious appearance at the First National Convention of the National Black Music Caucus,[1] March 30, 1989, performing works by Mussorgsky and black composer William Dawson ("Negro Folk Symphony," 1934). Most revealing for the hundreds of attendees was the fact that at the helm was the young black conductor Kirk E.

Smith. He had made history earlier when, in October 1987, he conducted the combined forces (instrumental and vocal) of Georgia State University (historically white) and Spelman and Morehouse Colleges (both historically Black) in two programs devoted to the music of black composer Alvin Singleton, who was then in his third year as composer-in-residence with the Atlanta Symphony.[2]

Smith had arrived in Atlanta July 1986 as assistant professor at Georgia State and conductor of the university's orchestra and wind ensemble. His appointment represented the first full-time black membership in GSU's music school. (During his final year of Georgia residency, Smith also served as Assistant Conductor of Atlanta's Sandy Springs Chamber Orchestra.)

He arrived in Atlanta from Denver, Colorado, where he worked as a freelance conductor and a staff member of radio station KVOD. Following receipt of the master's degree in conducting from the University of Denver, he spent a year studying for his Doctor of Arts in conducting at Ball State University in Muncie, Indiana.

Though he planned completing the degree during subsequent summer months, the summers of 1985, 1986, 1987, and 1988 were spent at various conducting workshops, including the Pierre Monteux and American Symphony Orchestra League programs. The value of such programs was realized when Smith participated in the Aspen Music Festival's conducting program immediately following graduation from Shenandoah Conservatory (1980).

The son of a violinist mother and a jazz devotee father (now deceased), Smith listened to all types of music as a child in his native city of Baltimore. He began studying piano at age six, when he received one year of piano lessons as a birthday present. The agreement was that if he still liked the piano after that year, he would pay for all future study. He bought into the idea and paid for thirteen additional years of piano lessons himself.

Study of the clarinet began in high school, followed soon thereafter by a firm decision to make music his career. Enrolled at the Gilman School, Smith was a member of the band, the glee club, and a barbershop quartet.

While enrolled at the Shenandoah Conservatory in Winchester, Virginia, Smith participated as clarinetist in the concert band, wind ensemble, orchestra, and various chamber groups; he was also assistant conductor of the school's symphony and chamber orchestras.

Following graduation (magna cum laude), he taught in the public schools of Mercersburg, Pennsylvania. But conducting was his interest, having been strongly influenced and encouraged by Harold Farberman (principal guest conductor of the Bournemouth Sinfonietta and founder/director of the Conductors' Guild Summer Institute) and the late black conductor Calvin Simmons* (former conductor of the Oakland Symphony).

His years in Denver, 1983 to 1986, provided extremely beneficial experience in many roles: conductor, Colorado Youth String Orchestra; assistant conductor, Denver Chamber Orchestra; and guest conductor, Denver Children's Ballet, Colorado Youth String Orchestra, and the Golden Youth Symphony. Throughout the residency, Smith served as guest rehearsal conductor of the Denver Young Artist's Orchestra.

By his professors and associates, Smith is perceived as "gifted, highly skilled, well-versed, and articulate; the possessor of a fine, clear technique." Overall, he is respected for his musicality.[3]

Smith left Georgia State University and the Sandy Springs Chamber Orchestra during the fall of 1989, to accept the position of assistant professor of music and director of orchestra at Iowa State University in Ames. Since arriving in Iowa, his conducting opportunities have increased. Guest conducting assignments have included several university orchestras (University of Central Florida, University of Northern Colorado, University of Wisconsin at Stevens Point, and the National Taiwan Normal University). Other guest conducting included the Southeastern Music Center Orchestra (Georgia), Adrian Symphony Orchestra (Michigan), the National Black Arts Festival (Atlanta), and the Black Music Repertory Ensemble (Chicago-based).

During the first year of his Iowa residency, he accepted the position of music director of the Central Iowa Symphony Orchestra. The following year he accepted the position of music director of the Fort Dodge (Iowa) Area Symphony Orchestra. On the agenda for 1992 was a guest conducting appearance with the Nashville Symphony Orchestra.

Work at Iowa State University was overwhelmingly successful. He took over a university orchestra whose numbers had dwindled to ten; within a short period, enrollment increased dramatically and the ensemble became one of the music department's most popular ensembles. Typical of the kind of praise extended to the young maestro is the following press review of an ISU Orchestra concert:

> The conductor provided a winning balance between orchestra and soloist [Brahms's First Piano Concerto]. . . . [T]he orchestra . . . was impressively on top of the various scores throughout the evening. This attests to the conducting and rehearsing prowess of Kirk Smith whose interpretations struck me as being well-attuned to the character of each composition.[4]

Further recognition of his contribution to the University (as well as the community) took place in May 1992. During the Spring Convocation and Awards Ceremony, Smith was one of thirty-nine faculty and staff members honored. The Iowa State University Foundation for Early Achievement in Teaching recognized the young conductor for "a vital role in increased enrollment and quality in orchestra programs." Also acknowledged were his many outreach activities across the country and even in Taiwan.

Press Comments

"There has been a significant improvement this year of the GSU Symphony Orchestra under the leadership of its new conductor, Kirk E. Smith."

Southline

"Mr. Smith extracted an elegant performance from his players . . . imparting an uplifting character."

Southline

". . . the performances were outstanding and exceptionally communicative. . . ."

Atlanta Journal-Constitution

"{C}onductor Kirk Edward Smith drew a stunning performance from the combined forces of GSU, Spelman and Morehouse. . . ."

Atlanta Journal-Constitution

". . . Saturday evening's concert was an excellent example of what the ASO {Adrian Symphony Orchestra} can do, and Smith's fine conducting was an extra highlight. He put the orchestra through its paces, and it met the challenge well."

Daily Telegram (Lenawee, Michigan)

"Kirk Smith . . . has a quiet, steady beat and a remarkable presence. . . . There was an intensity and grandeur in the sound as a result of this rare conductor-orchestra collaboration."

Spotlight (Hancock, Maine)

Notes

1. An affiliate of the Music Educators National Conference.
2. Derrick Henry, "Singleton Program by College Artists a Stunning Success," *Atlanta Journal-Constitution,* October 21, 1987, p. C-2.
3. Letters of recommendation for Kirk Edward Smith.
4. Peter S. Murano, "Symphony Orchestra Gives Great Performance," *Ames Tribune,* April 13, 1992, p. A3.

Leon Everette Thompson (Courtesy: Jewel Thompson)

LEON EVERETTE THOMPSON

BIRTHDATE/PLACE: August 1, 1928; Newport News, Virginia.
DEATH DATE/PLACE: June 23, 1983; Massanetta Springs, Virginia.
EDUCATION: B.S. Virginia State College (now Virginia State University), 1948; M.Mus., Eastman School of Music, 1952; D.M.A. in Conducting, University of Southern California, 1966.
FURTHER STUDY: L'Ecole Monteux, 1951–53; Paris National Conservatory of Music (Conducting), 1955–57.
MAJOR INSTRUCTORS/COACHES Pierre Monteux, George Szell, Walter Ducloux, Jean Fournier, Ingolf Dahl, Richard Lert, Conducting; Howard Hanson, Composition; Nadia Boulanger, Piano Accompaniment.
MAJOR APPOINTMENTS: Supervisor of Instrumental Music, Raleigh, North Carolina, 1948–51; Director of Instrumental Music, West Virginia State College, 1952–62; Music Director and Conductor, Southeast (California) Symphony Orchestra, 1963–66; Professor and Chair, Department of Music, West Virginia State College, 1966–70; Director, Fine Arts Institute, West Virginia State College, 1968–70; Director of Educational Activities and Assistant Conductor, New York Philharmonic Orchestra 1970–80; Professor of Music, Brooklyn College, 1972–75; Music Director, Opera South (Jackson, Mississippi), 1973–74; Minister of Music, Abyssinian Baptist Church (New York City), 1975–83; Principal Guest Conductor, Symphony of the New World, 1975–77.
GUEST CONDUCTOR: Orchestre Internationale de Paris, Los Angeles Philharmonic, French National Radio Orchestra; National, American, Richmond, and Indianapolis Symphony Orchestras; Miami Philharmonic; Detroit Symphony; Symphony of the New World; Orchestre de Chambre de Paris; Orchestre de Société das Concerts de Basonçon; Olsztyn Philharmonic (Poland); Virginia All-State Music Festival; Hollywood Opera Showcase.
AWARDS/HONORS: Fulbright Fellowship (Conducting), 1955; Fulbright Prize Award, 1956; Pi Delta Phi National French Honor Society; Pi Kappa Lambda National Honorary Music Society; Phi Delta Kappa National Educational Fraternity; Knight in the Grand Sovereign Dynastic Hospitaller Order of St. John, Knights of Malta.

THROUGHOUT HIS LIFETIME, LEON THOMPSON possessed a deep concern for the plight of black musical artists in America—singers,

434

instrumentalists, and conductors. He contributed an article on the subject to the *Black Perspective in Music*'s "Birthday Offering to William Grant Still, Upon the Occasion of His Eightieth Anniversary" in May 1975. (The subject of Thompson's 1964 doctoral dissertation at the University of Southern California had been "The Music of William Grant Still.") Titled "The Black Performing Artist and Achievement," Thompson's article addressed the black conductor's plight:

> Of all the black performing artists, the conductor was the last to receive the chance to practice his profession. While the choirs of black colleges have been noted in the past for their outstanding choral conductors, there has been no outlet for orchestral conductors. . . . It is a sad commentary on the United States that [Dean] Dixon* had to go to Europe in order to pursue his career as a conductor. . . . Another conductor who found it necessary to practice his profession in Europe is Everett Lee.*

Reflecting on progress in the conducting arena, Thompson highlighted the recent achievements of Henry Lewis,* Paul Freeman,* George Byrd, Denis De Coteau* [sic], James Frazier,* and Isaiah Jackson.*[1] To this list should be added the name of Leon Everette Thompson himself.

In a press release dated November 15, 1970, the New York Philharmonic Orchestra (New York City) announced the appointment of Leon Thompson to the newly-created post of director of the department of educational activities. That position, which would hold responsibility for continuing to "study the Orchestra's overall educational program and establish a closer relationship between the Orchestra and the educational forces of the City"[2] would also provide Thompson the opportunity to engage in that activity which was for him the most rewarding of musical pursuits—conducting.[3]

His interest in conducting was first stimulated by experiences witnessed in his father's church (Greater Mount Moriah Baptist Church, Richmond, Virginia), where he often provided piano accompaniment to his father's singing. By his sophomore year in high school, he both conducted the choir in rehearsal and played cello and bass in the school orchestra and band.[4]

With the benefit of church music experience and public school music preparation, Thompson enrolled at Virginia State College (now Virginia State University), from which he graduated in 1948, with a major in instrumental music education. His first appointment following graduation was to the position of supervisor of instrumental music in the public schools of Raleigh, North Carolina. During his tenure in Raleigh he began graduate studies at the Eastman School of Music and received the Master of Music degree with a major in theory and composition in 1952.

Eastman was crucial for both the development of Thompson's conducting skills and the encouragement to consider conducting as a component of his future professional life. Howard Hanson, who taught him composition, arranged for Thompson to have an audience with the revered conductor Pierre Monteux. Thompson recalled that Monteux handed him a score (Mozart's "Eine Kleine Nachtmusik") to read. Fortuitously the work was one Thompson already knew and he conducted the score from memory. He was less successful when queried by the maestro about the instrumentation for the opening measures of Beethoven's *Fifth Symphony;* Thompson did not know.[5] Monteux was apparently more impressed by Thompson's reading of the Mozart than by his not knowing the instrumentation for the Beethoven. The result was an invitation for Thompson to study with the maestro at the latter's private summer academy, L'Ecole Monteux, in Hancock, Maine. Thompson accepted the invitation for the summers of 1951, 1952, and 1953.

Maestro Monteux continued to be pleased by the progress of his protégé and recommended him for a Fulbright Scholarship, which Thompson won. The honor and the additional prize award allowed Thompson to study at the Paris National Conservatory of Music for two years, where his teachers included Jean Fournier (conductor of the Paris Opera) and the venerable Nadia Boulanger, who taught him piano accompaniment.

The Paris years provided Thompson not only the occasion to study with some of the world's finest teachers but also the opportunity to conduct throughout France; to lecture on jazz, spirituals and other American music for the American Embassy; and to program the music of black composers, of whom he was always a strong advocate. On his debut concert with the Orchestre Internationale de Paris, Thompson programmed Howard Swanson's *First Symphony* and a work by William Grant Still.[6]

Thompson returned to the United States in 1957, euphoric about his European experience and optimistic about the possibilities of conducting in this country. He made the rounds of managers, only to discover that in the late 1950s, interest in signing a black conductor was nil. He entered competitions of all kinds, and in 1960 received one of five Rockefeller awards in conducting. That prize allowed him to study with the revered and formidable George Szell, conductor of the Cleveland Orchestra. Thompson recalled Szell as a "taskmaster" and his three months' experience with him as "not the nicest."[7]

Though his first love was conducting, Thompson was always extremely aware of the realities—and hazards—of pursuing a conducting career. Competition among aspirants for the few conducting posts that come available during one's productive lifetime is always keen. For a black candidate in the 1950s, the likelihood of an appointment as even an apprentice conductor was remote. But Thompson had thoroughly prepared himself for an academic career as well and in 1952, he accepted an appointment as director of instrumental music at West Virginia State College at Institute, West Virginia. In 1959 he was elevated to associate professor of music. Throughout his year of postgraduate study, Thompson maintained his faculty position at West Virginia State.

Thompson continued to seek out situations that would provide conducting opportunities, and in the summer of 1959 he participated in conductors' workshops in Los Angeles, sponsored by the American Symphony Orchestra League and directed by Richard Lert, then music director of the Pasadena Symphony. That experience in Southern California, reinforced by the advice of black composer Ulysses Kay, persuaded Thompson to undertake doctoral studies at the University of Southern California. There Thompson studied with Walter Ducloux who, despite his enthusiasm for Thompson's talents, tried to dissuade him from pursuing conducting any further. Ducloux felt that odds were too greatly stacked against him. Nonetheless, Ducloux did assist Thompson in securing the position as conductor of the Southeast Los Angeles Orchestra, which he held for three seasons, and an opportunity to guest conduct the Los Angeles Philharmonic.[8]

During his Los Angeles years, Thompson's conducting activities embraced not only symphonic music but opera as well. His work at the University and for the Hollywood Opera Showcase included both conducting performances and vocal coaching. Thompson left Los Angeles, having earned the doctor of musical arts degree, with a major in conducting, in 1966, and returned to West Virginia State as professor and chair, Department of Music. In 1968, his duties were expanded to include directorship of the College's Fine Arts Institute. Thompson maintained these positions (while guest conducting when the opportunity presented itself) until 1970.

In 1969, Thompson received a telephone call that ultimately changed the course of his career. The caller was Helen Thompson of the New York Philharmonic, whom Thompson had known from the time of his participation in the American Symphony Orchestra League's summer workshop. Helen Thompson, then executive vice president of the League, explained to Thompson that the Philharmonic was considering increasing the staff and that she wanted to talk with him about a position.[9] At a subsequent meeting, Thompson recalled:

> She explained to me that Pierre Boulez would be the next music director, replacing [Leonard] Bernstein. But, he had already indicated that his primary interest was in the avant-garde—the unusual. He would be giving it much of his attention which left a void in the educational program because there was already nobody to take over the work that Bernstein was doing. We talked about what he [Bernstein] was doing and how it might be changed and what the needs were at that time [1970] in the New York City Schools.[10]

Helen Thompson indicated that the position had not been offered to anyone yet and that a search would begin only if Thompson was not interested. According to Thompson, "The minute she offered I already had my mind made up."[11]

Thompson's ten-year tenure as Director of Educational Activities was eventful and productive. The basic administrative responsibilities of his position included management of the Young People's Concerts, including selecting the repertoire and recommending conductors. Early in his tenure Thompson revamped the Young People's Concerts to make them more appropriate and meaningful to a school audience, which was increasingly composed of minorities and of listeners unaccustomed to attending symphony concerts. He instituted the New York All-City High School Orchestra and Joint Concert Project. This program allowed 100 students to study and work on a regular basis with the principal players of the New York Philharmonic and to play one concert each year with their New York Philharmonic teachers and to be seated in the first chairs ahead of their mentors. Thompson created the Orchestra's Repertoire Institute, which provided minority musicians with a five-day program of reading and coaching sessions with New York Philharmonic members. Thompson also administered the

Music Assistance Fund, which provides scholarship support to highly talented minority musicians for their professional training at conservatories, schools of music, and universities. In 1975 Thompson expanded this program of assistance of minority musicians aspiring to orchestra careers by creating the Music Assistance Fund Orchestral Fellowship Program. The Fellowship Program provides conservatory and university school of music graduates with one or more years' experience in symphony orchestras, learning repertory and coaching with players of the orchestras to which the fellows are invited. As of 1980 (the end of Thompson's management of the two Music Assistance Fund programs), more than $500,000 had been granted to 300 musicians at forty institutions.[12]

Concurrent with his designation as Director of Educational Activities, Thompson carried the title of assistant conductor. In that capacity, he led the New York Philharmonic in numerous Young People's Concerts at Lincoln Center and performances at schools and other sites in the New York metropolitan area. Thompson continued to champion the music of black composers and programmed their works whenever he had the opportunity. In 1977, he organized a week of New York Philharmonic concerts that featured the works of black composers covering a 200-year span. The concerts included eleven world premieres (one of which Thompson conducted).

Leon Thompson left the New York Philharmonic in 1980, feeling a strong sense of accomplishment, but eager to pursue other musical interests—largely conducting—for which his responsibilities at the Philharmonic had not allowed him adequate time. He died of a heart attack June 23, 1983, in Massanetta Springs, Virginia, where he was guest conducting at the All-State Music Festival.

Press Comments

"Leon Thompson . . . shaped performances of Berlioz's 'Roman Carnival' Overture and Liszt's 'Les Preludes' that were . . . somber, sonorous and satisfying."
     New York Times

"Dr. Leon E. Thompson . . . proved himself to be a musician with a depth of feeling, and a warmth of interpretation . . . All the facets of tonal color and dynamics were clearly delineated."
     Richmond News Leader

Notes

1. Leon Thompson, "The Black Performing Artist and Achievement," *Black Perspective in Music,* May 1975, pp. 162–163.
2. Press release. New York Philharmonic. November 15, 1970.
3. Lecture, Leon Thompson, "The Emergence of the Black Conductor," Virginia State College (The Black Man in American Music Project), March 24, 1970.
4. *Ibid.*
5. *Ibid.*
6. *Ibid.*
7. *Ibid.*
8. *Ibid.*
9. Luther Lincoln Henderson, III, "The Role of the New York Philharmonic's Director of Educational Activities: A New Dimension for the Conductor," D.M.A. dissertation, University of Texas at Austin, 1980, p. 7.
10. *Ibid.*
11. *Ibid.*
12. *Ibid.,* p. 44.

Will(iam) Vodery (Courtesy: Frank Driggs)

WILL(IAM) HENRY BENNETT VODERY (VODREY)

BIRTHDATE/PLACE: October 8, 1885; Philadelphia, Pennsylvania.
DEATH DATE/PLACE: November 18, 1951, New York.
EDUCATION: Central High School (Philadelphia), University of Pennsylvania and Bandmaster's School (Chaumont, France).
MAJOR INSTRUCTORS: Theory—Hugh Clarke (University of Pennsylvania); Harmony and Orchestration—Frederick Stock (Chicago Symphony Orchestra).
MAJOR APPOINTMENTS: Music Director (and arranger), Jolly John Larkin Show (St. Louis); Charles K. Harris's Publishing Company (Chicago); Librarian, Chicago Symphony Orchestra (1905); Music Director, George Walker/Bert Williams Productions; Music Director, Howard Theatre (Washington) and Academy Theatre (Baltimore); Music Director, Hertig and Seamon's Enterprises; Music Director (and arranger), Florenz Ziegfeld's "Follies" (1911–32); leader, Century Roof Garden Dance Orchestra and Vodery's Plantation Orchestra ("Plantation Revue" and "Dixie to Broadway"); arranger and Music Director, Fox Film Company (Hollywood) (1929–3?); leader, Jubilee Singers and Will Vodery Singers (late 1920s, early 1930s respectively); Music Director (and arranger), "The Cotton Club Parade" revue (1940).
AWARD: Composition Prize (Tone Poem, "Two Months in the Old Mill"), France.

WILL VODERY CAME IN EARLY CONTACT with the leading black entertainers of his era, simply because his family ran a theatrical boarding house in Philadelphia:

> During the early days of show business, people in cities that had large houses, would set aside rooms to take care of the colored performers. Every week during the theatrical season colored show and vaudeville performers would visit their cities. Bill Vodrey's house was one of those places.[1]

Two frequent visitors were entertainers George Walker and Bert Williams. The fact that his father was a professor of Greek at Lincoln

442

University in Pennsylvania brought to the young Will little more than his classic style and an appreciation for the finer things in life.

Vodery studied piano as a child and performed in numerous local concerts while in his early teens. Serious study took place at the University of Pennsylvania where he was a student of Hugh Clarke and where he organized his first orchestra. Later study of harmony and orchestration was undertaken with Frederick Stock, music director of the Chicago Symphony Orchestra. The year was 1905, when Vodery was working as a librarian for the symphony. He also worked as an arranger for Charles K. Harris's publishing company.

Prior to his Chicago experience, Vodery was initiated into the music directing business through opportunities afforded by the Walker and Williams Companies (1904), followed by a brief period in St. Louis with the Jolly John Larkin show. By 1907, Vodery was settled in New York City, where he established himself as one of the city's principal arrangers and songwriters. For a period, he resided at the residence of Will Marion Cook* and affiliated himself with Cook's Clef Club (a black musician's association founded in 1910).

Vodery served as music director for Walker and Williams's "In Bandanna Land" (1907) and various J. Lubrie Hill productions (1911–1914). He trained the chorus and directed the orchestra for the "Smart Set" company, starring S. H. Dudley and Ada Overton Walker (wife of George Walker). When the Howard Theatre opened in Washington, D.C., in August 1910, "[i]n the pit the orchestra was under the direction of Will Vodery who was billed in the program as 'Professor Will Vodery'."[2] Early in the second decade, he led a dance orchestra on the Century Roof Garden in New York City.

During World War I, Vodery organized the 807th Pioneer Infantry Band. The band performed throughout Europe, appearing before royalty in Belgium and Monaco, and the President of France. He had earlier attended the Bandmaster School at Chaumont, France, and according to several sources, he graduated with high honors and was recommended to the Paris National Conservatory. Of his post-World War I experience, entertainer and show business historian Tom Fletcher wrote:

> When the war was over he and other band leaders were sent to Fort Betev, France, to receive an award from [pianist] Robert Casadesus. Vodery was the only colored man there.[3]

While in France he won a composition prize for his tone poem "Two Months in the Old Mill."

Returning to the States, he easily resumed both his work and his musical status. He organized the Plantation Orchestra, for the cabaret in the Winter Garden Building at Broadway and 50th Street in 1922 and remained there until 1925. He was music director for the shows "Dover Street to Dixie" (1923), "Dixie to Broadway" (1924), and "Brown Skin Quinan Revue" (1925).

Vodery departed for Hollywood in 1929, where he was employed as a film composer and arranger with Fox Studios. This represented a first for a black American. Wrote musicologist Doris McGinty:

> Vodery was known for his exciting musicianship, brilliant arranging skills, and support of younger musicians, among them Duke Ellington.*[4]

Ellington paid tribute to Vodery in his book *Music Is My Mistress*. He credits Vodery with having secured for him

> the gig in "Show Girl" at the Ziegfeld Theatre simply by mentioning my name to Flo Ziegfeld. . . . Will Vodery was a very strict and very precise musician. He would stand up and write an orchestration without a score, and guarantee every note. . . . He used to give me valuable lectures in orchestration.[5]

W. C. Handy wrote in his autobiography that it was Vodery who introduced him to Ziegfeld and to the circle of black celebrities.[6]

Vodery's association with Flo Ziegfeld, the dean of revue producers, began in 1911 and lasted for over two decades. His assignments included arrangements and orchestrations for the featured performers, as well as coaching for Ziegfeld's musicians. Wrote Fletcher, "Not a tune was played on an opening of any big musical shows until the O.K. was given by Vodery."[7]

As a composer, Vodery contributed the scores for various productions: "A Trip to Africa," "The Oyster Man," "The Isle of Bang-Bang," "South Africa," "Time, Place and the Girl," "Girls from Happy Land," "Saucy Maid," and "Men, Her and I!", and contributed to the popular "Shuffle Along" (1921) and "Cotton Club Express" (1937). Various music publishers hired him to do orchestrations.

Not often recalled is the fact that Vodery assisted George Gershwin in getting work with a music publisher and as pianist in a downtown theater. He also orchestrated Gershwin's first opera, "Blue Monday."[8] Others who benefited from Vodery's assistance were composer William Grant Still and singers/actors Jules Bledsoe and Paul Robeson:

> When "Show Boat" was being produced [1927 on stage, 1929 on film], Bill received a telegram from Ziegfeld to get 32 colored singers, the best that he could get his hands on. He discovered Jules Bledsoe and also cleared the road for Paul Robeson for the European Company.[9]

"The Cotton Club Parade" revue of 1940, featuring dancers Bill Robinson and the Nicholas Brothers, along with Cabell ("Cab") Calloway and his band, was Vodery's last major assignment. Soon after he retired to Saratoga Springs, New York, where he bought property and ran several amusement places. The loss to the music world was tremendous when Vodery died on November 18, 1951.

Notes

1. Tom Fletcher, *The Tom Fletcher Story: 100 Years of the Negro in Show Business,* New York: Burdge, 1954, p. 154. (Reprint, New York: Da Capo Press, 1984).
2. Henry T. Sampson, *Blacks in Blackface: A Source Book on Early Black Musical Shows,* Metuchen, N.J.: The Scarecrow Press, Inc., 1980, p. 124.
3. Fletcher, *op. cit.,* p. 156.
4. Doris McGinty, "Vodery, Will(iam Henry Bennett), *New Grove Dictionary of American Music,* Vol. 4, New York, N.Y.: Macmillan Press, 1986, p. 461.
5. Duke Ellington, *Music Is My Mistress,* Garden City, N.Y.: Doubleday and Company, 1973, p. 98.
6. W. C. Handy, *Father of the Blues: An Autobiography,* New York, N.Y.: The Macmillan Co., 1941, p. 195.
7. Fletcher, *op. cit.*
8. Morroe Berger, Edward Berger, and James Patrick, *Benny Carter: A Life in American Music,* Metuchen, N.J.: Scarecrow Press and the Institute of Jazz Studies (Rutgers), 1982, pp. 27–28.
9. Fletcher, *op. cit.*

Willie Anthony Waters (Courtesy: Sheldon Soffer Management)

WILLIE ANTHONY WATERS

BIRTHDATE/PLACE: October 11, 1951; Goulds, Florida.

EDUCATION: B.Mus.Ed., University of Miami (Major, Piano; Minor, Conducting); Memphis State University, Conducting.

MAJOR INSTRUCTORS: Ivan Davis, piano; Mary Henderson Buckley, voice; Lee Kjelson, Robert Hines, Paul Eisenhart, Erich Leinsdorf, conducting.

MAJOR APPOINTMENTS: Assistant Conductor and Chorus Master, Memphis Opera (now Opera Memphis), 1973–75; Music Assistant to Kurt Herbert Adler, General Director, San Francisco Opera, 1975–79; Music Administrator (1981–83), Music Director (1983–84), Artistic Director (1984–92), Principal Guest Conductor (1992—), Greater Miami Opera; Acting Dean, New World School for the Arts (Miami) (1992–93); Music Director, Chautauqua Opera Company (1993—).

GUEST CONDUCTOR: New Lyric Theater, Michigan Opera Theater; Utah, Connecticut, San Diego, Tulsa, and Fort Worth Opera Companies; San Francisco Opera Center; Cologne and Australian Opera Companies; Austin, Miami Chamber, Fort Lauderdale, Jacksonville, Shreveport, San Antonio (San Antonio Festival), and Detroit Symphony Orchestras; Norwegian Radio Orchestra (Bergen Festival), Essen Philharmonic (Germany), Auckland Philharmonic (Australia), and Bavarian Radio Orchestra; Spoleto (USA) Festival.

AWARDS/HONORS: Prix de Martell, 1991 (Recognizing contributions of classical musicians to their communities).

STAFF WRITER JANE WOOLDRIDGE of the *Miami Herald* contributed an impressive article in early 1985 titled simply "Willie Waters." The focus was on the relatively new thirty-three-year-old artistic director of the Greater Miami Opera Company, an organization that Waters joined in 1981 as music administrator. "Willie Waters" was the feature story in the *Herald*'s "Élan" section—gifted, spirited, poised, vivacious, energetic, and imaginative, all traits applicable to Wooldridge's subject:

> At six feet four and more than 220 pounds, Waters is a substantive man both literally and—in his present position with the sixth

447

biggest-budgeted opera company in the country—professionally. There are approximately 120 U.S. opera companies, but there is only one black artistic director.

Waters's response was:

> I think it's still a novelty. People probably still don't know quite how to deal with it in Miami, but there it is. The idea of [anyone's being] a conductor is sort of strange to most people anyway.[1]

Six and a half years later (Winter 1991), Greater Miami Opera's own *Il Libretto* wrote:

> The passing of the baton at the Greater Miami Opera made history throughout the world. Willie Anthony Waters became the first black Artistic Director of a major opera company. . . . During his tenure, Maestro Waters has expanded the Opera's repertoire and enhanced its reputation. . . . Maestro Waters' creative impact has also been evidenced by the quality of singers and stage directors engaged by the Opera.[2]

A native of Goulds, Florida, Willie Waters is the youngest of six gifted children whose parents were a packing company shipping and receiving clerk and a beautician. Both parents were members of New Bethel A.M.E. Church and both sang in the choir. Joined by their children, they traveled around the area, singing for various social and religious functions.

On one of the family's entertainment outings, Waters's piano playing attracted the attention of a wealthy St. Louis judge who was visiting friends in Miami Beach. It was the judge's opinion that the seven-year-old's talent warranted encouragement. He subsequently defrayed the cost of Waters's music lessons until young Waters completed high school.[3] The family had recognized talent at a very early age. Well before his fifth birthday, he inherited a piano, originally purchased for an older sister, who by this time had lost interest. According to Waters:

> My grandmother, already an established piano teacher in Goulds, taught me the basics of piano technique and also how to read music. My parents and teachers in elementary and high school provided me with as much musical training and experience as they could. And, of course, I played piano (and later organ) in church, starting when I was six years old.[4]

Waters's piano studies continued through high school, along with added training on organ, violin, and trumpet. By the time he entered the University of Miami, he had selected the piano for his instrumental concentration, with additional study of voice and conducting. Waters excelled in all areas. Both teachers and students recognized outstanding leadership qualities and as Waters observed, "Conducting was the only musical activity in which I was involved that I didn't get nervous about."[5] Voice teacher Mary Buckley encouraged her student to pursue operatic conducting.

Following graduation from the University of Miami, Willie Waters enrolled at Memphis State University for the master's degree, but left two months short of completing all requirements. He majored in conducting, not necessarily opera, though he had been fascinated with the art form since seeing his first live opera, Puccini's "Madama Butterfly," while in the tenth grade.

The Memphis years (1973–75) were good ones; during that time he served as assistant conductor and chorus master of the Memphis Opera (a partly professional, partly collegiate outfit). But in 1975 when the opportunity came for Waters to serve as assistant to the San Francisco Opera's legendary general director Kurt Adler, there was no refusing. Though he had successfully completed all the course work and comprehensive examinations, one paper stood between him and the degree. He left Memphis for San Francisco.

Without hesitation, Waters cites his appointment as artistic director of the Greater Miami Opera as his most significant achievement to date. During the 1981–82 season (while serving as music administrator) he conducted productions of "Trouble in Tahiti," "Simon Boccanegra," and "La Traviata." During the 1982–83 season he led performances of "The Impressario," "Andrea Chenier," "Faust," and "Un Ballo in Maschera." Waters was elevated to the position of Music Director of the Greater Miami Opera in 1983 and one year later, to the position of artistic director. Among other works that he has conducted in Miami are "Lucia de Lammermoor," "L'Amore dei Tre Re," "Il Trovatore," "La Gioconda," "Hamlet," "Aida," "Of Mice and Men," "The Fantasticks," and "Salome."

Though he was once fearful of Richard Strauss's "Salome," Waters conducted five performances in February 1987, based heavily on his 1983 experience with one of today's leading Strauss exponents, Erich Leinsdorf. The Greater Miami Opera's publication *Voice* asked Waters "How technically demanding is the score?" Waters replied:

Extremely. It's an 85-minute one-act opera with no intermission and that alone makes it strenuous. . . . It's hard work from beginning to end. Then you have all the rhythmic difficulties—within one page there may be five different meters. . . . The amount of concentration necessary is astounding, not to mention the sheer technical difficulties of keeping the whole thing together.[6]

A local critic responded to the performances:

Waters conducted with assurance and attentiveness to the myriad details that go into the score. He shaped the final scene with particular care, bringing out all its perverse sensuality. The expanded orchestra met with remarkable poise the heady challenge Strauss posed; it was the most consistent, vibrant playing I have yet heard at a Miami Opera performance.[7]

Opening night of the company's 1987–88 season, the curtain rose on the American premiere of Rossini's thirtieth opera "Bianca e Falliera." Willie Waters was in the pit. The performance was covered by National Public Radio, and "Bianca" was recorded for broadcast during the summer of 1988. The Greater Miami Opera was heard by more people in one evening than in the company's previous forty-seven years. Live broadcasts of the company were inaugurated by radio station WTMI-FM in 1985. These transmissions enabled many in South Florida to experience the Miami Opera (and the conducting of Willie Waters) for the first time.

On October 12, 1988, the Greater Miami Opera's new program "Opera Tonight," hosted by Waters, was premiered on WTMI-FM. In a series of 26 bi-weekly programs, Waters would

introduce music lovers of every background not only to opera's musical and dramatic passion, but to the creativity and humanity that make all of its diverse elements come together and come alive. "Grand Opera is just plain good entertainment," says Maestro Waters. "It deals with our most basic feelings and desires in some very sophisticated ways, and it has something for everyone—that's what I want listeners to feel when they join me for 'Opera Tonight'."[8]

Waters would go into the orchestra pit, mount the stage, converse with guests, singers, and designers—a format designed to bring the company's productions to a new and wider audience, in easily accessible and interesting ways. As he frequently states, "Our older patrons are dying off. We have to find people to replace them."

Waters considers as a highlight of his career a program that he started and administered for high school inner-city youngsters, sponsored solely by the Greater Miami Opera. Talented but economically disadvantaged students were selected and trained in music, drama, and dance for a period of four weeks, at no cost to the participants. The program continued for three summers. Recalls Waters:

> The program was very successful, though by choice, low-key. We opted for training, providing an intense experience rather than exploiting it to the press and community. I am very proud of the achievements of the students involved.[9]

Another ambitious program launched by the Greater Miami Opera in 1983 (and one in which Waters is extensively involved) is an Apprentice Program for young American singers and technicians. Known as the "Young Artist Program," participants receive instruction in acting, movement, and diction, take part in the company's productions in smaller roles and choruses, sing leading roles in the company's In-School Opera, are highlighted in their own productions, are trained in various technical aspects of opera production, and are contracted by other arts organizations. By its fourth season, the program was able to report:

> Historically, young American singers travelled to Europe to obtain extensive professional training and experience. Since the inception of this program, . . . up-and-coming performers and technicians have been able to receive excellent experience and training without ever leaving home.[10]

The 1987–88 roster of young artists included fourteen participants from twelve states.

Waters's guest appearances have been numerous: New Lyric Theater (Memphis); Michigan Opera (Detroit); Utah, San Diego, Fort Worth, and Shreveport Opera Companies; Opera Omaha; Austin, Miami Chamber, Fort Lauderdale, Utah, Jacksonville, Shreveport, and San Antonio Symphony Orchestras. Waters also participated (as conductor of the Detroit Symphony) in the historically significant "Black American Music Symposium" held during the summer of 1985 at The University of Michigan. He made his European debut conducting the Norwegian Radio Orchestra in 1987.

Three appearances with the Connecticut Opera (1980, 1981, and 1986) have been particularly gratifying to Waters. It was the company's general director, George Osborne, who gave Waters his real start in Memphis; Waters remembers, "Those years were important, because I was allowed to just go out and do it, and I learned a lot."[11]

New vistas, broader horizons—these Waters designates as essential if he is to have "a truly big-league career." In an interview with Steve Metcalf of *The Hartford Courant* (1986), he stated:

> The only way I'll ever be taken seriously as a conductor, in this country at least, is to do more symphony repertoire, and that's what I'm looking to do. . . . It's not easy, though.[12]

Willie Anthony Waters had made his debut with the Detroit Symphony in 1985, conducting a special program, "Classical Roots," devoted to music by black composers. He returned in 1986 to preside over a concert of gospel music, "Gospel Celebration," featuring the orchestra and several black church choirs. But he is cautious about accepting too many such performances and awaits an invitation to preside over a regular series concert:

> There's a great danger, a very great danger, in doing a lot of these kinds of concerts. . . . If I'm not careful, I could end up making a career out of them. In fact, I've already told my agent that after I do two more of these gospel evenings that I've already lined up, I don't want to take any more of them. It's just too easy to get pegged early on in the music business. I'm a conductor—not an opera conductor, or a gospel conductor, or a pops conductor.[13]

An invitation to preside over a regular series concert came in 1988. Willie Anthony Waters, Artistic Director of the Greater Miami Opera Association, would make his debut as conductor at a Philharmonic Orchestra of Florida Celebrity Concert. On January 2–6, 1989, Maestro Waters led the orchestra in a program featuring cellist Ralph Kirshbaum in a performance of Dvorak's Cello Concerto, as well as Barber's Overture to "School for Scandal" and Copland's "Appalachian Spring."[14] Other 1989 conducting assignments included the Tulsa Opera (Floyd's "Susanna"), San Francisco Opera Center (Verdi's "Rigoletto"), and the Australian Opera Company (Puccini's "La Boheme"). He made his debut at the Spoleto

U.S.A. Festival in May 1990, conducting Beethoven's Ninth Symphony and Choral Fantasy. He recently completed his first recording, for the Philips label, "Songs from Broadway," with bass-baritone Simon Estes, soprano Shirley Verrett, and the Bavarian Radio Orchestra of Munich.

Widening his horizons, Waters debuted with the Cologne Opera and the Essen Philharmonic during the Fall of 1991. On the international experience, Waters commented:

> I need to validate my stature as a conductor, therefore I have to have European connections. It means I'm no longer considered just 'a local talent'. . . . [T]he only way to grow artistically and technically is by conducting as much as possible. . . . Going to Europe means exposure to a lot of repertoire, a lot of different styles.[15]

Waters recalls that as he sat before his stereo as a youngster, waving his arms, his family thought he was slightly abnormal. A brother assured other family members that it was "just a passing phase." More than a fantasy, Waters insists:

> [Conducting] is my love and I feel this is what I was born to do. I feel that this is where I'm supposed to be and it's what I want to do.[16]

Following his effort at reshaping the Greater Miami Opera's future, Waters, in 1993, set out to chart new directions for the Chautauqua Opera Company. In the interim, he served as Acting Dean of the New World School for the Arts in Miami (1992–93). He maintains nevertheless that his ultimate goal is to become music director of a symphony orchestra.

Press Comments

"Waters conducted with brio and understanding."

New York Times

"Willie Anthony Waters and the Philharmonic Orchestra of Florida stirred up a storm, . . ."

Miami Herald

"Through it all, Waters conducted with assurance and attentiveness to the myriad details that go into the score. He shaped the final scene with particular care, bringing

all its ("Salome") perverse sensuality. . . . A commendable achievement, a coming-of-age for the company {Greater Miami Opera}."

Sun-Sentinel

"Willie Anthony Waters . . .gave Wagner's first act 'Prelude' to 'Die Meistersinger' a touch of martial majesty and was a deeply sensitive accompanist for {Shirley} Verrett."

Miami Herald

"Waters. . . . conducted exquisitely, synchronizing accompaniments to help the singers tell you what their lyrics were about."

Miami Herald

"Waters. . . . conducted, as always, with a keen ear for the inner pulse of a score."

Sun-Sentinel

"To conductor Willie Anthony Waters goes the credit for most of the evening's subtlety . . . Verdi at his most atmospheric"

Miami Herald

"{S}uperlative conducting. . . . It was definitely Waters' conducting which made the performance come to life, giving Gounod's familiar score an added measure of expansiveness and sonority."

Miami News

"Willie Anthony Waters was in peak form on the podium, conducting with equal proportions of drive and musical poetry."

Sun-Sentinel

"Willie Anthony Waters did one of his best conducting jobs ever in the orchestra pit, pouring a wealth of galvanizing energy into the powerhouse score."

Miami Herald

"Two events of monumental importance to Greater Miami Opera have been the advent of Robert Herman as general manager . . . and the recent appointment of Willie Anthony Waters as artistic director. . . . The orchestra and chorus have rarely sounded better, but even more impressive were his love and understanding of the voice; he enveloped each singer in an accompaniment crafted to highlight individual strengths and minimize flaws. . . ."

Opera News

Notes

1. Jane Wooldridge, "Willie Waters," *The Miami Herald* (Élan), March 20, 1985, Section E, p. 1.
2. "Maestro Willie Waters: Making His Mark Both Here and Abroad," *Il Libretto* (News from the Greater Miami Opera), Winter 1991, p. 2.
3. Wooldridge, *op. cit.*
4. Correspondence, Waters/Handy, June 10, 1987.
5. *Ibid.*
6. "Salome–An Interview With Willie Anthony Waters," *Voice,* December 1986, p. 3.
7. Tim Smith, "Despite Ending, 'Salome' A Triumph," *Sun-Sentinel,* February 11, 1987, p. 8E (Lifestyle/Entertainment.)
8. "Opera Takes Over the Airwaves," *Il Libretto,* published by GMO's Marketing Department, n.d., p. 2.
9. Correspondence, *op. cit.*
10. Press Release, Greater Miami Opera, April 30, 1987, p. 3.
11. Steve Metcalf, "Conductor Looks Forward to His Turn in the Big Leagues," *The Hartford Courant,* October 20, 1986, p. D1.
12. *Ibid.,* p. D2.
13. *Ibid.*
14. "Season Preview," *Philharmonic Images,* Vol. 2, Number 1, p. 5.
15. "Maestro Willie Waters," *op. cit.*
16. *Ibid.*

William Henry ("Chick") Webb (Courtesy: Institute of Jazz Studies)

WILLIAM HENRY ("CHICK") WEBB

BIRTHDATE/PLACE: February 10, 1909; Baltimore, Maryland.
DEATH DATE/PLACE: June 16, 1939; Baltimore.
EDUCATION: School 105 (elementary); the streets of Baltimore.
CAREER HIGHLIGHT: Leader of the Chick Webb Band, 1926–39;
AWARDS/HONORS: Honorary doctorate, Yale University, 1937.

ACCORDING TO JAZZ CRITIC GARY GIDDINS, Chick Webb

was the first great drummer of the Swing era, the leader of a fiercely competitive and innovative orchestra, a pacesetter for dancers during the golden age of ballroom dancing, and a nurturer of talent whose fabled generosity was rewarded when he discovered and groomed Ella Fitzgerald.[1]

Born at Johns Hopkins Hospital in Baltimore, Maryland, indications were that Chick Webb would be a hopeless cripple for the remainder of his life, forever deprived of the use of his legs. A preteen operation made walking possible, though it was relatively certain that his growth would be stunted and his back would be forever deformed. The problem was caused by a birth defect, namely, spinal tuberculosis, the same ailment that caused his death at age thirty.

Another version of his illness is that "he was dropped when he was still small. He fell on his back and several vertebrae were smashed." The same writers attribute a liver ailment, plus overwork, as the cause of death.[2] And a slightly different version was issued by his hometown newspaper in 1977. Wrote the *Baltimore Afro-American,* "He was born a hunchback, grew to only four feet, and a tumble down the stairs at age 5 left him permanently crippled."[3]

At the height of his short-lived career, *Down Beat* magazine offered over a period of three months a series of praiseworthy articles entitled "The Rise of A Crippled Genius."[4] Such recognition was fully warranted, since, even today, whenever one refers to "the swing era" or "the big-band tradition," the name Chick Webb is always included.

At the time of his death, many journalists wrote that Webb's reign as a band leader was "unparalleled in the history of jazz." For close to a decade, the Webb band was second only to Ellington's in popularity. Webb was one of the first leaders to sign with Decca Recording Company (1935) and remained one of the company's biggest profit-makers until his death in 1939. He rose to national prominence in 1935, when NBC featured his band on a weekly coast-to-coast program called "Good Time Society." So successful was the band that it continued for roughly three years following his death. Finally, none will forget that Chick Webb was the one person "willing to take a chance" on the incomparable Ella Fitzgerald (1934) and who had the foresight to organize his band around her voice.

Webb began developing his talent at age three by beating out rhythms on kitchen pots and pans, soon graduating to tin cans. By age eleven, Webb was playing for neighborhood dances, having purchased his first drum set with money saved from selling newspapers. Before long, he was drumming on an excursion boat, crossing back and forth on Chesapeake Bay.

At age sixteen, Chick Webb headed for New York City. His first real job was at the Black Bottom Club, where he led a band of five, including alto saxophonist Johnny Hodges (a distant relative). Moving on to the Paddock Club (upon the recommendation of Duke Ellington*), he attracted the attention of Moe Gale,[5] who eventually placed him into the Savoy Ballroom. Other jazz talents who were alumni of the Webb outfit included trombonist Jimmy Harrison, cornetist/trumpeter Taft Jordan, saxophonists Louis Jordan and Benny Carter, and bassist John Kirby.

The Chick Webb Band was a swinging band, for the simple reason that the leader was a premier swinger. As Ellington wrote in *Music Is My Mistress:*

> As a drummer, Chick had his own ideas about what he wanted to do. Some musicians are dancers, and Chick was. You can dance with a lot of things besides your feet. . . . The reason why Chick Webb had such control, such command of his audiences at the Savoy ballroom, was because he was always in communication with the dancers and felt it the way they did. And that is probably the biggest reason why he could cut all the other bands that went in there.[6]

The band reigned at the Savoy Ballroom throughout the 1930s and regularly defeated competing ensembles in various "cutting contests." Often written about is the May 11, 1937, battle of the Benny Goodman and Chick Webb Bands. The declared winner was Webb, with Goodman's drummer, Gene Krupa, declaring:

> I'll never forget that night. . . . He just cut me to ribbons—made me feel awfully small. . . . That man was dynamic; he could reach the most amazing heights. When he really let go, you had a feeling that the entire atmosphere in the place was being charged. When he felt like it, he could cut down any of us.[7]

The following year, the Webb Band battled the Count Basie Band. The verdict was once more in favor of Webb.

Webb led his band from the center of the ensemble, on a raised platform, using specially constructed bass drum pedals and cymbal holders. According to *The New Grove Dictionary of American Music* (1986), he was universally admired as a drummer because of his "forceful swing, accurate technique, control of dynamics, and imaginative breaks and fills."[8] Yet he never indulged in drum fireworks or drumming exhibitionism. Webb led with a firm swinging beat; without fanfare, he acquired and sustained both the respect and response from those who accepted him as leader. Together they "stomped" at the "home of the happy feet," packing them in night after night.

Chick Webb and his men had mastered the ability to play "jazz for dancing." The resulting dance creations included the Lindy Hop, the Susie Q, and the Big Apple.

His death on June 16, 1939, was headlined:

> 10,000 Bid Farewell to Chick Webb; From Newsboy to King, Chick Webb, Whose Genius Triumphed Over Terrific Odds; 40 Cops Taxed Handling Crowd at Webb Funeral.[9]

Pallbearers and honorary pallbearers included Fletcher Henderson,* Jimmie Lunceford,* Cab Calloway,* Benny Carter, and Duke Ellington.*

Notes

1. Gary Giddins, "Chick Webb, King of the Savoy," *The Village Voice/Jazz Special,* August 30, 1988, p. 5.

2.   Samuel B. Charters and Leonard Kunstadt, *Jazz: A History of the New York Scene,* New York, N.Y.: Da Capo Press, 1981, p. 254 (originally published, Garden City, N.Y.: Doubleday, 1962).

3.   "The Day They Buried Chick Webb," *Baltimore Afro-American,* Part I, Magazine Section, April 19–23, 1977, p. 21.

4.   "The Rise of a Crippled Genius," *Down Beat,* December 1937, p. 14; January 1938, p. 9; and February 1938, pp. 9, 31.

5.   Moe Gale was Chick Webb's manager and owner of the Savoy Ballroom.

6.   Edward Kennedy Ellington, *Music Is My Mistress,* Garden City, New York: Doubleday and Company, Inc., 1973, p. 100.

7.   George T. Simon, *The Big Bands,* rev. ed., New York: Collier Books, 1974, p. 440.

8.   "William Henry 'Chick' Webb," *The New Grove Dictionary of American Music,* Vol. IV, New York: Grove's Dictionaries of Music Inc., 1986, pp. 495–496.

9.   "The Day They Buried Chick Webb," *Baltimore Afro-American,* Part II, Magazine Section, April 26–30, 1977, p. 21.

Thomas Alphonso Wilkins

THOMAS ALPHONSO WILKINS

BIRTHDATE/PLACE: September 10, 1956; Norfolk, Virginia.
EDUCATION: B.Mus.Ed., Shenandoah Conservatory of Music (Winchester, Virginia), 1978 (Certification, Tuba Performance); M.Mus., New England Conservatory of Music (Boston), 1982 (Conducting).
MAJOR INSTRUCTOR: Richard Pittman.
CONDUCTOR TRAINING PROGRAMS: American Symphony Orchestra League Conducting Workshops, 1985, 1986, 1988; Conductors' Guild Summer Institutes, 1986, 1987; Conductors' Guild Workshops, 1987, 1988.
WORKSHOP INSTRUCTORS: Gerhardt Samuel, Daniel Lewis, Maurice Abravanel, Leonard Slatkin, Jorge Mester, Pierre Boulez, Otto-Werner Mueller, Edo de Waart, Ricardo Muti, Samuel Jones, Ole Schmidt, Bernard Rubenstein, Frank Brieff, Harold Farberman, Irwin Hoffman, Gunther Schuller, and Henry Holt (Conducting); Charles Wuorinen (Composition).
MAJOR APPOINTMENTS: Assistant Conductor, Community Symphony of Boston, 1982; Music Director, North Park College Orchestra, 1982–86; Music Director, Northwest Indiana Youth Orchestra, 1983–87; Music Director, University of Tennessee at Chattanooga Orchestra, 1987–89; Interim Music Director, Du Page Symphony Orchestra, 1986; Assistant Conductor, Northwest Indiana Symphony, 1983–87; Assistant Conductor, 1989–91/Associate Conductor, Richmond (Virginia) Symphony Orchestra, 1991–94; Resident Conductor, Florida Orchestra (Tampa), 1994—.
GUEST CONDUCTOR: College of William and Mary Brass Choir, 1979; New England Conservatory Commencement Orchestra, 1982; Jugendkammerorchester, Stuttgart (American Tour), 1984; Glenbard Festival Orchestra (Wheaton, Illinois), 1986; Walla Walla Symphony (Washington), 1987; Southwest Michigan Symphony, 1987; Classical Symphony Orchestra (Chicago), 1988; Williamsburg Symphonia, 1991.

THE NAME THOMAS WILKINS ACHIEVED national· recognition in March 1989 with the announcement that he had been selected as assistant conductor of the Richmond (Virginia) Symphony. He would assume his duties at the beginning of the 1989–90 season. According to George Manahan, the orchestra's music director,

"Wilkins was one of four finalists among more than 150 applicants for the assistant conductor's post."[1]

Wilkins was then enjoying tremendous success at the University of Tennessee in Chattanooga. Arriving at the University for the academic year 1987–88, his first conducting of the orchestra garnered laudatory comments from his musical peers and top university officials. Wrote one music professor:

> The musical growth of the orchestra under your direction has been outstanding. . . . Your musicianship, conducting expertise and teaching skills were clearly evident in this fine performance.[2]

An assessment of his performance as assistant professor brought a unanimous vote of support for retention from the music faculty:

> Mr. Wilkins has already instilled in the Orchestra a sense of identity and pride which it has not had for some time. . . . [His] service activities are concentrated . . . in the areas of recruitment and renewing and cementing relationships with the public school string communities. . . . Without any qualifications, [we are] pleased to recommend retention for Assistant Professor Thomas Wilkins.[3]

Wilkins had prepared well for the challenges that awaited him. In his native Norfolk, Virginia, he began studying the cello at age nine and the tuba at age fourteen. He was exposed to fine music-making through youth concerts given by the Norfolk Symphony. Commenting on his decision to become a professional musician, Wilkins said:

> [I make my living as a musician] not because as a young kid in the "projects" I saw music as my ticket out, nor because I participated in a music education program. I became a professional musician because as a result of such participation, I learned that my appetite for music was insatiable. I was captured, immersed, even perhaps consumed by something that, as Beethoven said, understood and knew me, though I not it.[4]

Postsecondary study took place at Shenandoah Conservatory in Winchester, Virginia, and the New England Conservatory in Boston, Massachusetts (B.Mus.Ed. and M.Mus., respectively). Following graduation from the latter, Wilkins joined the faculty of North Park College in Chicago, conducting the school's orchestra and serving as assistant conductor of the Northwest Indiana Symphony and music director of its youth orchestra.

Wilkins was at the helm when the North Park College Orchestra toured Scandinavia in 1984 and made its yearly appearances at Chicago's Orchestra Hall (1983–86). During this same period, Wilkins guest conducted many youth orchestras, including the Jugendkammerorchester of Stuttgart's 1984 performance in Chicago, Illinois during its American tour. Additional work experiences included Wilkins serving as interim minister of music at the Northbrook Evangelical Church in Northbrook, Illinois, in 1985 and minister of music at the Cuyler Covenant Church in Chicago from 1986 to 1988.

Wilkins also took advantage of every opportunity for continued study and development. He participated in various American Symphony Orchestra League Conducting Workshops: Cincinnati, Ohio (1985); St. Louis and Cleveland (1986); and Minneapolis and Philadelphia (1988). Summers permitted his participation in the Conductors' Guild Workshops at the Universities of South Carolina and Oregon in 1987 and 1988 and the Conductors' Guild Summer Institutes in 1986 and 1987. Harold Farberman, Director of the Conductors' Guild Workshops at the University of South Carolina's Conductors' Institute wrote:

> Mr. Wilkins is a first rate, natural conductor. He is a musician of excellence and integrity. The results he achieves on the podium reflect his own attitudes as a human being; he gets the best out of his musicians because he is a genuinely whole person of quality.[5]

Richmond represented a new challenge; and it was obvious that the thirty-two-year-old conductor was up to the task. According to music director Manahan:

> In the interviews . . . Wilkins showed us a lot of virtues. . . . The orchestra likes him, and his credentials are very strong. . . . He'll give us what we need, not only in conducting but in being here for day-to-day work as well.[6]

His duties included youth concerts, in-school and promotional engagements, pops concerts, suburban "run-outs," and special events. But as local music critic Clarke Bustard wrote:

The music in those programs isn't the most demanding the
symphony plays, but the circumstances are the toughest—fewer
rehearsals, concerts that might be staged in unfamiliar surroundings,
[and] audiences that might need some gentle persuasion in order to
enjoy the classics.[7]

Toward the end of Wilkins's first two-year contract with the
Richmond Symphony, *Richmond News Leader* music critic Francis
Church wrote:

The Richmond Symphony's Young Performers Program is looking
onward and upward. In a time when music programs are being cut
back because of the sagging economy, when arts budgets are being
slashed, the symphony is making an act of faith. The catalyst is
Thomas Wilkins, the symphony's assistant conductor. When Wilkins speaks of what is planned for the youth orchestra program, he
means business.[8]

Now artistic director of the Symphony's Youth Program, Wilkins
saw himself as the common denominator. The Richmond Symphony
Youth Orchestra, the senior ensemble, would be renamed the Greater
Richmond Youth Symphony; the Junior Youth Orchestra would be
called the Young Artists Orchestra; the ensemble of primarily
elementary-school musicians would retain its name, the String
Sinfonietta. Wilkins intended to strengthen the ties between the
symphony's musicians and the young performers. He believed that

Symphony players should do more than merely give concerts. . . .
They must have a greater impact on the music education of the kids
in the community. There's not a professional ensemble in the country
that can survive without a strong youth program.

The local press believed that Wilkins would be able to bring this
about. He worked well with young people. He had wowed teachers
and pupils alike as he went "out into the hustings with Richmond
Symphony players to introduce young listeners, from elementary-
school age upwards, in the wonders of music."[9]

Thomas Wilkins was making a significant contribution to the
city of Richmond and its environs; he was a true asset to the Richmond Symphony's roster. In July 1991, his position title was
elevated to that of assistant conductor and a new two-year contract
was signed.

Beginning with the 1994–95 season, Wilkins joins the conducting staff as Resident Conductor of the Florida Orchestra in Tampa,
Florida.

Press Comments

*"He is a no-nonsense conductor—economical and concise in his every movement—and
his flair for programming should be emulated by some other folks at the symphony's
office."*

Richmond Times-Dispatch

"Under the skillful baton of Thomas A. Wilkins, the orchestra excelled."

Richmond Times-Dispatch

*"Wilkins and the orchestra deserve plaudits for making a historic day {'Viennese
Gala'} all the more significant, serving up the best 'champagne' this side of Vienna."*

Richmond Times-Dispatch

*"The marches of such composers as Tchaikovsky, Sousa, Elgar, Mendelssohn, Herbert,
etc., were made majestic under the magic baton of Maestro Wilkins."*

Richmond Afro-American

*"What's the most enjoyable concert given here this season? A top candidate would
have to be the Symphony Sundays performance by the Richmond Sinfonia under
Assistant Conductor Thomas Wilkins yesterday afternoon in the Virginia Museum
auditorium."*

Richmond News Leader

*"Thomas Wilkins . . . kept the music on the money . . . {H}e conducted efficiently and
with assurance. . . ."*

Richmond Times-Dispatch

Notes

1. Clarke Bustard, "Symphony Taps Wilkins As Assistant Conductor,"
   Richmond Times-Dispatch, Weekend, March 31, 1989, p. 1.
2. Personal letter to Wilkins, October 29, 1987.
3. Memorandum for Retention of Thomas Wilkins, University of
   Tennessee at Chattanooga, February 3, 1988.

4. Thomas Wilkins, "Arts Education Isn't Just A Frill," *Richmond News Leader,* May 23, 1991, p. 18.
5. Letter of Recommendation for Thomas Wilkins from Harold Farberman, November 1987.
6. Bustard, *op. cit.,* p. 4.
7. Clarke Bustard, "Upbeat: Personality Propels Symphony's Assistant Conductor," *Richmond Times-Dispatch,* January 14, 1990, p. 1, Section K.
8. Francis Church, "Richmond Symphony's Youth Program Raises Sights," *Richmond News Leader,* May 11, 1991., p. A 39.
9. *Ibid.*

Julius Penson Williams

JULIUS PENSON WILLIAMS

BIRTHDATE/PLACE: June 22, 1954; Bronx, New York.

EDUCATION: B.S., City University of New York, Lehman College (Music Education and Composition), 1977; M.Mus.Ed., Hartt School of Music, University of Hartford, 1980; Aspen Music Festival (Orchestral Conducting Scholarship), Summer 1984; Aspen Music Festival (Composition and Conducting Professional Fellowship), Summer 1985.

MAJOR INSTRUCTORS: Choral Technique—Carl Benjamin and John Motley; Orchestration—Fred Norman; Composition—John Corigliano, Charles Bell, and Coleridge-Taylor Perkinson; Piano—Anna Gelfand and Watson Morrison; Jazz Piano—Jaki Byard; Schillinger Jazz Arranging—Richard Benda (New School for Social Research); Orchestral and Choral Conducting—Murry Sidlin, Gerald Mack, Coleridge-Taylor Perkinson, Charles Bruck, Vytausus Marijosius, Hugh Ross, John Motley, and Kurt Klippstatter.

MAJOR APPOINTMENTS (Professorships, Lecturer/Clinician, Visiting Scholar, Artist-in-Residence): Wesleyan University (Middletown, Connecticut), 1979–80; Middlesex Community College (Middlesex, Connecticut), 1979–80; Artists' Collective (Hartford, Connecticut), 1980–86; Hartt School of Music, University of Hartford (Connecticut)—Composition, Piano, Theory, and Conducting, 1980–85; Repertory Community Orchestra, Hartt School of Music, 1982–84; Peabody Conservatory (Baltimore, Maryland), Summer 1983; Central Connecticut State University (New Britain, Connecticut), Summer 1986; University of Vermont (Burlington, Vermont), 1988; Music Director, Royal Ethiopian Philharmonic, 1992—.

ARTISTIC DIRECTOR: Festival of the Costa Del Sol (Spain), Summer 1987.

MUSIC DIRECTOR/CONDUCTOR: New York Fred Astaire Dance and Connecticut Arts Awards Ceremonies; Nutmeg Ballet Company (Torrington, Connecticut); Symphony Saint Paulia (1989); The Royal Ethiopian Philharmonic (debut performance, Washington, D.C., March 1992); New York State Summer School of Choral Studies (Western Connecticut State University), Summers 1989—.

GUEST CONDUCTOR: Opus, Inc., The Amor Artist Chamber Orchestra; Connecticut Opera Association; Camerata Youth Orchestra of New York; Torrington Festival Orchestra; Association of Connecticut Choruses; New

Haven, Savannah, Detroit, Tulsa, Knoxville, and Dallas Symphony Orchestras.

RECORDING: Bohuslav Martinu Philharmonic, Albany Records, "African American Composers," 1993.

AWARDS/FELLOWSHIPS/GRANTS: ASCAP Popular Award Grant for Music Composition, 1979–80, 1981–87; ASCAP Standard Award Grant, 1987–88; Astral Foundation Grants, 1985 and 1986; Aspen Music Festival, Professional Studies Fellowship, 1985; Outstanding Young Men of America Awards, 1982 and 1983.

TELEVISION JOURNALIST CHARLES KURALT stated the following on September 11, 1988:

> We are not accustomed to seeing a black musician with a baton in his hand. Black orchestra conductors are about as rare as black quarterbacks. Billy Taylor is about to introduce us to a man who would like to change that.[1]

These remarks led into jazz pianist/television personality Billy Taylor's introduction of Julius Williams, featured musical subject on the CBS television program "Sunday Morning."

Said Taylor:

> This jack of so many musical trades is Julius Williams . . . a gifted young American conductor and composer. He's been commissioned to compose music for major symphony orchestras, ballets, operas, soloists, and chamber groups. Julius has the demanding control and repertoire to be the conductor of a major orchestra.

On the subject of "jack-of-so-many-musical-trades," Williams himself commented:

> I'm really not. I just do music. I've grown up in an environment where I was able to do all different types of things—playing jazz, conducting concerts, writing, arranging for musicals, or being music director on Broadway. And so it comes naturally, being able to do so many different things.[2]

Such national exposure as "Sunday Morning" would serve as a major boost to Williams's conducting career.

Prominent recognition of Williams as a composer came earlier, in 1985, when maestro Zubin Mehta conducted the New York

Philharmonic in a performance of his "A Norman Overture." The performance was given at Harlem's Abyssinian Baptist Church, where Williams had previously served as assistant minister of music.[3]

Though Williams once aspired to be a rock star, the lack of sufficient challenge led to boredom. A more than adequate pianist, he used these skills in several Broadway shows and in 1982 appeared as piano soloist with the Albany Symphony Orchestra. He was engaged from time to time for appearances with pop artists Ashford and Simpson, soul performer James Brown, and jazz immortal Dizzy Gillespie. Of his eclectic background as performer, accompanist, teacher, composer, and conductor, Williams says, "such versatility was essential for survival in New York City."[4]

On the "Sunday Morning" telecast, Williams had more to say on the subject:

> My blackness has helped . . . playing in church, doing all different types of music. Just the black audience itself. When you are in front of a black audience, they don't let you get away with anything. You can't do anything half. . . . I think that has helped me as a conductor, because when you get in front of a symphony orchestra, they don't let you get up there and just wave your arms. You've got to know what you're doing and you have to do it well.[5]

Williams' formal training included a B.S. degree in music education and music composition from Lehman College of the City University of New York in 1977 and a M.Mus.Ed. degree in orchestral conducting from the Hartt School of Music of the University of Hartford in 1980, with piano as his major instrument. He was a scholarship student in orchestral conducting at the Aspen Music School during the summers of 1984 and 1985. He participated during the second summer as a professional fellow, concentrating in composition and conducting, a status that afforded Williams the opportunity to work with two Aspen Festival Orchestra conductors, Sergiu Comissiona and James DePreist.*

In 1984, for the second consecutive year, Williams was named conductor for the Connecticut Commission on the Arts Awards Ceremony. For this "second time around," the program featured tributes to two Connecticut composers, past and present: Charles Ives and Julius Williams. The occasion marked the opening of New Haven's new Shubert Theatre. The ceremony was broadcast the following evening on Connecticut's PBS-TV affiliate.[6]

Williams served as conductor for the Dallas Symphony Orchestra's 1986 "Symphony in Black," an annual project of the Junior Black Academy of Arts and Letters. The concert, the orchestra's fourth such event, began with Williams' "Toccatina" for string orchestra. With a Special Project grant from the Connecticut Commission on the Arts, Williams provided the score for the three-act ballet "Cinderella." Premiered May 2, 1987 in Torrington, Connecticut, the work was danced by members of the ten-year-old student dance company Nutmeg Ballet, for which Williams served as composer-in-residence, with an ensemble made up of New Haven Symphony Orchestra musicians. An additional performance took place at Yale's University Theatre. On this occasion, Julius Williams was on the podium.

Act I, Scene I, of his opera "Guinevere" was premiered as an Aspen Music Festival Opera Workshop event on August 3, 1985. Act I of the same opera was a part of a May 27, 1987, concert offering at Alice Tully Hall, Lincoln Center. On both occasions, Williams conducted.

Preparing the city of Savannah for the Savannah Symphony Orchestra's first annual Black Heritage Concert in February 1987, the local newspaper conducted an interview with guest conductor Williams. In an article titled "Don't Expect the Blues From This Conductor," Arts/Entertainment writer Rosanne Howard pointed out that many concertgoers were in for a surprise if they were "expecting to hear gospel music, spirituals, jazz or anything remotely associated with easy listening."

During the course of the interview, Williams pointed out that he felt it important to emphasize black contributions in the classical tradition. His program therefore included works by black composers Adolphus Hailstork, Coleridge-Taylor Perkinson, the Chevalier de Saint-Georges (b. 1739 of Franco-African parentage), Julia Perry, Ulysses Kay, and William Grant Still. Though he was excited about the Savannah Symphony's scheduling of the Black Heritage Concert (the first of a series of regularly scheduled February events), Williams indicated that such concerts can be "discouraging because such occasions ultimately can be limiting for a black musician seeking acceptance in the musical mainstream."[7]

A composer/conductor of strong convictions, Williams's goal was to "one day conduct a major orchestra in a metropolitan setting." His wife, Lenora, who holds degrees in music and biology, elected to pursue medicine as a career. Remarked husband Julius:

She didn't want to be poor like me. . . . Most of the time I get a lot of work and the money flows in. At other times, I'm broke. But that's the fun part—the uncertainty. It's the excitement that keeps me going.[8]

Some of the uncertainty was removed when he joined the University of Vermont's staff in the Fall of 1988, as artist-in-residence. According to the University's president:

[Julius Williams] is the quintessence of everything we hoped for in this program. He is creative; he is exciting; he likes students; he reaches out to the campus community. He brings a flare and an excitement, because he is clearly a very promising artist, already making his place.[9]

In early January 1989, the author received a letter (dated December 1988) soliciting "Friends" for Saintpaulia, Inc. from opera and concert singer Esther Hinds and announcing the newly-formed organization's inaugural concert, on January 14, 1989. The January 14 concert would take place at New York City's Apollo Theatre, followed on the January 15 and 16 by concerts at the Brooklyn Academy of Music and Carnegie Hall, respectively. The concerts would feature a 120-member Sacred and Concert Choir (Voices Saintpaulia) and a symphony orchestra conducted by Julius Williams. The featured works would be Brahm's "Schicksalslied," Verdi's "Te Deum" and "Stabat Mater," and black composer Undine Smith Moore's "Scenes from the Life of a Martyr."

A late 1989 tribute at Lehman College to black composer Ulysses Kay (distinguished professor emeritus of music at Lehman) featured a concert adaptation of Kay's opera "Jubilee." On the podium was Maestro Julius Williams.

At Constitution Hall in Washington, D.C., on March 27, 1992, the newly created Royal Ethiopian Philharmonic, "by special appointment of His Imperial Majesty Amha Selassie I, Emperor of Ethiopa . . . in response to the guest of the Ethiopian Royal Family-in-Exile," made its debut appearance. The fifty-piece "multi-ethnic, multi-national orchestra" was conducted by Julius Williams.[10]

Reaching a wider audience, Julius Williams was conductor on the 1993 Albany Records release, "African American Composers." Conducting the Bohuslav Martinu Philharmonic, the compact disc featured works by Harry T. Burleigh, David Baker, Adolphus Hailstork, Gary Nash, and Williams.

Only time will tell if these various conducting opportunities will move Williams closer toward his professional goal. In the meantime, he continues to compose and enjoy notification of occasional performances of his many compositions.

Press Comments

"Williams led a dramatic performance . . . and the Dallas Symphony played well."
Dallas Times Herald

"Julius Williams . . . a rising star . . . {an} auspicious debut, . . ."
Savannah News-Press

"Conductor Julius P. Williams has gotten a wonderful sound from the {Connecticut Opera} ensemble and the orchestra."
Hartford Courant

"Williams was a pleasure to watch. His exciting direction was mirrored in the Vermont Symphony which seemed to become enkindled . . ."
Burlington Free Press

Notes

1. On May 15, 1988, television journalist/flutist Eugenia Zukerman did a feature story on the same CBS program "Sunday Morning" on black conductor James DePreist.
2. William "Billy" Taylor, feature story on Julius Williams, September 11, 1988, "Sunday Morning," CBS.
3. Kathy Rivard, "Local Composer Receives Boost in Musical Career," *Bristol Press,* May 10, 1985, p. 7. Note: Since 1980, the New York Philharmonic has performed one concert yearly at the Abyssinian Baptist Church, as a part of its outreach efforts. In more recent years, this annual event has taken place at the Apollo Theater in Harlem.
4. C. W. Vrtacek, "The Music Man Behind Torrington's New Ballet," *Litchfield-County Times,* October 31, 1986, p. 23.
5. "Sunday Morning," *op. cit.*
6. "Williams to Conduct," *Bristol/Valley Press,* October 19, 1984, p. 13.

7. Rosanne Howard, "Don't Expect the Blues From This Conductor," *Savannah Morning News,* January 30, 1987, pp. 1, 10.

8. Rivard, *op. cit.*

9. "Sunday Morning," *op. cit.*

10. Program, newly created Royal Ethiopian Philharmonic's debut performance, March 27, 1992.

Warren George Wilson

WARREN GEORGE WILSON

BIRTHDATE/PLACE: October 21, 1934; New York, New York.

EDUCATION: B.S. and M.S. Juilliard School of Music, 1959 and 1960.

MAJOR INSTRUCTORS: Adele Marcus, Piano; Sergius Kagen, Louis Persinger, Pierre Bernac, Paul Ulanoswsky, Vocal and Instrumental Chamber Music Repertoire.

MAJOR APPOINTMENTS: Music Director, Turnau Opera Company (Woodstock, New York), 1961–1969; The David Ensemble (founder), 1969–73; Associate Conductor, Lake George Opera Festival, 1973–75; Music Director, Opera Program, Boston University, 1975–1984.

GUEST CONDUCTOR: Dallas Symphony, Opera Ebony, Wolf Trap Festival, Opera Theater of Boston University.

PIANIST FOR: Reri Grist, Shirley Verrett, Anna Moffo, William Warfield, Mary Costa, Mattiwilda Dobbs. Pianist for all U.S.A. entries in the Tschaikowsky International Competitions, 1976.

AWARDS/HONORS: Grants from Hattie M. Strong Foundation, National Association of Negro Musicians; John Hay Whitney Fellowship.

WARREN GEORGE WILSON WAS BORN IN NEW YORK CITY and grew up in the Bronx and on Long Island. He describes his West Indian immigrant parents as "devoted and supportive." Of them he says, "Like most immigrants, they were devoted to the idea that their children have everything possible, and I did."[1]

But emotional and material support for Wilson's musical aspirations were not all that his parents provided; they also imbued him with a confidence that he could succeed based on his own talents, and not because of other considerations. Wilson reports that he was ". . . instilled with the feeling that I could do anything; that being black was not a problem. I would be lying to say it hasn't caused some difficulties, but I decided long ago that I wouldn't take time to focus on them. I've had lots of opportunities that other people haven't had."[2]

One of those opportunities was studying piano with Adele Marcus at the Juilliard School of Music. Wilson actually began his study with Marcus while he was a student at City College of New York, preparing for a career as a psychiatrist. Music gradually emerged as preeminent, and Wilson enrolled as a full-time student at Juilliard, where he earned both bachelor's and master's degrees.

After his Juilliard studies, Wilson embarked upon a multifaceted musical career. He served as the musical director of the Turnau Opera Company in Woodstock, New York (a post he held from 1961 to 1969). He began to perform in recital with prominent vocalists, including soprano Anna Moffo, black bass-baritone William Warfield, black coloratura soprano Mattiwilda Dobbs, and black mezzo-soprano Shirley Verrett. (He continues his collaboration with Miss Verrett, and in May 1991 performed two concerts with her in Moscow.) In 1976 he was chosen by the International Institute of Education as pianist to accompany all entrants from the United States in the Tschaikowsky International Competitions in Moscow.

In 1969, Wilson founded The David Ensemble, a choral chamber music group that performed in the United States and England. In 1975 Wilson became music director of the opera program at Boston University, a position he found stimulating but extremely time-consuming. However, Wilson continued the accompanying and other performing (including White House engagements), commuting back and forth between New York and Boston until the mid-1980s. During his tenure in Boston, Wilson conducted orchestral performances of twenty-seven operas, in addition to semi-annual scene recitals.

While occupying permanent posts, Warren George Wilson developed an active career as a guest conductor. In July 1982, he conducted the new production of "Cosi Fan Tutte" that inaugurated the new Barns Theatre at the Wolf Trap Festival Park in Vienna, Virginia, and during the 1983–84 season he conducted the New York company of Opera Ebony in "Faust" at Wolf Trap. In July 1984, Wilson made his debut with the Dallas Symphony, and in June 1985 conducted Opera Ebony in Saint-Saens' "Samson and Delilah." Of the performance, *Philadelphia Inquirer* music critic Daniel Webster wrote:

> Last night was the local debut of conductor Warren George Wilson. He is a well-routined conductor who was able to hold together the large forces involved with considerable skill. The chorus . . . presented a challenge which Wilson met ably.[3]

Later that month he conducted Opera Ebony in the world premiere of black composer Dorothy Rudd Moore's "Frederick Douglass."

During this period, Wilson conducted a series of concerts focused on the music of Bach and Mozart and employing the musical forces of the Boys Choir of Harlem, the Orchestra of Saint Luke, and soloists.

Wilson's guest conducting continued in 1986 with a production of "Madame Butterfly" in New York, and then seventeen performances of a new staging of "Porgy and Bess" for the Theatro Municipal in Rio de Janeiro. In 1987, Wilson conducted the New York premiere of Ned Rorem's chamber opera "Hearing" in concert version.

Throughout his career, Warren George Wilson has expressed his particular dedication to music of the 20th century and has either commissioned or been responsible for the commissioning of works by Thomas Pasatieri, Henri Sauguet, Ned Rorem, and black composers George Walker and Hale Smith.

Press Comments

"Warren George Wilson is a master of understatement, tact, exquisite detailing and refinement."

San Francisco Chronicle

"This was arresting music making that was sheer pleasure. Debussy once described Bach's style as 'the divine arabesque.' Mr. Wilson's conducting created just this kind of sinuous accentuation and athletic grace."

New York Times

"Every element of Opera Ebony's world premiere of Dorothy Rudd Moore's FREDERICK DOUGLASS bespoke poise, vigor, even nobility—precisely the qualities of the black abolitionist and journalist whose story provides the central action of the opera . . . the orchestra played with generous warmth under Warren George Wilson."

Opera News

"With the superb orchestra under the baton of Warren George Wilson, the outstanding vocal ensemble poured out streams of glorious sound in arias, duets and trios . . ."

Amsterdam News

Notes

1. Michael Kimmelman, " 'Samson' conductor making debut here," *Philadelphia Inquirer,* June 7, 1985, p. 1D.
2. *Ibid.*
3. Daniel Webster, "Opera Ebony Marks 10th Anniversary," *Philadelphia Inquirer,* June 7, 1985, p. 3E.

PART IV: MORE CONDUCTOR PROFILES

The following conductors are included here (rather than in the previous sections) for any of the following reasons: sufficient information was unavailable, their conducting activities were secondary to their other musical or nonmusical involvements, or their conducting associations were peripheral. Nevertheless, their contribution to the conducting universe merits recognition and recall.

Alton Augustus Adams

(Born November 4, 1889, in St. Thomas, Virgin Islands; died 1987 in St. Thomas.) Adams was the first black bandmaster in the United States Navy; his band was the Navy's first black unit. He began his musical studies at age nine with self-instruction on the flageolet. He later studied flute and was introduced to band leadership by the shoemaker with whom he apprenticed. His more advanced training was acquired through correspondence courses: Diploma, University of Pennsylvania; B.Mus., University Extension Conservatory of Music in Chicago; School of Musical Theory of Carnegie Hall in New York City; and the Royal Academy of Music in London. In 1910 he formed his first band—the St. Thomas Juvenile Band—which he developed into a first-rate ensemble. In 1917, when the United States purchased the Virgin Islands and placed them under U.S. supervision, Adams and his band entered the Navy as a unit, with Adams as Chief Musician. He served during the years 1917–37 and 1942–47. His band toured the United States and the West Indies and made radio appearances in New York City, Boston, and Washington. Adams was a composer of marches and contributor of articles to *Jacob's Band Monthly* (he was editor of the Band Department), *Metronome,* and *Army and Navy Musician.* He organized the Virgin Island's public school music program (1918) and served as music supervisor, 1918–31. (See Samuel A. Floyd, Jr., "Alton Augustus Adams: The First Black Bandmaster in the U.S. Navy," *The Black Perspective in Music,* Fall 1977, pp. 173–187.)

Edward Gilbert Anderson

(Born February 20, 1874, in Still Pond, Kent County, Maryland; died December 2, 1926, in Chester, Pennsylvania.) Anderson was active as an orchestral conductor in both Philadelphia, Pennsylvania (Philadelphia Concert Orchestra) and New York City (New Amsterdam Musical Association, Clef Club Orchestra, Harlem Symphony Orchestra, and the Renaissance Theater Orchestra).

Hallie Anderson

(Born 1885 in Lynchburg, Virginia; died 1927 in New York City.) Anderson distinguished herself as a conductor, pianist, and organist.

As regularly advertised in the *New York Age* in the early years of this century, Anderson assembled and led "orchestras for all occasions"—festivals, picnics, dances, and riverboats. She directed a five-piece male orchestra at Harlem's Lafayette Theatre in 1914 and a female band at the same theatre in 1919. During the 1920s, Anderson directed theatre orchestras in Philadelphia, Pennsylvania and served as organist at Harlem's Douglas Theatre in the late teens and early twenties.

Joseph G. Anderson

(Born c. 1816 in Philadelphia, Pennsylvania; died April 30, 1873, in Philadelphia.) He was initially associated with the Frank Johnson* String and Brass Bands in Philadelphia. A flutist, violinist, and cornet à piston player, upon Johnson's death (1844), he assumed leadership of the band. Anderson was employed by the government to train brass bands for black regiments stationed at Camp William Penn during the Civil War.

Lovie Austin (née Cora Calhoun)

(Born 1887 in Chattanooga, Tennessee; died 1972 in Chicago, Illinois.) Lovie Austin was a pioneering woman jazz musician and a consummate artist. She studied music at Knoxville and Roger Williams Colleges (Tennessee). Her early years were spent touring the vaudeville circuit, eventually settling in Chicago in the 1920s. She accompanied the world's finest blues singers, including Ida Cox, Gertrude "Ma" Rainey, Alberta Hunter, Bertha "Chippie" Hill, Edmonia Henderson, and Ethel Waters, as pianist or as leader of her own combo, the Blues Serenaders. She composed, arranged, and recorded extensively. Throughout the 1920s and 1930s, Austin worked as musical director of the Monogram, Gem, and Joyland Theaters, all in Chicago. The late pianist Mary Lou Williams said of Austin, "My entire concept was based on the few times I was around Lovie Austin. She was a fabulous woman and a fabulous musician, too. I don't believe there's any woman around now who could compete with her. She was a greater talent than many men of this period." (Liner notes for the album "Jazz Women: A Feminist Retrospective," Stash, ST-109).

David N. Baker

(Born December 21, 1931, in Indianapolis, Indiana.) Known best as an extremely prolific composer, David Baker is also a performer (trombone, tuba, bass, and cello), author, and educator. He has been commissioned by such artists and ensembles as Janos Starker, Josef Gingold, the Saint Paul Chamber Orchestra, and the New York Philharmonic and has authored more than fifty books on jazz. He is coeditor of the extremely valuable publication *The Black Composer Speaks* (Scarecrow, 1978). Baker has headed the jazz program at Indiana University School of Music since 1966, where he holds the rank of distinguished professor. As a clinician, his services are utilized worldwide. Baker is president of the National Jazz Service Organization, a Presidentially appointed member of the National Council on the Arts (1986–92), and a member of the Board of Directors of the American Symphony Orchestra League. He is co-musical director (with Gunther Schuller) of The Smithsonian Jazz Masterworks Orchestra, organized in 1991 as orchestra-in-residence at the Smithsonian's National Museum of American History.

Joyce Brown

(Born December 1, 1920, in New York, New York.) Conductor, pianist, composer, and arranger, Joyce Brown began studying piano at age three and later studied violin, cello, trumpet, saxophone, organ, and voice. She studied at New York College of Music, Columbia University Teachers College, and New York University. She was active in vocal and instrumental activities at Salem United Methodist Church in New York City. Brown served as music director at the city's Latin Quarter for 11 years and worked in the same capacity for singers Napoleon Reed, Joyce Bryant, Norman Atkins, and Diahann Carroll. She served briefly on the staff of CBS; was tour conductor of the Broadway shows "Golden Boy," "Hallelujah Baby," and "How Green Was My Valley"; and was music director of the Alvin Ailey Ballet Company. In March 1970, Joyce Brown became "the first black woman to conduct the opening of a Broadway musical," namely, "Purlie."

James "Tim" Brymn

(Born 1881, in Kingston, North Carolina; died 1946 in New York, New York.) Brymn was musical director of various George Walker and Bert Williams shows; leader of the 350th Field Artillery Regiment Band, known as the Seventy Black Devils; and a composer. Publicity concerning the Seventy Black Devils reads: "The only colored aggregation of musicians to appear before President Wilson and General Pershing by special request" during the Chief Executive's visit to France for the opening of the Peace Conference. He was often referred to as "Mr. Jazz Himself." The band is credited with having "introduced jazz in France" and was a jazz sensation in all parts of the Allied countries. The group made a triumphant return to the States with an appearance at The Academy of Music in Philadelphia. Its rival band was James Reese Europe's* 369th Infantry Band. Brymn led a twenty-piece jazz band at the New York Roof Garden in 1915.

George Byrd

(Born 1927.) Since the early 1950s, Byrd's professional activity has taken place primarily abroad, leading orchestras and opera companies: France, Belgium, Switzerland, England, West Germany, East Germany, Denmark, Norway, Sweden, Poland, and Yugoslavia. For a brief period, he served as assistant conductor of the American Ballet Theatre (1968–???). He conducted the Symphony of the New World in New York City in December 1971. With assistance from UNESCO, Byrd participated in the establishment of a music school in Ethiopia in 1963. He graduated from the Juilliard School of Music in 1951 and engaged in further study at Paris National Conservatory. He also studied briefly with maestro Herbert von Karajan. (See Allen Hughes, "And Now There Are Three," the *New York Times,* March 17, 1968, p. D19.)

Bennett "Benny" Lester Carter

(Born August 8, 1907 in New York City.) Alto saxophonist/ trumpeter, composer/arranger, and bandleader Benny Carter was primarily self-taught. Some early guidance was provided by his mother and neighborhood teachers. Already a professional, he joined Horace Henderson's Wilberforce Collegians in 1925. In the early years he played with and arranged for Fletcher Henderson,* McKinney's Cotton Pickers, and Chick Webb.* Carter organized his first band in 1932, which included such future giants as Chu Berry, Dickie Wells, Ben Webster, Teddy Wilson, and Sid Catlett. In 1934 he moved to Europe (minus his band) where he did arrangements for the British Broadcasting Corporation. Carter organized and led a multinational jazz band in the Netherlands in 1937 and returned to the States in 1938. He formed a new orchestra in 1939 that took up residency at the Savoy Ballroom in Harlem. This band continued through much of 1940. Soon after, Carter left for the West Coast and settled permanently in Los Angeles. He continued to lead stellar orchestras that through the years included such brilliant performers (and future leaders) as Gerald Wilson, Snooky Young, J. J. Johnson, and Max Roach. As a bandleader, he received the nickname "The King" and was throughout his career held in high esteem by his peers. He was extremely successful as a composer and arranger, including scores for such films as "A Man Called Adam" and "Buck and the Preacher", and such television programs as "Ironside" and "Bob Hope Presents." During the 1970s, he frequently served as visiting professor: Yale, Cornell, and Princeton Universities. He received many honors and awards, including *Metronome* Poll and *Esquire* Awards, honorary doctorates from Princeton and Rutgers Universities, and the American Jazz Master Award (National Endowment for the Arts, 1988). (See M. Berger, E. Berger, and J. Patrick, *Benny Carter: A Life* in *American Music,* 2 volumes, Metuchen, N.J.: Scarecrow Press, 1982.)

Consuella Carter

(Born April 16, 1902, in Haynesville, Alabama; died January 22, 1989, in Clarksdale, Mississippi.) We associate the name Consuella Carter primarily with the International Sweethearts of Rhythm, a fully capable and highly competitive "ladies" jazz band. Though contemporary historians place emphasis on the group after April 1941 (at which time the band—under new leadership—severed its relationship with Piney Woods Country Life School and included many non-Piney Woods students and non-blacks), the foundation was laid by Consuella Carter. Organized in 1937 at Piney Woods Country Life School in Piney Woods, Mississippi, the band was touring extensively (and successfully) as early as 1938. The girls' ages ranged from fourteen to nineteen, all high school enrollees. Carter taught all of the instruments and directed the school's marching band as well as the school's "adventures into the world of jazz" (both male and female). She attended Snow Hill Institute (Alabama) prior to entering Piney Woods. Both Institutions offered "work-your-way-through" programs for Blacks. Preparation for a career in music began at age nineteen, with encouragement from the school's President, Laurence C. Jones (also conceiver of the idea of sending out student vocal and instrumental groups to be the school's traveling messengers and chief fundraisers). Carter received music degrees from Rust College and Vandercook College of Music. Her principal instrument was the trumpet. Following her years of teaching and band directing at Piney Woods, she joined the faculty of Coahoma Junior College and Agricultural High School in Clarksdale, Mississippi, from which she retired in 1976.

Paul Elliott Cobbs

Cobbs received the B.S. degree in instrumental music education from Wayne State University (1973), Master's degree and D.M.A. in symphonic conducting from the University of Washington (1980 and 1991). Additional conducting study took place in Austria, Germany, and Italy. His conducting career included associate conductor, Detroit Metropolitan Symphony Orchestra (1973–75); Music Director/Conductor, Everett (Washington) Youth Symphony Orchestra (1981–85); Festival Chamber Orchestra (1983—); Everett Symphony Orchestra (1984—); and the Junior Seattle Youth Symphony Orchestra (1987—).

Walter F. Craig

(Born 1854; Died 192?) Solo and ensemble violinist, conductor, and presenter of black talent, Craig established himself in New York City as leader of society dance orchestras. He appeared throughout the country as solo violinist with black vocal talent, e.g., Sissieretta Jones ("Black Patti"), Harry T. Burleigh, and Flora Batson-Bergen. Craig was the first Black admitted to the Musician's Mutual Protective Union (1886).

Jacques Constantin Deburque

Deburque was a violinist, music educator, and co-conductor of the Negro Philharmonic Society of New Orleans, an 1830s all-Negro group of instrumentalists of over 100 members. The group was "organized for the study and presentation of the classics." Members of the group provided music at the Theatre de la Renaissance for "free colored." On various occasions, the orchestra was augmented by professional white musicians. Wrote James Monroe Trotter in his 1881 publication *Music and Some Highly Musical People:* "This was really a scholarly body of musicians, with whom the very best artists of any race might well be proud to associate" (New York, N.Y.: Johnson Reprint Corporation, 1968, p. 351).

Edmond Dédé

(Born 1827 in New Orleans; died 1903 in Bordeaux, France.) A violinist who studied at Paris Conservatory and settled in Bordeaux, France in 1857, Dédé became music director of the L'Alcazar Theatre Orchestra. Before leaving for France, he made his living as a cigarmaker. Dédé returned to New Orleans briefly in 1893 to give a series of concerts.

Leonard DePaur

(Born November 18, 1915 in Summit, New Jersey.) Conductor (choral and instrumental), composer, lecturer, writer, and arts administrator, DePaur studied at the Institute of Musical Art, Columbia University, the Université Laval, and privately with Henry Cowell, Hall Johnson, Sergei Radamsky, and Pierre Monteux. Multigifted DePaur was the recipient of numerous honors and awards: honorary doctorates from Lewis and Clark College and

Morehouse College; New York City Mayor's Award of Honor for Arts and Culture; and an Award of Merit from the University of Pennsylvania Glee Club. His many musical activities have been featured in such national publications as *Time, Newsweek, Musical America, Etude, Ebony, Biographical Dictionary of Afro-American and African Musicians,* and *Who's Who Among Black Americans.*

Amsterdam News (New York City) music critic and journalist Raoul Abdul did a feature article for the paper in February 1989 entitled "Leonard DePaur: Lifetime of Musical Achievement," based on a recent interview. Abdul concluded the article with this inquiry of the musical achiever: "[Had] he ever stopped to think of possible racial barriers before he set about a project in the musical world?" DePaur's response was, "It never entered my mind that I couldn't accomplish something to which I set my mind. I just went ahead and did it." Perhaps best remembered for his leadership of the famous DePaur Infantry Chorus, he "went ahead and did" many things: lecturing, commenting (television, radio, and film), teaching, consulting (Epcot Center, Walt Disney World; New York City, Board of Education; Cultural Development, Republic of Tunisia); and co-chairing the American Committee for the First World Festival of Negro Art in Dakar, Senegal.

DePaur was assistant conductor of the famous Hall Johnson Choir (1932–36) and music director of the Federal Theater Project in New York City (1936–39). In 1943 he became choral director of the Air Force show "Winged Victory," an association which led to the creation of and conducting responsibilities for the DePaur Infantry Chorus (1947–68). DePaur's orchestral experiences included appearances with the Cincinnati, Miami Beach, and Minnesota Symphony Orchestras; Symphony of the New World; Buffalo Philharmonic; Orchestra of America; and Opera/South. He conducted the National Company of the production "Hallelujah Baby" and guest conducted the Broadway and national tour of the production "Purlie."

According to *New York Times* music journalist Raymond Ericson, DePaur "was on the verge of getting a position as associate conductor with a Midwestern orchestra. . . . [Said DePaur] 'if there had been one more race riot, I would have gotten the job. As it was, things quieted down, the job offer was reduced in status, with too little pay, and I had to refuse'" ("Changing Lincoln Center's Image," *New York Times,* October 10, 1971, p. D29).

In 1970 DePaur was appointed Associate Director of Lincoln Center's (New York City) International University Choral Festival and worked with the Center's Street Theater Festival. He was soon appointed Lincoln Center's Director of Community Relations. This affiliation continued until his retirement in 1988.

Walter Henri Dyett

(Born 1901 in St. Joseph, Missouri; died 1969 in Chicago.) Dyett began studying piano and violin at an early age and continued his studies at the University of California at Los Angeles, Vandercook School of Music (B.Mus.), and Chicago Musical College (M.Mus.). Settling in Chicago, Dyett played with groups led by such prominent musical Chicagoans as Erskine Tate, Dave Peyton, and Charles Cooke. In 1922, he began leading his own organizations, most prominent of which were the Pickford Orchestra, the U.S. Eighth Infantry Band, and the 184th Field Artillery Band. He is perhaps best remembered for his leadership of two Chicago high school instrumental music programs: Wendell Phillips (1931–35) and DuSable (1935–69). Under his guidance were such outstanding talents as singer/pianist Nat "King" Cole, tenor saxophonist Gene Ammons, bassist Richard Davis, and flutist Harold Jones.

Mercer Kennedy Ellington

(Born March 11, 1919, in Washington, D.C.) Trumpeter, composer/arranger, manager, and son of Edward Kennedy "Duke" Ellington, young Mercer Ellington received training from members of his father's band and at the Institute of Musical Arts (the Juilliard School of Music). He originally played alto saxophone but switched to trumpet under the influence of Charles "Cootie" Williams. Intermittently he led his own groups from 1939 until officially joining Duke's band in 1965 as business manager/trumpeter. Mercer Ellington had previously played with the band in 1950 and between 1955 and 1959. After his father's death in 1974, he became the band's leader and devoted additional energies to preserving his father's legacy.

Anthony Elliott

Anthony Elliott is a solo, chamber, and orchestral cellist, as well as a cello instructor. Prizewinner in the 1979 Cassado Competition in Italy and winner of the First Emanuel Feuermann International Cello Competition (1987), Elliott has appeared as soloist with such outstanding orchestras as the Detroit, Minnesota, Vancouver, and CBC Toronto Symphony Orchestras. He served a five-year tenure as associate principal cellist with the Minnesota Orchestra and four years as principal cellist of the Vancouver Symphony Orchestra. He previously served on the faculty of Western Michigan University, where he conducted the University Symphony Orchestra and currently serves on the faculty of the School of Music at the University of Houston. Elliott participated in master conducting classes led by André Previn and Pierre Boulez and subsequently established himself as a conductor to be reckoned with. While at Western Michigan University, he conducted fully staged productions of Menotti's "The Consul" and Mozart's "Cosi Fan Tutte." He served seven seasons as assistant music director of the Marrowstone Music Festival. Other conducting affiliations include music leadership of the Vancouver Chamber Players, the All-Michigan Honors Orchestra, the University of Houston's Symphony Orchestra, the Michigan Youth Arts Festival Orchestra, and the Blue Lake Fine Arts Festival Faculty Orchestra.

Wendell English

English served as Music Director of the Concert Orchestra of Concerts in Black and White, Inc., based in Boston, Massachusetts during the late 1970s.

Harrison Herbert Ferrell

(Born c. 1901 in Chicago; died November 18, 1976, in Institute, West Virginia.) Harrison Ferrell began studying the violin at age eight and made his debut as a violin soloist at age 14. In later years he made his living as a college language professor and administrator, having obtained the B.A., M.A., and Ph.D. degrees from Northwestern University. He founded and directed the Ferrell Symphony Orchestra (Chicago) in 1923 and continued the affiliation until 1928, at which time he became head of the Language Department at West Virginia State College. He returned frequently to Chicago to conduct Ferrell Symphony Orchestra rehearsals and to stage various concerts. Ferrell organized and led the West Virginia College Strings (1939–46). Worth noting is the fact that Ferrell was one of three recipients of the National Association of Negro Musicians' (NANM) first Scholarship Awards (1927), along with Marian Anderson (voice) and J. Harold Brown (composition).

Theodore Finney

(Born September 1, 1837, in Columbus, Ohio; Died May 1899 in Detroit, Michigan). Most of Finney's professional life was spent in Detroit where he directed and managed many society dance bands and served the instrumental needs for all of Detroit (both black and white). Finney's Famous Orchestra toured extensively throughout the Midwest. Following his death, Finney Orchestras were led by former members Ben Shook and Fred Stone.

William Fitzpatrick

(Born c. 1950 in California.) Fitzpatrick grew up in Nashville, Tennessee, where he studied the violin and became a member of the Cremona Strings, Nashville Youth Orchestra, and, later, the Nashville Symphony. He received a diploma from the Juilliard School of Music and organized the New York String Quartet. With Fitzpatrick as the group's first violinist, the quartet was in residence at the Aspen Music Festival and the University of Southern California at Irvine (late 1970s–early 1980s). He has appeared as violin soloist with the Midland-Odessa (Texas), American, Irvine and Nashville Symphony Orchestras. He was conductor of the Nashville Symphony Chamber Orchestra, assistant conductor and associate concertmaster with the Nashville Symphony Orchestra (1983–84), and for a brief period, a member of the faculty at the Sewanee Summer Music Center (Tennessee). Since 1984, Fitzpatrick has established residence in France, fulfilling varying conducting assignments and performing as a solo recitalist. Other activities include artistic director of l'Ensemble Fitzpatrick (formerly l'Ensemble des Deux Mondes) and Professor of Chamber Music at the American Conservatory in Fontainebleau.

Frank (Benjamin) Foster III

(Born September 23, 1928, in Cincinnati, Ohio.) Tenor saxophonist, composer, arranger, band leader Foster originally played clarinet and alto saxophone. He was for many years principal soloist with the Count Basie* Band. He formed his own band in 1964, an organization that came to be known as The Loud Minority. Since 1986, Foster has successfully fronted the Count Basie Band.

William Patrick Foster

(Born August 25, 1919, in Kansas City, Kansas.) Band director, clinician, lecturer, adjudicator, composer Foster has been professionally active since the late 1940s. For more than four decades, he has been a preeminent band director, credited with revolutionizing marching band techniques. For a number of years, Foster has been chairperson of the Department of Music and director of bands at Florida A & M University. He and his band have been featured in *Ebony* Magazine and *The Chronicle of Higher Education,* as well as on CBS's "60 Minutes" and ABC's "20/20." Foster received the B.Mus.Ed. from the University of Kansas, M.A. from Wayne State University, and the Ed.D. from Columbia University. He is a former president of The College Band Directors National Association, a former member of the Florida Arts Council, and special assistant to the Secretary of State of Florida for Cultural Affairs. Among the many honors that he has received are the national Kappa Kappa Psi Band Fraternity's Distinguished Service to Music Medal; United States Achievement Academy's (USAA) American Achievement Hall of Fame Award; and induction into the Hall of Fame, Florida Music Educators Association. He has been director of the McDonald's All-American High School Band and guest conductor of the United States Air Force Band, Gamergori Municipal Band of Japan, United States Army Band, and the United States Inter-service Band.

Harry Lawrence Freeman

(Born October 9, 1869, in Cleveland, Ohio; died March 21, 1954, in New York City) Though Freeman is perhaps best remembered as a composer (salon pieces, ballets, cantatas, songs, instrumental pieces, and no fewer than fourteen operas), he was also a music director for various vaudeville and musical comedy companies, including the Cole-Johnson Brothers Company and Pekin Stock Company. Additionally, he conducted performances of many of his own operas.

D. Jerlene Harding

Harding is founder and director of the Tidewater Area Musicians (TAM) Youth Orchestra, organized in 1975 to perform at the Regional Conference of the National Association of Negro Musicians, Inc. Made up of high school, college, and community musicians, TAM is now an annual feature at the National Association of Negro Musician's annual meetings. Members are residents of the Tidewater Virginia cities of Norfolk, Portsmouth, and Chesapeake. Harding is a string teacher and orchestra director in the public schools of Portsmouth.

Charles Harris

Harris was the first conductor of the Baltimore (Maryland) City Colored Orchestra, a 1930s organization maintained by the city's Municipal Department of Music for its "colored" citizens.

Erskine ("The Hawk") Ramsey Hawkins

(Born July 26, 1914, in Birmingham, Alabama; died November 11, 1993, in Willingboro, New Jersey.) Hawkins began playing trumpet at age 13. He enrolled at Alabama State Teachers College (now Alabama State University) in Montgomery and played with the 'Bama State Collegians. The band made its first real impact in New York City in 1936, with Hawkins as leader. The band recorded extensively (Vocalion and Bluebird) and is best remembered for its recording of "Tuxedo Junction" and "After Hours." The Hawkins Band was one of the most popular of the swing era (particularly at the Savoy Ballroom in Harlem), remaining in the forefront from the late 1930s until the early 1950s. Beginning in 1953, Hawkins led various small ensembles, with Hawkins big bands being reassembled for special occasions. Early in his career, he was billed as "The Twentieth Century Gabriel." Alabama State University awarded Hawkins an honorary doctorate in 1947 and issued a "Certificate of Accomplishment in Music" in 1973. Other honors included the *Pittsburgh Courier* Award (1949); Mayor's Award, Birmingham (1972); and induction into Birmingham's Hall of Arts (1973).

William Henderson

Violinist, composer, arranger, and studio musician Henderson is founder and music director of the Los Angeles Modern String Orchestra. He received his education at Howard University (B.Mus.) and the University of Southern California (Ph.D.). He was professionally active in Hollywood, California during the 1970s and 1980s.

Robert Jackson

(Born c. 1949 in Portsmouth, Virginia.) Though best known as a bass-baritone, Jackson was music director of the 1970 world company production of "Porgy and Bess," touring twenty-two European countries. He made his conducting debut as music director for the Gold Mask production of "Little Mary Sunshine." He previously served as consultant to New York City Mayor's Council Against Poverty. Jackson received the B.A. degree in theater arts and music from Adelphi University and the M.A. degree from New York University.

Thaddeus ("Thad") Joseph Jones

(Born March 28, 1923, in Pontiac, Michigan; died August 20, 1986, in Copenhagen, Denmark.) Thad Jones, trumpeter, cornetist, flugelhornist, composer, and bandleader, was one of the three famous Jones brothers: Thad, drummer Elvin, and pianist Hank. Self-taught, Thad played professionally with both of his brothers. He also played with Charles Mingus's Jazz Composers Workshop (1954–55) and Count Basie's* Orchestra (1954–63). Along with Mel Lewis, Thad Jones organized an eighteen-piece band in 1965. The band played at New York City's Village Vanguard for over a decade. The band later toured the college and festival circuit, Japan, the U.S.S.R. and Europe. Settling in Denmark in 1978, Jones led the big band Radioens and, in 1979, the Thad Jones Eclipse, also a big band. He returned to America in 1985 to assume leadership of the Count Basie Orchestra, which he fronted until his death in 1986. (See W. R. Stokes, "Thad Jones: At the Helm of the Basie Band," *Jazz Times,* June 1985, p. 10.)

Andrew ("Andy") Dewey Kirk

(Born May 28, 1898, in Newport, Kentucky; died December 11, 1992 in New York, New York.) Kirk grew up in Denver, Colorado, and as a child, studied piano and alto saxophone. For a brief period he played tuba and bass saxophone with George Morrison's Band. Later Kirk joined a band led by Terrence Holder. When Holder left the band (1929), Kirk assumed the leadership. By this time, the group had adopted the name Clouds of Joy. Though the band was most popular in the Midwest, it toured nationwide and recorded extensively. Kirk's Twelve Clouds of Joy existed from 1930 to 1948 and was one of Kansas City's most important units. Its most popular member was Mary Lou Williams (pianist/arranger, 1929–42). Andrew Dewey Kirk was the recipient of an American Jazz Masters Award from the National Endowment for the Arts in 1991. (See Andy Kirk, *Twenty Years on Wheels,* Ann Arbor: The University of Michigan Press, 1989.)

Ulysses Kirksey

Cellist/conductor Kirksey joined the Petersburg (Virginia) Symphony Orchestra in 1980 as principal cellist. He was named the orchestra's assistant conductor in 1986 and principal conductor in

1989 (following the sudden death of its founder/conductor F. Nathaniel Gatlin).* A native of Richmond, Virginia, Kirksey received his Bachelor's and Master's degrees in cello performance from Manhattan School of Music. He studied conducting and orchestral repertoire with Anton Coppola, Nicholas Flagello, and Lukas Foss. As a cellist, Kirksey toured Europe with the Pro Arte Chamber Orchestra (1971 and 1974); was a member of the Symphony of the New World, and the Alvin Ailey and Paul Taylor Dance Company Orchestras (NYC); and upon his return to Richmond, substituted with the Richmond Symphony Orchestra. He also served as a member of the chamber group Trio Pro Viva (specializing in the music of black composers) and the Richmond Chamber Players, and performed as a baroque cellist for the Governor's Palace Music Series in Williamsburg (Virginia). In addition to his earlier experience as assistant conductor of the Petersburg Symphony, Kirksey frequently conducted the Richmond Community Orchestra.

Irene Armstrong Kitchings

(Born in Marietta, Ohio; died in the mid-70s in Cleveland, Ohio.) Kitchings is perhaps best remembered as a pianist, songwriter ("Some Other Spring"), friend of Billie Holiday and, for a period, wife of Teddy Wilson. She is here included because of her band leadership (Chicago, 1920s). Kitchings began studying the piano at a very early age and was soon assisting at Sunday school. She moved first to Muncie, Indiana, then Detroit, and at about age eighteen, to Chicago (during the years of Prohibition). Within a short time, she was leading a band (all-male) at the Vogue, later another at the Cottage Cafe, and still later, another at the Vogue again. In the early 1930s, she met and married pianist Teddy Wilson, moving with him to New York City and moving out of the business except as a songwriter. She nevertheless fronted an all-male band that performed at the 1933 World's Fair. In later years she became afflicted with Eale's disease, eventually losing her sight. (See Stanley Dance, *The World of Earl Hines,* New York: Charles Scribner's Sons, 1977: entry "Irene Kitchings" by Helen Oakley Dance, pp. 179–182.)

Richard Lambert

Music teacher, patriarch of a family of prominent professional musicians, Richard Lambert was co-conductor of the Negro Philharmonic Society of New Orleans, an 1830s all-Negro group of instrumentalists of over 100 members, "organized for the study and presentation of the classics." (See entry Jacques Constantin Deburque.)

P. H. Loveridge

Loveridge was conductor of the Philharmonic Society of New York City, organized in 1876.

Marie Lucas

(Born in the 1880s in Denver, Colorado; died April 1947 in New York City.) Society dance-orchestra leader, trombonist, and pianist, Marie Lucas was the daughter of celebrated minstrelman Sam Lucas and violinist/cornetist Carrie Melvin Lucas. She received training from her parents, at various schools in Europe, and at Boston Conservatory. She was musical director for the Quality Amusement Corporation (managers of black theaters on the eastern seaboard). She was the conducting starlet of the Lafayette Theatre's Ladies Orchestra, 1914–1916. Advertisements circulated the announcement of Lucas' availability to teach and train "all young women with even the slightest knowledge of music" for female theatre orchestras in Boston, Baltimore, Philadelphia, and Washington, D.C. She led male orchestras at D.C.'s Howard Theatre (1919–20) and, in the early 1930s, a male group known as Lucas's Merry Makers.

George Morrison

(Born September 9, 1891, in Fayette, Missouri; died November 5, 1974, in Denver, Colorado.) Morrison's father and uncles were all fiddlers. He emerged as a more than adequate violinist, music educator, and dance band leader. He and a brother joined his sister in Boulder, Colorado, at around the age of ten. Prior to engaging in formal study, Morrison played guitar in the Morrison Brothers String Band. Shortly after purchasing a violin (from earnings acquired shining shoes in a barbershop), he began studying with Nellie Greenwood and Horace Tureman, conductor of the Denver Symphony. He later studied with Carl Becker at the Columbia Conservatory in Chicago (along with Eddie South, "Angel of the Violin") and secured arranging guidance from Dave Peyton (with whose band he also played). While in New York City, he received several lessons from concert violinist Fritz Kreisler, who heard Morrison playing at the Carlton Terrace and offered him instruction. Morrison won a scholarship to attend New England Conservatory of Music, but chose marriage instead. During the late teens, Morrison returned to Denver, where he led a three-piece band, which he gradually expanded to ten pieces. Bands under Morrison's leadership were in great demand in Denver and included in their membership future band leaders Andy Kirk, Alphonse Trent, and Jimmie Lunceford.* Holding brief membership in a Morrison band was Jelly Roll Morton. But as Morrison said to jazz historian, composer, and music educator Gunther Schuller in a 1962 interview, "Of course, he [Morton] didn't last long. He couldn't stay in one band too long because he was too eccentric and too temperamental, and he was a one-man band himself. . . ." Morrison's band completed a residency in New York City in 1920, during which time the band made its recording debut (Columbia). Unfortunately the results were never released. In the mid-twenties, the Morrison Band toured widely on the Pantages vaudeville circuit, with actress Hattie McDaniel as the featured entertainer. The billing read "George Morrison, the colored Paul Whiteman, and Hattie McDaniel, the female Bert Williams." Before retirement, Morrison taught instrumental music in the Denver Public Schools and conducted a music studio. (See "Appendix" in Gunther Schuller, *Early Jazz: Its Roots and Musical Development,* New York: Oxford University Press, 1968.)

Bennie Moten

(Born November 13, 1894, in Kansas City, Missouri; Died April 2, 1935 in Kansas City, Missouri.) As a youth, Moten played baritone horn in Blackburn's Juvenile Brass Band and later studied piano with local teachers. He soon organized his own band, a ragtime trio (BB&D). He expanded the group to six pieces and then to ten. Before long, Moten's Band was the leading jazz band in Kansas City, touring widely and including such celebrated personalities as Ben Webster, Walter Page, "Hot Lips" Page, Eddie Durham, Count Basie,* brother Buster Moten, and Jimmy Rushing. When Bennie Moten died suddenly, leadership of the band was taken over by Basie and Buster Moten. From 1936 on, the band, under the leadership of Basie, became one of the greatest ensembles of all times.

William Joseph Nickerson

(Born November 10, 1865, in New Orleans, Louisiana; died February 7, 1928, in New Orleans.) Nickerson was a music teacher and orchestra conductor. He taught privately and at Southern University (then only a high school). He was founder/director of the Nickerson School of Music. In the late 1890s he led the Nickerson Orchestra and Concert Company. The Nickerson Ladies Orchestra performed throughout the city of New Orleans; at the 1900 Great Congress in Atlanta, Georgia, and in 1901 in Chicago, Illinois. He was the husband of cellist Julia Lewis Nickerson and father of Howard University professor, pianist, arranger (of Creole Songs) and folklorist Camille Nickerson. His sons Henry and Philip were also practicing musicians.

Nevilla Ottley

Ms. Ottley is cofounder, music director, and principal conductor of the Takoma Park (Maryland) Symphony Orchestra, a community ensemble founded in 1989. Ottley earlier founded the Nevilla Ottley Singers, remembered in the nation's capitol particularly for its 1986 performance of Scott Joplin's "Treemonisha" at the Kennedy Center. For several years keyboardist Ottley directed the Choral Society and Orchestra of the World Bank/International Monetary Fund. With a background in music history and conducting (Catholic University), Ottley is "dedicated to creating performance opportunities for promising artists and to presenting the 'Classical' work of minority composers" (Program Notes, Takoma Park Symphony Orchestra's "The Sound of Ebony" Concert, February 18, 1990.) Nevilla Ottley conducted the Ottley Singers and Takoma Park Symphony Orchestra, featured at the first "Kwame" Awards Ceremony honoring Minority performers, March 1992. The Terrace Theater/Kennedy Center for the Performing Arts event was sponsored jointly by the D.C. Commission on the Arts and Humanities, National Endowment for the Arts, and the Kennedy Center Office of Cultural Diversity Affairs. A student of Lloyd Geisler, J. Jeanette Wells, Evelyn White, Herbert Blomstedt, and Robert Page, since May 1976 she has produced and hosted WCTS-FM's weekly program "Classics of Ebony." She previously coached the opera workshop at Washington's Duke Ellington School of the Arts.

John T. Peek

A native Atlantan, trumpeter Peek organized the Music South Orchestra in October 1989. Atlanta's "first all-black professional orchestra" is a non-profit organization "devoted to the dissemination of black music." The group, with Peek at the helm, made its concert debut February 24, 1990. According to Peek, the first concert was designed "to synopsize the whole black musical culture in the symphonic mode."

Corilla Rochon

Pianist Madame Corilla Rochan organized and led a ladies symphony orchestra in Houston, Texas, in existence between 1915 and 1920.

Andrew Fletcher Rosemond

(Born c. 1897 in New Orleans, Louisiana; died January 17, 1976 in Gloucester, Virginia.) Violinist, educator, conductor Rosemond studied at the Nickerson School of Music and Straight University in New Orleans, and at the Ecole Normale de Musique in Paris. He engaged in additional study in Berlin, Germany. He was instructor of strings and leader of instrumental ensembles at Tuskegee Institute (Alabama), Coppin State Teachers College (Baltimore, Maryland), and in the public schools of Baltimore. He led a dance orchestra in the Far East. In the early 1940s, Rosemond served as conductor of the Baltimore National Youth Administration (NYA) Negro Symphony Orchestra and the Baltimore City Colored Chorus and Orchestra.

Luis Carl Russell

(Born 1902 in Careening Cay, Panama; died 1963 in New York City.) Bandleader, pianist, arranger Russell got his start as a music professional playing for silent movies in local theaters in Panama. In the mid-1920s, he played with Charles "Doc" Cooke and the famous King Oliver Band in Chicago, having earlier been a part of the music-making scene in New Orleans's Storyville. He moved to New York City in the late 1920s and took over the leadership of George Howe's band, one that backed Louis Armstrong between 1935 and 1943. Persons who played with Russell included Henry "Red" Allen, Albert Nicholas, J. C. Higginbotham, Sid Catlett, and George "Pops" Foster. He was married to the outstanding guitarist/bassist/vocalist Carline Ray (member of the International Sweethearts of Rhythm and musical associate of Mary Lou Williams and later, Ruth Brown).

Noble Lee Sissle

(Born July 19, 1889, in Indianapolis, Indiana; died December 17, 1975, in Tampa, Florida.) Band leader, singer, composer, lyricist Noble Sissle organized a glee club while still in high school. He attended Butler University to prepare for the ministry but dropped out to support his family upon the death of his father. He toured for two years with the Thomas Jubilee Singers. He was guitarist/vocalist in James Reese Europe's* Clef Club Orchestra and, upon Europe's insistence, joined the U.S. Army in 1916, serving as drum major with Europe's popular 369th Band. Sissle remained in musical contact with Europe until the maestro's death in 1919. Sissle was also a music associate of James Hubert ("Eubie") Blake. Sissle and Blake began working as a team in 1915, writing popular music and touring as a vaudeville unit. Sissle and Blake wrote and produced the successful Broadway musicals "Shuffle Along" (1921) and "Chocolate Dandies" (1924). The two dissolved their partnership in the mid-1920s. Sissle-led bands completed several successful residences both in the United States and abroad, including appearances at The Kit Kat Club, 1926 (London); Les Ambassadeurs, 1928 (Paris); and the Park Central Hotel, 1931, and Billy Rose's Diamond Horseshoe, 1938 (New York City). Other involvements included managing his own publishing company and running his own night club ("Noble's"). He was founder and first president of the Negro Actor's Guild of America and was known as the unofficial Mayor of Harlem.

[Major] N. Clark Smith

(Born July 31, 1877, in Fort Leavenworth, Kansas; died October 8, 1933, in St. Louis, Missouri.) Conductor, composer, educator, and band master (8th Regiment, Illinois State Militia), Smith began his career as a young employee of Lyon and Healy Instrument Manufacturing Company, with access to all parts of the plant. The company supported Smith's career development and, following his formal training period, hired him as an agent for the firm and utilized his skills to work with newly organized bands that the Lyon and Healy Company equipped. He received the B.Mus. degree from Chicago Musical College, the M.Mus. from Sherwood School of Music, and additional training at the Horner Institute of Fine Arts, University of Kansas, and Guild Hall (London). He was a member of the faculties at Lincoln High School (Kansas City), Wendell Phillips High School (Chicago), and Sumner High School (St. Louis). His pupils included Bennie Moten, Milt Hinton, and Ray Nance, all future jazz celebrities. Following a request from educator Booker T. Washington, Smith went to Tuskegee Institute to develop a band in 1907. His reputation for "high standards of excellence" and instrumental development skills were well known throughout the country. Other instrumental groups that he organized and directed were the Little Symphony Orchestra in Chicago (1892); the Ladies Mandolin and String Instrument Club in Chicago (1904); the Ladies Orchestra in Chicago (1905); and the Pullman Porter Band, Orchestra, and Glee Club (1922–24).

Jesse Stone (a/k/a Charles Calhoun)

(Born 1901 in Atchison, Kansas.) Stone was a popular composer, arranger, and band leader throughout the 1920s, 1930s, and 1940s. He was born into a musical family and began performing on stage at age four. He was a significant contributor to the birth and history of Rock 'n Roll. He began leading bands at the age of fifteen, but is perhaps best remembered for his leadership of the band Jesse Stone and His Blues Serenaders, based in St. Joseph, Missouri. Later, based in Chicago, he led the band Jesse Stone and His Cyclones, under the management of Joe Glaser. For a period, based in Kansas City, Missouri, Stone led (on occasion) the famous George Lee Orchestra and did arrangements for the band. Other bands for which he did arrangements were those led by Earl "Fatha" Hines,* Chick Webb,* Louis Jordan, and Jimmie Lunceford,* to name a few. With the late 1970s/early 1980s attention on female instrumentalists, the name Jesse Stone was frequently recalled in connection with the International Sweethearts of Rhythm (early 1940s); for this popular group (originally from Piney Woods Country Life School in Piney Woods, Mississippi) he served as arranger and coach. In remembrance of this affiliation, Jesse Stone (along with the ladies) was honored at the Women's Jazz Festival in Kansas City, Missouri, March 1980. Following his association with the Sweethearts, Stone led a band (all-male) on an extended USO Tour of the Pacific.

Sun Ra (Herman "Sonny" Blount, Le Sony)

(Born c. 1915 in Birmingham, Alabama; died May 30, 1993 in Birmingham.) Keyboardist, composer, band leader Sun Ra for more than four decades delved musically into the universal and spiritual realms. In the 1950s he organized the Solar Arkestra (also known as Space Arkestra or Intergalactic Myth-Science Arkestra), around the same time that he adopted the name Sun Ra. His "Arkestra" included singers and dancers, as well as instrumentalists. The thirty or more performers focused heavily on theatrics. According to Sun Ra, "[T]he planet is in danger. . . . They've got trouble, not from man, but from some other source which is in control. . . . [T]hey sent me here to change the planet and I'm supposed to do it." But he asked not to be considered a leader; "coordinator" or "adjuster" he would consider. Sun Ra toured widely and recorded extensively. He was well respected by the music industry and was the recipient of many awards, including an American Jazz Masters Award from the National Endowment for the Arts. (See Art Sato, "Sun Ra Interview," *Konceptualization,* April/May/June 1989, pp. 18–20 and "Sun Ra, 79, Versatile Jazz Artist; A Pioneer With a Surrealist Bent," *New York Times* obituary, May 31, 1993.)

William ("Billy") Edward Taylor

(Born July 24, 1921, in Greenville, North Carolina.) Pianist, composer, disc jockey, program director, teacher, lecturer, author, television personality, and executive Billy Taylor is widely referred to as "Mr. Jazz." He mastered every activity in which he ever engaged and constantly expanded jazz awareness and the entire jazz scene for performers, creators, and listeners alike. He grew up in Washington, D.C., where he studied with high school bandmaster and local teacher Henry Grant. He began playing jazz semiprofessionally around age eleven or twelve. Having graduated from Virginia State College (now University) in Petersburg, he arrived in New York City in 1943. Two days following his arrival, he became pianist with the Ben Webster Quartet. Recognized world-wide as a superb pianist, outstanding lecturer, exciting composer, recognized author, knowledgeable disc jockey, and arts correspondent for the CBS news program "Sunday Morning," his accomplishments and recognitions include: membership on the National Council of the National Endowment for the Arts (a Presidential appointment), five guest appearances at the White House, recipient of the first International Critics' Award for "Best Pianist" from *Down Beat* magazine, designated as "Man of the Year" by the National (now International) Association of Jazz Educators, recipient of an American Jazz Masters Award from the National Endowment for the Arts, winner of two Peabodys, an Emmy, and the first Certificate of Recognition given by the United States Congressional Arts Caucus. Taylor is founder/president of Harlem's Jazzmobile.

But we are here focusing on "Billy Taylor the Conductor." He was music director of the PBS-TV special "Memories of Eubie." He led an eighteen-piece big band for the special "Salute to Duke," produced for public television in Pittsburgh. He was the first guest to conduct the Duke Ellington Orchestra following Ellington's 1974 death. Not to be forgotten is his leadership of the twelve-piece band for the award-winning "David Frost Show" (1969–72). Since 1975, the "Mr. Jazz" has been referred to as "Dr. Jazz," having earned the Ed.D. degree from the University of Massachusetts. (See Barbara Campbell, "How Mr. Taylor Broke the Ice With Mr. Frost," *New York Times,* January 3, 1971, p. D15, and Dan Morgenstern, "Taylor-Made Frostings," *Down Beat,* March 4, 1971, pp. 18–19.)

A(lfred) Jack Thomas

(Born April 14, 1884, in Pittsburgh, Pennsylvania; died April 19, 1962, in Baltimore, Maryland.) Composer, educator, conductor Thomas studied the mandolin, trumpet, and violin as a child in Pittsburgh. Advanced musical training was acquired at Washington and Jefferson College (Pennsylvania), the National Conservatory of Music (Manila, Philippines), the Institute of Musical Art (New York City), and the Bandmasters School at Chaumont, France. He joined the United States Army in 1903 and was soon appointed bandmaster of the Tenth Calvary. He later became bandmaster of the 368th Infantry (The Buffaloes), active in Europe during World War I. Thomas was later commissioned bandmaster in the Allied Expeditionary Forces.

Following his military service, he settled in Baltimore, Maryland, organizing and leading community bands and establishing the Aeolian Conservatory of Music. He is credited with having established the city's first black municipal band (1921). Between 1924–27, he served as head of the Music Department at Morgan College (now Morgan State University) and at some point was a member of the Howard University (Washington) music faculty. Following a brief period in New York City (where he conducted a studio), he returned to Baltimore to establish the Baltimore Institute of Musical Arts (1946).

A February 2, 1946, issue of the *Baltimore Afro-American* newspaper (p. 11) reported, "A. Jack Thomas Conducts White Baltimore Symphony." According to the article, "Musical history was made . . . when A. Jack Thomas, teacher-composer and master musician, directed the Baltimore Symphony Orchestra, white. In this achievement, Mr. Thomas became the first colored ever to conduct an all-white symphony orchestra locally. [The article cited two earlier examples: Layton Turner conducting the Hiawatha Club of Washington and S. Coleridge-Taylor conducting the Marine Band, 40 years earlier.]. . . . Featured on the program was Mr. Thomas's own composition "Etude en Noire. . . ."

Egbert E. Thompson

(Born c. 1883 in Sierra Leone, West Africa; Died August 22, 1927, in Paris.) Thompson grew up in Jamaica and studied at Kneller Hall, the British Army's School of Music in Hounslow, England, and the Institute of Musical Art in New York City. He played a variety of instruments, including the saxophone. Settling in New York City in 1907, he became very involved in black musical circles. For a brief period, he led the New Amsterdam Musical Association (the oldest black music organization in the United States, paralleling the segregated musicians' union) and was active with the black Clef and Tempo Clubs. Thompson was one of the select group of black men to be commissioned in the U.S. Army as a bandmaster during the early years of this century. He led the U.S. Fifteenth Infantry, later renamed the 367th "Buffaloes." During the war, he served in France. Following the war, he settled again in New York City. Returning to Europe in 1919, he replaced Will Marion Cook* as director of the Southern Syncopated Orchestra. Thompson and his jazz orchestra were a sensation in Copenhagen, 1923–24. (See Morten Clausen, "Egbert E. Thompson: He Introduced Copenhageners to Real Jazz Music," *Black Perspective in Music,* Fall 1988, pp. 151–175.)

Edythe Turnham

(Born c. 1890 in Topeka, Kansas; died 1950.) Turnham was professionally active during the first decade of this century through the mid-1930s, around Spokane, Seattle, and Los Angeles. She was a pianist and jazz band leader, working on the Orpheum and Pantages Circuits. Originally a family band, her expanded outfit worked under the names of Knights of Syncopation and the Dixie Aces. In addition to fulfilling club dates, bands under Turnham's leadership were staff players for radio stations WFWB, WFOX, and KGFJ. (See Sally Placksin, *American Women in Jazz: 1900 to Present (Their Words, Lives, and Music),* New York: Seaview Books, 1982, pp. 47–49.)

Linda Twine

(Born c. 1947 in Muskogee, Oklahoma.) Conductor, pianist, composer, and arranger Twine currently resides in New York City. From a musical family, she received her undergraduate training at Oklahoma City University and the Master's degree from Manhattan School of Music. One of a handful of women conductors working in the theater in the 1980s, she was inspired when she saw black female Joyce Brown conducting the Broadway musical "Purlie." Twine was assistant conductor/pianist for the Broadway musicals "The Wiz" "Ain't Misbehavin'," and "Bring Back Birdie." National attention was forthcoming when she was hired as conductor of a sixteen-piece orchestra for "Lena Horne: The Lady and Her Music," running more than two years on Broadway, enjoying a seven-week run in Los Angeles, followed by a national tour (including Chicago, Washington, Detroit, Seattle, Denver, San Francisco, and New Orleans). (See Ruthe Stein, "Lena's Conductor," *Ebony,* December 1982, pp. 46, 50.)

Harold Wheeler

(Born 1944 in St. Louis, Missouri.) Conductor/arranger Wheeler received his training at Howard University and Manhattan School of Music. He made his Broadway debut as conductor of the musical "Promises, Promises" (1968). He was music supervisor for the films "Cotton Comes to Harlem" and "Fortune and Men's Eyes" and orchestrator and music supervisor for the productions "Two Gentlemen of Verona," "Ain't Supposed to Die a Natural Death," "Don't Play Us Cheap," "Coco," and "The Wiz." Wheeler arranged over 500 radio and television commercials and was musical director of the Broadway production "Lena Horne: The Lady and Her Music." He arranged and conducted record albums for Lena Horne, Nina Simone, Billy Taylor, and numerous others.

Earl H. Williams

During the 1970s, Williams was conductor of the Boston Orchestra and Chorale in Boston. The well-integrated group performed annual concerts at the city's Judson Hall. The group recorded Samuel Coleridge-Taylor's "Hiawatha's Wedding Feast." Trained at Tuskegee Institute, Williams devoted his life's energies to "promoting and keeping alive serious music written by black composers." In his declining years, he sought diligently to perform "Hiawatha's Wedding Feast" with black college choirs, believing that the experience would be educational and informative, and could contribute greatly to the "preservation of a musical classic." Unfortunately this dream never materialized.

Henry ("Harry") A. Williams

(Born 1850s in Cleveland, Ohio [?]; died 1930s or 1940s in New York, New York) Williams is primarily remembered as a tenor who studied in his native Cleveland, Ohio; Paris; and London. After a period of study, he was appointed teacher of voice at the London Academy of Music. Returning to the United States, he first settled in Cleveland, where he was a successful voice teacher. He was soon invited to head the vocal department of the Washington Conservatory of Music, established in the nation's capitol by Harriet Gibbs Marshall in 1903. "The need of a well equipped, high class orchestra [had] been a long felt one in Washington. . . . Realizing the great need, Mr. Harry A. Williams [arranged] the first concert which he conducted in March, 1912, at Howard Theatre under the auspices of the Washington Conservatory of Music, [and] began a propaganda among the musicians. . . . In May [1912], the first meeting was held and an independent organization established under its present name with a membership of sixteen. Since that time rehearsals have been regularly kept up, with an ever increasing interest as the men began to realize the wonderful possibilities before them in the field of high class orchestral work." (Program Notes, December 28, 1913 Concert, The Washington Concert Orchestra—First Season.)

Judith Williams-Gartrell

A Fulbright Fellow, Williams-Gartrell has enjoyed conducting affiliations with the Brockport Symphony Orchestra, the Seattle Civic Light Opera, Prometheus Symphony Orchestra, Cascade Youth Symphony, and the Frohnburg Chamber Orchestra (Austria).

Anna Mae Darden Winburn

(Born August 13, 1913, in Port Royal, Tennessee.) Vocalist/bandleader Winburn is best remembered for her leadership of the International Sweethearts of Rhythm, 1941–48 (See Handy, *International Sweethearts of Rhythm,* Metuchen, N.J.: Scarecrow Press, 1983). Upon the group's demise, she organized and led the group Anna Mae Winburn and Her Sweethearts of Rhythm, 1950–56. Prior to joining the International Sweethearts of Rhythm, Winburn worked as a singer in Kokomo, Fort Wayne, and Indianapolis, Indiana; Chicago; and Omaha, Nebraska. In Omaha she worked as vocalist and/or leader with Frank Shelton "Red" Perkins's Dixie Ramblers and Lloyd Hunter's Serenaders.

Appendix A: Black Conductors Attend "Toward Greater Participation of Black Americans in Symphony Orchestras" Conference—Arden House in Harriman, New York, September 16–18, 1988 (Sponsored by the Music Assistance Fund, New York Philharmonic)

Keynote Speaker James DePreist (Photo by Frederico Diaz/Courtesy New York
Philharmonic)

James DePreist (seated) chats with Michael Morgan

William Curry (r) with violinist Jack Bradley (former member Denver Symphony, 1946–49)

Kermit Moore listens intently to discussion.

Michael Morgan (left) and William Curry at Avery Fisher Hall (Lincoln Center, NYC) await departure for Harriman, New York.

Raymond Harvey (left) and Julius Williams participate in round table discussion

Breaktime, Raymond Harvey (left) and Wayne Brown (Executive Director, Louisville Symphony)

APPENDIX B: LETTER TO BLACK CONDUCTORS

Dear

We, D. Antoinette Handy and William E. Terry*, are writing a book that will focus on American conductors of African descent. (Biographical material about the authors is enclosed.) The book, tentatively titled *On the Podium: Black Conductors**, will be published by Scarecrow Press (primarily a librarians' publisher).

For this publication, "conductor" will be defined as leaders of ensembles performing in all genres of music, including traditional Western European, jazz, and musical theatre. All conductors will be leaders of instrumental ensembles (even though the ensemble might support vocal music, such as opera, oratorio, and musical theatre). Thus, conductors of symphony orchestras, big bands, pit orchestras for musical theatre, dance, opera, minstrel or other variety shows, chamber orchestras, dance bands, and stage bands backing vocalists or instrumentalists, are all eligible for inclusion. Though the conductors might have led smaller forces during their careers, they must have made conducting instrumental groups of at least ten players the primary focus of their musical activities.

The book will include a historical overview of black conductors in all genres. The time frame will be the 19th century to the present. We feel that it is essential to approach our treatment of the subject from a strong historical perspective and to consider the circumstances and experiences of black conductors in a broad context. The historical overview will provide the background for the presentation of a series of profiles of black conductors (both living and deceased) whose

---

Black Conductors had originally been contracted as a co-authored manuscript with the working title cited above.

519

careers we feel are highly significant for understanding and appreciating the opportunities and obstacles presented to those of African descent who elected to venture into the highly competitive and traditionally exclusionary world of instrumental conducting.

Since *we intend to include you in this publication,* we are asking you to help shape your profile's content. Your response is crucial for assuring that your profile is accurate and complete and that it reflects the attitudes and special concerns that have influenced you as a vital and creative artist in contemporary society.

Not all of the response you provide will be included in your personal profile; some of the information (particularly that that is more philosophical and attitudinal) will be incorporated in the introductory and overview portions of the book that will treat (in a collective way) the attitudes of black conductors about the music they conduct, the institutions that support their efforts, and their relations with other conductors who share their musical universe.

We certainly realize that your schedule is a busy one and that our requests are time consuming. Please feel free to respond to the philosophical and attitudinal questions by way of tape.

ADDITIONALLY, WE WILL NEED THE FOLLOWING:

1. A GLOSSY PHOTOGRAPH (portrait or "in conducting action");

2. PRESS REVIEWS AND CLIPPINGS (with complete citations).

Kindly place us on your mailing list.

WE SINCERELY THANK YOU.

Respectively yours,

D. Antoinette Handy

William E. Terry

APPENDIX C: SURVEY INSTRUMENT

QUESTIONNAIRE——— *ON THE PODIUM: BLACK CONDUCTORS*

Full Name _____

Place of Birth _____ *Date of Birth* _____

Address _____ *Telephone Number(s)* _____

_____

FAMILY DATA (indicating if any others pursued careers in music); *Parents* (full names, including mother's maiden name, and their involvements)

_____
_____
_____

Siblings (indicating your position, i.e., oldest/youngest)

_____
_____
_____
_____ (Use reverse side if needed)

How did you initially become interested in music? In pursuing music as a career? How were you influenced (both positively and negatively) by family, teachers, friends, others?

How/where did you secure your training?

Were you ever discouraged from pursuing a career as a "serious musician", particularly as a conductor?

What factors influenced your decision to become a conductor primarily (rather than to concentrate in some other area of music—performance, composition, arranging, teaching)?

Do you feel that your race has affected (positively or negatively) your opportunities to conduct? If so, in what way?

Have you considered the creation of your own ensemble as a mechanism for increasing your own conducting opportunities? Have you created such an ensemble? If so, please provide details.

Are there other conductors who have served (serve) as sources of encouragement and inspiration to you?

Do relationships with other black conductors provide any sort of support/network for you? Is association with other black conductors important to you? More important than with your non-black colleagues? (Are relationships with any other conductors important?)

What is your personal identity? Black? Black Conductor? Conductor? American (with other identifications in combination)? American? Other?

What do you consider to be the most significant milestone(s) you have achieved in your conducting career?

What is your most significant achievement to date (other than conducting)?

What is your favorite repertoire to program and conduct?

Does the music you program reflect any personal philosophy (musical or otherwise)?

Have you had the opportunity to program the music of black composers? Do you feel any special obligation? Please elaborate.

Do you feel any special responsibility to engage musicians of African descent (orchestral members or soloists)?

What advice would you offer to aspiring black conductors?

CONDUCTORS WHO YOU FEEL SHOULD DEFINITELY BE
PROFILED IN THIS PUBLICATION
(Address & telephone number would be appreciated)

_____
_____
_____
_____
_____
_____
_____

SELECTIVE BIBLIOGRAPHY

Books

Abdul, Raoul. *Blacks in Classical Music: A Personal History.* New York: Dodd, Mead and Company, 1977.

Bamberger, Carl, ed. *The Conductor's Art.* New York: McGraw-Hill, 1965.

Bernstein, Leonard. *The Joy of Music.* New York: New American Library, 1959. (Part II, "The Art of Conducting").

Blaukopf, Kurt. *Great Conductors.* London: Arco Publishers Limited, 1955.

Boult, Adrian. *Thoughts On Conducting.* London: Phoenix House/Dent, 1963.

Carse, Adam. *The Orchestra.* New York: Chanticleer Press, Inc., 1949.

―――. *Orchestral Conducting.* London: Augener Ltd., 1935 (reprint, Greenwood Press, 1971).

Charters, Samuel B. and Leonard Kunstadt. *Jazz: A History of the New York Scene.* Garden City, N.Y.: Doubleday, 1962 (reprint, Da Capo Press, 1981).

Epstein, Helen. *Music Talks: Conversations With Musicians.* New York: McGraw-Hill Book Company, 1987 (chapter "Learning to Conduct at Tanglewood").

Ewen, David. *Dictators of the Baton,* rev. and expanded. Chicago/New York: Ziff-Davis Publishing Company, 1948.

―――. *The Man With the Baton.* New York: Thomas Y. Crowell, 1936.

Feather, Leonard. *The Encyclopedia of Jazz.* New York: Bonanza Books, 1960.

―――. *The Book of Jazz: From Then Till Now,* rev. ed. New York: Dell Publishing Co., Inc., 1976.

Fernett, Gene. *Swing Out: Great Negro Dance Bands.* Midland, Michigan: Pendell, 1970.

Fletcher, Tom. *The Tom Fletcher Story: 100 Years of the Negro in Show Business.* New York: Burdge, 1954 (reprint, Da Capo Press, 1984).

Galkin, Elliott. *A History of Orchestral Conducting In Theory and Practice.* New York: Pendragon Press, 1988.

Handy, D. Antoinette. *Black Women in American Bands & Orchestras.* Metuchen, N.J.: Scarecrow Press, 1981.

Hart, Philip. *Conductors: A New Generation.* New York: Charles Scribner's Sons, 1979.

Hitchcock, H. Wiley and Stanley Sadie, eds. *The New Grove Dictionary of American Music.* New York: Macmillan Press Limited, 1986, vols. 1–4.

Johnson, James Weldon. *Black Manhattan.* New York: Alfred A. Knopf, 1930.

Keepnews, Orrin and Bill Grauer, Jr. *A Pictorial History of Jazz: People and Places from New Orleans to Modern Jazz,* rev. ed. New York: Crown Publishers, 1966.

Kernfeld, Barry, ed. *The New Grove Dictionary of Jazz.* New York: Macmillan Press Limited, 1988, vols. 1 and 2.

Krueger, Karl. *The Way of the Conductor.* New York: Charles Scribner's Sons, 1958.

Lebrecht, Norman. *The Maestro Myth: Great Conductors in Pursuit of Power.* New York: Carol Publishing Group, 1991.

Mapp, Edward. *Directory of Blacks in the Performing Arts.* Metuchen, N.J.: Scarecrow Press, 1978.

Sampson, Henry T. *Blacks in Blackface: A Source Book of Early Black Musical Shows,* Metuchen, N.J.: Scarecrow Press, Inc., 1980.

Schonberg, Harold C. *The Great Conductors.* New York: Simon and Schuster, Inc., 1967.

Schuller, Gunther. *Early Jazz: Its Roots and Musical Development.* New York: Oxford University Press, 1968.

Selecting A Music Director (A Handbook for Trustees and Management). Washington, D.C.: American Symphony Orchestra League, 1985.

Seltzer, George. *The Professional Symphony Orchestra in the United States,* Metuchen, N.J.: Scarecrow Press, Inc., 1975 (chapter II, "The Conductor: The Ultimate Autocrat in a Democratic World").

Simon, George T. *The Big Bands,* rev. ed. New York: Collier Books, 1974.

Southern, Eileen, ed. *Biographical Dictionary of Afro-American and African Musicians.* Westport, Conn.: Greenwood Press, 1982.

———. *The Music of Black Americans: A History.* 2nd ed. New York: W. W. Norton and Company, 1983.

Tirro, Frank. *Jazz: A History.* New York: W. W. Norton and Company, Inc. 1977.

Articles and Periodicals

"Black Conductors Are Optimistic About Appointment to Orchestras," *The Sun,* May 31, 1977, p. B5.

Bockman, Chris and Nick J. Hall, "The New Black Symphony Conductors," *Sepia,* October 1974, pp. 18–29.

Calloway, Earl, "Black Conductors Making Progress," *Chicago Daily Defender,* January 8–14, 1972, p. 36.

de Lerma, Dominique-Rene, "Black Conductors and Concert Instrumentalists," *Tarakan Music Letter,* Vol 5, #1, September/October 1983, pp. 1, 4–6.

Harreld, Kemper. "Starting an Orchestra," *Negro Musician,* September 1920, p. 13.

Hughes, Allen, "And Now There Are Three," *New York Times,* March 17, 1968, p. D19.

———. "For Black Conductors, A Future? Or Frustrations," *New York Times,* March 15, 1970, pp. D19, 32.

Jennings, Patricia Prattis, ed., *Symphonium* (For and About the African-American Symphony Musician), Pittsburgh, Pennsylvania (Published three times annually since 1988—)

Lundy, Anne, "Conversations With Three Symphonic Conductors: Denis de Coteau, Tania León, Jon Robinson [sic]," *Black Perspective in Music,* Vol. 16, #2, Fall 1988, pp. 213–226.

Mason, Bryant S. "And the Beat Goes On," *Essence,* November 1972, pp. 50–51, 81, 86.

Narine, Dalton, "The Maestros (Black Symphony Conductors Are Making A Name for Themselves)," *Ebony,* February 1989, pp. 54, 56, 60, 62.

Pareles, Jon, "Re-creating A Night When History Was Made," *New York Times,* July 17, 1989, C13.

Schwarz, K. Robert, "Black Maestros On the Podiums, But No Pedestal," *New York Times,* October 11, 1992, section 2, pp. 1, 27. (See also "Letters" re: Black Conductors, *New York Times,* October 25, 1992, section 2, p. 4)

Thompson, Leon, "The Black Performing Artist and Achievement," *Black Perspective in Music,* Vol. 3, Special Issue, May 1975, pp. 160–164.

INDEX

Note: Neither the "quick reference" that precedes each "Major" profile nor the Press Comments and Notes that follow each "Major" profile have been indexed.
Profiled individuals and profile pages (Parts II, III, and IV) are indicated by **boldface type.**

ABOUT THE AUTHOR

D. ANTOINETTE HANDY (B. Mus., New England Conservatory of Music; M. Mus., Northwestern University; Diploma, Paris National Conservatory) is a native of New Orleans, Louisiana. A flutist, Ms. Handy spent more than twenty years as a symphony musician, both in the United States and abroad. She served as organizer, manager, and flutist with the chamber group Trio Pro Viva (specializing in the music of black composers) for three decades. Her teaching tenures include Florida A & M, Tuskegee, Jackson State, Southern (New Orleans), and Virginia State Universities. In 1971, Ms. Handy was a Ford Foundation Humanities Fellow at North Carolina and Duke Universities. She joined the staff of the National Endowment for the Arts in 1985 as Assistant Director of the Music Program and assumed the duties of Director in 1990. Ms. Handy retired in July 1993. Also in 1993, she received an honorary Doctor of Music degree from the Cleveland Institute of Music and delivered the commencement address. She is a frequent lecturer, has published articles and book reviews in numerous professional journals, and authored *Black Women in American Bands and Orchestras* (1981) and *The International Sweethearts of Rhythm* (1983), both published by Scarecrow Press.